WESTHOUGHTON
01942 634640

ADULT
GRAPHIC
NOVEL

**Bolton
Council**

BY FRED PERRY

KU-072-867

CONTENTS

BOLTON LIBRARIES
BT 136 3969 2

By: FRED PERRY

Creator - Fred Perry
Graphic Designer - GURU-eFX
Cover Design - GURU-eFX
Layout - Doug Dlin

Editor in Chief - Jochen Weltjens
President of Sales and Marketing - Lee Duhig
Art Direction - GURU-eFX
VP of Production - Wes Hartman
Publishing Manager - Robby Bevard
Publisher - Joe Dunn
Founder - Ben Dunn

Come visit us online at www.antarctic-press.com

Gold Digger II Pocket Manga Vol. 2 by Fred Perry
An Antarctic Press Pocket Manga

Antarctic Press
7272 Wurzbach Suite 204 San Antonio, TX 78240

Collects *Gold Digger* Vol. 3 issues 9-16.
First published in 2000 by Antarctic Press.

Gold Digger II Pocket Manga Vol. 2, September 2007.
Gold Digger and all related characters are ™ and ® Fred Perry. All other
material is ™ and ©2006 Antarctic Press. No similarity to any actual
character(s) and/or place(s) is intended, and any such similarity is purely
coincidental. All rights reserved. Nothing from this book may be repro-
duced or transmitted without the express written consent of the authors,
except for the purposes of review and promotion.
"I like Spawn *a lot." "Well, there goes your tip."*

ISBN: 978-0-9792723-0-1
Printed and bound in Canada.

VOLUME 2

MAIN CHARACTERS

Gina Diggers

Brilliant and sexy, she's the total package. She might be a little boy-crazy, but that doesn't stop her from charging into fantastic archaeological adventures that reach not only all over the Earth, but into dimensions beyond! Long before Tomb Raider, Gina was on the case!

Britanny "Cheetah" Diggers

Britanny is a were-cheetah endowed with lightning speed and rapid reflexes. She's Gina's adopted sister and loyal bodyguard. Sexier than Gina (at least she thinks so), she often has to tear herself away from her alien Kryn fiancé Stripe to pull her sister out of the frying pan!

Brianna Diggers

Brianna, the third sister, the ultimate warrior, a clone-fusion of Gina and Cheetah's abilities. This makes her a brilliant scientist and weapons specialist with fantastic reflexes and the speed of an Olympic athlete!

Penny Pincer

Gina's one-time rival and now sometime partner, Penny is one of the few people who could go head-to-head with Gina on matters academic and archaeological. Both of them are equally intelligent, though with some different specialties. Penny has developed a relationship with Kevin "Ace" Koss, the Diggers sisters' friend and transport manager, and has taken in a bioengineered harpy named Charlotte as her partner/bodyguard.

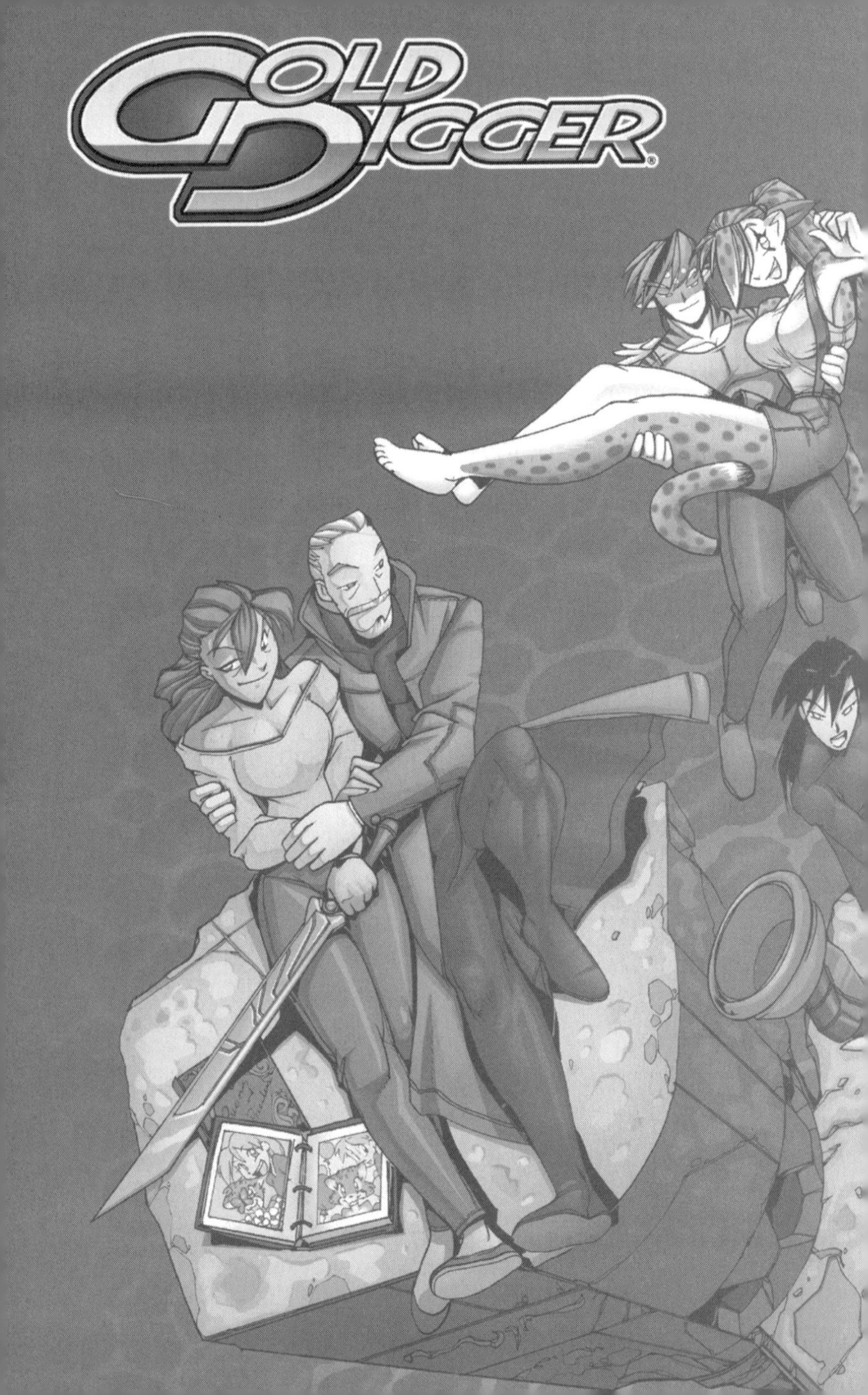
GOLD DIGGER®

BOLTON LIBRARIES

13639692

Bertrams	10.12.07
AF/GN	£9.99
WM	

THE STORY SO FAR...

Super-scientist/archaeologist/adventurer Gina Diggers,
her adopted were-cheetah sister Britanny, and their clone-
fusion sister Brianna regularly travel around the world, to
other dimensions, and across time and space in pursuit of
discoveries and treasure.

Gina takes a group to the sunken city of Muthia, but Pee Wee
Talon and his goons pursue them, hoping to find a relic of the
mythical Djinn. Instead, they all find a living statue who puts
them in a game-show competition for Muthia's treasures.
With a little help from the statue, Gina's group wins, and
despite Brit's objections, Gina goes for the "mystery box,"
which contains an old, iron pot. The pot turns out to contain
the guardian "statue", actually a gamester Djinn named Dao.
Gina eagerly prepares to present Dao at the annual Explorers' Society Banquet, but is upstaged by a snooty newcomer
named Fauntleroy who presents his own Djinn, a female
named Madrid. Pee Wee then has his ninja, Daishi, snatch
Madrid's lamp, and convinces half the room that Gina did it.
During the ensuing free-for-all (an annual tradition anyway),
Pee Wee and Daishi are "convinced" to hand over the lamp
by the society chairman, the enormous Monty. Monty then
proclaims Gina winner of that year's award and his successor
as chairman. The next day, he hands over Madrid's lamp to
Gina as well. Dao warns Gina that his unfaithful ex-wife is not
to be trusted, but uses a magic viewer to assure Madrid's
story is truthful. Gina learns that Fauntleroy's a young dragon
cursed to stay in human form. Control over Djinn power could
restore him and then some. Gina is convinced to seek out
Uhm di Turrok, the Halls of the Extremely Dead, to gain the
secrets of the Djinn before Fauntleroy can. However, Faunty
and his two sub-dragon wives are waiting for them...

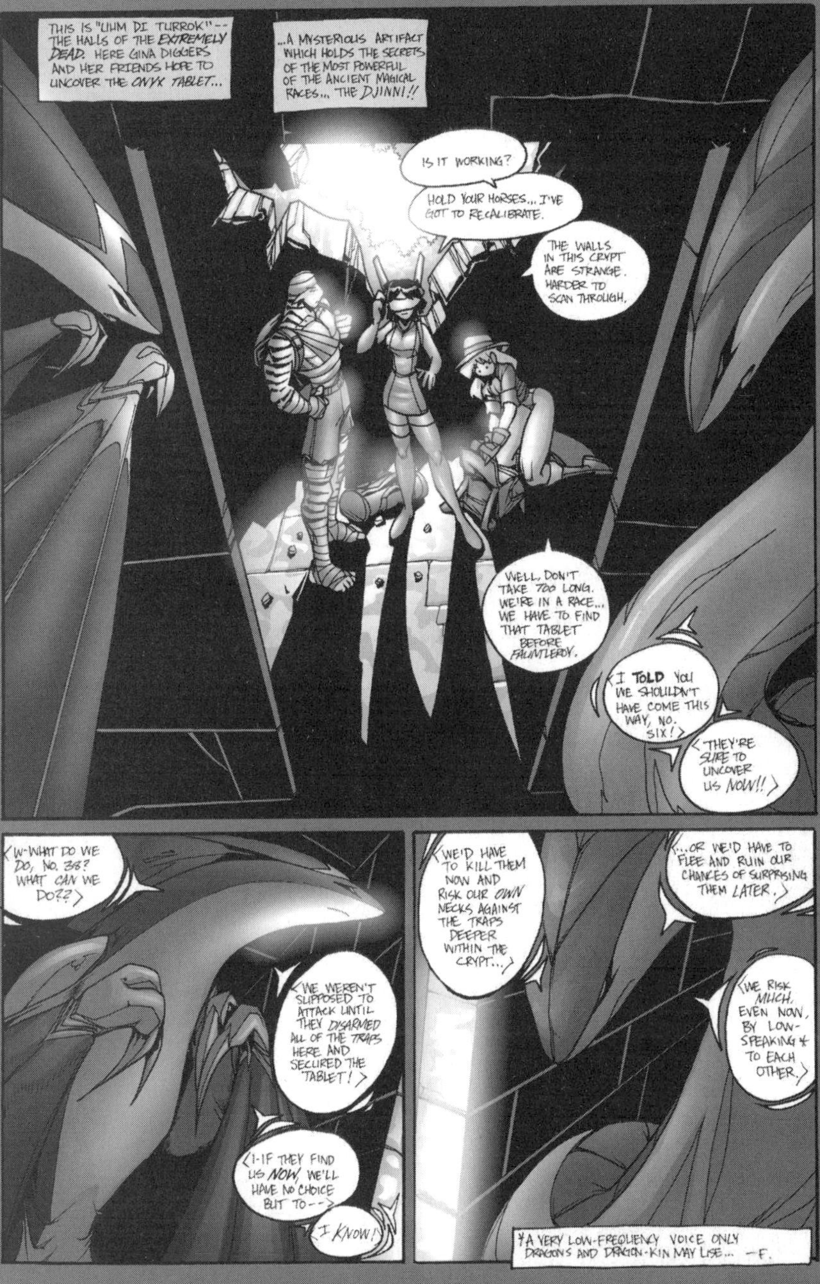

THIS IS "LIHM DI TURROK"-- THE HALLS OF THE *EXTREMELY DEAD*. HERE GINA DIGGERS AND HER FRIENDS HOPE TO UNCOVER THE *ONYX TABLET*...
...A MYSTERIOUS ARTIFACT WHICH HOLDS THE SECRETS OF THE MOST POWERFUL OF THE ANCIENT MAGICAL RACES... THE *DJINNI*!!
IS IT WORKING?
HOLD YOUR HORSES... I'VE GOT TO RECALIBRATE.
THE WALLS IN THIS CRYPT ARE STRANGE. HARDER TO SCAN THROUGH.
WELL, DON'T TAKE *TOO* LONG. WE'RE IN A RACE... WE HAVE TO FIND THAT TABLET BEFORE *FAUNTLEROY*.
<I **TOLD** YOU WE SHOULDN'T HAVE COME THIS WAY, NO. SIX!>
<THEY'RE *SURE* TO UNCOVER US *NOW*!!>
<W-WHAT DO WE *DO*, NO. 38? WHAT *CAN* WE DO??>
<WE WEREN'T *SUPPOSED* TO ATTACK UNTIL THEY *DISARMED* ALL OF THE *TRAPS* HERE AND SECURED THE TABLET!>
<I-IF THEY FIND US *NOW*, WE'LL HAVE NO CHOICE BUT TO-->
<I *KNOW*!>
<WE'D HAVE TO KILL THEM NOW AND RISK OUR *OWN* NECKS AGAINST THE TRAPS DEEPER WITHIN THE CRYPT...>
<...OR WE'D HAVE TO FLEE AND RUIN OUR CHANCES OF SURPRISING THEM *LATER*.>
<WE RISK *MUCH*, EVEN NOW, BY LOW-SPEAKING* TO EACH OTHER.>
*A VERY LOW-FREQUENCY VOICE ONLY DRAGONS AND DRAGON-KIN MAY USE... -F.

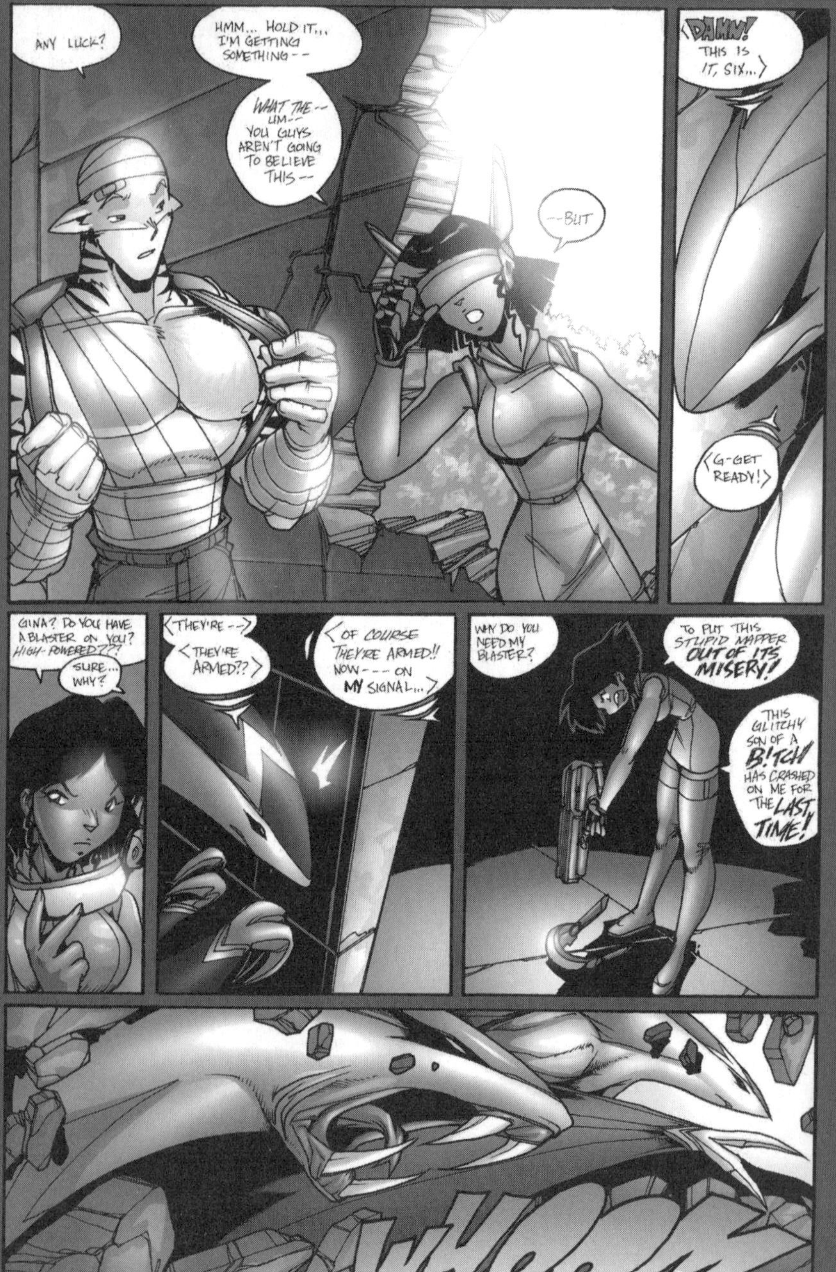
ANY LUCK?
HMM... HOLD IT... I'M GETTING SOMETHING--
WHAT THE-- UM-- YOU GUYS AREN'T GOING TO BELIEVE THIS--
--BUT
⟨DAMN! THIS IS IT, SIX...⟩
⟨G-GET READY!⟩
GINA? DO YOU HAVE A BLASTER ON YOU? HIGH-POWERED???
SURE... WHY?
⟨THEY'RE--⟩
⟨THEY'RE ARMED??⟩
⟨OF COURSE THEY'RE ARMED!! NOW--- ON MY SIGNAL...⟩
WHY DO YOU NEED MY BLASTER?
TO PUT THIS STUPID MAPPER OUT OF ITS MISERY!
THIS GLITCHY SON OF A B!TCH HAS CRASHED ON ME FOR THE LAST TIME!
WHOOM

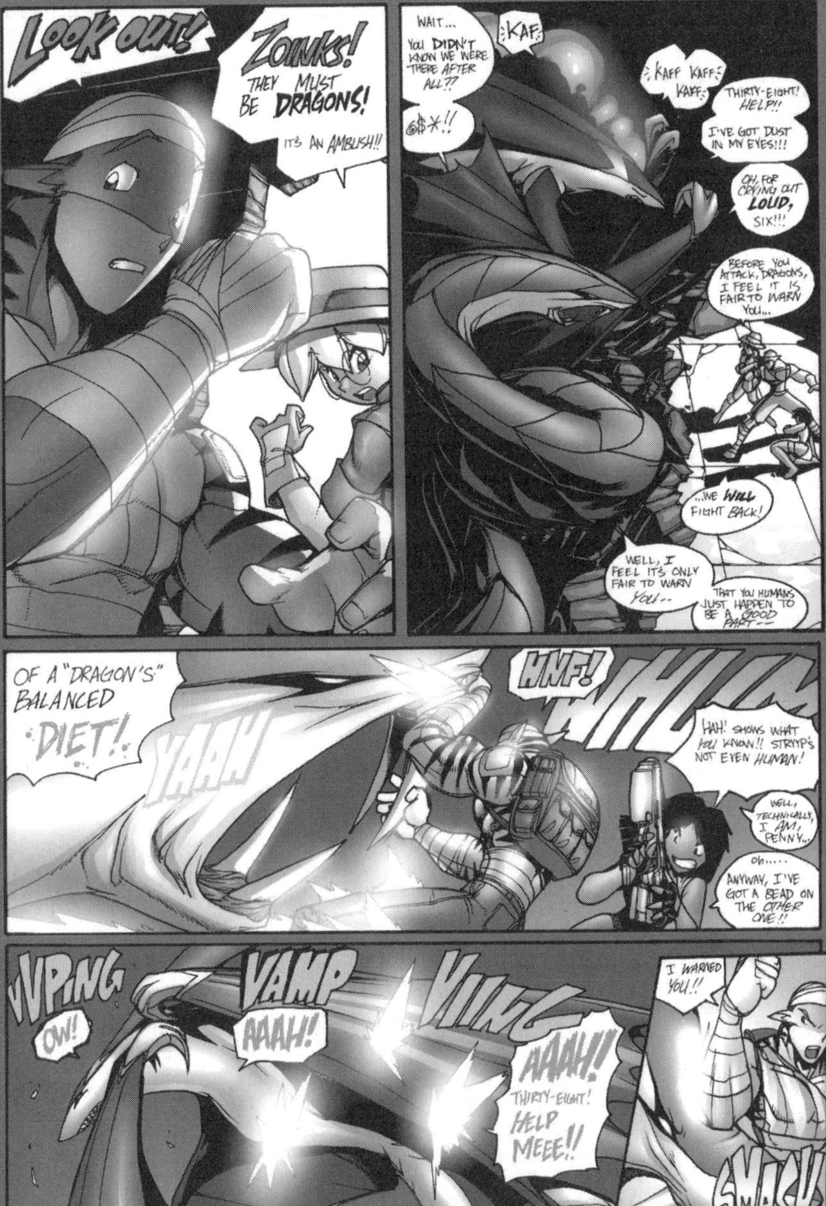
LOOK OUT!
ZOINKS! THEY MUST BE DRAGONS!
IT'S AN AMBUSH!!
WAIT... YOU DIDN'T KNOW WE WERE THERE AFTER ALL??
KAF
KAFF KAFF KAFF
THIRTY-EIGHT! HELP!!
I'VE GOT DUST IN MY EYES!!!
OH, FOR CRYING OUT LOUD, SIX!!!
BEFORE YOU ATTACK, DRAGONS, I FEEL IT IS FAIR TO WARN YOU...
...WE WILL FIGHT BACK!
WELL, I FEEL IT'S ONLY FAIR TO WARN YOU--
THAT YOU HUMANS JUST HAPPEN TO BE A GOOD PART--
OF A "DRAGON'S" BALANCED DIET!
YAAAH
HNF!
WHUM
HAH! SHOWS WHAT YOU KNOW!! STRYYP'S NOT EVEN HUMAN!
WELL, TECHNICALLY, I AM, PENNY...
OH.....
ANYWAY, I'VE GOT A BEAD ON THE OTHER ONE!!
VVPING
OW!
VAMP
AAAH!
VIING
AAAH! THIRTY-EIGHT! HELP MEEE!!
I WARNED YOU!!
SMASH
AUGHH

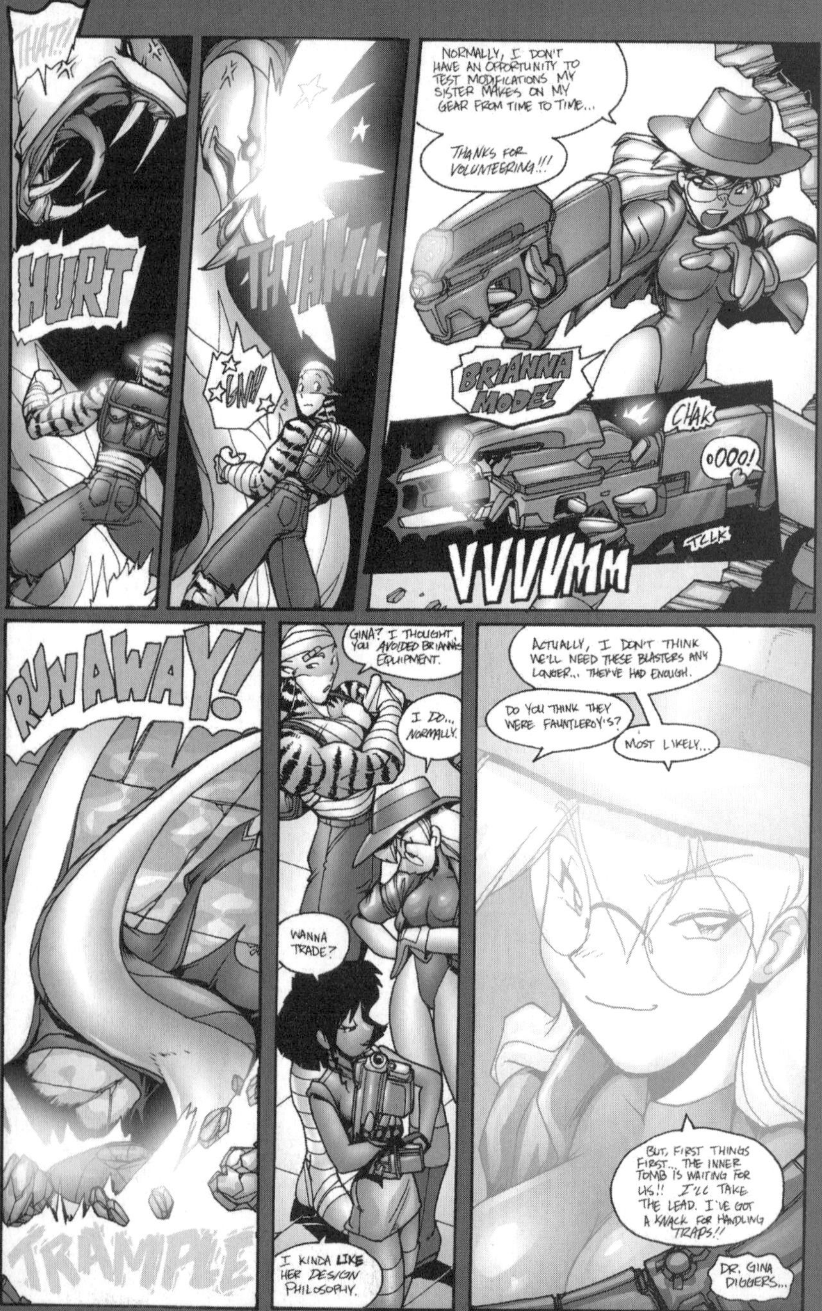
THAT!!
HURT
THTAMM
UNH!
NORMALLY, I DON'T HAVE AN OPPORTUNITY TO TEST MODIFICATIONS MY SISTER MAKES ON MY GEAR FROM TIME TO TIME...
THANKS FOR VOLUNTEERING!!!
BRIANNA MODE!
CHAK
OOOO!
TCLK
VVVVMM
RUN AWAY!
TRAMPLE
GINA? I THOUGHT YOU AVOIDED BRIANNA'S EQUIPMENT.
I DO... NORMALLY.
WANNA TRADE?
I KINDA LIKE HER DESIGN PHILOSOPHY.
ACTUALLY, I DON'T THINK WE'LL NEED THESE BLASTERS ANY LONGER... THEY'VE HAD ENOUGH.
DO YOU THINK THEY WERE FAUNTLEROY'S?
MOST LIKELY...
BUT, FIRST THINGS FIRST... THE INNER TOMB IS WAITING FOR US!! I'LL TAKE THE LEAD. I'VE GOT A KNACK FOR HANDLING TRAPS!!
DR. GINA DIGGERS...

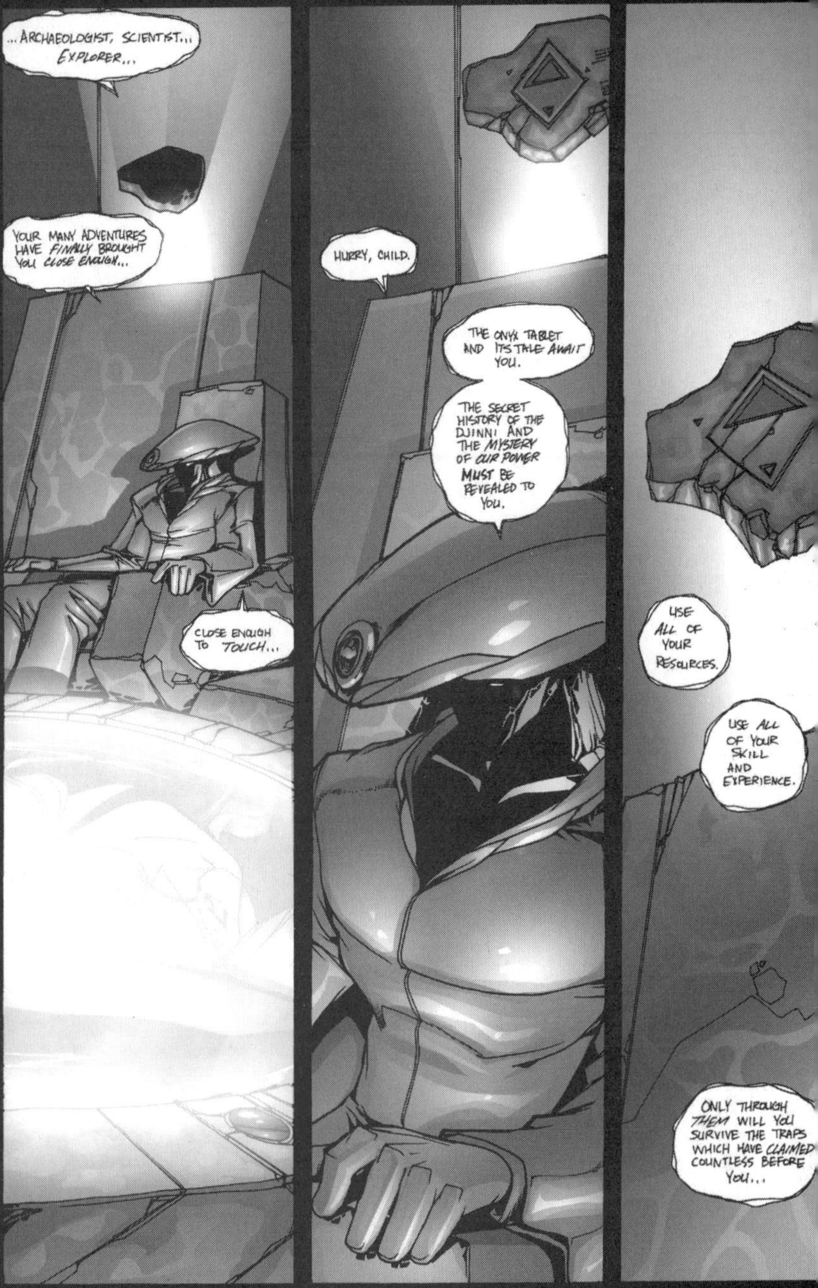
...ARCHAEOLOGIST, SCIENTIST... EXPLORER...
YOUR MANY ADVENTURES HAVE FINALLY BROUGHT YOU CLOSE ENOUGH...
CLOSE ENOUGH TO TOUCH...
HURRY, CHILD.
THE ONYX TABLET AND ITS TALE AWAIT YOU.
THE SECRET HISTORY OF THE DJINNI AND THE MYSTERY OF OUR POWER MUST BE REVEALED TO YOU.
USE ALL OF YOUR RESOURCES.
USE ALL OF YOUR SKILL AND EXPERIENCE.
ONLY THROUGH THEM WILL YOU SURVIVE THE TRAPS WHICH HAVE CLAIMED COUNTLESS BEFORE YOU...

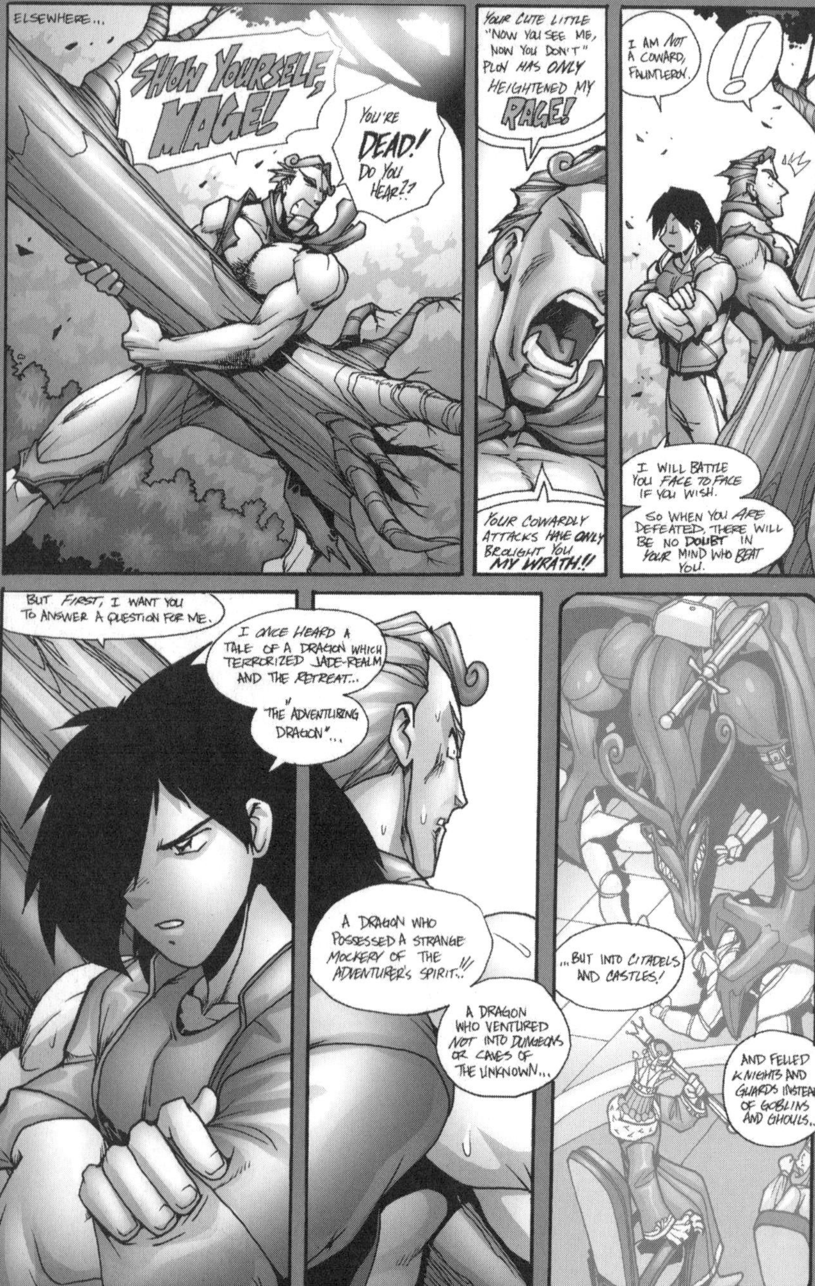
ELSEWHERE...
SHOW YOURSELF, MAGE!
YOU'RE DEAD! DO YOU HEAR?!?
YOUR CUTE LITTLE "NOW YOU SEE ME, NOW YOU DON'T" PLOY HAS ONLY HEIGHTENED MY RAGE!
YOUR COWARDLY ATTACKS HAVE ONLY BROUGHT YOU MY WRATH!!
I AM NOT A COWARD, FAUNTLEROY.
!
I WILL BATTLE YOU FACE TO FACE IF YOU WISH.
SO WHEN YOU ARE DEFEATED, THERE WILL BE NO DOUBT IN YOUR MIND WHO BEAT YOU.
BUT FIRST, I WANT YOU TO ANSWER A QUESTION FOR ME.
I ONCE HEARD A TALE OF A DRAGON WHICH TERRORIZED JADE-REALM AND THE RETREAT...
"THE ADVENTURING DRAGON"...
A DRAGON WHO POSSESSED A STRANGE MOCKERY OF THE ADVENTURER'S SPIRIT...!!
A DRAGON WHO VENTURED NOT INTO DUNGEONS OR CAVES OF THE UNKNOWN...
...BUT INTO CITADELS AND CASTLES!
AND FELLED KNIGHTS AND GUARDS INSTEAD OF GOBLINS AND GHOULS...

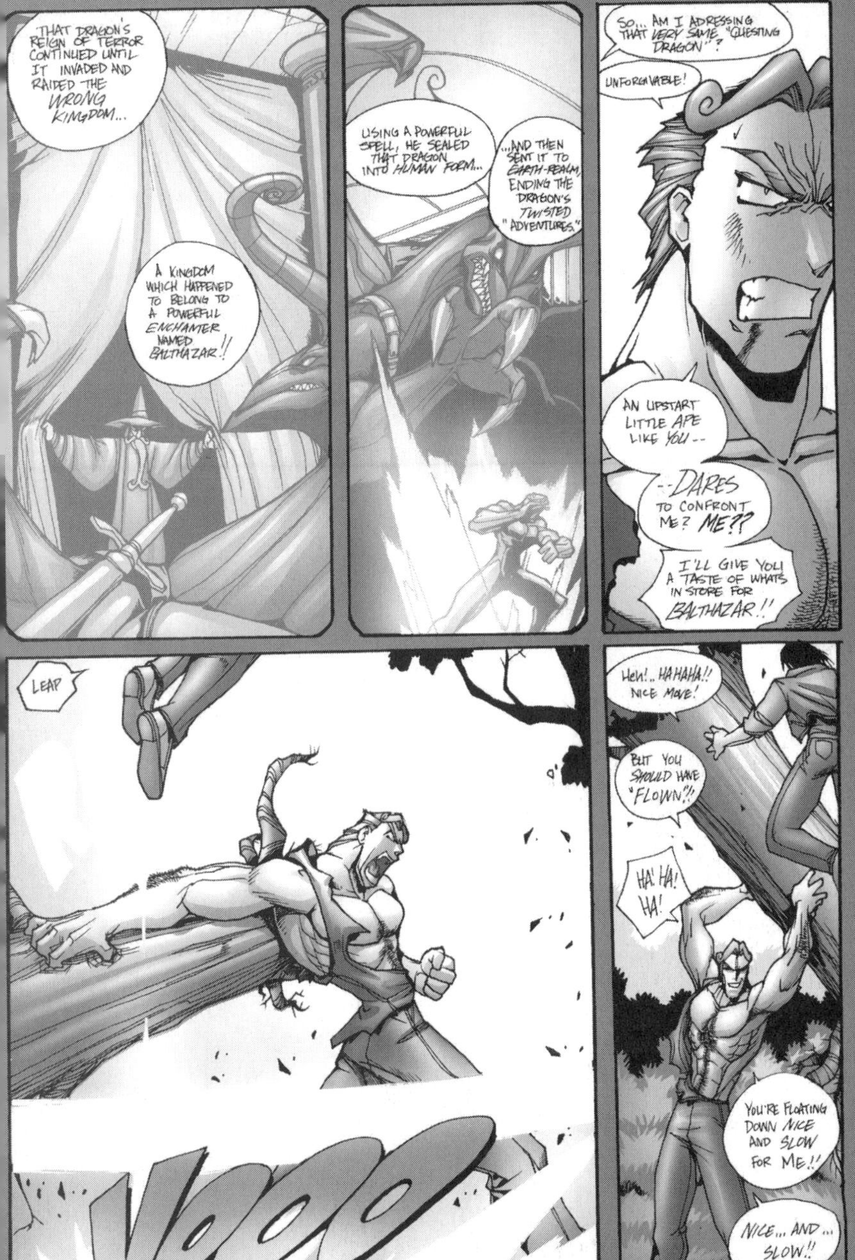
THAT DRAGON'S REIGN OF TERROR CONTINUED UNTIL IT INVADED AND RAIDED THE WRONG KINGDOM...
A KINGDOM WHICH HAPPENED TO BELONG TO A POWERFUL ENCHANTER NAMED BALTHAZAR!!
USING A POWERFUL SPELL, HE SEALED THAT DRAGON INTO HUMAN FORM...
...AND THEN SENT IT TO EARTH-REALM, ENDING THE DRAGON'S TWISTED "ADVENTURES."
SO... AM I ADRESSING THAT VERY SAME "QUESTING DRAGON"?
UNFORGIVABLE!
AN UPSTART LITTLE APE LIKE YOU--
--DARES TO CONFRONT ME? ME??
I'LL GIVE YOU A TASTE OF WHATS IN STORE FOR BALTHAZAR!!
LEAP
VOOO
Heh!.. HAHAHA!! NICE MOVE!
BUT YOU SHOULD HAVE "FLOWN"!!
HA! HA! HA!
YOU'RE FLOATING DOWN NICE AND SLOW FOR ME!!
NICE... AND... SLOW!!

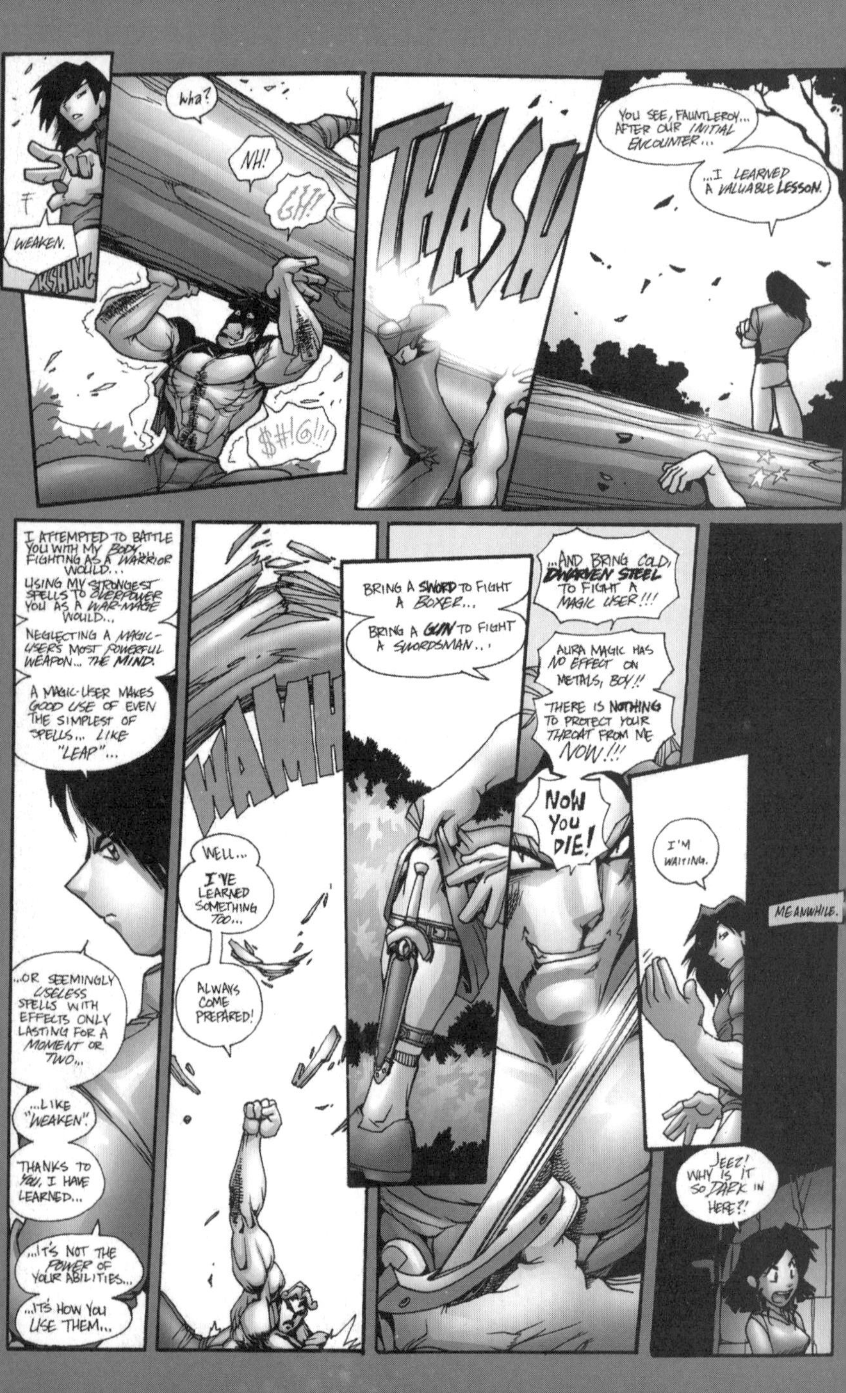
WEAKEN.
KSHING
Wha?
NH!
GH!
$#!@!!!
THASH
YOU SEE, FAUNTLEROY... AFTER OUR INITIAL ENCOUNTER...
...I LEARNED A VALUABLE LESSON.
I ATTEMPTED TO BATTLE YOU WITH MY BODY... FIGHTING AS A WARRIOR WOULD...
USING MY STRONGEST SPELLS TO OVERPOWER YOU AS A WAR-MAGE WOULD...
NEGLECTING A MAGIC-USER'S MOST POWERFUL WEAPON... THE MIND.
A MAGIC-USER MAKES GOOD USE OF EVEN THE SIMPLEST OF SPELLS... LIKE "LEAP"...
...OR SEEMINGLY USELESS SPELLS WITH EFFECTS ONLY LASTING FOR A MOMENT OR TWO...
...LIKE "WEAKEN".
THANKS TO YOU, I HAVE LEARNED...
...IT'S NOT THE POWER OF YOUR ABILITIES...
...IT'S HOW YOU USE THEM...
WAMH
WELL... I'VE LEARNED SOMETHING TOO...
ALWAYS COME PREPARED!
BRING A SWORD TO FIGHT A BOXER...
BRING A GUN TO FIGHT A SWORDSMAN...
...AND BRING COLD, DWARVEN STEEL TO FIGHT A MAGIC USER!!!
AURA MAGIC HAS NO EFFECT ON METALS, BOY!!
THERE IS NOTHING TO PROTECT YOUR THROAT FROM ME NOW!!!
NOW YOU DIE!
I'M WAITING.
MEANWHILE.
JEEZ! WHY IS IT SO DARK IN HERE?!

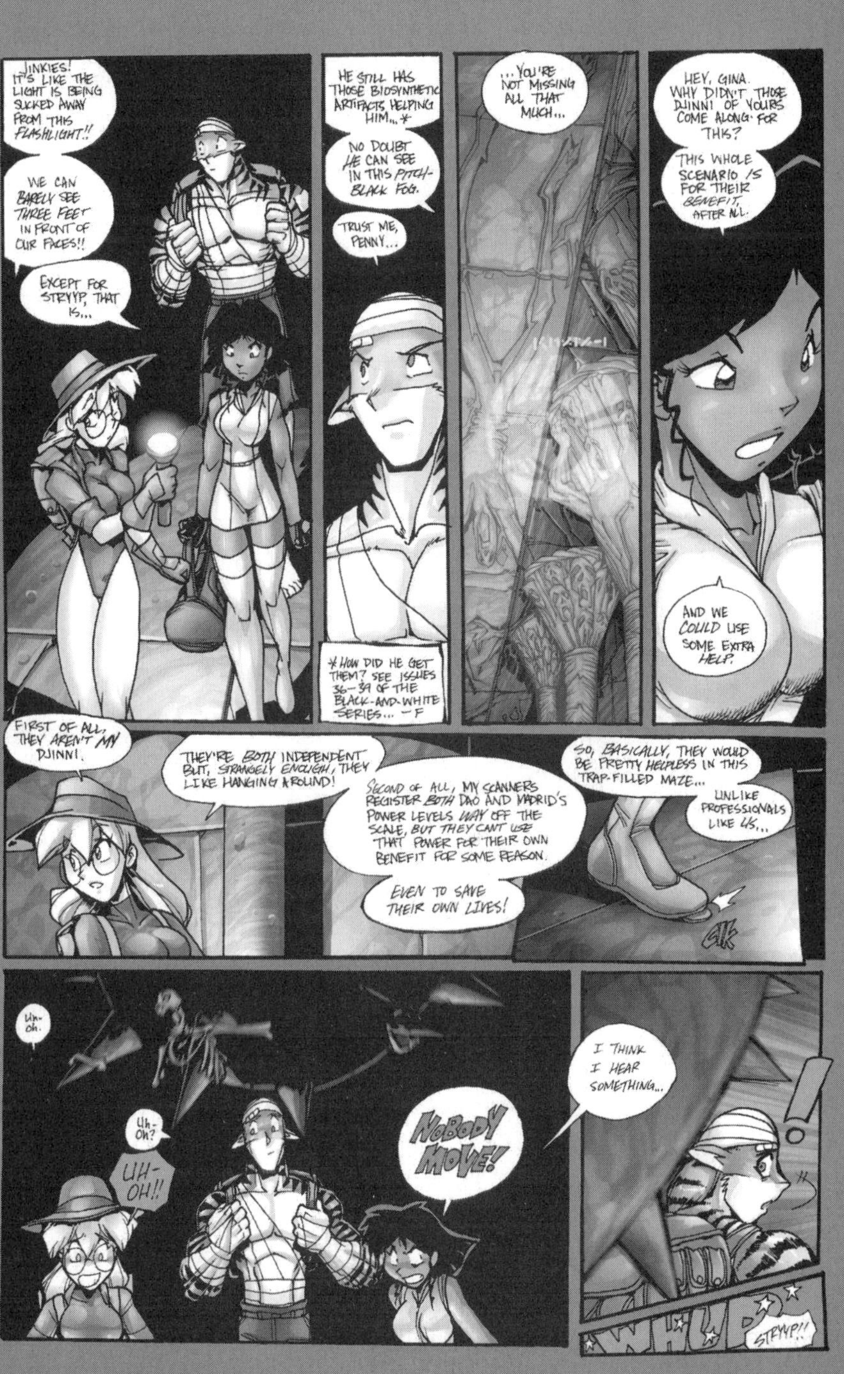

JINKIES! IT'S LIKE THE LIGHT IS BEING SUCKED AWAY FROM THIS FLASHLIGHT!!
WE CAN BARELY SEE THREE FEET IN FRONT OF OUR FACES!!
EXCEPT FOR STRYYP, THAT IS...
HE STILL HAS THOSE BIOSYNTHETIC ARTIFACTS HELPING HIM... *
NO DOUBT HE CAN SEE IN THIS PITCH-BLACK FOG.
TRUST ME, PENNY...
* HOW DID HE GET THEM? SEE ISSUES 36-39 OF THE BLACK-AND-WHITE SERIES... -F
...YOU'RE NOT MISSING ALL THAT MUCH...
HEY, GINA. WHY DIDN'T THOSE DJINNI OF YOURS COME ALONG FOR THIS?
THIS WHOLE SCENARIO IS FOR THEIR BENEFIT, AFTER ALL.
AND WE COULD USE SOME EXTRA HELP.
FIRST OF ALL, THEY AREN'T MY DJINNI.
THEY'RE BOTH INDEPENDENT BUT, STRANGELY ENOUGH, THEY LIKE HANGING AROUND!
SECOND OF ALL, MY SCANNERS REGISTER BOTH DAO AND MADRID'S POWER LEVELS WAY OFF THE SCALE, BUT THEY CANT USE THAT POWER FOR THEIR OWN BENEFIT FOR SOME REASON.
EVEN TO SAVE THEIR OWN LIVES!
SO, BASICALLY, THEY WOULD BE PRETTY HELPLESS IN THIS TRAP-FILLED MAZE...
UNLIKE PROFESSIONALS LIKE US...
CLIK
UH-OH.
UH-OH?
UH-OH!!
NOBODY MOVE!
I THINK I HEAR SOMETHING...
!
WHUD
STRYYP!!

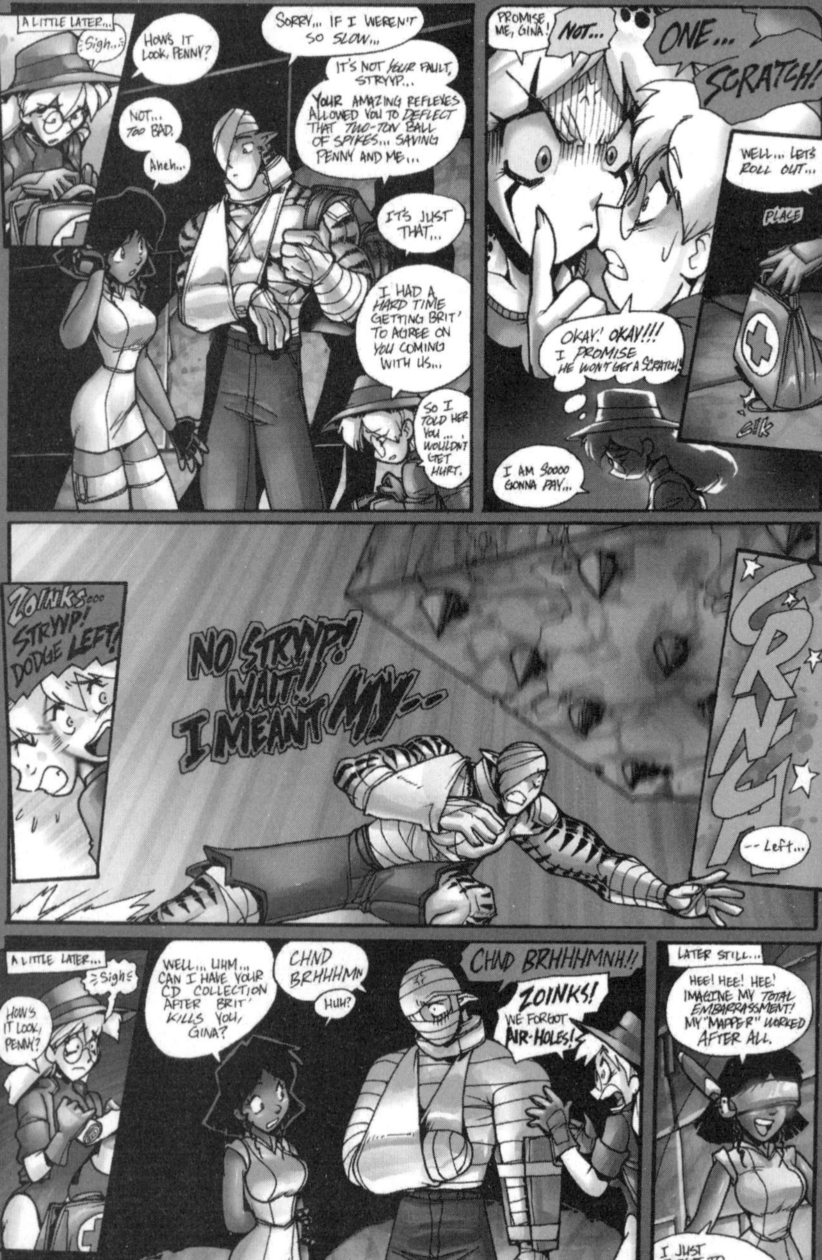
A LITTLE LATER...
Sigh...
HOW'S IT LOOK, PENNY?
NOT... TOO BAD.
Aheh...
SORRY... IF I WEREN'T SO SLOW...
IT'S NOT YOUR FAULT, STRYYP...
YOUR AMAZING REFLEXES ALLOWED YOU TO DEFLECT THAT TWO-TON BALL OF SPIKES... SAVING PENNY AND ME...
IT'S JUST THAT...
I HAD A HARD TIME GETTING BRIT' TO AGREE ON YOU COMING WITH US...
SO I TOLD HER YOU... WOULDN'T GET HURT.
PROMISE ME, GINA!
NOT...
ONE...
SCRATCH!!
OKAY! OKAY!!! I PROMISE HE WON'T GET A SCRATCH!
I AM SOOOO GONNA PAY...
WELL... LETS ROLL OUT...
PLACE
ZOINKSooo STRYYP! DODGE LEFT!
NO STRYYP! WAIT!! I MEANT MY--
CRNG
--Left...
A LITTLE LATER...
Sigh
HOW'S IT LOOK, PENNY?
WELL... UHM... CAN I HAVE YOUR CD COLLECTION AFTER BRIT' KILLS YOU, GINA?
CHND BRHHHMN
HUH?
CHND BRHHHMNH!!
ZOINKS! WE FORGOT AIR-HOLES!
LATER STILL...
HEE! HEE! HEE! IMAGINE MY TOTAL EMBARRASSMENT! MY "MAPPER" WORKED AFTER ALL.
I JUST FORGOT TO TURN OFF THE STUPID SCREEN-SAVER!

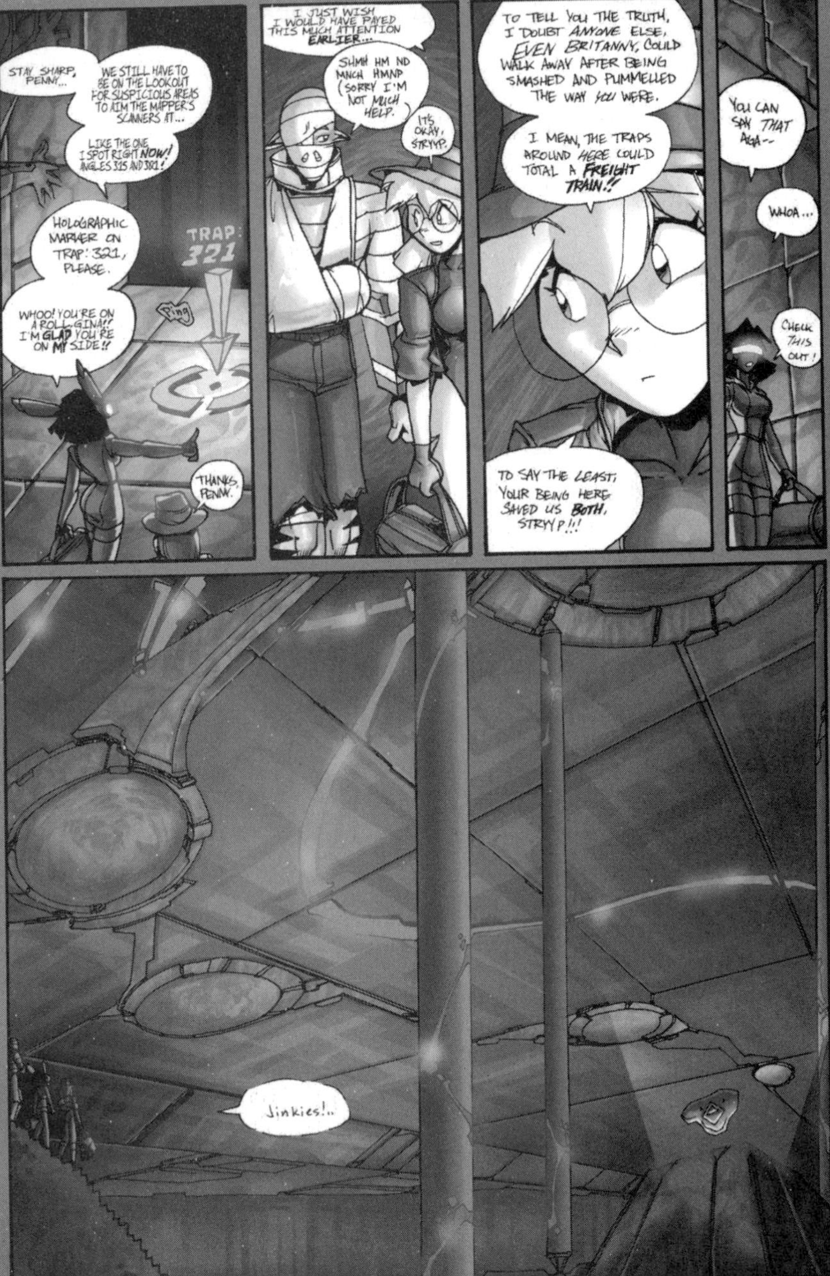
STAY SHARP, PENNY...
WE STILL HAVE TO BE ON THE LOOKOUT FOR SUSPICIOUS AREAS TO AIM THE MAPPER'S SCANNERS AT...
LIKE THE ONE I SPOT RIGHT NOW! ANGLES 315 AND 321!
HOLOGRAPHIC MARKER ON TRAP: 321, PLEASE.
TRAP: 321
Ping
WHOO! YOU'RE ON A ROLL, GINA!! I'M GLAD YOU'RE ON MY SIDE!!
THANKS, PENNY.
I JUST WISH I WOULD HAVE PAYED THIS MUCH ATTENTION EARLIER...
SHMH HM ND MNCH HMNP (SORRY I'M NOT MUCH HELP.)
IT'S OKAY, STRYYP.
TO TELL YOU THE TRUTH, I DOUBT ANYONE ELSE, EVEN BRITANNY, COULD WALK AWAY AFTER BEING SMASHED AND PUMMELLED THE WAY YOU WERE.
I MEAN, THE TRAPS AROUND HERE COULD TOTAL A FREIGHT TRAIN!!
TO SAY THE LEAST, YOUR BEING HERE SAVED US BOTH, STRYYP!!!
YOU CAN SAY THAT AGA--
WHOA...
CHECK THIS OUT!
Jinkies!..

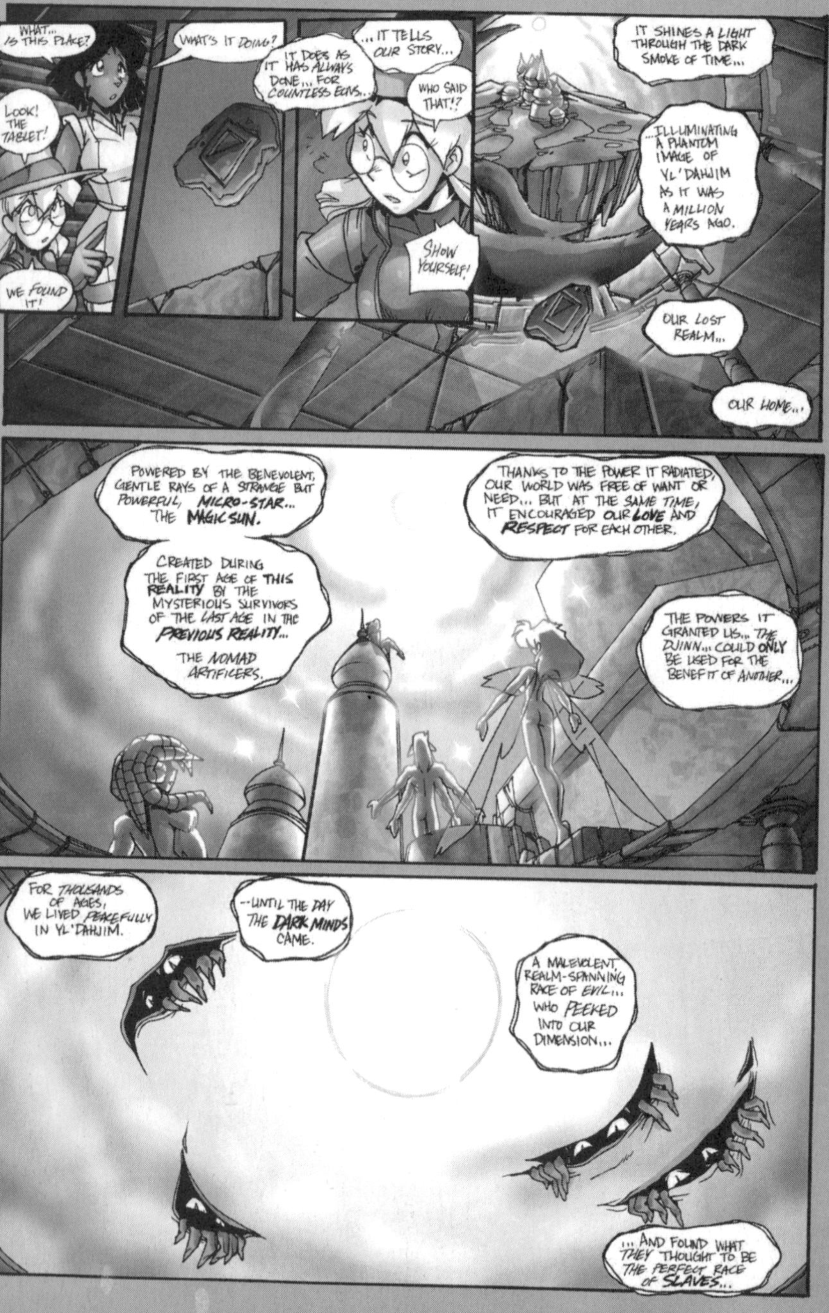

WHAT... IS THIS PLACE?
LOOK! THE TABLET!
WE FOUND IT!
WHAT'S IT DOING?
IT DOES AS IT HAS ALWAYS DONE... FOR COUNTLESS EONS...
...IT TELLS OUR STORY...
WHO SAID THAT!?
SHOW YOURSELF!
IT SHINES A LIGHT THROUGH THE DARK SMOKE OF TIME...
...ILLUMINATING A PHANTOM IMAGE OF YL'DAHJIM AS IT WAS A MILLION YEARS AGO.
OUR LOST REALM...
OUR HOME...
POWERED BY THE BENEVOLENT, GENTLE RAYS OF A STRANGE BUT POWERFUL, MICRO-STAR... THE MAGIC SUN.
CREATED DURING THE FIRST AGE OF THIS REALITY BY THE MYSTERIOUS SURVIVORS OF THE LAST AGE IN THE PREVIOUS REALITY... THE NOMAD ARTIFICERS.
THANKS TO THE POWER IT RADIATED, OUR WORLD WAS FREE OF WANT OR NEED... BUT AT THE SAME TIME, IT ENCOURAGED OUR LOVE AND RESPECT FOR EACH OTHER.
THE POWERS IT GRANTED US... THE DJINN... COULD ONLY BE USED FOR THE BENEFIT OF ANOTHER...
FOR THOUSANDS OF AGES, WE LIVED PEACEFULLY IN YL'DAHJIM.
--UNTIL THE DAY THE DARK MINDS CAME.
A MALEVOLENT, REALM-SPANNING RACE OF EVIL... WHO PEEKED INTO OUR DIMENSION...
...AND FOUND WHAT THEY THOUGHT TO BE THE PERFECT RACE OF SLAVES...

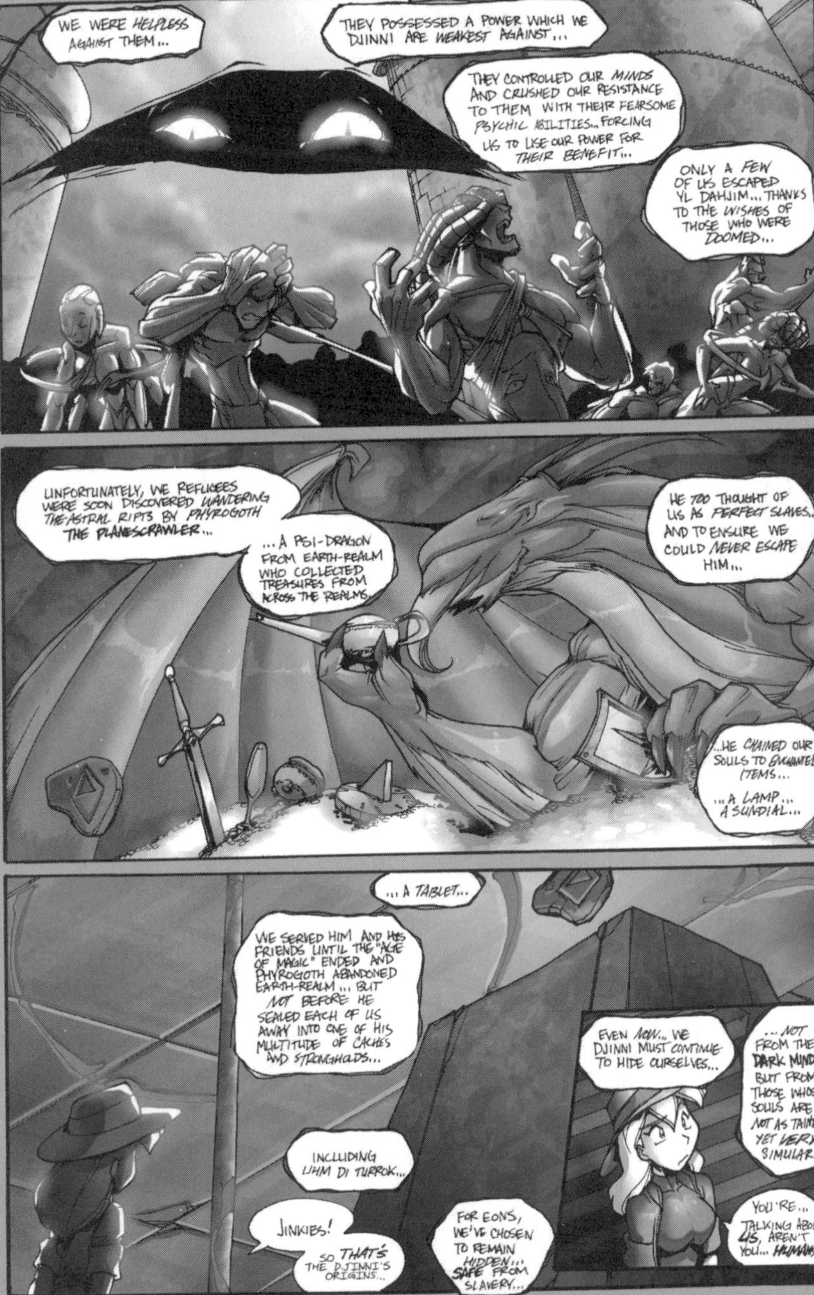
WE WERE HELPLESS AGAINST THEM...
THEY POSSESSED A POWER WHICH WE DJINNI ARE WEAKEST AGAINST...
THEY CONTROLLED OUR MINDS AND CRUSHED OUR RESISTANCE TO THEM WITH THEIR FEARSOME PSYCHIC ABILITIES... FORCING US TO USE OUR POWER FOR THEIR BENEFIT...
ONLY A FEW OF US ESCAPED YL DAHJIM... THANKS TO THE WISHES OF THOSE WHO WERE DOOMED...
UNFORTUNATELY, WE REFUGEES WERE SOON DISCOVERED WANDERING THE ASTRAL RIPTS BY PHYROGOTH THE PLANESCRAWLER...
...A PSI-DRAGON FROM EARTH-REALM WHO COLLECTED TREASURES FROM ACROSS THE REALMS.
HE TOO THOUGHT OF US AS PERFECT SLAVES. AND TO ENSURE WE COULD NEVER ESCAPE HIM...
...HE CHAINED OUR SOULS TO ENCHANTED ITEMS...
...A LAMP... A SUNDIAL...
...A TABLET...
WE SERVED HIM AND HIS FRIENDS UNTIL THE "AGE OF MAGIC" ENDED AND PHYROGOTH ABANDONED EARTH-REALM... BUT NOT BEFORE HE SEALED EACH OF US AWAY INTO ONE OF HIS MULTITUDE OF CACHES AND STRONGHOLDS...
INCLUDING UHM DI TURROK...
JINKIES!
SO THAT'S THE DJINNI'S ORIGINS...
FOR EONS, WE'VE CHOSEN TO REMAIN HIDDEN... SAFE FROM SLAVERY...
EVEN NOW... WE DJINNI MUST CONTINUE TO HIDE OURSELVES...
...NOT FROM THE DARK MINDS BUT FROM THOSE WHOSE SOULS ARE NOT AS TAINTED, YET VERY SIMULAR...
YOU'RE... TALKING ABOUT US, AREN'T YOU... HUMANS...

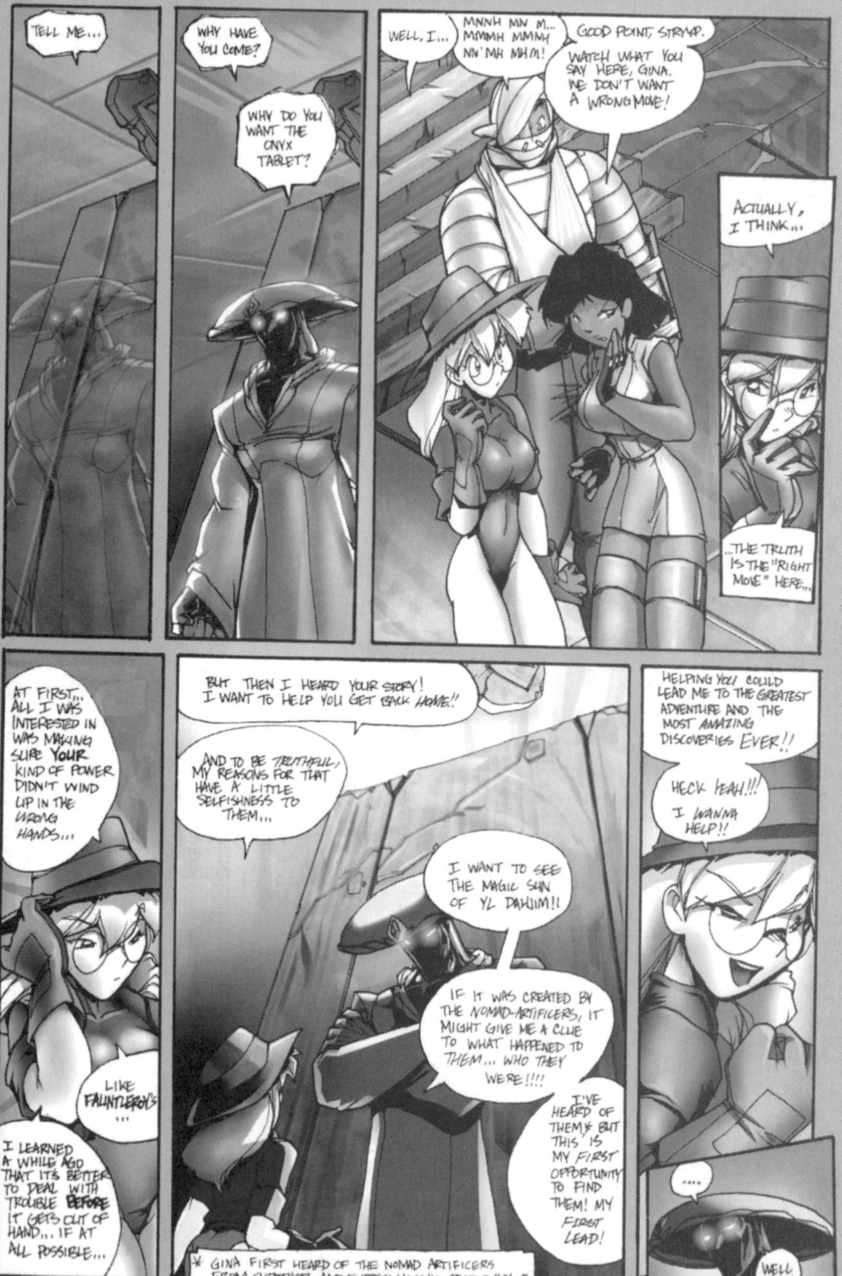

TELL ME...
WHY HAVE YOU COME?
WHY DO YOU WANT THE ONYX TABLET?
WELL, I...
MNNH MN M... MMMH MMMH NN'MH MHM!
GOOD POINT, STRYKP.
WATCH WHAT YOU SAY HERE, GINA. WE DON'T WANT A WRONG MOVE!
ACTUALLY, I THINK...
...THE TRUTH IS THE "RIGHT MOVE" HERE...
AT FIRST... ALL I WAS INTERESTED IN WAS MAKING SURE YOUR KIND OF POWER DIDN'T WIND UP IN THE WRONG HANDS...
LIKE FAUNTLEROY'S ...
I LEARNED A WHILE AGO THAT IT'S BETTER TO DEAL WITH TROUBLE BEFORE IT GETS OUT OF HAND... IF AT ALL POSSIBLE...
BUT THEN I HEARD YOUR STORY! I WANT TO HELP YOU GET BACK HOME!!
AND TO BE TRUTHFUL, MY REASONS FOR THAT HAVE A LITTLE SELFISHNESS TO THEM...
I WANT TO SEE THE MAGIC SUN OF YL DAHJIM!!
IF IT WAS CREATED BY THE NOMAD-ARTIFICERS, IT MIGHT GIVE ME A CLUE TO WHAT HAPPENED TO THEM... WHO THEY WERE!!!!
I'VE HEARD OF THEM,* BUT THIS IS MY FIRST OPPORTUNITY TO FIND THEM! MY FIRST LEAD!
* GINA FIRST HEARD OF THE NOMAD ARTIFICERS FROM SUBTRACTO AND EMPRESS LYNN IN GD VOL.2 #26-F.
HELPING YOU COULD LEAD ME TO THE GREATEST ADVENTURE AND THE MOST AMAZING DISCOVERIES EVER!!
HECK YEAH!!!
I WANNA HELP!!
....
WELL SAID!

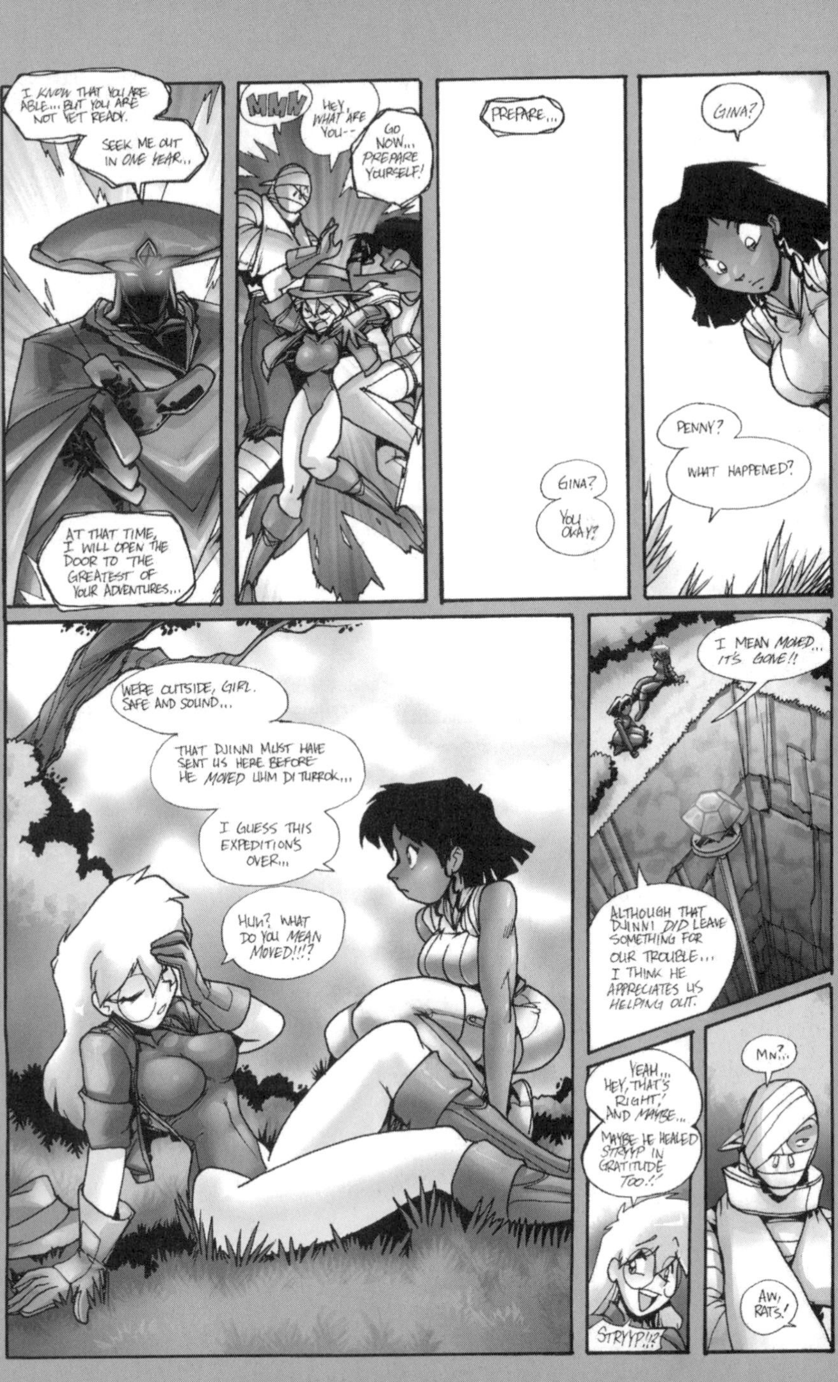

I KNOW THAT YOU ARE ABLE... BUT YOU ARE NOT YET READY.
SEEK ME OUT IN ONE YEAR...
AT THAT TIME, I WILL OPEN THE DOOR TO THE GREATEST OF YOUR ADVENTURES...
MMW
HEY, WHAT ARE YOU--
GO NOW... PREPARE YOURSELF!
PREPARE...
GINA? YOU OKAY?
GINA?
PENNY? WHAT HAPPENED?
WERE OUTSIDE, GIRL. SAFE AND SOUND...
THAT DJINNI MUST HAVE SENT US HERE BEFORE HE MOVED UHM DI TURROK...
I GUESS THIS EXPEDITION'S OVER...
HUH? WHAT DO YOU MEAN MOVED!!!?
I MEAN MOVED... IT'S GONE!!
ALTHOUGH THAT DJINNI DID LEAVE SOMETHING FOR OUR TROUBLE... I THINK HE APPRECIATES US HELPING OUT.
YEAH... HEY, THAT'S RIGHT! AND MAYBE...
MAYBE HE HEALED STRYYP IN GRATITUDE TOO!!
STRYYP!!?
MN?...
AW, RATS!

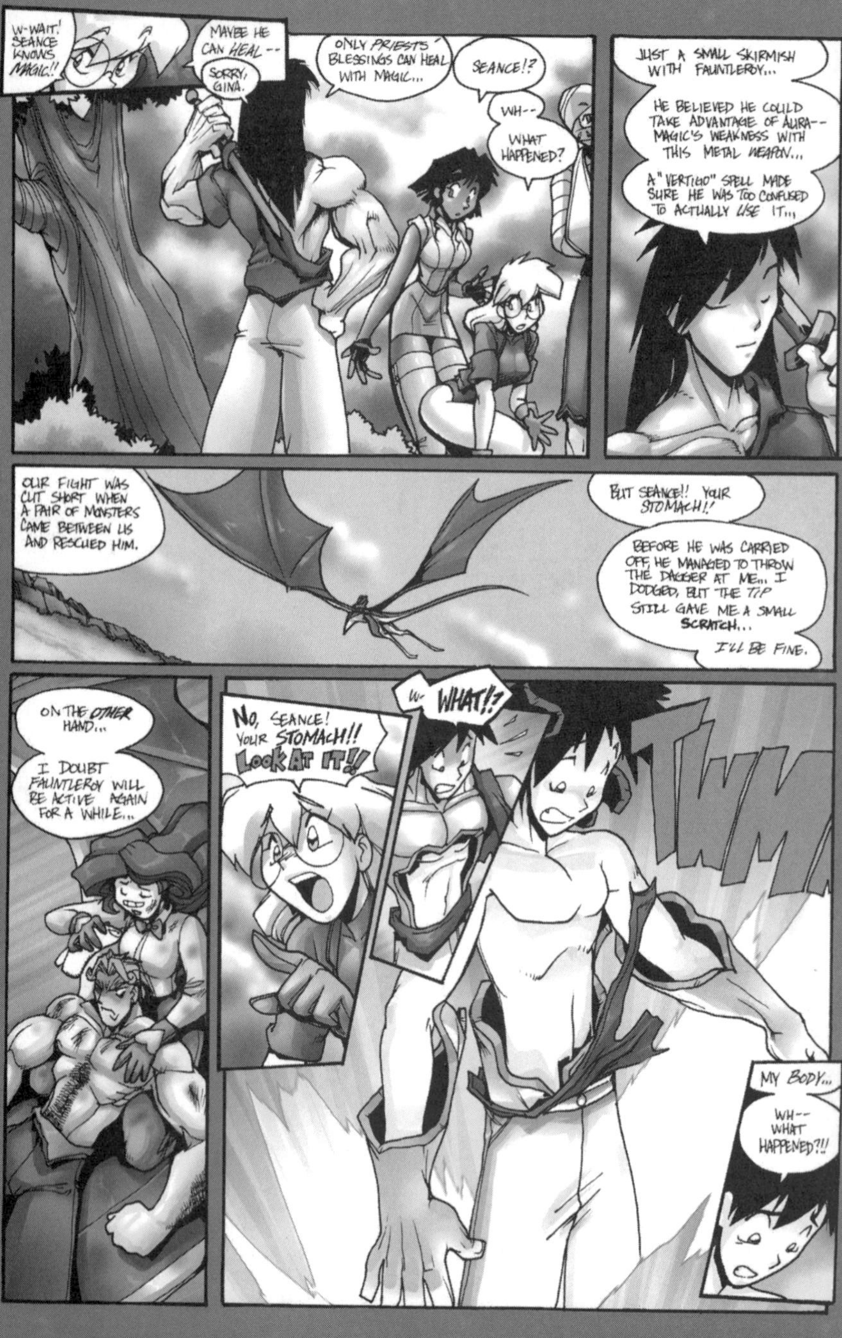
W-WAIT! SEANCE KNOWS MAGIC!!
MAYBE HE CAN HEAL--
SORRY, GINA.
ONLY PRIESTS' BLESSINGS CAN HEAL WITH MAGIC...
SEANCE!?
WH--
WHAT HAPPENED?
JUST A SMALL SKIRMISH WITH FAUNTLEROY...
HE BELIEVED HE COULD TAKE ADVANTAGE OF AURA-MAGIC'S WEAKNESS WITH THIS METAL WEAPON...
A "VERTIGO" SPELL MADE SURE HE WAS TOO CONFUSED TO ACTUALLY USE IT...
OUR FIGHT WAS CUT SHORT WHEN A PAIR OF MONSTERS CAME BETWEEN US AND RESCUED HIM.
BUT SEANCE!! YOUR STOMACH!!
BEFORE HE WAS CARRIED OFF, HE MANAGED TO THROW THE DAGGER AT ME... I DODGED, BUT THE TIP STILL GAVE ME A SMALL SCRATCH...
I'LL BE FINE.
ON THE OTHER HAND...
I DOUBT FAUNTLEROY WILL BE ACTIVE AGAIN FOR A WHILE...
NO, SEANCE! YOUR STOMACH!! LOOK AT IT!!
W- WHAT!?
THWM
MY BODY...
WH-- WHAT HAPPENED?!!

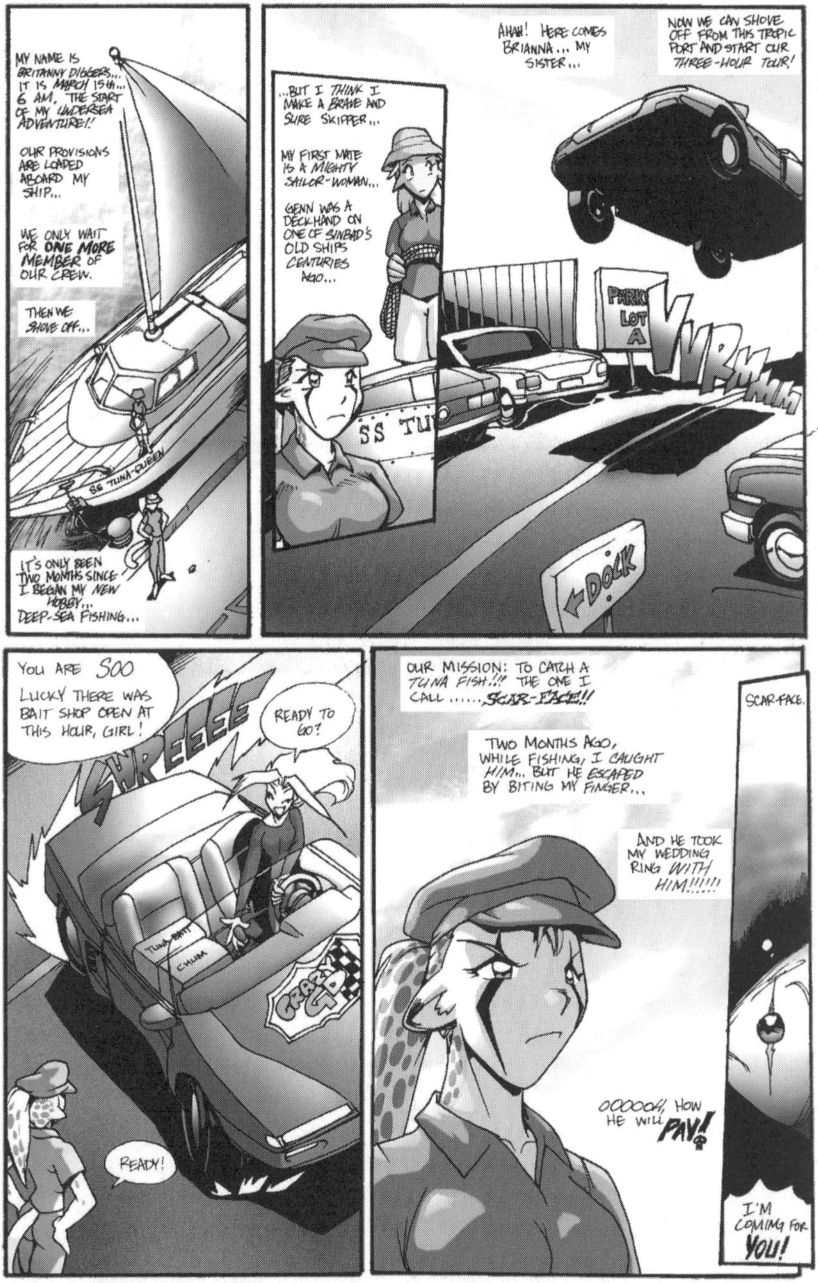

MY NAME IS BRITANNY DIGGERS... IT IS MARCH 15th... 6 AM, THE START OF MY UNDERSEA ADVENTURE!
OUR PROVISIONS ARE LOADED ABOARD MY SHIP...
WE ONLY WAIT FOR ONE MORE MEMBER OF OUR CREW.
THEN WE SHOVE OFF...
SS TUNA-QUEEN
IT'S ONLY BEEN TWO MONTHS SINCE I BEGAN MY NEW HOBBY... DEEP-SEA FISHING...
...BUT I THINK I MAKE A BRAVE AND SURE SKIPPER...
MY FIRST MATE IS A MIGHTY SAILOR-WOMAN...
GENN WAS A DECKHAND ON ONE OF SINBAD'S OLD SHIPS CENTURIES AGO...
SS TU
AHAH! HERE COMES BRIANNA... MY SISTER...
NOW WE CAN SHOVE OFF FROM THIS TROPIC PORT AND START OUR THREE-HOUR TOUR!
LOT A
VVRMMMM
DOCK
YOU ARE SOO LUCKY THERE WAS BAIT SHOP OPEN AT THIS HOUR, GIRL!
SHREEEE
READY TO GO?
TUNA BAIT
CHUM
READY!
OUR MISSION: TO CATCH A TUNA FISH!!! THE ONE I CALL ...... SCAR-FACE!!
TWO MONTHS AGO, WHILE FISHING, I CAUGHT HIM... BUT HE ESCAPED BY BITING MY FINGER...
AND HE TOOK MY WEDDING RING WITH HIM!!!!!!
OOOOOH, HOW HE WILL PAY!
SCAR-FACE.
I'M COMING FOR YOU!

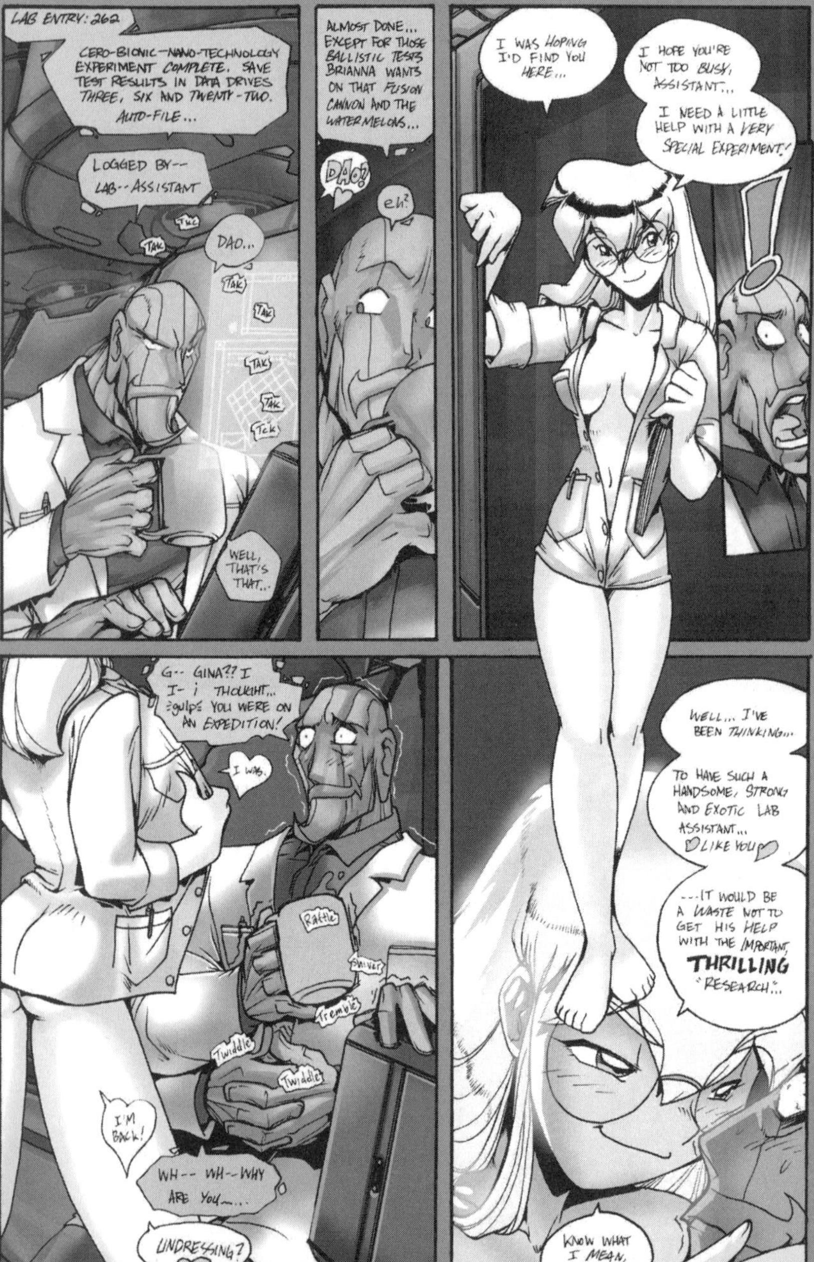
LAB ENTRY: 262
CERO-BIONIC-NANO-TECHNOLOGY EXPERIMENT COMPLETE. SAVE TEST RESULTS IN DATA DRIVES THREE, SIX AND TWENTY-TWO. AUTO-FILE...
LOGGED BY-- LAB--ASSISTANT
TAK
TAK
DAO...
TAK
TAK
TAK
TAK
Tck
WELL, THAT'S THAT...
ALMOST DONE... EXCEPT FOR THOSE BALLISTIC TESTS BRIANNA WANTS ON THAT FUSION CANNON AND THE WATERMELONS...
DAO?!
eh?
I WAS HOPING I'D FIND YOU HERE...
I HOPE YOU'RE NOT TOO BUSY, ASSISTANT...
I NEED A LITTLE HELP WITH A VERY SPECIAL EXPERIMENT!
G-- GINA?!? I I- i THOUGHT... gulp YOU WERE ON AN EXPEDITION!
I WAS.
Rattle
Shiver
Tremble
Twiddle
Twiddle
I'M BACK!
WH-- WH--WHY ARE YOU.....
UNDRESSING?
WELL... I'VE BEEN THINKING...
TO HAVE SUCH A HANDSOME, STRONG AND EXOTIC LAB ASSISTANT... LIKE YOU
...IT WOULD BE A WASTE NOT TO GET HIS HELP WITH THE IMPORTANT, THRILLING "RESEARCH"...
KNOW WHAT I MEAN, DARLING?

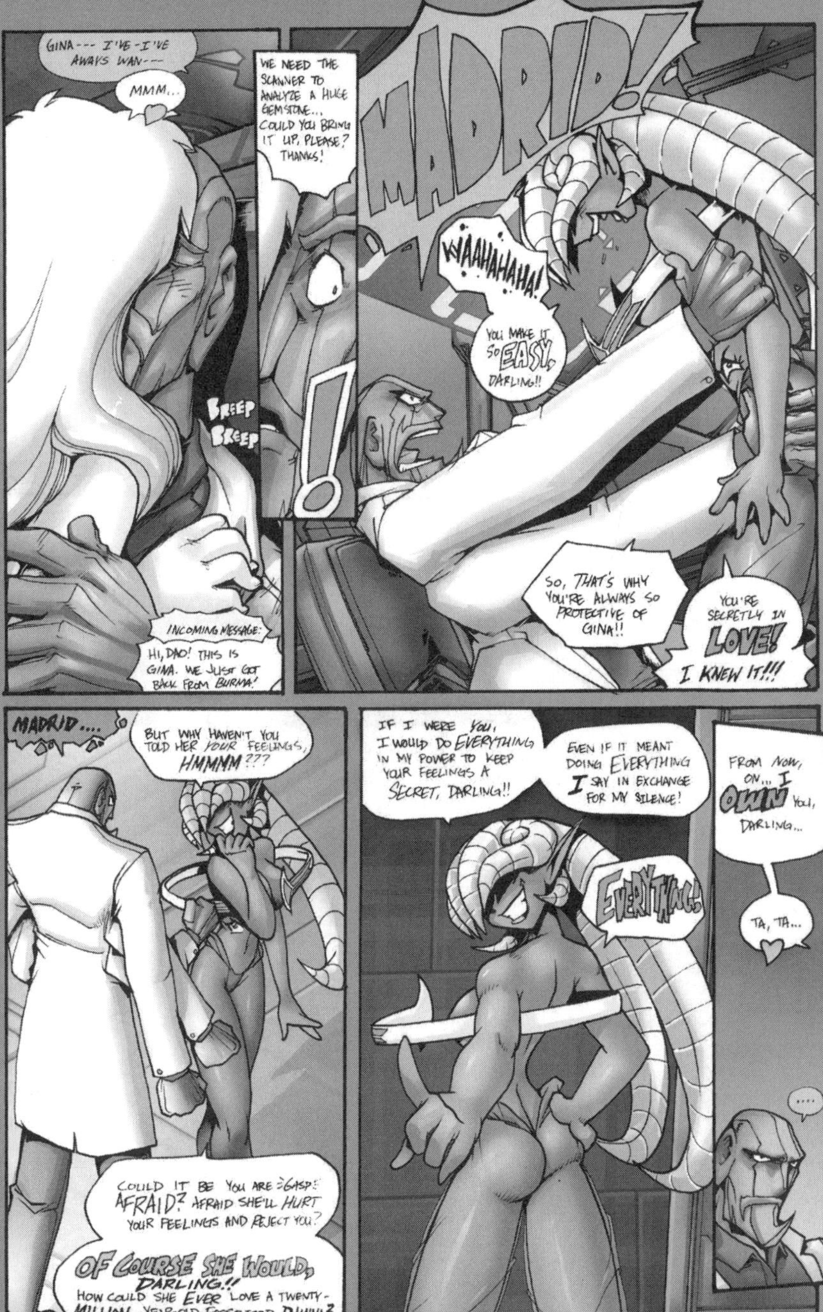
GINA--- I'VE-I'VE AWAYS WAN---
MMM...
BREEP BREEP
INCOMING MESSAGE:
HI, DAO! THIS IS GINA. WE JUST GOT BACK FROM BURMA!
WE NEED THE SCANNER TO ANALYZE A HUGE GEMSTONE... COULD YOU BRING IT UP, PLEASE? THANKS!
!
MADRID!
WAAHAHAHA!
YOU MAKE IT SO EASY, DARLING!!
SO, THAT'S WHY YOU'RE ALWAYS SO PROTECTIVE OF GINA!!
YOU'RE SECRETLY IN LOVE! I KNEW IT!!!
MADRID....
BUT WHY HAVEN'T YOU TOLD HER YOUR FEELINGS, HMMMM???
COULD IT BE YOU ARE GASP AFRAID? AFRAID SHE'LL HURT YOUR FEELINGS AND REJECT YOU?
OF COURSE SHE WOULD, DARLING!! HOW COULD SHE EVER LOVE A TWENTY-MILLION-YEAR-OLD FOSSILIZED DJINNI?
IF I WERE YOU, I WOULD DO EVERYTHING IN MY POWER TO KEEP YOUR FEELINGS A SECRET, DARLING!!
EVEN IF IT MEANT DOING EVERYTHING I SAY IN EXCHANGE FOR MY SILENCE!
EVERYTHING!
FROM NOW, ON... I OWN YOU, DARLING...
TA, TA...
....

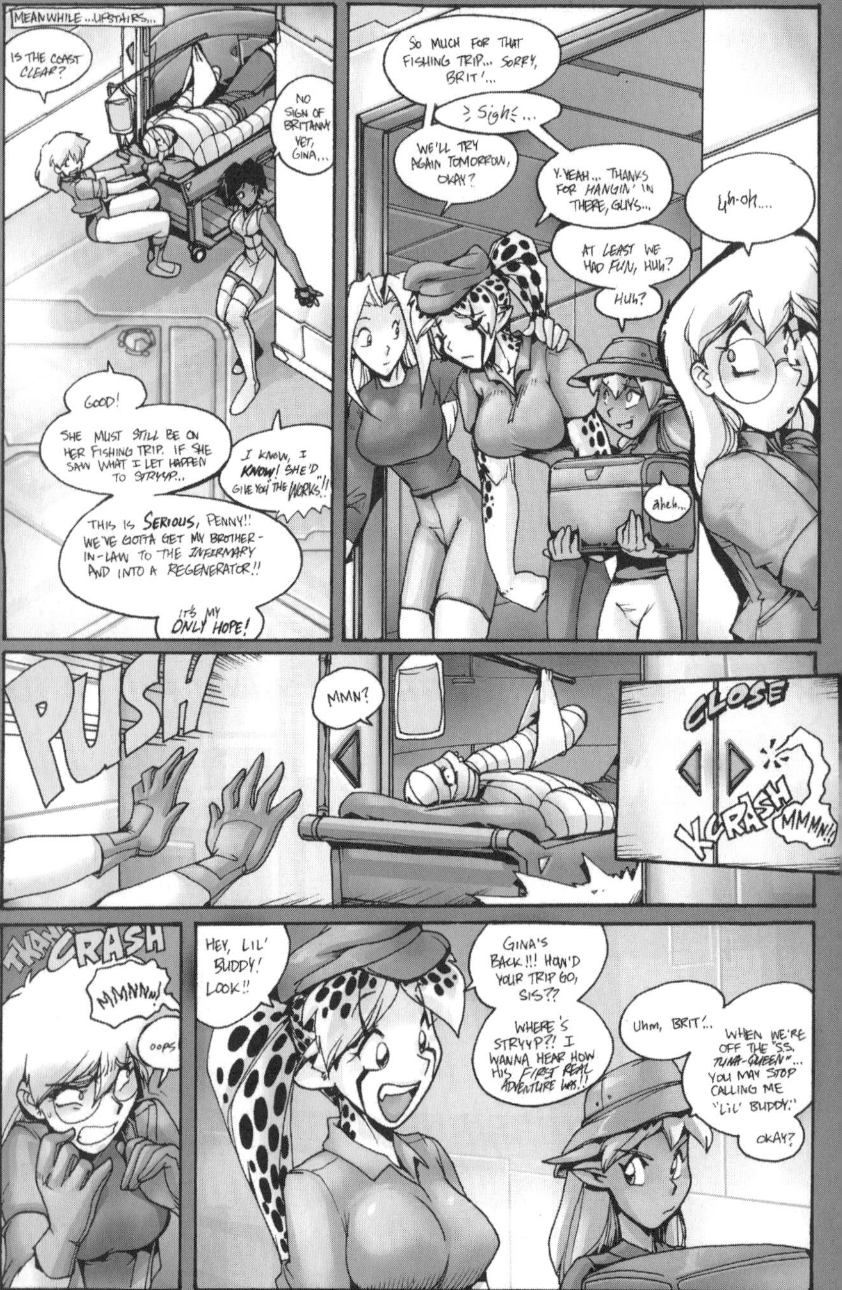
MEANWHILE... UPSTAIRS...
IS THE COAST CLEAR?
NO SIGN OF BRITANNY YET, GINA...
GOOD!
SHE MUST STILL BE ON HER FISHING TRIP. IF SHE SAW WHAT I LET HAPPEN TO STRYYP...
I KNOW, I KNOW! SHE'D GIVE YOU THE WORKS!!
THIS IS SERIOUS, PENNY!! WE'VE GOTTA GET MY BROTHER-IN-LAW TO THE INFIRMARY AND INTO A REGENERATOR!!
IT'S MY ONLY HOPE!
SO MUCH FOR THAT FISHING TRIP... SORRY, BRIT'...
≷ Sigh ≶ ...
WE'LL TRY AGAIN TOMORROW, OKAY?
Y-YEAH... THANKS FOR HANGIN' IN THERE, GUYS...
Uh-oh....
AT LEAST WE HAD FUN, HUH?
HUH?
aheh...
PUSH
MMN?
CLOSE
KRASH
MMMN!!
CRASH
MMNNN!
oops
HEY, LIL' BUDDY! LOOK!!
GINA'S BACK!!! HOW'D YOUR TRIP GO, SIS??
WHERE'S STRYYP?! I WANNA HEAR HOW HIS FIRST REAL ADVENTURE WAS!!
UHM, BRIT'...
WHEN WE'RE OFF THE "S.S. TUNA-QUEEN"... YOU MAY STOP CALLING ME "LIL' BUDDY."
OKAY?

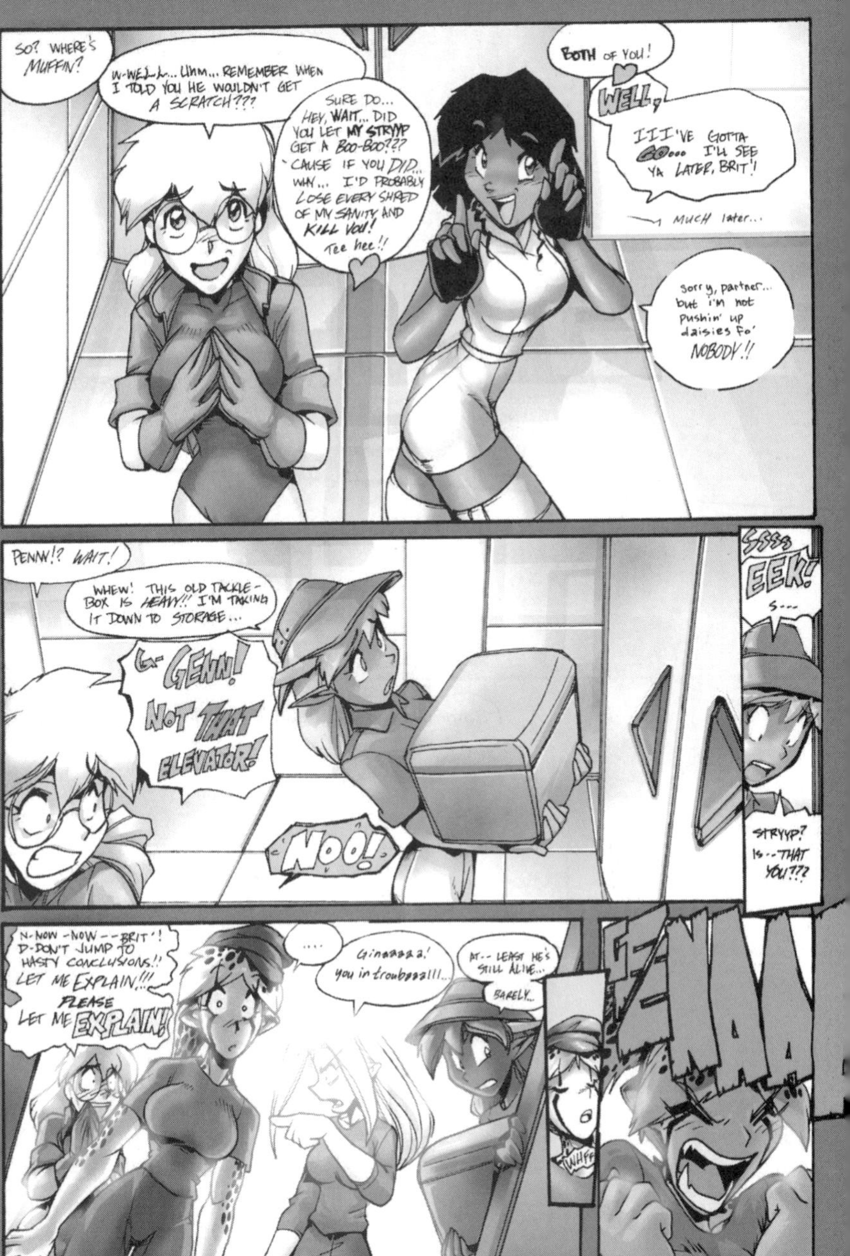
SO? WHERE'S MUFFIN?
W-WELL... Uhm... REMEMBER WHEN I TOLD YOU HE WOULDN'T GET A SCRATCH???
SURE DO... HEY, WAIT... DID YOU LET MY STRYYP GET A BOO-BOO??? 'CAUSE IF YOU DID... WHY... I'D PROBABLY LOSE EVERY SHRED OF MY SANITY AND KILL YOU! Tee hee!!
BOTH OF YOU!
WELL,
III'VE GOTTA GOooo I'LL SEE YA LATER, BRIT'!
MUCH later...
sorry, partner... but i'm not pushin' up daisies fo' NOBODY!!
PENNY!? WAIT!
WHEW! THIS OLD TACKLE-BOX IS HEAVY!! I'M TAKING IT DOWN TO STORAGE...
G-GENN! NOT THAT ELEVATOR!
NOO!
SSSS
EEK!
S...
STRYYP? IS--THAT YOU???
N-NOW-NOW--BRIT'! D-DON'T JUMP TO HASTY CONCLUSIONS!! LET ME EXPLAIN!!! PLEASE LET ME EXPLAIN!
....
Ginaaaaa! you in troubaaa!!!...
AT-- LEAST HE'S STILL ALIVE...
BARELY...
WHFF
GENAA

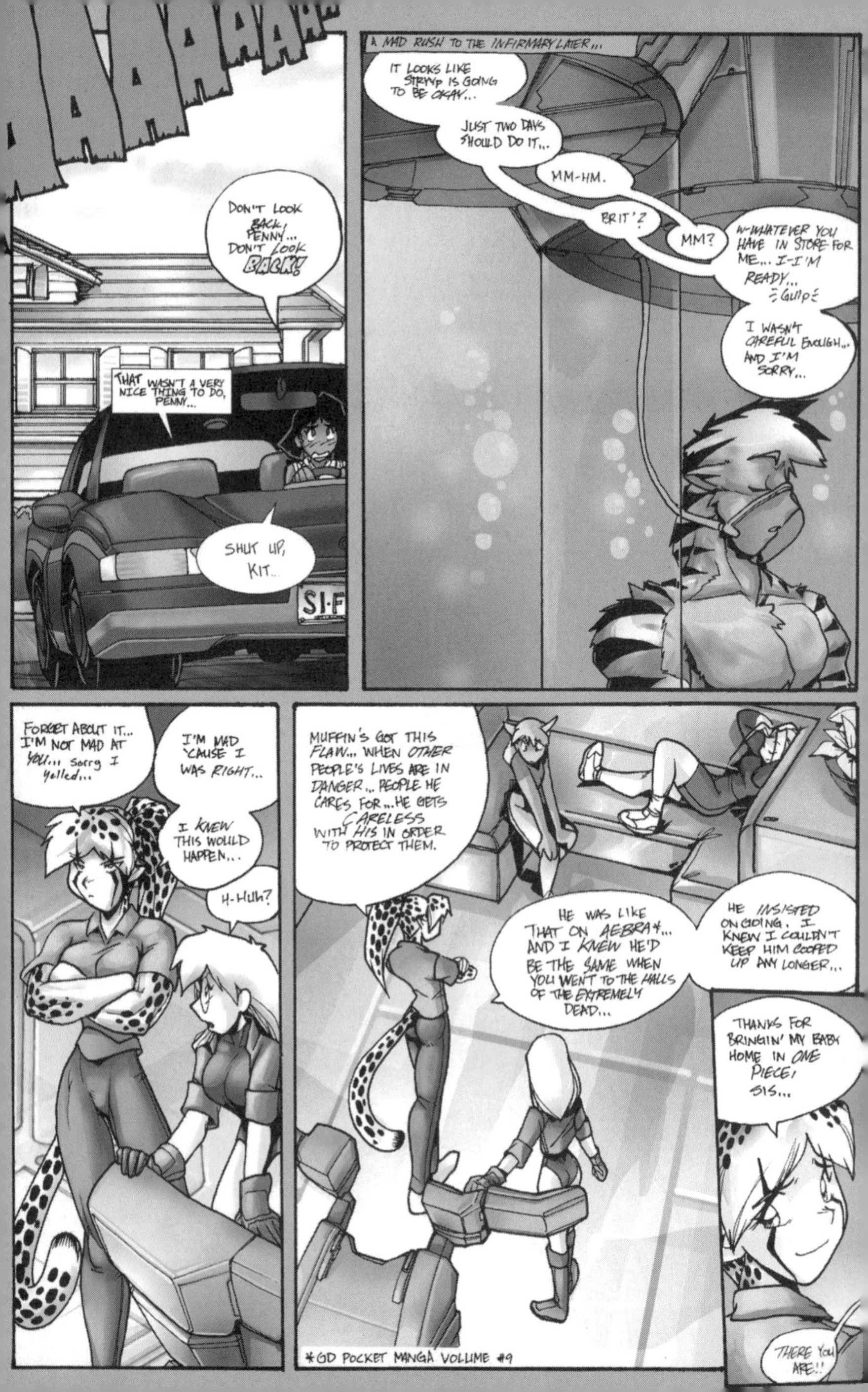
AAAAAAAH...
DON'T LOOK BACK, PENNY... DON'T LOOK BACK!
THAT WASN'T A VERY NICE THING TO DO, PENNY...
SHUT UP, KIT...
SI·F
A MAD RUSH TO THE INFIRMARY LATER...
IT LOOKS LIKE STRYYP IS GOING TO BE OKAY...
JUST TWO DAYS SHOULD DO IT...
MM-HM.
BRIT'?
MM?
W-WHATEVER YOU HAVE IN STORE FOR ME... I-I'M READY...
GULP
I WASN'T CAREFUL ENOUGH... AND I'M SORRY...
FORGET ABOUT IT... I'M NOT MAD AT YOU... sorry I yelled...
I'M MAD 'CAUSE I WAS RIGHT...
I KNEW THIS WOULD HAPPEN...
H-Huh?
MUFFIN'S GOT THIS FLAW... WHEN OTHER PEOPLE'S LIVES ARE IN DANGER... PEOPLE HE CARES FOR... HE GETS CARELESS WITH HIS IN ORDER TO PROTECT THEM.
HE WAS LIKE THAT ON AEBRA*... AND I KNEW HE'D BE THE SAME WHEN YOU WENT TO THE HALLS OF THE EXTREMELY DEAD...
HE INSISTED ON GOING. I KNEW I COULDN'T KEEP HIM COOPED UP ANY LONGER...
*GD POCKET MANGA VOLUME #9
THANKS FOR BRINGIN' MY BABY HOME IN ONE PIECE, SIS...
THERE YOU ARE!!

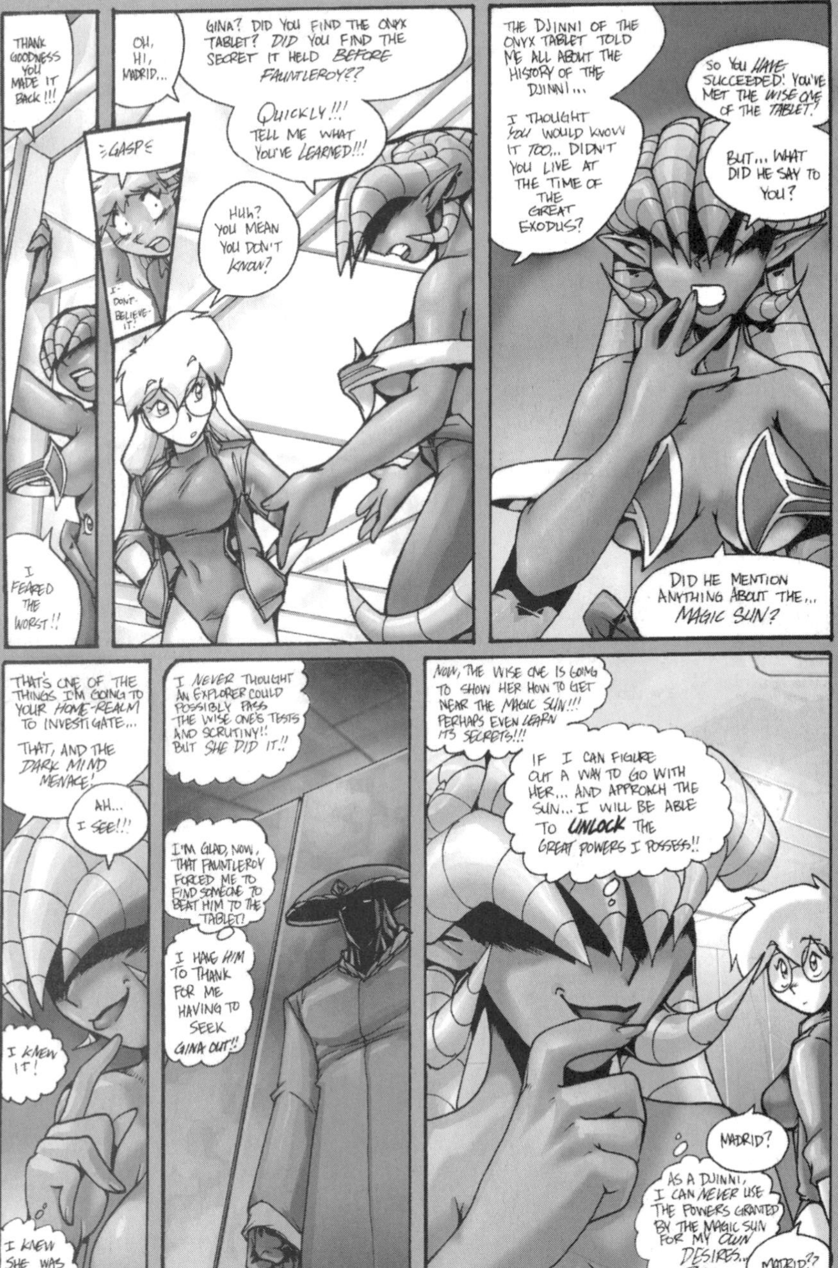
THANK GOODNESS YOU MADE IT BACK!!!
I FEARED THE WORST!!
OH, HI, MADRID...
GINA? DID YOU FIND THE ONYX TABLET? DID YOU FIND THE SECRET IT HELD BEFORE FAUNTLEROY??
QUICKLY!!! TELL ME WHAT YOU'VE LEARNED!!!
GASP
I- DON'T- BELIEVE- IT!
HUH? YOU MEAN YOU DON'T KNOW?
THE DJINNI OF THE ONYX TABLET TOLD ME ALL ABOUT THE HISTORY OF THE DJINNI...
I THOUGHT YOU WOULD KNOW IT TOO... DIDN'T YOU LIVE AT THE TIME OF THE GREAT EXODUS?
SO YOU HAVE SUCCEEDED! YOU'VE MET THE WISE ONE OF THE TABLET!
BUT... WHAT DID HE SAY TO YOU?
DID HE MENTION ANYTHING ABOUT THE... MAGIC SUN?
THAT'S ONE OF THE THINGS I'M GOING TO YOUR HOME-REALM TO INVESTIGATE...
THAT, AND THE DARK MIND MENACE!
AH... I SEE!!!
I KNEW IT!
I KNEW SHE WAS THE ONE!!
I NEVER THOUGHT AN EXPLORER COULD POSSIBLY PASS THE WISE ONE'S TESTS AND SCRUTINY!! BUT SHE DID IT!!
I'M GLAD, NOW, THAT FAUNTLEROY FORCED ME TO FIND SOMEONE TO BEAT HIM TO THE TABLET!
I HAVE HIM TO THANK FOR ME HAVING TO SEEK GINA OUT!!
NOW, THE WISE ONE IS GOING TO SHOW HER HOW TO GET NEAR THE MAGIC SUN!!! PERHAPS EVEN LEARN ITS SECRETS!!!
IF I CAN FIGURE OUT A WAY TO GO WITH HER... AND APPROACH THE SUN... I WILL BE ABLE TO UNLOCK THE GREAT POWERS I POSSESS!!
MADRID?
AS A DJINNI, I CAN NEVER USE THE POWERS GRANTED BY THE MAGIC SUN FOR MY OWN DESIRES... BUT....
MADRID??

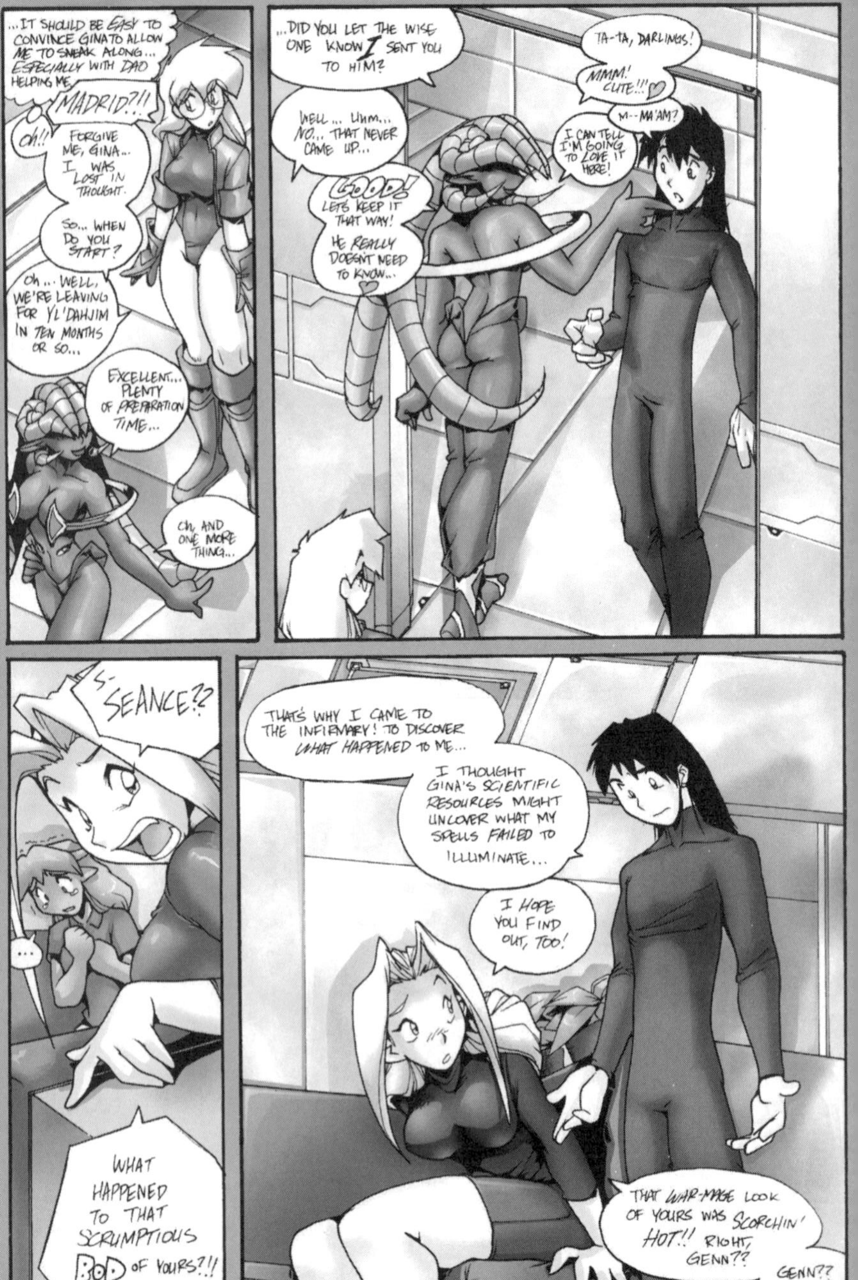
...IT SHOULD BE EASY TO CONVINCE GINA TO ALLOW ME TO SNEAK ALONG... ESPECIALLY WITH DAO HELPING ME.
MADRID?!!
Oh!!
FORGIVE ME, GINA... I WAS LOST IN THOUGHT.
SO... WHEN DO YOU START?
Oh... WELL, WE'RE LEAVING FOR YL'DAHJIM IN TEN MONTHS OR SO...
EXCELLENT... PLENTY OF PREPARATION TIME...
Oh, AND ONE MORE THING...
...DID YOU LET THE WISE ONE KNOW I SENT YOU TO HIM?
WELL... UHM... NO... THAT NEVER CAME UP...
GOOD! LET'S KEEP IT THAT WAY!
HE REALLY DOESN'T NEED TO KNOW...
TA-TA, DARLINGS!
MMM! CUTE!!!
M--MA'AM?
I CAN TELL I'M GOING TO LOVE IT HERE!
S-SEANCE?!?
...
WHAT HAPPENED TO THAT SCRUMPTIOUS BOD OF YOURS?!!
THAT'S WHY I CAME TO THE INFIRMARY! TO DISCOVER WHAT HAPPENED TO ME...
I THOUGHT GINA'S SCIENTIFIC RESOURCES MIGHT UNCOVER WHAT MY SPELLS FAILED TO ILLUMINATE...
I HOPE YOU FIND OUT, TOO!
THAT WAR-MAGE LOOK OF YOURS WAS SCORCHIN' HOT!! RIGHT, GENN??
GENN??

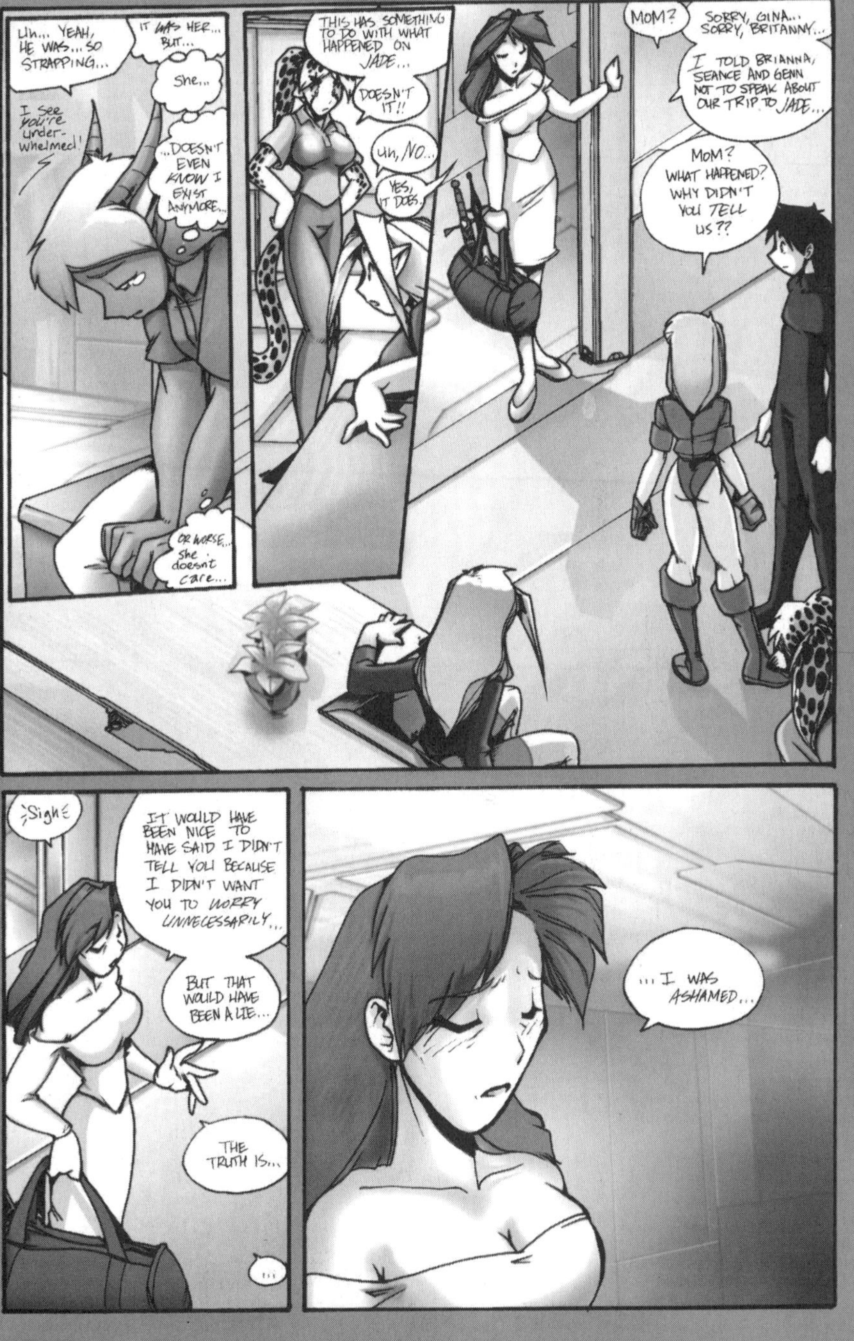
Uh... YEAH, HE WAS... SO STRAPPING...
IT WAS HER... BUT...
She...
...DOESN'T EVEN KNOW I EXIST ANYMORE...
I see you're under-whelmed!
OR WORSE... she doesn't care...
THIS HAS SOMETHING TO DO WITH WHAT HAPPENED ON JADE...
DOESN'T IT!!
Uh, NO...
YES, IT DOES...
MOM?
SORRY, GINA... SORRY, BRITANNY...
I TOLD BRIANNA, SEANCE AND GENN NOT TO SPEAK ABOUT OUR TRIP TO JADE...
MOM? WHAT HAPPENED? WHY DIDN'T YOU TELL US??
Sigh
IT WOULD HAVE BEEN NICE TO HAVE SAID I DIDN'T TELL YOU BECAUSE I DIDN'T WANT YOU TO WORRY UNNECESSARILY...
BUT THAT WOULD HAVE BEEN A LIE...
THE TRUTH IS...
...
...I WAS ASHAMED...

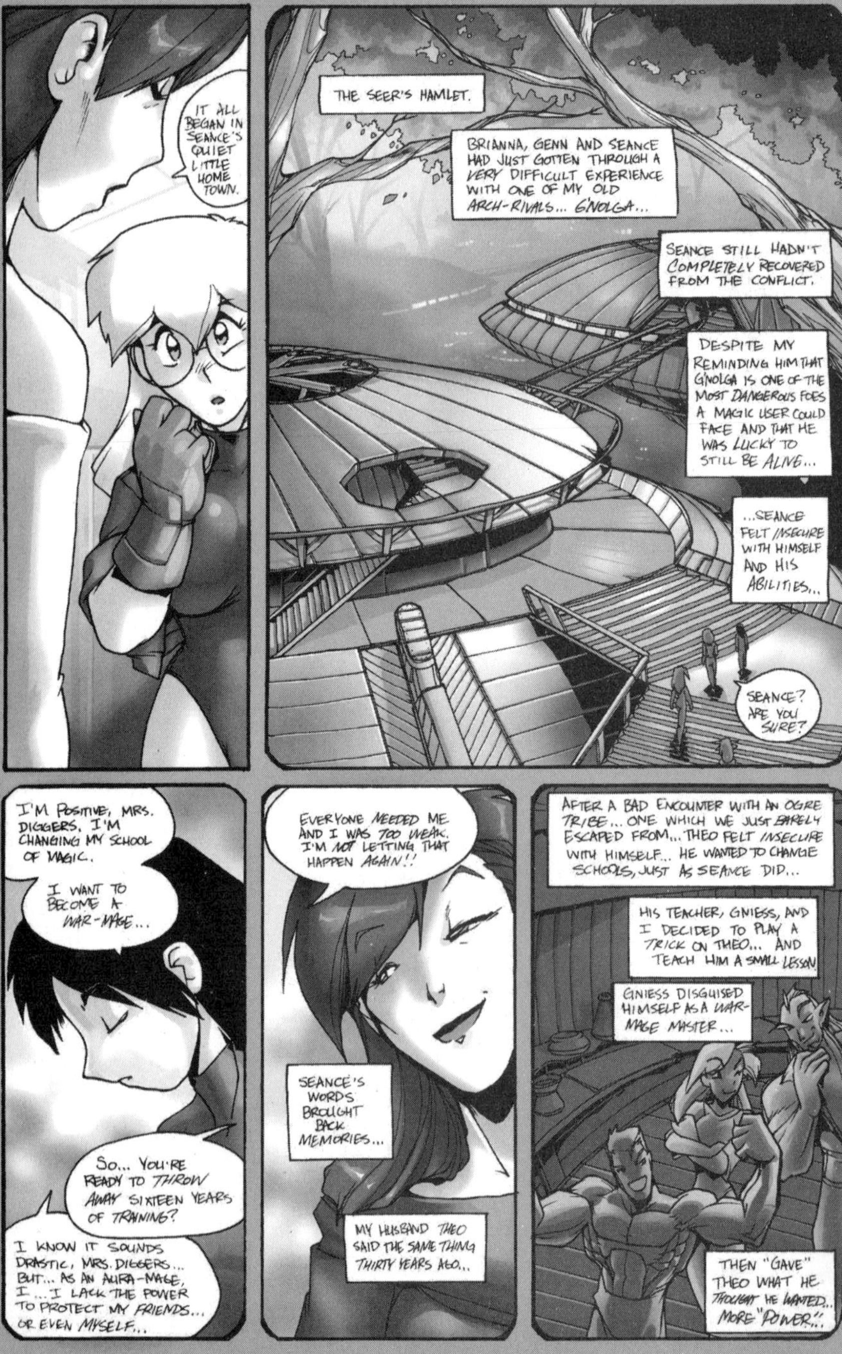
IT ALL BEGAN IN SEANCE'S QUIET LITTLE HOME TOWN.
THE SEER'S HAMLET.
BRIANNA, GENN AND SEANCE HAD JUST GOTTEN THROUGH A VERY DIFFICULT EXPERIENCE WITH ONE OF MY OLD ARCH-RIVALS... G'NOLGA...
SEANCE STILL HADN'T COMPLETELY RECOVERED FROM THE CONFLICT.
DESPITE MY REMINDING HIM THAT G'NOLGA IS ONE OF THE MOST DANGEROUS FOES A MAGIC USER COULD FACE AND THAT HE WAS LUCKY TO STILL BE ALIVE...
...SEANCE FELT INSECURE WITH HIMSELF AND HIS ABILITIES...
SEANCE? ARE YOU SURE?
I'M POSITIVE, MRS. DIGGERS. I'M CHANGING MY SCHOOL OF MAGIC.
I WANT TO BECOME A WAR-MAGE...
SO... YOU'RE READY TO THROW AWAY SIXTEEN YEARS OF TRAINING?
I KNOW IT SOUNDS DRASTIC, MRS. DIGGERS... BUT... AS AN AURA-MAGE, I... I LACK THE POWER TO PROTECT MY FRIENDS... OR EVEN MYSELF...
EVERYONE NEEDED ME AND I WAS TOO WEAK. I'M NOT LETTING THAT HAPPEN AGAIN!!
SEANCE'S WORDS BROUGHT BACK MEMORIES...
MY HUSBAND THEO SAID THE SAME THING THIRTY YEARS AGO...
AFTER A BAD ENCOUNTER WITH AN OGRE TRIBE... ONE WHICH WE JUST BARELY ESCAPED FROM... THEO FELT INSECURE WITH HIMSELF... HE WANTED TO CHANGE SCHOOLS, JUST AS SEANCE DID...
HIS TEACHER, GNIESS, AND I DECIDED TO PLAY A TRICK ON THEO... AND TEACH HIM A SMALL LESSON.
GNIESS DISGUISED HIMSELF AS A WAR-MAGE MASTER...
THEN "GAVE" THEO WHAT HE THOUGHT HE WANTED... MORE "POWER"!!

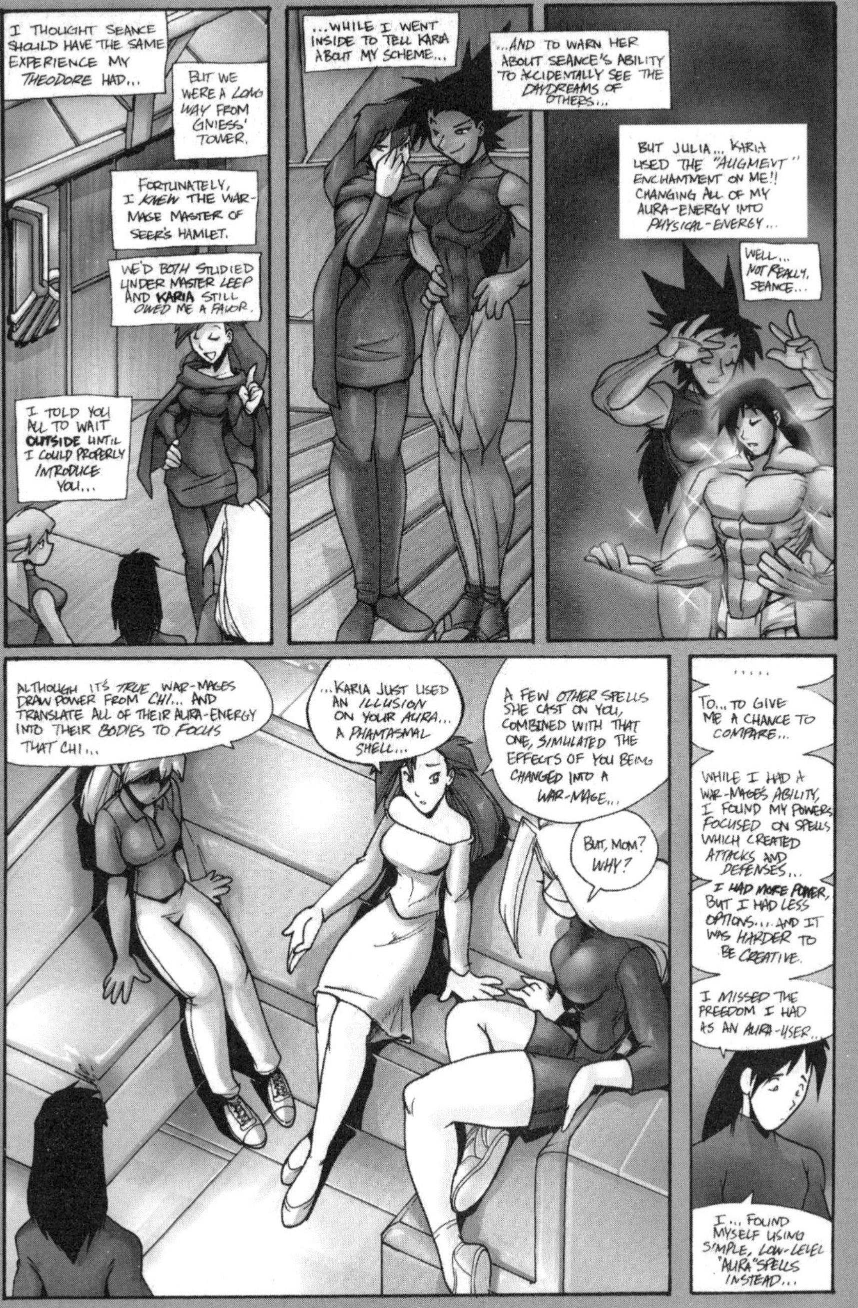
I THOUGHT SEANCE SHOULD HAVE THE SAME EXPERIENCE MY THEODORE HAD...
BUT WE WERE A LONG WAY FROM GNIESS' TOWER.
FORTUNATELY, I KNEW THE WAR-MAGE MASTER OF SEER'S HAMLET.
WE'D BOTH STUDIED UNDER MASTER LEEP AND KARIA STILL OWED ME A FAVOR.
I TOLD YOU ALL TO WAIT OUTSIDE UNTIL I COULD PROPERLY INTRODUCE YOU...
...WHILE I WENT INSIDE TO TELL KARIA ABOUT MY SCHEME...
...AND TO WARN HER ABOUT SEANCE'S ABILITY TO ACCIDENTALLY SEE THE DAYDREAMS OF OTHERS...
BUT JULIA... KARIA USED THE "AUGMENT" ENCHANTMENT ON ME!! CHANGING ALL OF MY AURA-ENERGY INTO PHYSICAL-ENERGY...
WELL... NOT REALLY, SEANCE...
ALTHOUGH IT'S TRUE WAR-MAGES DRAW POWER FROM CHI... AND TRANSLATE ALL OF THEIR AURA-ENERGY INTO THEIR BODIES TO FOCUS THAT CHI...
...KARIA JUST USED AN ILLUSION ON YOUR AURA... A PHANTASMAL SHELL...
A FEW OTHER SPELLS SHE CAST ON YOU, COMBINED WITH THAT ONE, SIMULATED THE EFFECTS OF YOU BEING CHANGED INTO A WAR-MAGE...
BUT, MOM? WHY?
.....
TO... TO GIVE ME A CHANCE TO COMPARE...
WHILE I HAD A WAR-MAGE'S ABILITY, I FOUND MY POWERS FOCUSED ON SPELLS WHICH CREATED ATTACKS AND DEFENSES...
I HAD MORE POWER, BUT I HAD LESS OPTIONS... AND IT WAS HARDER TO BE CREATIVE.
I MISSED THE FREEDOM I HAD AS AN AURA-USER...
I... FOUND MYSELF USING SIMPLE, LOW-LEVEL "AURA" SPELLS INSTEAD...

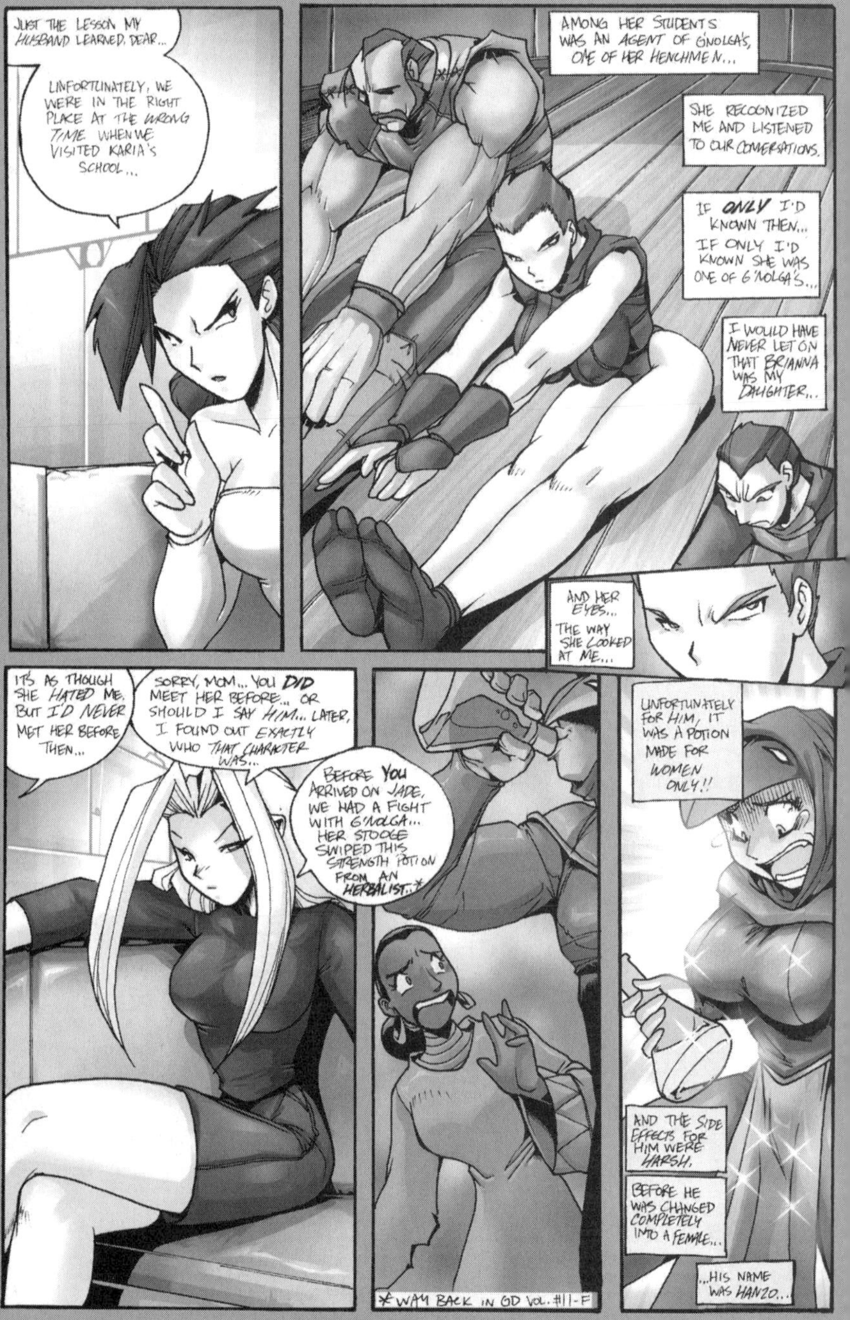
JUST THE LESSON MY HUSBAND LEARNED, DEAR...
UNFORTUNATELY, WE WERE IN THE RIGHT PLACE AT THE WRONG TIME WHEN WE VISITED KARIA'S SCHOOL...
AMONG HER STUDENTS WAS AN AGENT OF G'NOLGA'S, ONE OF HER HENCHMEN...
SHE RECOGNIZED ME AND LISTENED TO OUR CONVERSATIONS.
IF ONLY I'D KNOWN THEN... IF ONLY I'D KNOWN SHE WAS ONE OF G'NOLGA'S...
I WOULD HAVE NEVER LET ON THAT BRIANNA WAS MY DAUGHTER...
AND HER EYES... THE WAY SHE LOOKED AT ME...
IT'S AS THOUGH SHE HATED ME. BUT I'D NEVER MET HER BEFORE THEN...
SORRY, MOM... YOU DID MEET HER BEFORE... OR SHOULD I SAY HIM... LATER, I FOUND OUT EXACTLY WHO THAT CHARACTER WAS...
BEFORE YOU ARRIVED ON JADE, WE HAD A FIGHT WITH G'NOLGA... HER STOOGE SWIPED THIS STRENGTH POTION FROM AN HERBALIST...*
*WAY BACK IN GD VOL. #11-F
UNFORTUNATELY FOR HIM, IT WAS A POTION MADE FOR WOMEN ONLY!!
AND THE SIDE EFFECTS FOR HIM WERE HARSH.
BEFORE HE WAS CHANGED COMPLETELY INTO A FEMALE...
...HIS NAME WAS HANZO...

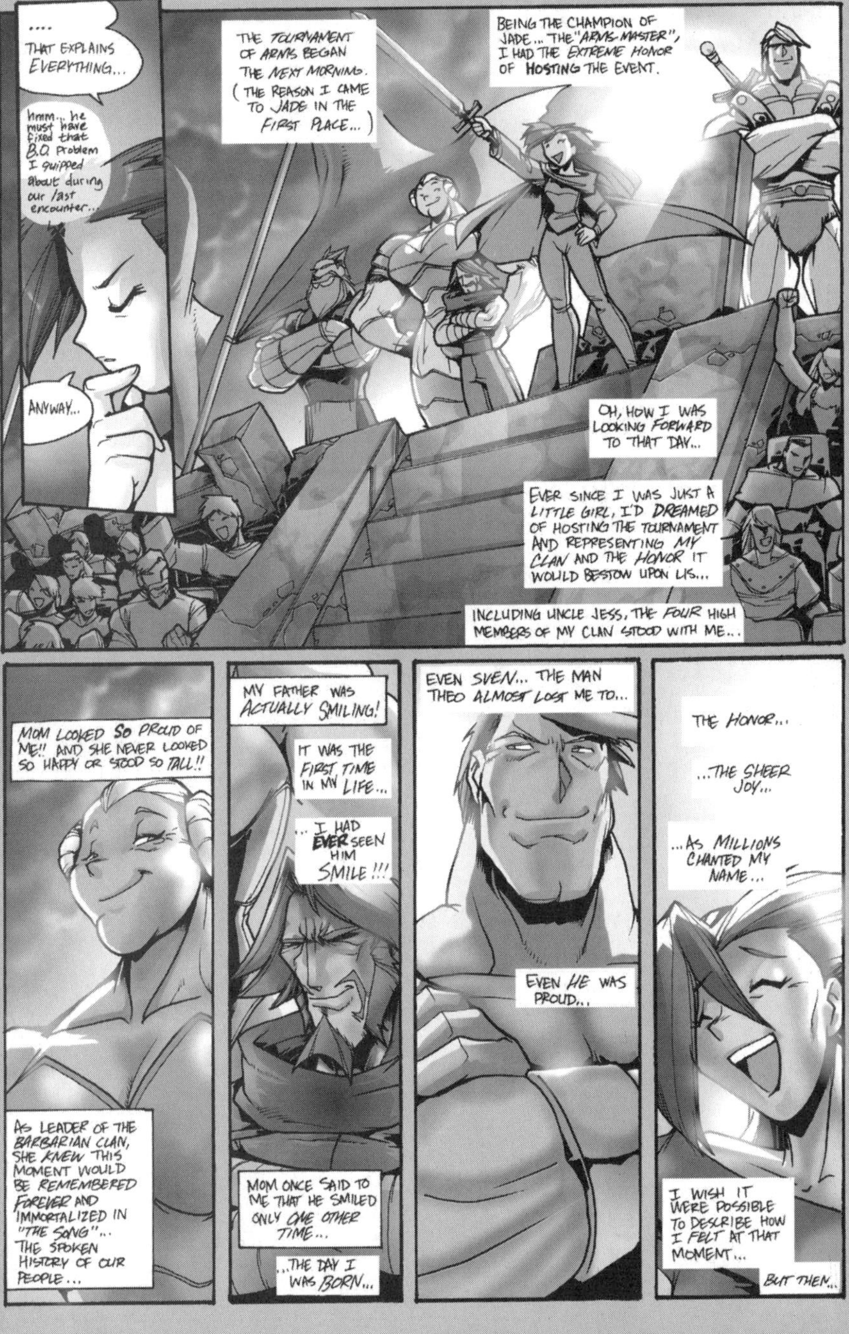
....
THAT EXPLAINS EVERYTHING...
hmm... he must have fixed that B.O. problem I quipped about during our last encounter...
ANYWAY...
THE TOURNAMENT OF ARMS BEGAN THE NEXT MORNING. (THE REASON I CAME TO JADE IN THE FIRST PLACE...)
BEING THE CHAMPION OF JADE... THE "ARMS-MASTER", I HAD THE EXTREME HONOR OF HOSTING THE EVENT.
OH, HOW I WAS LOOKING FORWARD TO THAT DAY...
EVER SINCE I WAS JUST A LITTLE GIRL, I'D DREAMED OF HOSTING THE TOURNAMENT AND REPRESENTING MY CLAN AND THE HONOR IT WOULD BESTOW UPON US...
INCLUDING UNCLE JESS, THE FOUR HIGH MEMBERS OF MY CLAN STOOD WITH ME...
MOM LOOKED SO PROUD OF ME!! AND SHE NEVER LOOKED SO HAPPY OR STOOD SO TALL!!
AS LEADER OF THE BARBARIAN CLAN, SHE KNEW THIS MOMENT WOULD BE REMEMBERED FOREVER AND IMMORTALIZED IN "THE SONG"... THE SPOKEN HISTORY OF OUR PEOPLE...
MY FATHER WAS ACTUALLY SMILING!
IT WAS THE FIRST TIME IN MY LIFE...
... I HAD EVER SEEN HIM SMILE!!!
MOM ONCE SAID TO ME THAT HE SMILED ONLY ONE OTHER TIME...
...THE DAY I WAS BORN...
EVEN SVEN... THE MAN THEO ALMOST LOST ME TO...
EVEN HE WAS PROUD...
THE HONOR...
...THE SHEER JOY...
...AS MILLIONS CHANTED MY NAME...
I WISH IT WERE POSSIBLE TO DESCRIBE HOW I FELT AT THAT MOMENT...
BUT THEN...

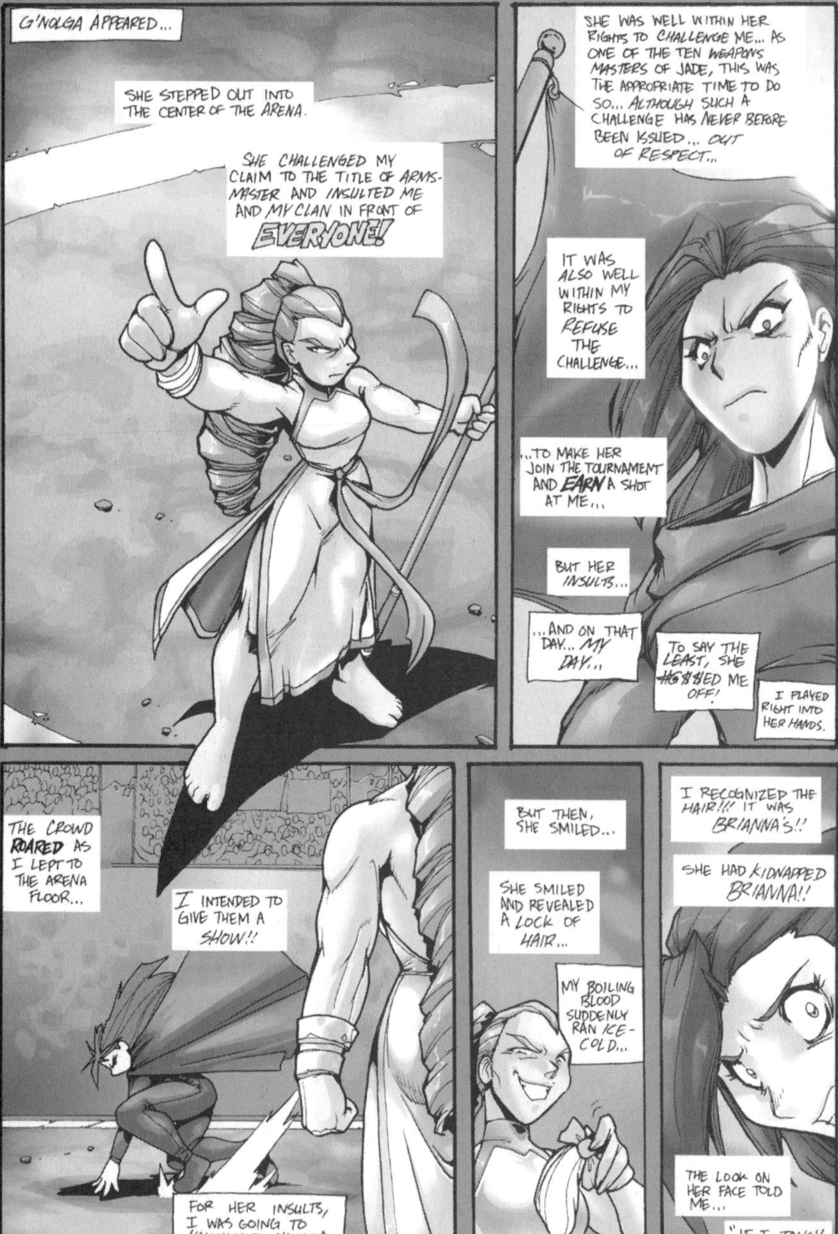
G'NOLGA APPEARED...
SHE STEPPED OUT INTO THE CENTER OF THE ARENA.
SHE CHALLENGED MY CLAIM TO THE TITLE OF ARMS-MASTER AND INSULTED ME AND MY CLAN IN FRONT OF EVERYONE!
SHE WAS WELL WITHIN HER RIGHTS TO CHALLENGE ME... AS ONE OF THE TEN WEAPONS MASTERS OF JADE, THIS WAS THE APPROPRIATE TIME TO DO SO... ALTHOUGH SUCH A CHALLENGE HAS NEVER BEFORE BEEN ISSUED... OUT OF RESPECT...
IT WAS ALSO WELL WITHIN MY RIGHTS TO REFUSE THE CHALLENGE...
...TO MAKE HER JOIN THE TOURNAMENT AND EARN A SHOT AT ME...
BUT HER INSULTS...
...AND ON THAT DAY... MY DAY...
TO SAY THE LEAST, SHE #G$$ED ME OFF!
I PLAYED RIGHT INTO HER HANDS.
THE CROWD ROARED AS I LEPT TO THE ARENA FLOOR...
I INTENDED TO GIVE THEM A SHOW!!
FOR HER INSULTS, I WAS GOING TO HUMILIATE G'NOLGA AS NO FIGHTER HAS EVER BEEN HUMILIATED BEFORE!!!
BUT THEN, SHE SMILED...
SHE SMILED AND REVEALED A LOCK OF HAIR...
MY BOILING BLOOD SUDDENLY RAN ICE-COLD...
I RECOGNIZED THE HAIR!!! IT WAS BRIANNA'S!!
SHE HAD KIDNAPPED BRIANNA!!
THE LOOK ON HER FACE TOLD ME...
"IF I TOUCH HER, BRIANNA DIES!!!"

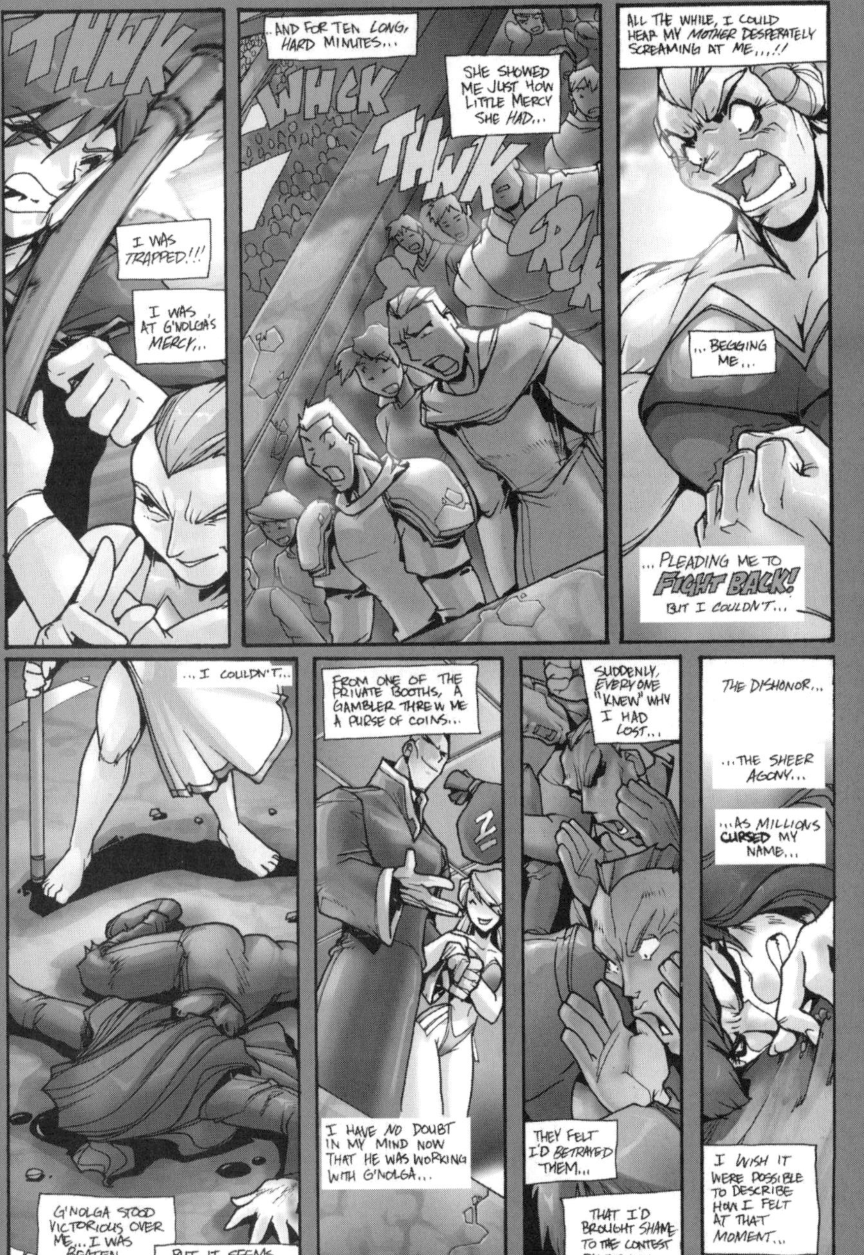
THWK
I WAS TRAPPED!!!
I WAS AT G'NOLGA'S MERCY...
...AND FOR TEN LONG, HARD MINUTES...
WHCK
SHE SHOWED ME JUST HOW LITTLE MERCY SHE HAD...
THWK
ALL THE WHILE, I COULD HEAR MY MOTHER DESPERATELY SCREAMING AT ME...!!
...BEGGING ME...
...PLEADING ME TO FIGHT BACK! BUT I COULDN'T...
...I COULDN'T...
G'NOLGA STOOD VICTORIOUS OVER ME... I WAS BEATEN...
BUT IT SEEMS THAT WASN'T ENOUGH FOR HER...
FROM ONE OF THE PRIVATE BOOTHS, A GAMBLER THREW ME A PURSE OF COINS...
I HAVE NO DOUBT IN MY MIND NOW THAT HE WAS WORKING WITH G'NOLGA...
SUDDENLY, EVERYONE "KNEW" WHY I HAD LOST...
THEY FELT I'D BETRAYED THEM...
THAT I'D BROUGHT SHAME TO THE CONTEST BY THROWING THE FIGHT...
THE DISHONOR...
...THE SHEER AGONY...
...AS MILLIONS CURSED MY NAME...
I WISH IT WERE POSSIBLE TO DESCRIBE HOW I FELT AT THAT MOMENT...

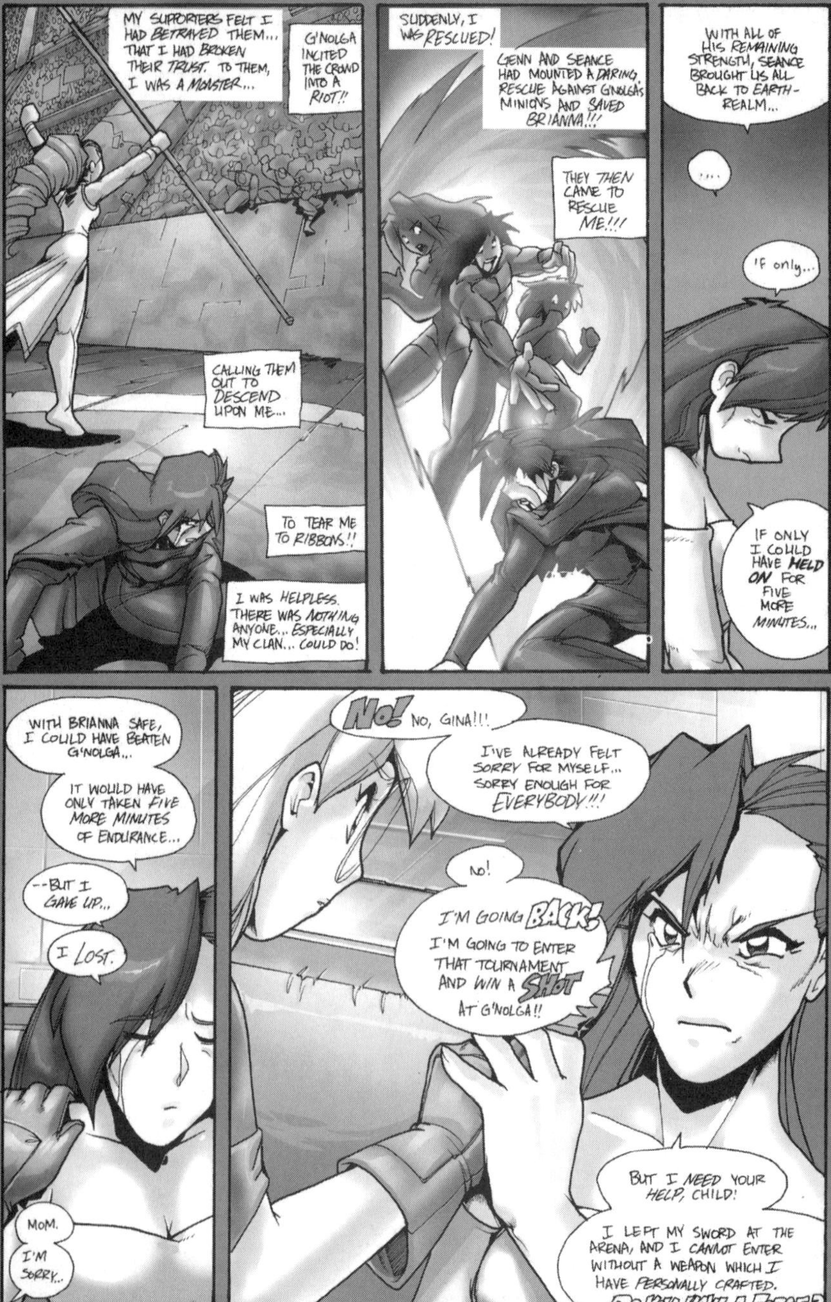
MY SUPPORTERS FELT I HAD BETRAYED THEM... THAT I HAD BROKEN THEIR TRUST. TO THEM, I WAS A MONSTER...
G'NOLGA INCITED THE CROWD INTO A RIOT!!
CALLING THEM OUT TO DESCEND UPON ME...
TO TEAR ME TO RIBBONS!!
I WAS HELPLESS. THERE WAS NOTHING ANYONE... ESPECIALLY MY CLAN... COULD DO!
SUDDENLY, I WAS RESCUED!
GENN AND SEANCE HAD MOUNTED A DARING RESCUE AGAINST G'NOLGA'S MINIONS AND SAVED BRIANNA!!!
THEY THEN CAME TO RESCUE ME!!!
WITH ALL OF HIS REMAINING STRENGTH, SEANCE BROUGHT US ALL BACK TO EARTH-REALM...
....
'F only...
IF ONLY I COULD HAVE HELD ON FOR FIVE MORE MINUTES...
WITH BRIANNA SAFE, I COULD HAVE BEATEN G'NOLGA...
IT WOULD HAVE ONLY TAKEN FIVE MORE MINUTES OF ENDURANCE...
--BUT I GAVE UP...
I LOST.
MOM.
I'M SORRY...
NO! NO, GINA!!!
I'VE ALREADY FELT SORRY FOR MYSELF... SORRY ENOUGH FOR EVERYBODY!!!
NO!
I'M GOING BACK! I'M GOING TO ENTER THAT TOURNAMENT AND WIN A SHOT AT G'NOLGA!!
BUT I NEED YOUR HELP, CHILD!
I LEFT MY SWORD AT THE ARENA, AND I CANNOT ENTER WITHOUT A WEAPON WHICH I HAVE PERSONALLY CRAFTED.
DO YOU HAVE A FORGE?

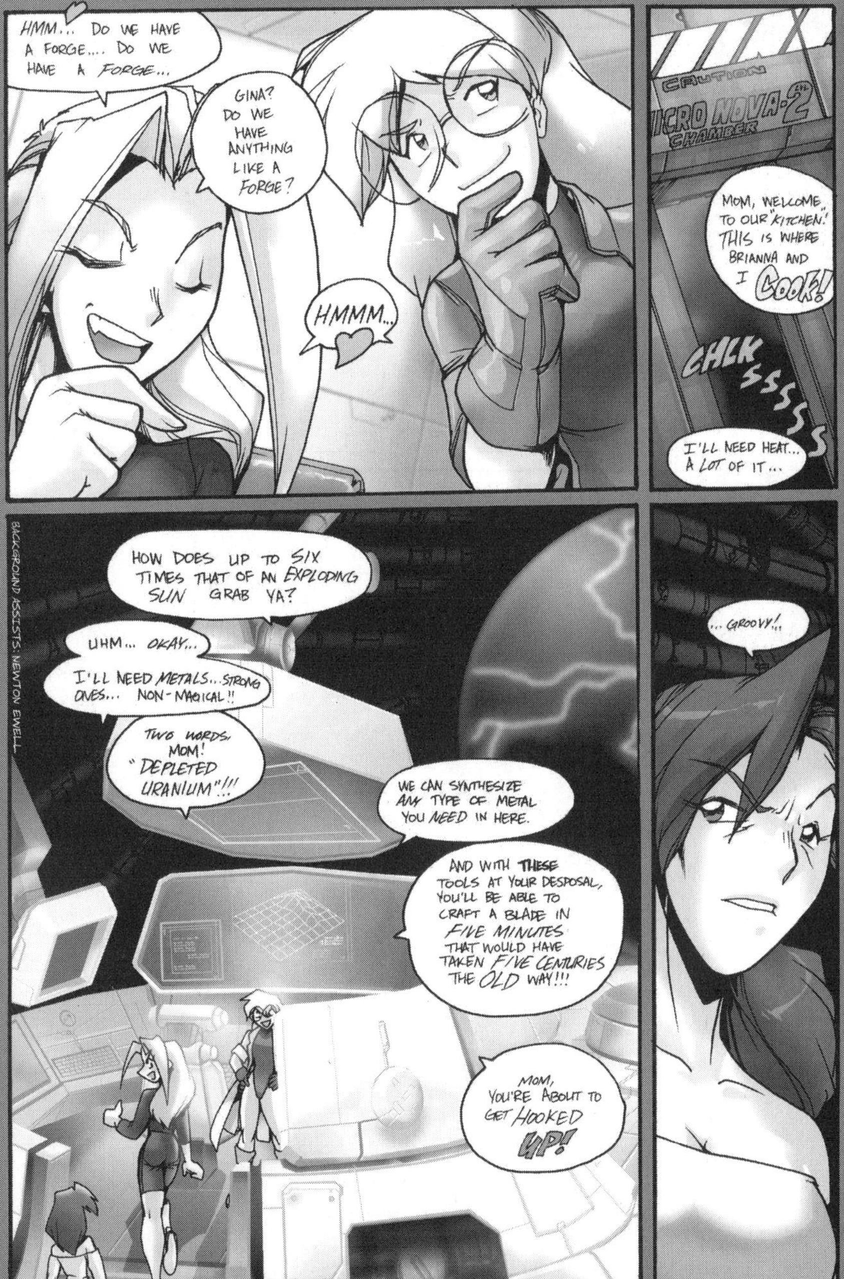
HMM... DO WE HAVE A FORGE.... DO WE HAVE A FORGE...
GINA? DO WE HAVE ANYTHING LIKE A FORGE?
HMMM...
CAUTION
ICRO NOVA-2
CHAMBER
MOM, WELCOME TO OUR "KITCHEN." THIS IS WHERE BRIANNA AND I COOK!
CHLK SSSSSS
I'LL NEED HEAT... A LOT OF IT...
BACKGROUND ASSISTS: NEWTON EWELL
HOW DOES UP TO SIX TIMES THAT OF AN EXPLODING SUN GRAB YA?
UHM... OKAY...
I'LL NEED METALS... STRONG ONES... NON-MAGICAL!!
TWO WORDS, MOM! "DEPLETED URANIUM"!!!
WE CAN SYNTHESIZE ANY TYPE OF METAL YOU NEED IN HERE.
AND WITH THESE TOOLS AT YOUR DESPOSAL, YOU'LL BE ABLE TO CRAFT A BLADE IN FIVE MINUTES THAT WOULD HAVE TAKEN FIVE CENTURIES THE OLD WAY!!!
MOM, YOU'RE ABOUT TO GET HOOKED UP!
...GROOVY!...

JADE SAGA: EPILOGUE

My dearest Theodore,

I didn't want to say goodbye.

Not like this. On a letter...

I knew you'd never let me return to Jade without you...

...and I ache not having you by my side. But there is no other way.

I'm entering the Tournament of Arms... to win back my title as Arms-master,

to win back my stolen honor,

and to have my revenge.

I know the odds will be against me...

I barely survived the tournament when I was in my PRIME...

It will be much harder for me now. I may not survive.

But I will never give up... never again!!!

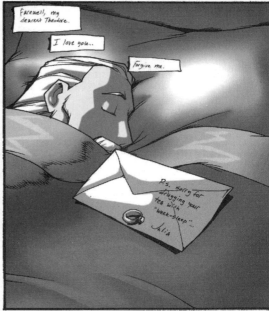

Farewell, my dearest Theodore.

I love you...

Forgive me.

P.s. Sorry for drugging your tea with "week-sleep".

Julia

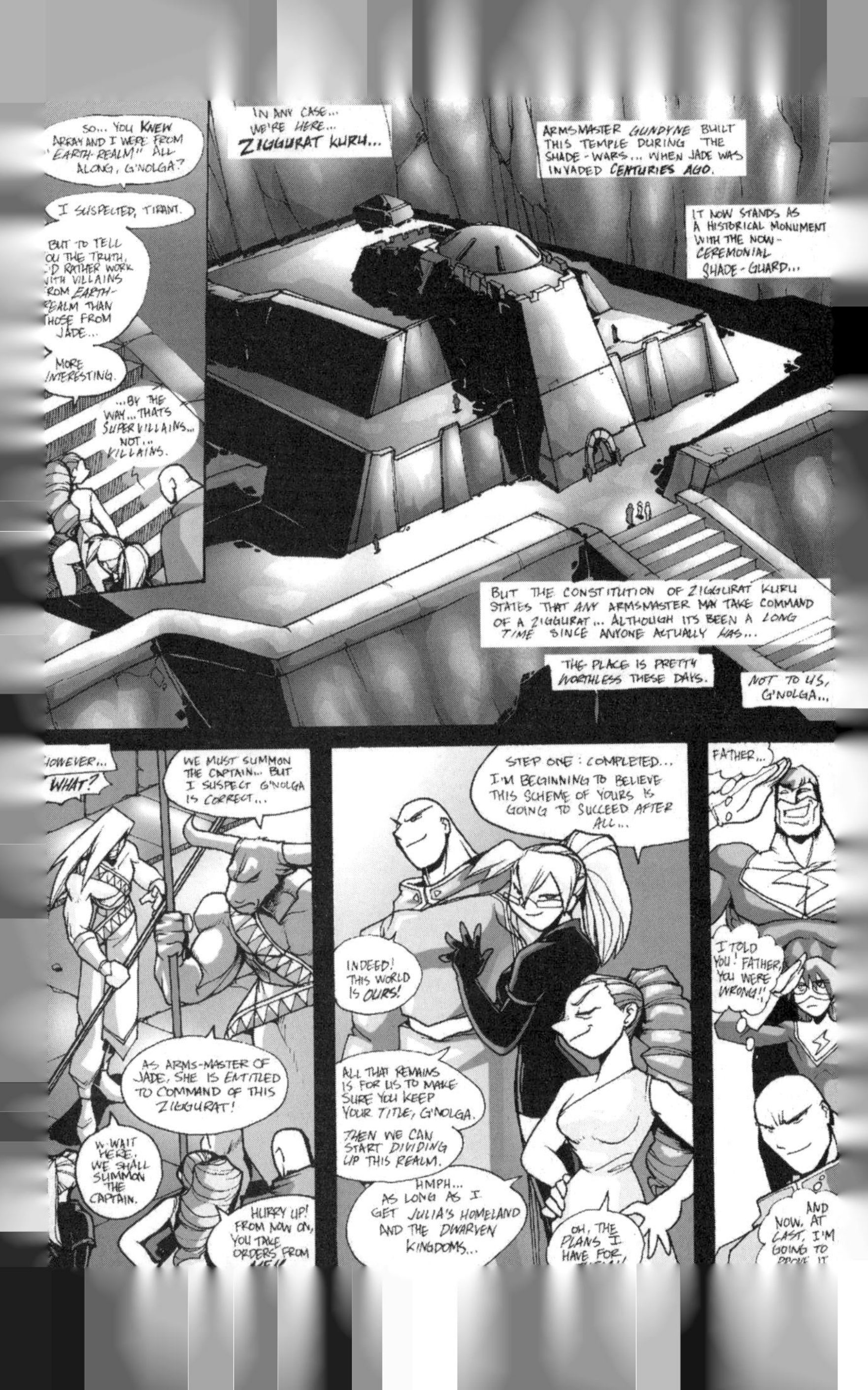
SO... YOU KNEW ARRAY AND I WERE FROM "EARTH-REALM" ALL ALONG, G'NOLGA?
I SUSPECTED, TIRANT.
BUT TO TELL YOU THE TRUTH, I'D RATHER WORK WITH VILLAINS FROM EARTH-REALM THAN THOSE FROM JADE...
MORE INTERESTING.
...BY THE WAY... THATS SUPERVILLAINS... NOT... VILLAINS.
IN ANY CASE... WE'RE HERE... ZIGGURAT KURU...
ARMSMASTER GUNDYNE BUILT THIS TEMPLE DURING THE SHADE-WARS... WHEN JADE WAS INVADED CENTURIES AGO.
IT NOW STANDS AS A HISTORICAL MONUMENT WITH THE NOW-CEREMONIAL SHADE-GUARD...
BUT THE CONSTITUTION OF ZIGGURAT KURU STATES THAT ANY ARMSMASTER MAY TAKE COMMAND OF A ZIGGURAT... ALTHOUGH ITS BEEN A LONG TIME SINCE ANYONE ACTUALLY HAS...
THE PLACE IS PRETTY WORTHLESS THESE DAYS.
NOT TO US, G'NOLGA...
HOWEVER...
WHAT?
WE MUST SUMMON THE CAPTAIN... BUT I SUSPECT G'NOLGA IS CORRECT...
AS ARMS-MASTER OF JADE, SHE IS ENTITLED TO COMMAND OF THIS ZIGGURAT!
W-WAIT HERE. WE SHALL SUMMON THE CAPTAIN.
HURRY UP! FROM NOW ON, YOU TAKE ORDERS FROM
STEP ONE: COMPLETED... I'M BEGINNING TO BELIEVE THIS SCHEME OF YOURS IS GOING TO SUCCEED AFTER ALL...
INDEED! THIS WORLD IS OURS!
ALL THAT REMAINS IS FOR US TO MAKE SURE YOU KEEP YOUR TITLE, G'NOLGA.
THEN WE CAN START DIVIDING UP THIS REALM.
HMPH... AS LONG AS I GET JULIA'S HOMELAND AND THE DWARVEN KINGDOMS...
OH, THE PLANS I HAVE FOR
FATHER...
I TOLD YOU! FATHER, YOU WERE WRONG!!
AND NOW, AT LAST, I'M GOING TO

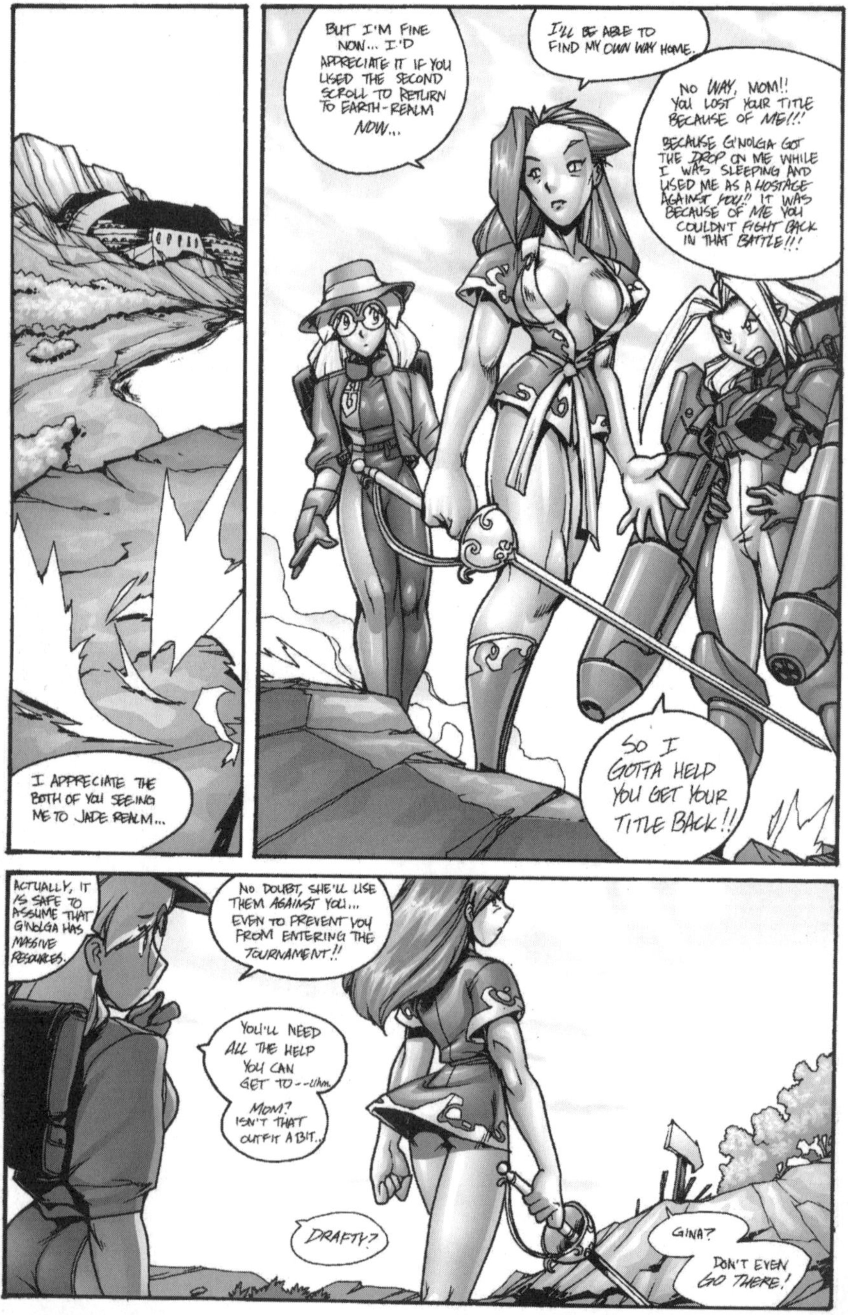

I APPRECIATE THE BOTH OF YOU SEEING ME TO JADE REALM...
BUT I'M FINE NOW... I'D APPRECIATE IT IF YOU USED THE SECOND SCROLL TO RETURN TO EARTH-REALM NOW...
I'LL BE ABLE TO FIND MY OWN WAY HOME.
NO WAY, MOM!! YOU LOST YOUR TITLE BECAUSE OF ME!!!
BECAUSE G'NOLGA GOT THE DROP ON ME WHILE I WAS SLEEPING AND USED ME AS A HOSTAGE AGAINST YOU!! IT WAS BECAUSE OF ME YOU COULDN'T FIGHT BACK IN THAT BATTLE!!!
SO I GOTTA HELP YOU GET YOUR TITLE BACK!!
ACTUALLY, IT IS SAFE TO ASSUME THAT G'NOLGA HAS MASSIVE RESOURCES.
NO DOUBT, SHE'LL USE THEM AGAINST YOU... EVEN TO PREVENT YOU FROM ENTERING THE TOURNAMENT!!
YOU'LL NEED ALL THE HELP YOU CAN GET TO--UHM.
MOM? ISN'T THAT OUTFIT A BIT...
DRAFTY?
GINA?
DON'T EVEN GO THERE!

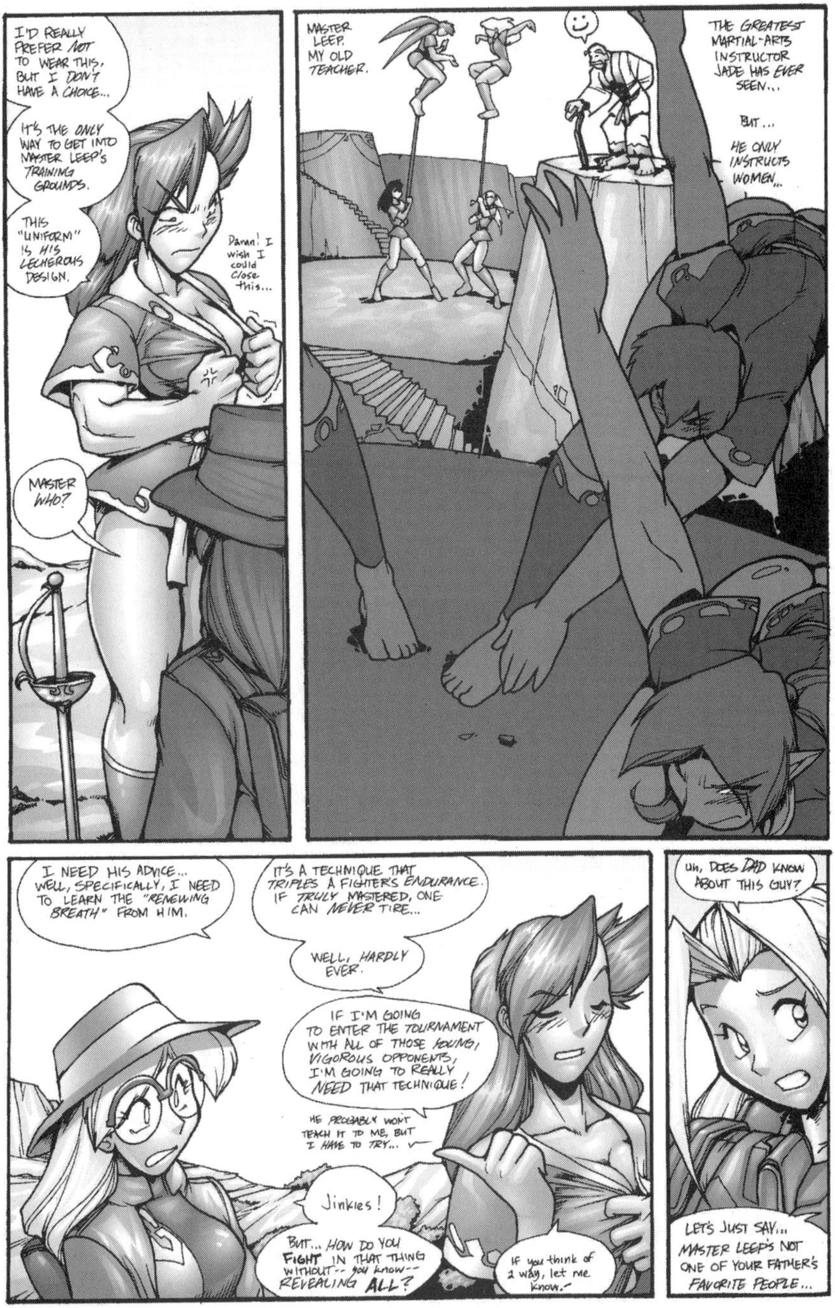
I'D REALLY PREFER NOT TO WEAR THIS, BUT I DON'T HAVE A CHOICE...
IT'S THE ONLY WAY TO GET INTO MASTER LEEP'S TRAINING GROUNDS.
THIS "UNIFORM" IS HIS LECHEROUS DESIGN.
Damn! I wish I could close this...
MASTER WHO?
MASTER LEEP. MY OLD TEACHER.
THE GREATEST MARTIAL-ARTS INSTRUCTOR JADE HAS EVER SEEN...
BUT... HE ONLY INSTRUCTS WOMEN...
I NEED HIS ADVICE... WELL, SPECIFICALLY, I NEED TO LEARN THE "RENEWING BREATH" FROM HIM.
IT'S A TECHNIQUE THAT TRIPLES A FIGHTER'S ENDURANCE. IF TRULY MASTERED, ONE CAN NEVER TIRE...
WELL, HARDLY EVER.
IF I'M GOING TO ENTER THE TOURNAMENT WITH ALL OF THOSE YOUNG, VIGOROUS OPPONENTS, I'M GOING TO REALLY NEED THAT TECHNIQUE!
HE PROBABLY WON'T TEACH IT TO ME, BUT I HAVE TO TRY...
Jinkies!
BUT... HOW DO YOU FIGHT IN THAT THING WITHOUT-- you know-- REVEALING ALL?
If you think of a way, let me know.
uh, DOES DAD KNOW ABOUT THIS GUY?
LET'S JUST SAY... MASTER LEEP'S NOT ONE OF YOUR FATHER'S FAVORITE PEOPLE...

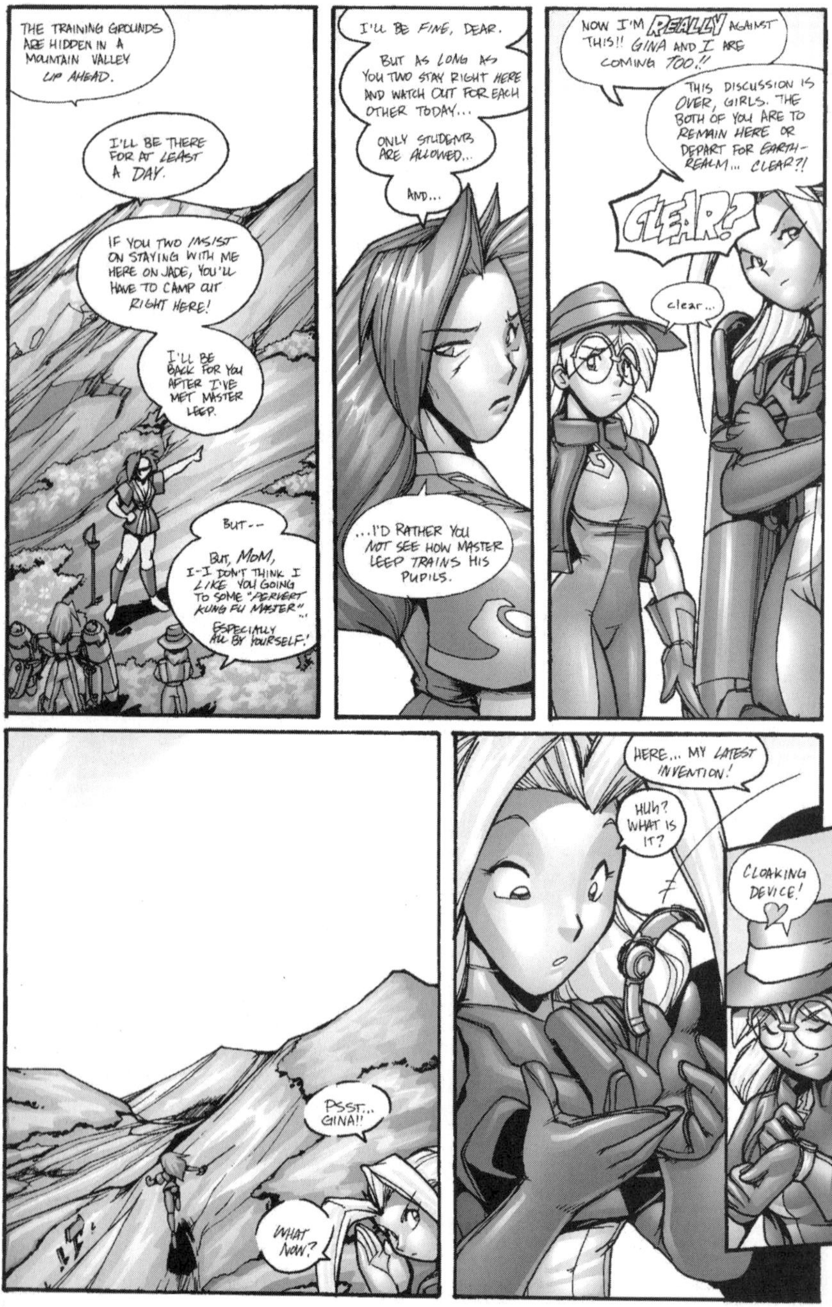
THE TRAINING GROUNDS ARE HIDDEN IN A MOUNTAIN VALLEY UP AHEAD.
I'LL BE THERE FOR AT LEAST A DAY.
IF YOU TWO INSIST ON STAYING WITH ME HERE ON JADE, YOU'LL HAVE TO CAMP OUT RIGHT HERE!
I'LL BE BACK FOR YOU AFTER I'VE MET MASTER LEEP.
BUT--
BUT, MOM, I-I DON'T THINK I LIKE YOU GOING TO SOME "PERVERT KUNG FU MASTER"..
ESPECIALLY ALL BY YOURSELF!
I'LL BE FINE, DEAR.
BUT AS LONG AS YOU TWO STAY RIGHT HERE AND WATCH OUT FOR EACH OTHER TODAY...
ONLY STUDENTS ARE ALLOWED...
AND...
...I'D RATHER YOU NOT SEE HOW MASTER LEEP TRAINS HIS PUPILS.
NOW I'M REALLY AGAINST THIS!! GINA AND I ARE COMING TOO!!
THIS DISCUSSION IS OVER, GIRLS. THE BOTH OF YOU ARE TO REMAIN HERE OR DEPART FOR EARTH-REALM... CLEAR?!
CLEAR?
clear...
PSST... GINA!!
WHAT NOW?
HERE... MY LATEST INVENTION!
HUH? WHAT IS IT?
CLOAKING DEVICE!

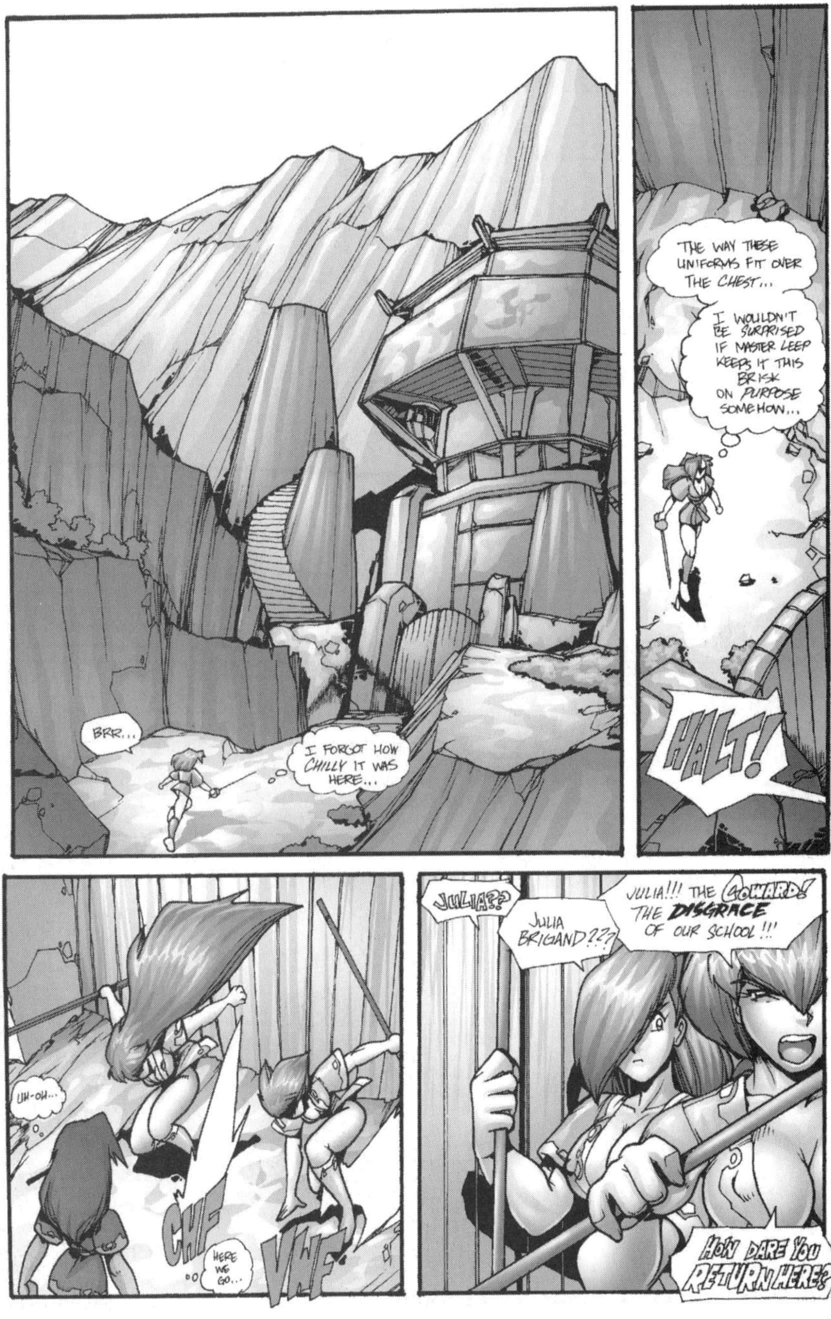
BRR...
I FORGOT HOW CHILLY IT WAS HERE...
THE WAY THESE UNIFORMS FIT OVER THE CHEST...
I WOULDN'T BE SURPRISED IF MASTER LEEP KEEPS IT THIS BRISK ON PURPOSE SOMEHOW...
HALT!
UH-OH...
CHF
HERE WE GO...
VNF
JULIA??
JULIA BRIGAND???
JULIA!!! THE COWARD! THE DISGRACE OF OUR SCHOOL!!!
HOW DARE YOU RETURN HERE?

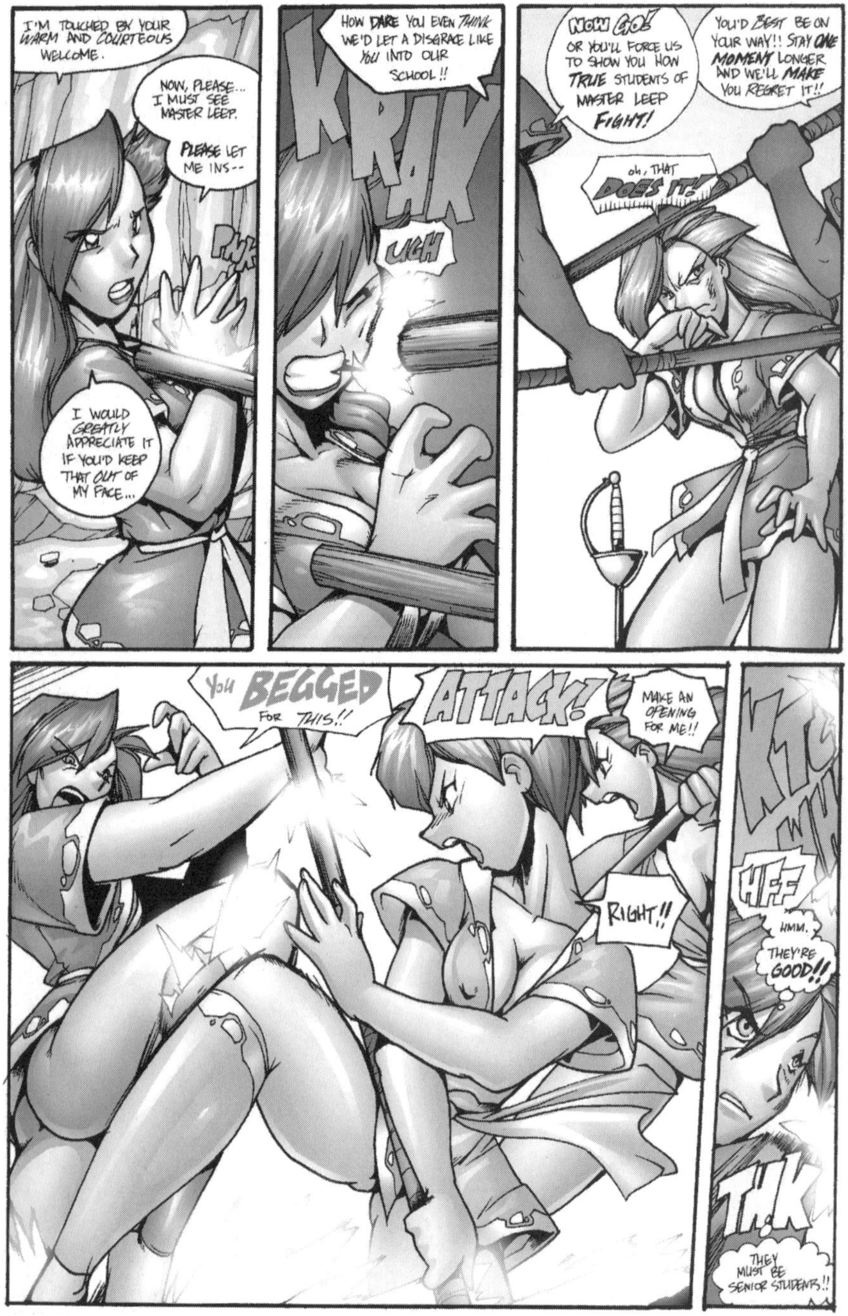

I'M TOUCHED BY YOUR WARM AND COURTEOUS WELCOME.
NOW, PLEASE... I MUST SEE MASTER LEEP.
PLEASE LET ME INS--
I WOULD GREATLY APPRECIATE IT IF YOU'D KEEP THAT OUT OF MY FACE...
KRAK
HOW DARE YOU EVEN THINK WE'D LET A DISGRACE LIKE YOU INTO OUR SCHOOL!!
UGH
NOW GO! OR YOU'LL FORCE US TO SHOW YOU HOW TRUE STUDENTS OF MASTER LEEP FIGHT!
YOU'D BEST BE ON YOUR WAY!! STAY ONE MOMENT LONGER AND WE'LL MAKE YOU REGRET IT!!
oh, THAT DOES IT!
YOU BEGGED FOR THIS!!
ATTACK!
MAKE AN OPENING FOR ME!!
RIGHT!!
HFF
HMM. THEY'RE GOOD!!
THK
THEY MUST BE SENIOR STUDENTS!!

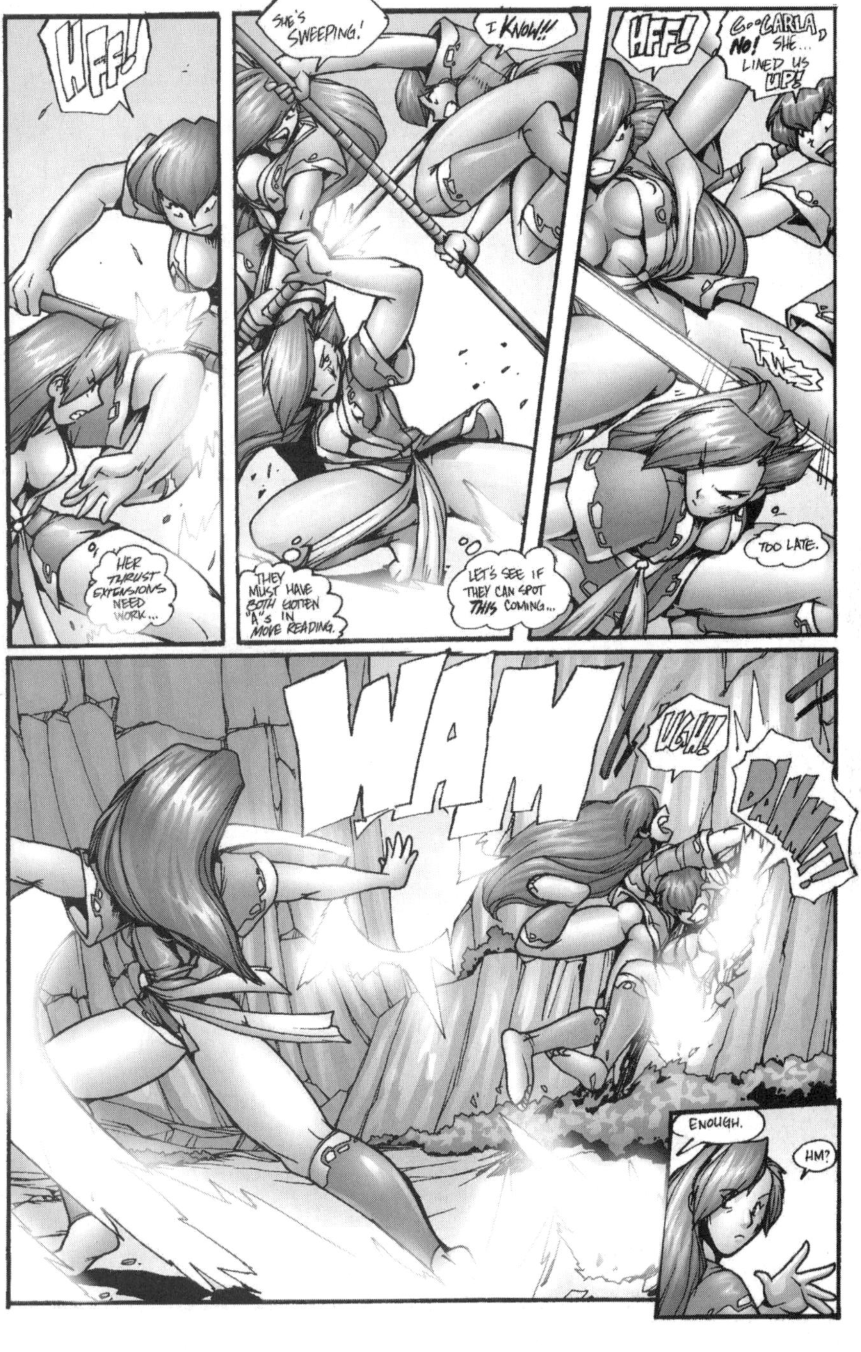
HFF!!
HER THRUST EXTENSIONS NEED WORK...
SHE'S SWEEPING!
I KNOW!!
THEY MUST HAVE BOTH GOTTEN "A"s IN MOVE READING.
LET'S SEE IF THEY CAN SPOT THIS COMING...
HFF!
C...CARLA, NO! SHE... LINED US UP!
TOO LATE.
WAM
UGH!!
DAMMIT!
ENOUGH.
HM?

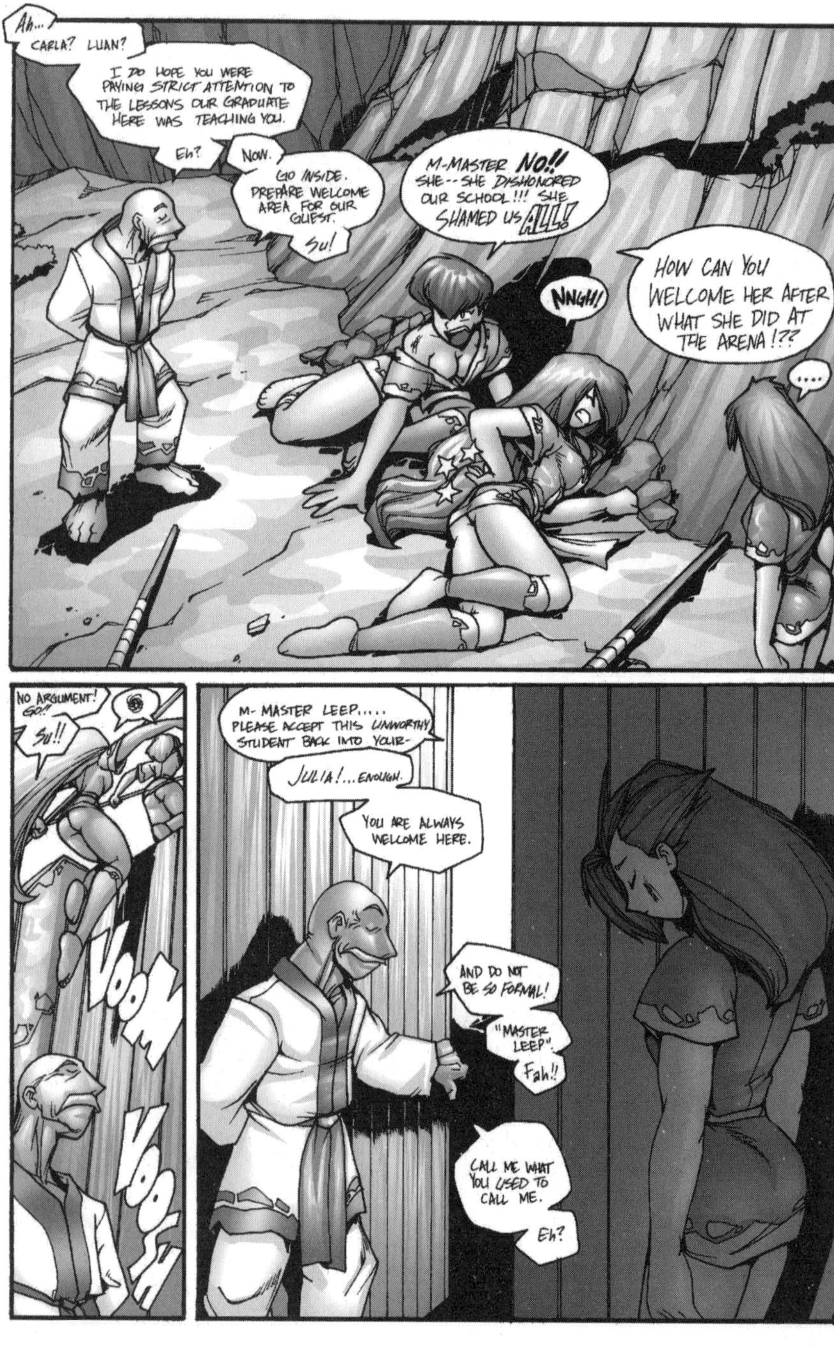
Ah...! CARLA? LUAN?
I DO HOPE YOU WERE PAYING STRICT ATTENTION TO THE LESSONS OUR GRADUATE HERE WAS TEACHING YOU.
Eh?
NOW.
GO INSIDE. PREPARE WELCOME AREA FOR OUR GUEST.
Su!
M-MASTER NO!! SHE--SHE DISHONORED OUR SCHOOL!!! SHE SHAMED US ALL!
NNGH!
HOW CAN YOU WELCOME HER AFTER WHAT SHE DID AT THE ARENA!??
....
NO ARGUMENT! GO!!
Su!!
VOOM
VOOM
M-MASTER LEEP..... PLEASE ACCEPT THIS UNWORTHY STUDENT BACK INTO YOUR-
JULIA!...ENOUGH.
YOU ARE ALWAYS WELCOME HERE.
AND DO NOT BE SO FORMAL!
"MASTER LEEP". Fah!!
CALL ME WHAT YOU USED TO CALL ME.
Eh?

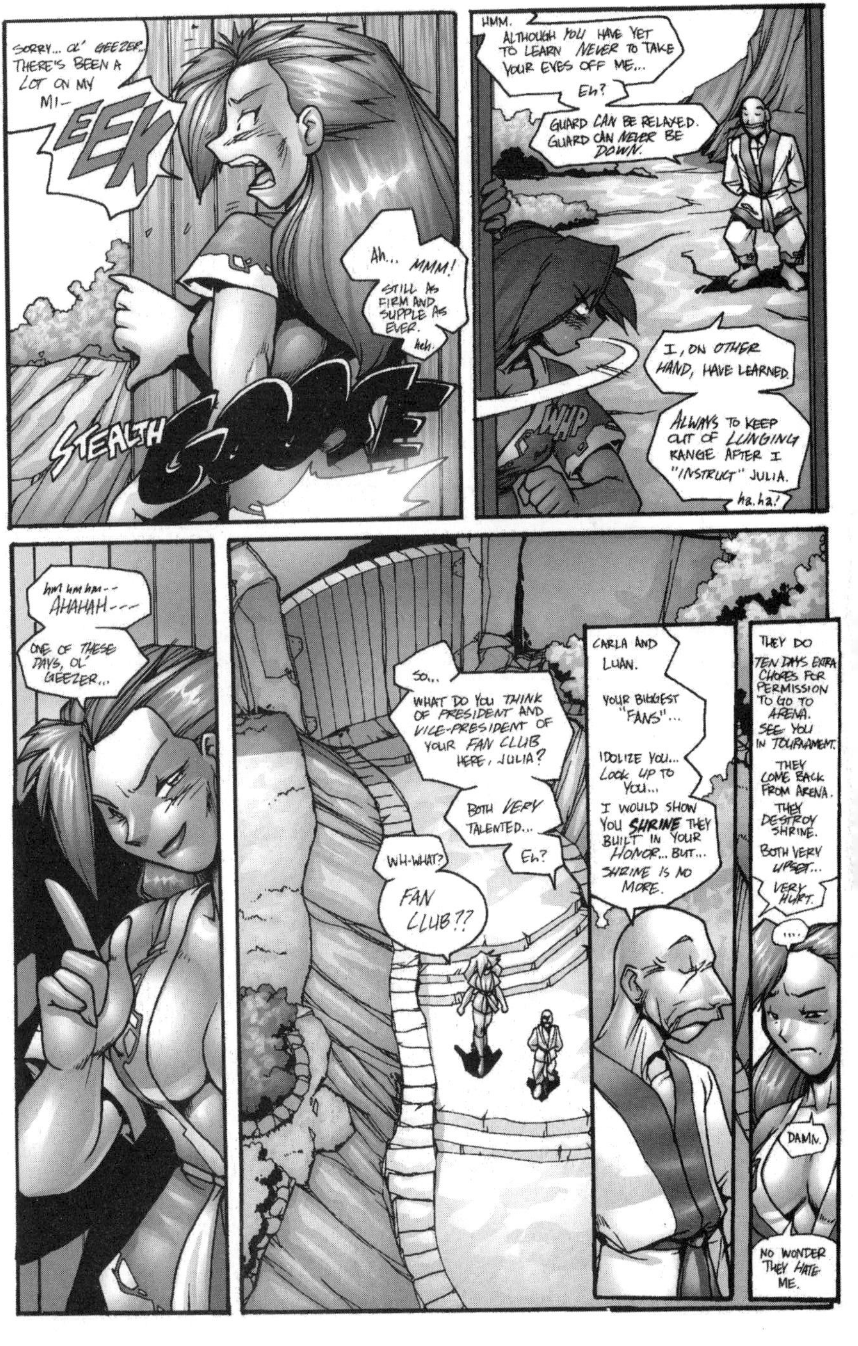
SORRY... OL' GEEZER... THERE'S BEEN A LOT ON MY MI-
EEK
Ah... MMM! STILL AS FIRM AND SUPPLE AS EVER. heh.
STEALTH
HMM. ALTHOUGH YOU HAVE YET TO LEARN NEVER TO TAKE YOUR EYES OFF ME...
Eh?
GUARD CAN BE RELAXED. GUARD CAN NEVER BE DOWN.
I, ON OTHER HAND, HAVE LEARNED.
WHP
ALWAYS TO KEEP OUT OF LUNGING RANGE AFTER I "INSTRUCT" JULIA.
ha, ha!
hm hm hm-- AHAHAH---
ONE OF THESE DAYS, OL' GEEZER...
SO... WHAT DO YOU THINK OF PRESIDENT AND VICE-PRESIDENT OF YOUR FAN CLUB HERE, JULIA?
BOTH VERY TALENTED...
Eh?
WH-WHAT?
FAN CLUB??
CARLA AND LUAN.
YOUR BIGGEST "FANS"...
IDOLIZE YOU... LOOK UP TO YOU...
I WOULD SHOW YOU SHRINE THEY BUILT IN YOUR HONOR... BUT... SHRINE IS NO MORE.
THEY DO TEN DAYS EXTRA CHORES FOR PERMISSION TO GO TO ARENA.
SEE YOU IN TOURNAMENT.
THEY COME BACK FROM ARENA.
THEY DESTROY SHRINE.
BOTH VERY UPSET...
VERY HURT.
....
DAMN.
NO WONDER THEY HATE ME.

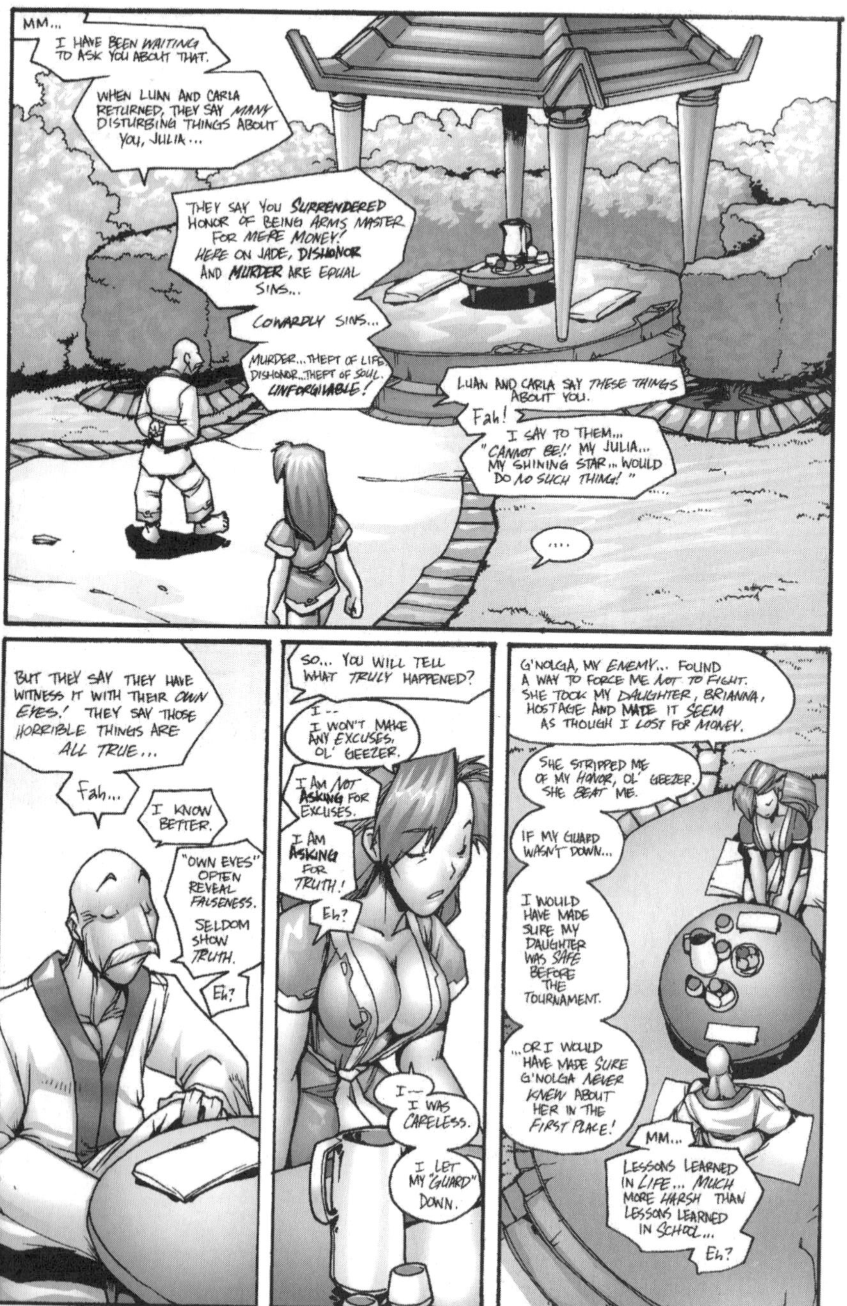
MM...
I HAVE BEEN WAITING TO ASK YOU ABOUT THAT.
WHEN LUAN AND CARLA RETURNED, THEY SAY MANY DISTURBING THINGS ABOUT YOU, JULIA...
THEY SAY YOU SURRENDERED HONOR OF BEING ARMS MASTER FOR MERE MONEY! HERE ON JADE, DISHONOR AND MURDER ARE EQUAL SINS...
COWARDLY SINS...
MURDER... THEFT OF LIFE. DISHONOR... THEFT OF SOUL. UNFORGIVABLE!
LUAN AND CARLA SAY THESE THINGS ABOUT YOU.
Fah!
I SAY TO THEM... "CANNOT BE!! MY JULIA... MY SHINING STAR... WOULD DO NO SUCH THING!"
....
BUT THEY SAY THEY HAVE WITNESS IT WITH THEIR OWN EYES! THEY SAY THOSE HORRIBLE THINGS ARE ALL TRUE...
Fah...
I KNOW BETTER.
"OWN EYES" OFTEN REVEAL FALSENESS.
SELDOM SHOW TRUTH.
Eh?
SO... YOU WILL TELL WHAT TRULY HAPPENED?
I -- I WON'T MAKE ANY EXCUSES, OL' GEEZER.
I AM NOT ASKING FOR EXCUSES.
I AM ASKING FOR TRUTH!
Eh?
I -- I WAS CARELESS.
I LET MY "GUARD" DOWN.
G'NOLGA, MY ENEMY... FOUND A WAY TO FORCE ME NOT TO FIGHT. SHE TOOK MY DAUGHTER, BRIANNA, HOSTAGE AND MADE IT SEEM AS THOUGH I LOST FOR MONEY.
SHE STRIPPED ME OF MY HONOR, OL' GEEZER. SHE BEAT ME.
IF MY GUARD WASN'T DOWN...
I WOULD HAVE MADE SURE MY DAUGHTER WAS SAFE BEFORE THE TOURNAMENT.
...OR I WOULD HAVE MADE SURE G'NOLGA NEVER KNEW ABOUT HER IN THE FIRST PLACE!
MM...
LESSONS LEARNED IN LIFE... MUCH MORE HARSH THAN LESSONS LEARNED IN SCHOOL...
Eh?

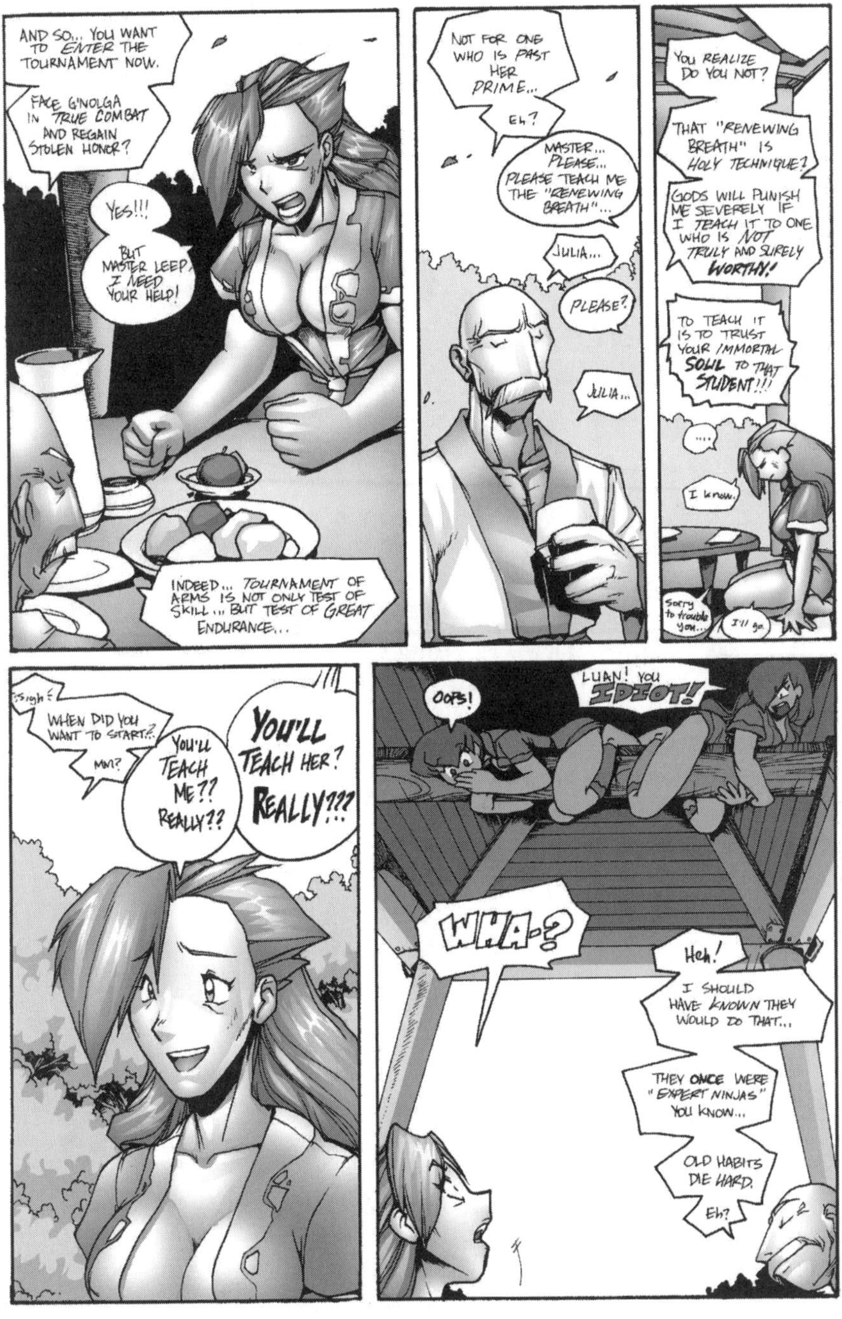
AND SO... YOU WANT TO ENTER THE TOURNAMENT NOW.
FACE G'NOLGA IN TRUE COMBAT AND REGAIN STOLEN HONOR?
YES!!!
BUT MASTER LEEP, I NEED YOUR HELP!
INDEED... TOURNAMENT OF ARMS IS NOT ONLY TEST OF SKILL... BUT TEST OF GREAT ENDURANCE...
NOT FOR ONE WHO IS PAST HER PRIME...
Eh?
MASTER... PLEASE... PLEASE TEACH ME THE "RENEWING BREATH"...
JULIA...
PLEASE?
JULIA...
YOU REALIZE DO YOU NOT?
THAT "RENEWING BREATH" IS HOLY TECHNIQUE?
GODS WILL PUNISH ME SEVERELY IF I TEACH IT TO ONE WHO IS NOT TRULY AND SURELY WORTHY!
TO TEACH IT IS TO TRUST YOUR IMMORTAL SOUL TO THAT STUDENT!!!
....
I know.
Sorry to trouble you...
I'll go.
Sigh
WHEN DID YOU WANT TO START...?
MM?
YOU'LL TEACH ME?? REALLY??
YOU'LL TEACH HER? REALLY???
OOPS!
LUAN! YOU IDIOT!
WHA-?
Heh!
I SHOULD HAVE KNOWN THEY WOULD DO THAT...
THEY ONCE WERE "EXPERT NINJAS" YOU KNOW...
OLD HABITS DIE HARD.
Eh?

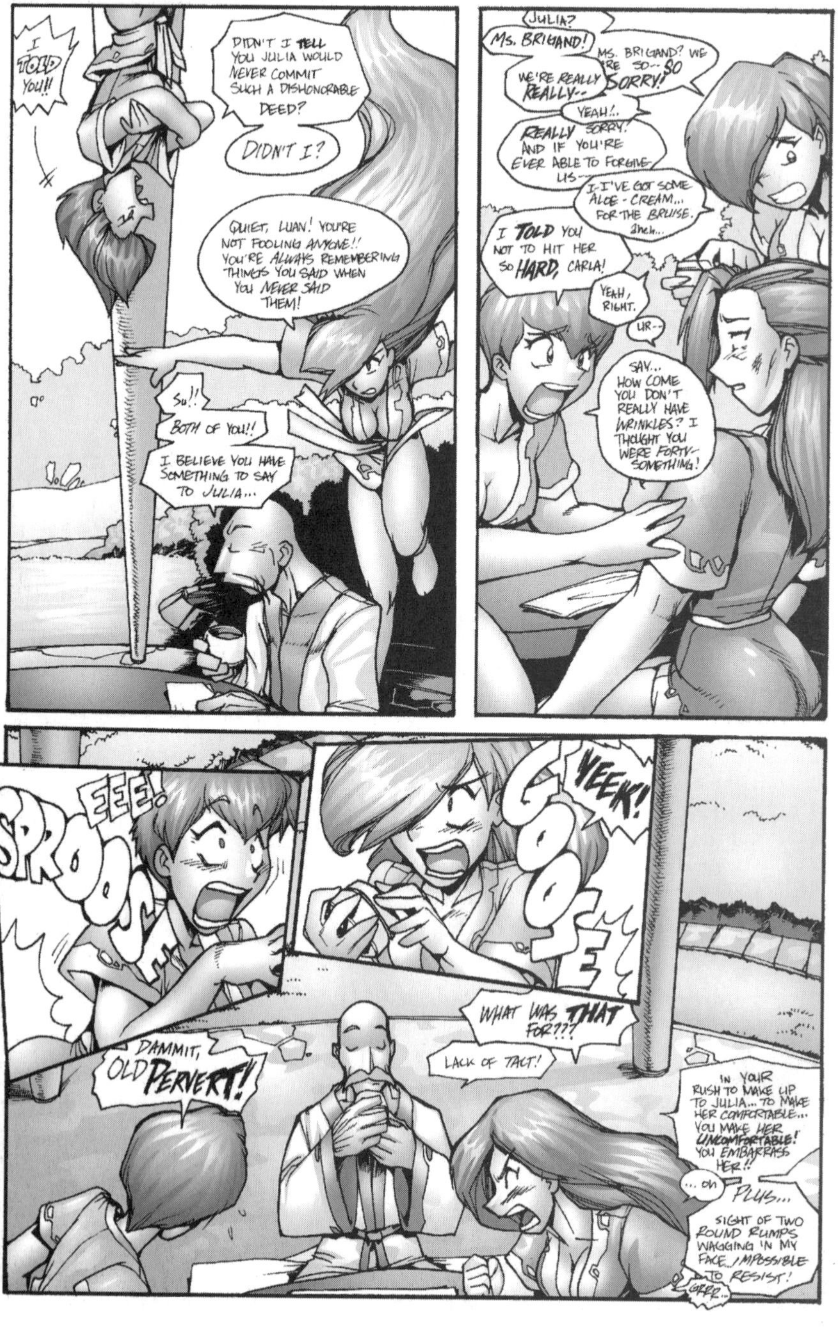
I TOLD YOU!!
DIDN'T I TELL YOU JULIA WOULD NEVER COMMIT SUCH A DISHONORABLE DEED?
DIDN'T I?
QUIET, LUAN! YOU'RE NOT FOOLING ANYONE!! YOU'RE ALWAYS REMEMBERING THINGS YOU SAID WHEN YOU NEVER SAID THEM!
SU!!
BOTH OF YOU!!
I BELIEVE YOU HAVE SOMETHING TO SAY TO JULIA...
JULIA?
MS. BRIGAND!
MS. BRIGAND? WE ARE SO-- SO SORRY!
WE'RE REALLY REALLY--
YEAH!..
REALLY SORRY! AND IF YOU'RE EVER ABLE TO FORGIVE US--
I-I'VE GOT SOME ALOE-CREAM... FOR THE BRUISE. eheh...
I TOLD YOU NOT TO HIT HER SO HARD, CARLA!
YEAH, RIGHT.
UR--
SAY... HOW COME YOU DON'T REALLY HAVE WRINKLES? I THOUGHT YOU WERE FORTY-SOMETHING!
EEE!
SPROOOSH
GOOOSE
YEEK!
WHAT WAS THAT FOR???
LACK OF TACT!
DAMMIT, OLD PERVERT!
IN YOUR RUSH TO MAKE UP TO JULIA... TO MAKE HER COMFORTABLE... YOU MAKE HER UNCOMFORTABLE! YOU EMBARRASS HER!!
...oh
PLUS...
SIGHT OF TWO ROUND RUMPS WAGGING IN MY FACE... IMPOSSIBLE TO RESIST!
GRRR...

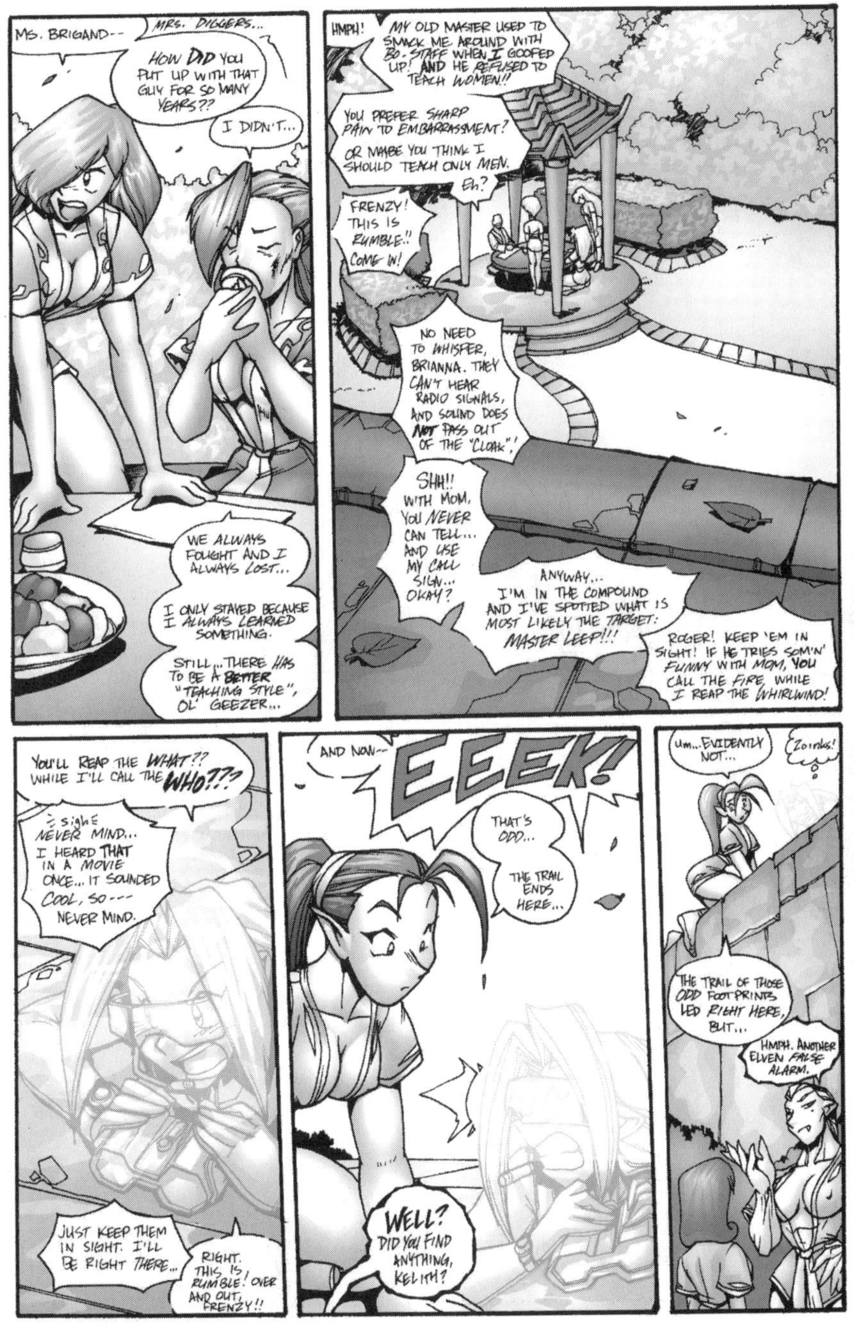
MS. BRIGAND--
MRS. DIGGERS...
HOW DID YOU PUT UP WITH THAT GUY FOR SO MANY YEARS??
I DIDN'T...
WE ALWAYS FOUGHT AND I ALWAYS LOST...
I ONLY STAYED BECAUSE I ALWAYS LEARNED SOMETHING.
STILL... THERE HAS TO BE A BETTER "TEACHING STYLE", OL' GEEZER...
HMPH!
MY OLD MASTER USED TO SMACK ME AROUND WITH BO-STAFF WHEN I GOOFED UP! AND HE REFUSED TO TEACH WOMEN!!
YOU PREFER SHARP PAIN TO EMBARRASSMENT?
OR MAYBE YOU THINK I SHOULD TEACH ONLY MEN.
EH?
FRENZY! THIS IS RUMBLE!! COME IN!
NO NEED TO WHISPER, BRIANNA. THEY CAN'T HEAR RADIO SIGNALS, AND SOUND DOES NOT PASS OUT OF THE "CLOAK".
SHH!! WITH MOM, YOU NEVER CAN TELL... AND USE MY CALL SIGN... OKAY?
ANYWAY... I'M IN THE COMPOUND AND I'VE SPOTTED WHAT IS MOST LIKELY THE TARGET: MASTER LEEP!!!
ROGER! KEEP 'EM IN SIGHT! IF HE TRIES SOM'N' FUNNY WITH MOM, YOU CALL THE FIRE, WHILE I REAP THE WHIRLWIND!
YOU'LL REAP THE WHAT?? WHILE I'LL CALL THE WHO???
=sigh= NEVER MIND... I HEARD THAT IN A MOVIE ONCE... IT SOUNDED COOL, SO--- NEVER MIND.
JUST KEEP THEM IN SIGHT. I'LL BE RIGHT THERE...
RIGHT. THIS IS RUMBLE! OVER AND OUT, FRENZY!!
AND NOW--
EEEK!
THAT'S ODD...
THE TRAIL ENDS HERE...
WELL? DID YOU FIND ANYTHING, KELITH?
UM... EVIDENTLY NOT...
Zoinks!
THE TRAIL OF THOSE ODD FOOTPRINTS LED RIGHT HERE, BUT...
HMPH. ANOTHER ELVEN FALSE ALARM.

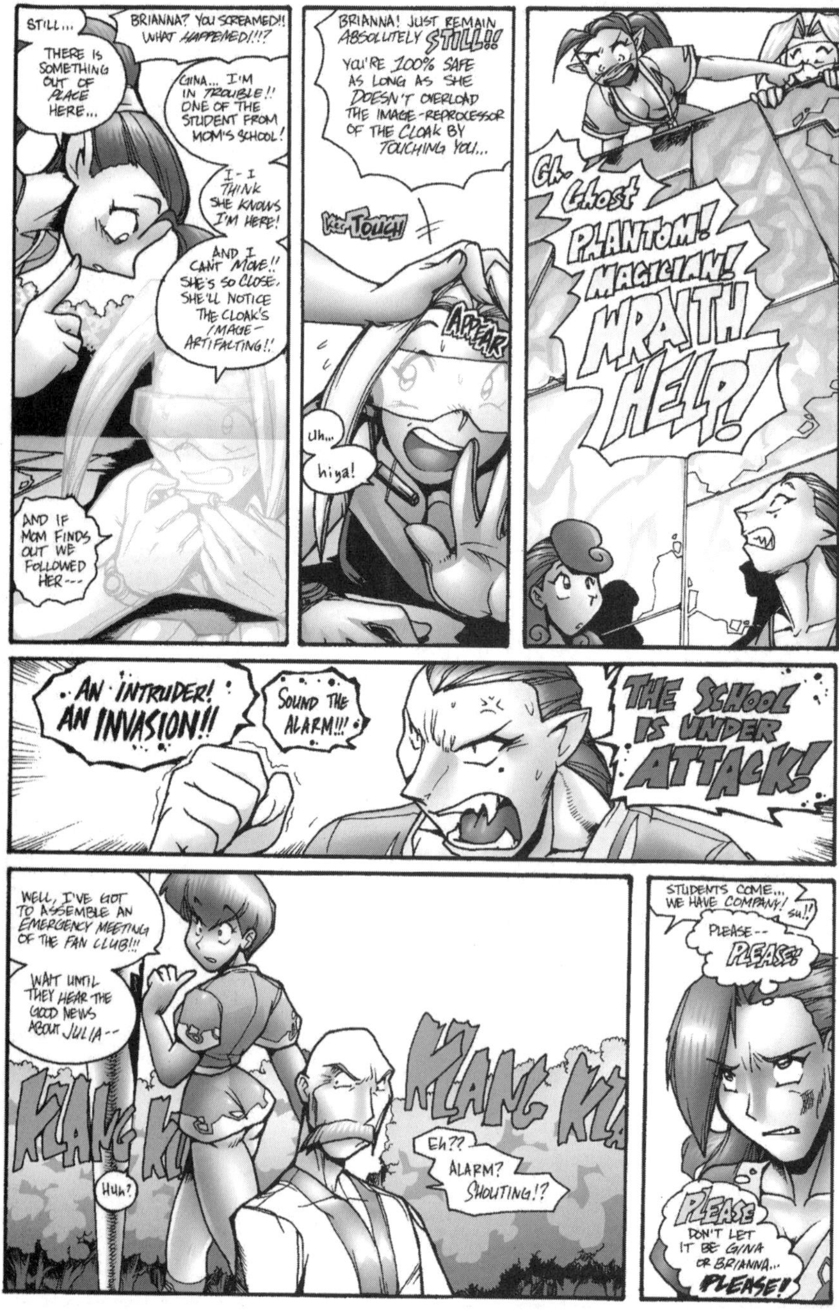
STILL...
THERE IS SOMETHING OUT OF PLACE HERE...
BRIANNA? YOU SCREAMED!! WHAT HAPPENED!!!?
GINA... I'M IN TROUBLE!! ONE OF THE STUDENT FROM MOM'S SCHOOL!
I - I THINK SHE KNOWS I'M HERE!
AND I CANT MOVE!! SHE'S SO CLOSE. SHE'LL NOTICE THE CLOAK'S IMAGE-ARTIFACTING!!
AND IF MOM FINDS OUT WE FOLLOWED HER---
BRIANNA! JUST REMAIN ABSOLUTELY STILL!!
YOU'RE 100% SAFE AS LONG AS SHE DOESN'T OVERLOAD THE IMAGE-REPROCESSOR OF THE CLOAK BY TOUCHING YOU...
TOUCH
APPEAR
uh... hiya!
Gh.. Ghost PLANTOM! MAGICIAN! WRAITH HELP!
AN INTRUDER! AN INVASION!!
SOUND THE ALARM!!!
THE SCHOOL IS UNDER ATTACK!
WELL, I'VE GOT TO ASSEMBLE AN EMERGENCY MEETING OF THE FAN CLUB!!!
WAIT UNTIL THEY HEAR THE GOOD NEWS ABOUT JULIA--
KLANG KL
KLANG KL
Huh?
Eh?? ALARM? SHOUTING!?
STUDENTS COME... WE HAVE COMPANY!
PLEASE-- PLEASE!
PLEASE DON'T LET IT BE GINA OR BRIANNA... PLEASE!

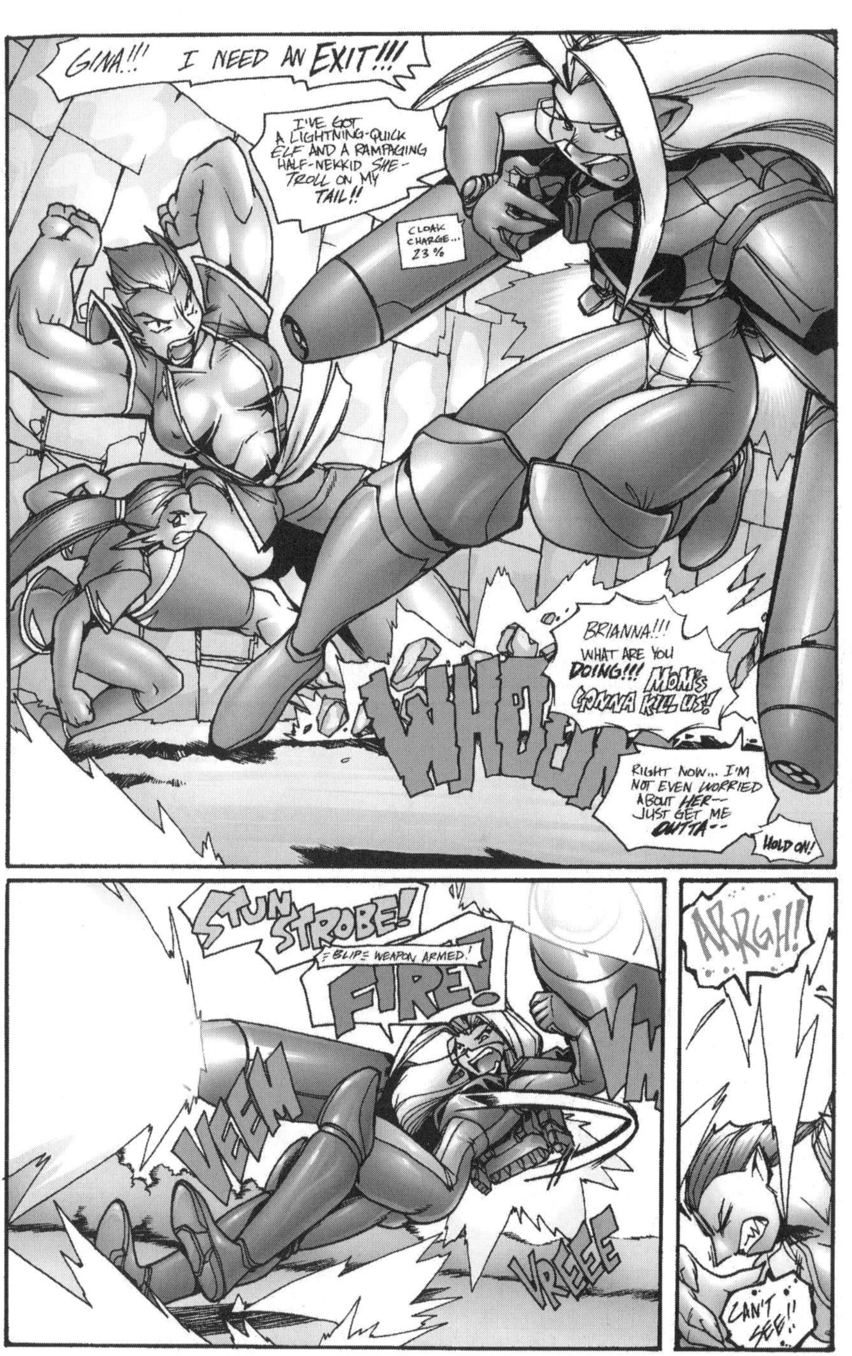
GINA!!! I NEED AN EXIT!!!
I'VE GOT A LIGHTNING-QUICK ELF AND A RAMPAGING HALF-NEKKID SHE-TROLL ON MY TAIL!!
CLOAK CHARGE... 23%
BRIANNA!!! WHAT ARE YOU DOING!!! MOM'S GONNA KILL US!
WHOOM
RIGHT NOW... I'M NOT EVEN WORRIED ABOUT HER-- JUST GET ME OUTTA--
HOLD ON!
STUN STROBE!
BLIP WEAPON ARMED.
FIRE!
VEEM
VREEE
ARRGH!!
CAN'T SEE!!

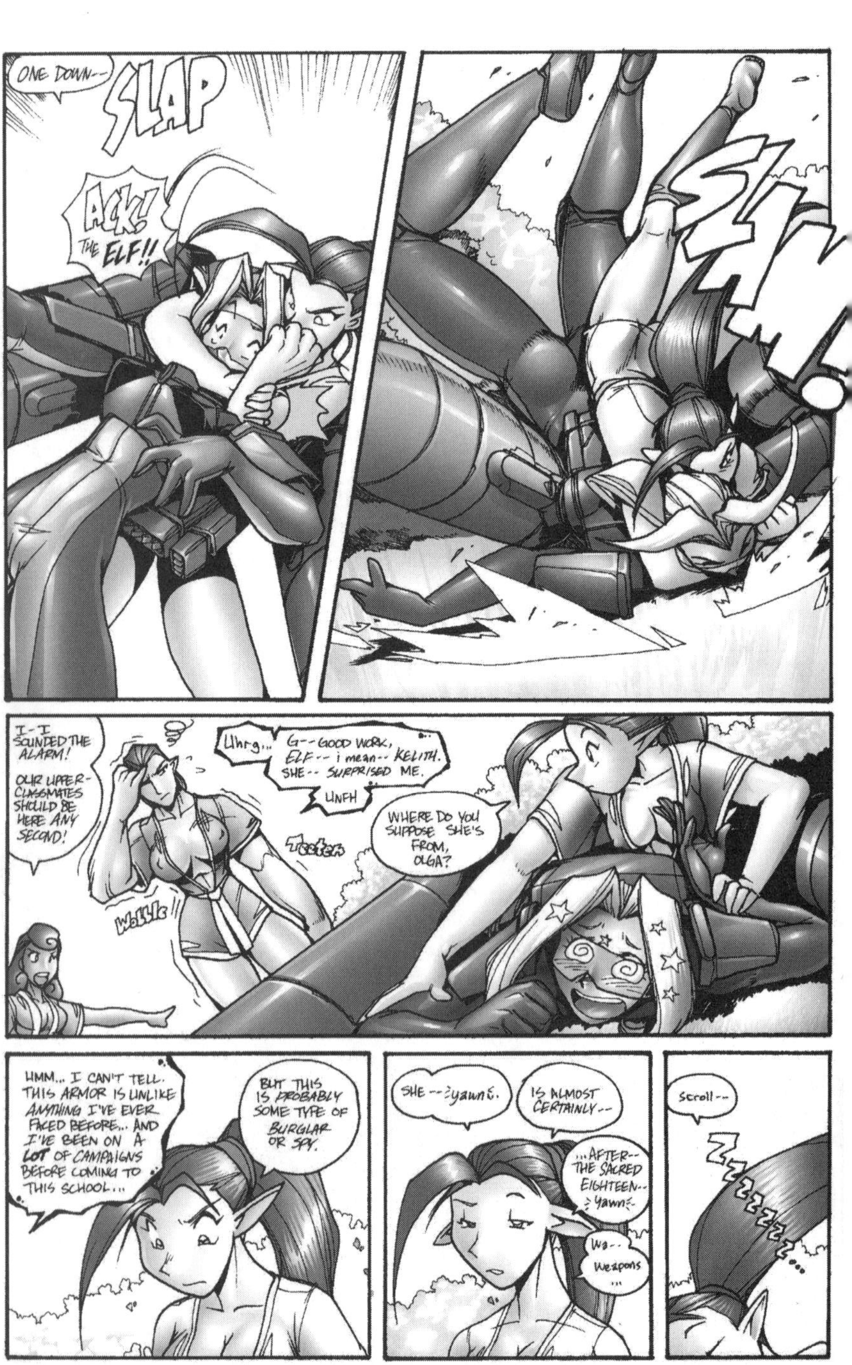

ONE DOWN--
SLAP
ACK! THE ELF!!
SLAM!
I- I SOUNDED THE ALARM!
OUR UPPER-CLASSMATES SHOULD BE HERE ANY SECOND!
Uhrg...
G--GOOD WORK, ELF-- i mean-- KELITH. SHE-- SURPRISED ME.
UNFH
Teeter
Wobble
WHERE DO YOU SUPPOSE SHE'S FROM, OLGA?
HMM... I CAN'T TELL. THIS ARMOR IS UNLIKE ANYTHING I'VE EVER FACED BEFORE... AND I'VE BEEN ON A LOT OF CAMPAIGNS BEFORE COMING TO THIS SCHOOL...
BUT THIS IS PROBABLY SOME TYPE OF BURGLAR OR SPY.
SHE -- yawn.
IS ALMOST CERTAINLY--
...AFTER-- THE SACRED EIGHTEEN-- yawn
Wa-- Weapons ...
Scroll--
Z Z Z Z Z Z Z...

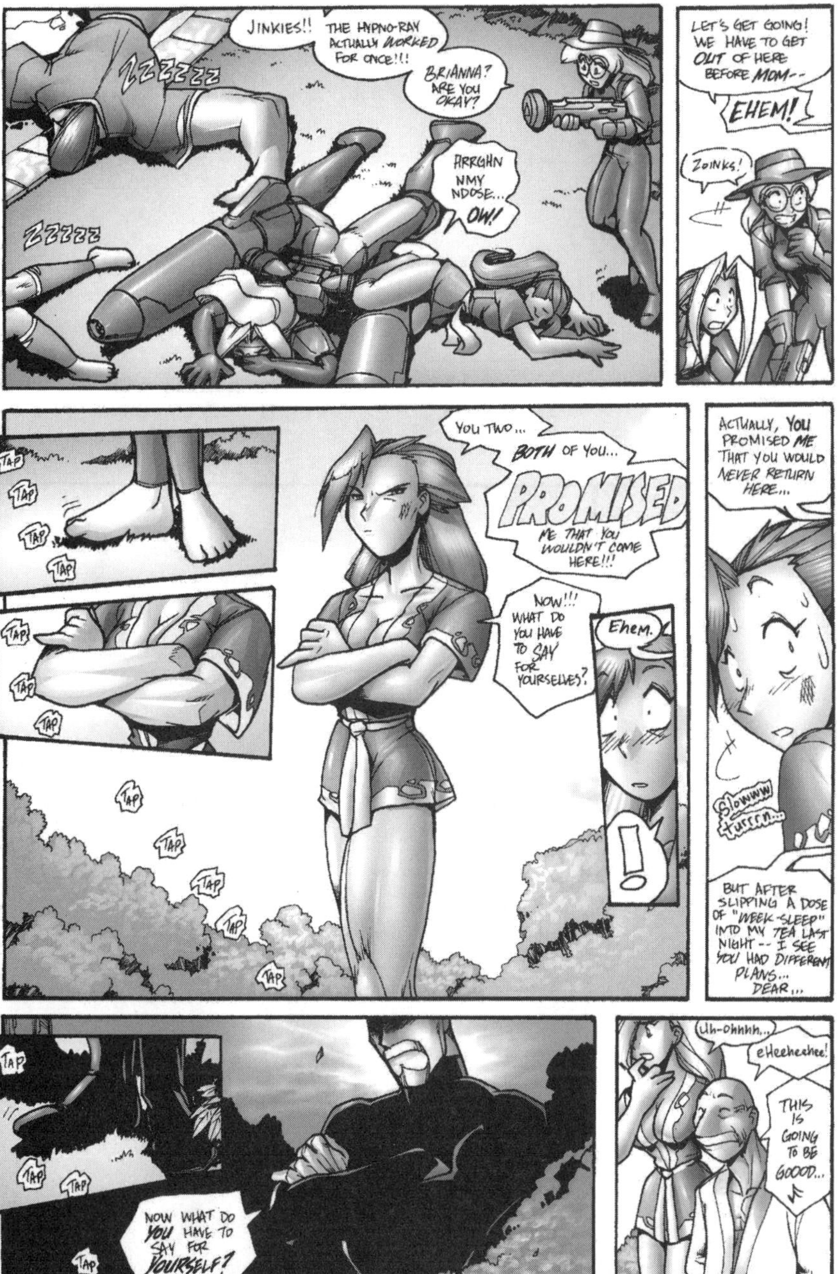

Jinkies!!
THE HYPNO-RAY ACTUALLY WORKED FOR ONCE!!!
BRIANNA? ARE YOU OKAY?
ZZZZZZ
ARRGHN NMY NDOSE... OW!
ZZZZZ
LET'S GET GOING! WE HAVE TO GET OUT OF HERE BEFORE MOM--
EHEM!
Zoinks!
TAP
TAP
TAP
TAP
TAP
TAP
TAP
YOU TWO...
BOTH OF YOU...
PROMISED
ME THAT YOU WOULDN'T COME HERE!!!
NOW!!! WHAT DO YOU HAVE TO SAY FOR YOURSELVES?
TAP
TAP
TAP
TAP
TAP
Ehem.
!
ACTUALLY, YOU PROMISED ME THAT YOU WOULD NEVER RETURN HERE...
Slowww turrrn...
BUT AFTER SLIPPING A DOSE OF "WEEK-SLEEP" INTO MY TEA LAST NIGHT -- I SEE YOU HAD DIFFERENT PLANS... DEAR...
TAP
TAP
TAP
NOW WHAT DO YOU HAVE TO SAY FOR YOURSELF?
TAP
TAP
Uh-ohhhh...
eHeeheehee!
THIS IS GOING TO BE GOOOD...

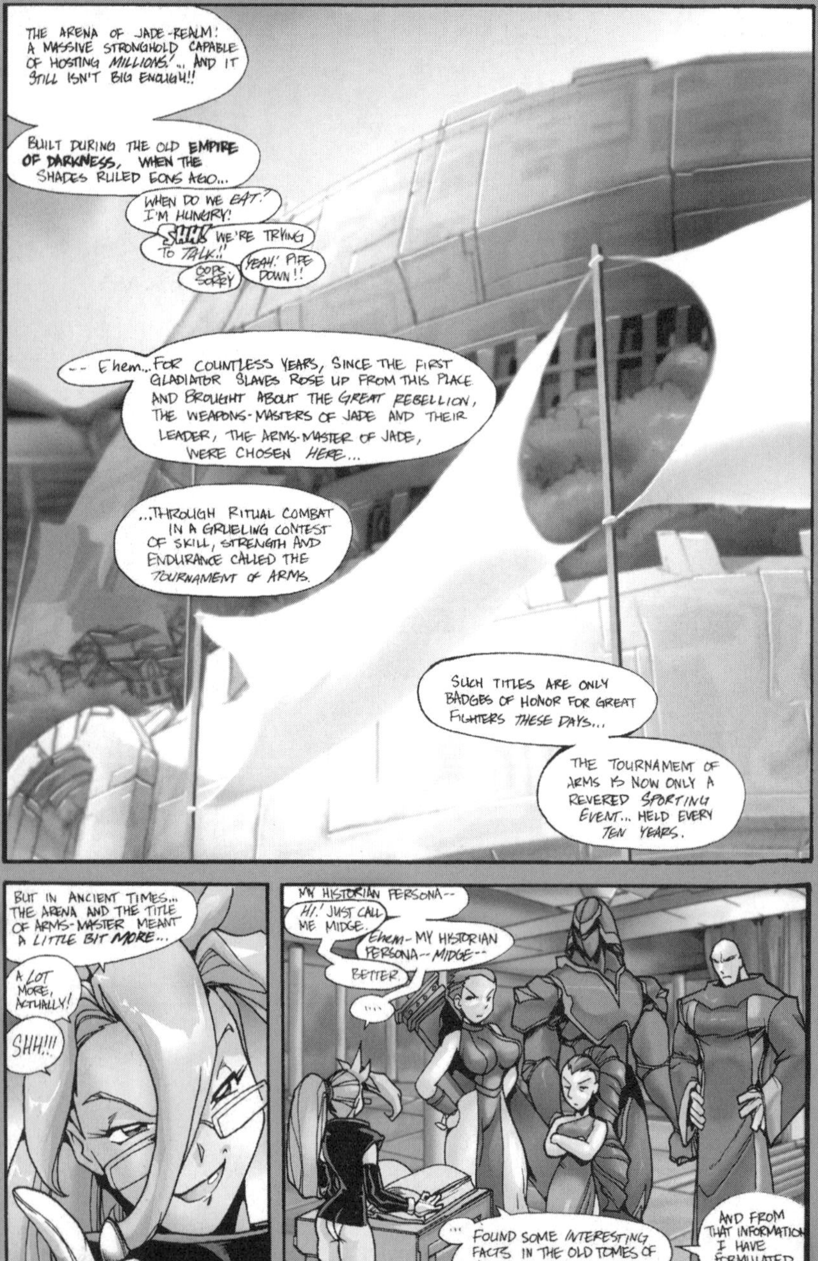
THE ARENA OF JADE-REALM! A MASSIVE STRONGHOLD CAPABLE OF HOSTING MILLIONS!... AND IT STILL ISN'T BIG ENOUGH!!
BUILT DURING THE OLD EMPIRE OF DARKNESS, WHEN THE SHADES RULED EONS AGO...
WHEN DO WE EAT? I'M HUNGRY!
SHH! WE'RE TRYING TO TALK!!
OOPS. SORRY
YEAH! PIPE DOWN!!
-- Ehem... FOR COUNTLESS YEARS, SINCE THE FIRST GLADIATOR SLAVES ROSE UP FROM THIS PLACE AND BROUGHT ABOUT THE GREAT REBELLION, THE WEAPONS-MASTERS OF JADE AND THEIR LEADER, THE ARMS-MASTER OF JADE, WERE CHOSEN HERE...
...THROUGH RITUAL COMBAT IN A GRUELING CONTEST OF SKILL, STRENGTH AND ENDURANCE CALLED THE TOURNAMENT OF ARMS.
SUCH TITLES ARE ONLY BADGES OF HONOR FOR GREAT FIGHTERS THESE DAYS...
THE TOURNAMENT OF ARMS IS NOW ONLY A REVERED SPORTING EVENT... HELD EVERY TEN YEARS.
BUT IN ANCIENT TIMES... THE ARENA AND THE TITLE OF ARMS-MASTER MEANT A LITTLE BIT MORE...
A LOT MORE, ACTUALLY!
SHH!!!
MY HISTORIAN PERSONA--
HI! JUST CALL ME MIDGE.
Ehem- MY HISTORIAN PERSONA-- MIDGE--
BETTER.
....
... FOUND SOME INTERESTING FACTS IN THE OLD TOMES OF JADE'S ANCIENT HISTORY...
AND FROM THAT INFORMATION I HAVE FORMULATED MY PLANS...

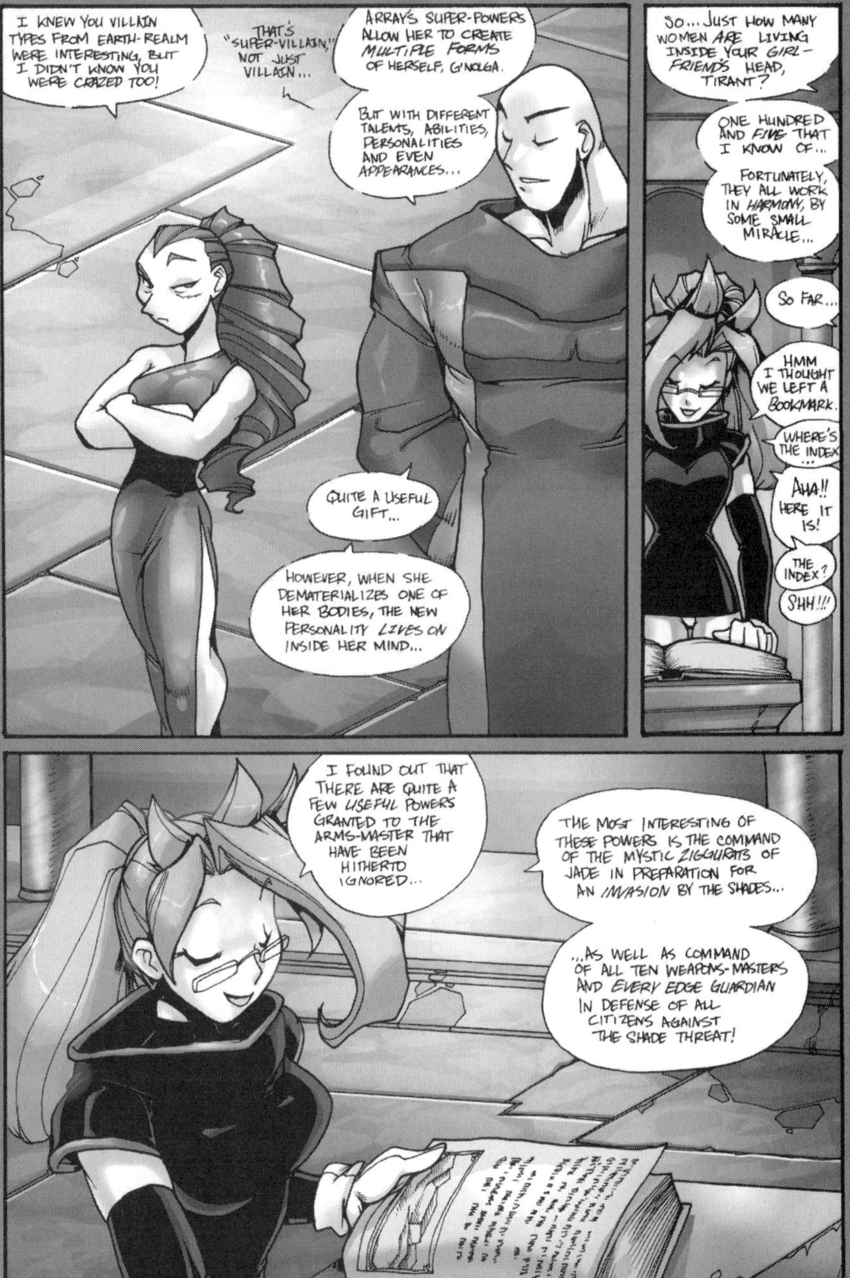
I KNEW YOU VILLAIN TYPES FROM EARTH-REALM WERE INTERESTING, BUT I DIDN'T KNOW YOU WERE CRAZED TOO!
THAT'S "SUPER-VILLAIN," NOT JUST VILLAIN...
ARRAY'S SUPER-POWERS ALLOW HER TO CREATE MULTIPLE FORMS OF HERSELF, G'NOLGA.
BUT WITH DIFFERENT TALENTS, ABILITIES, PERSONALITIES AND EVEN APPEARANCES...
QUITE A USEFUL GIFT...
HOWEVER, WHEN SHE DEMATERIALIZES ONE OF HER BODIES, THE NEW PERSONALITY LIVES ON INSIDE HER MIND...
SO... JUST HOW MANY WOMEN ARE LIVING INSIDE YOUR GIRL-FRIEND'S HEAD, TIRANT?
ONE HUNDRED AND FIVE THAT I KNOW OF...
FORTUNATELY, THEY ALL WORK IN HARMONY, BY SOME SMALL MIRACLE...
SO FAR...
HMM I THOUGHT WE LEFT A BOOKMARK.
WHERE'S THE INDEX...
AHA!! HERE IT IS!
THE INDEX?
SHH!!!
I FOUND OUT THAT THERE ARE QUITE A FEW USEFUL POWERS GRANTED TO THE ARMS-MASTER THAT HAVE BEEN HITHERTO IGNORED...
THE MOST INTERESTING OF THESE POWERS IS THE COMMAND OF THE MYSTIC ZIGGURATS OF JADE IN PREPARATION FOR AN INVASION BY THE SHADES...
...AS WELL AS COMMAND OF ALL TEN WEAPONS-MASTERS AND EVERY EDGE GUARDIAN IN DEFENSE OF ALL CITIZENS AGAINST THE SHADE THREAT!

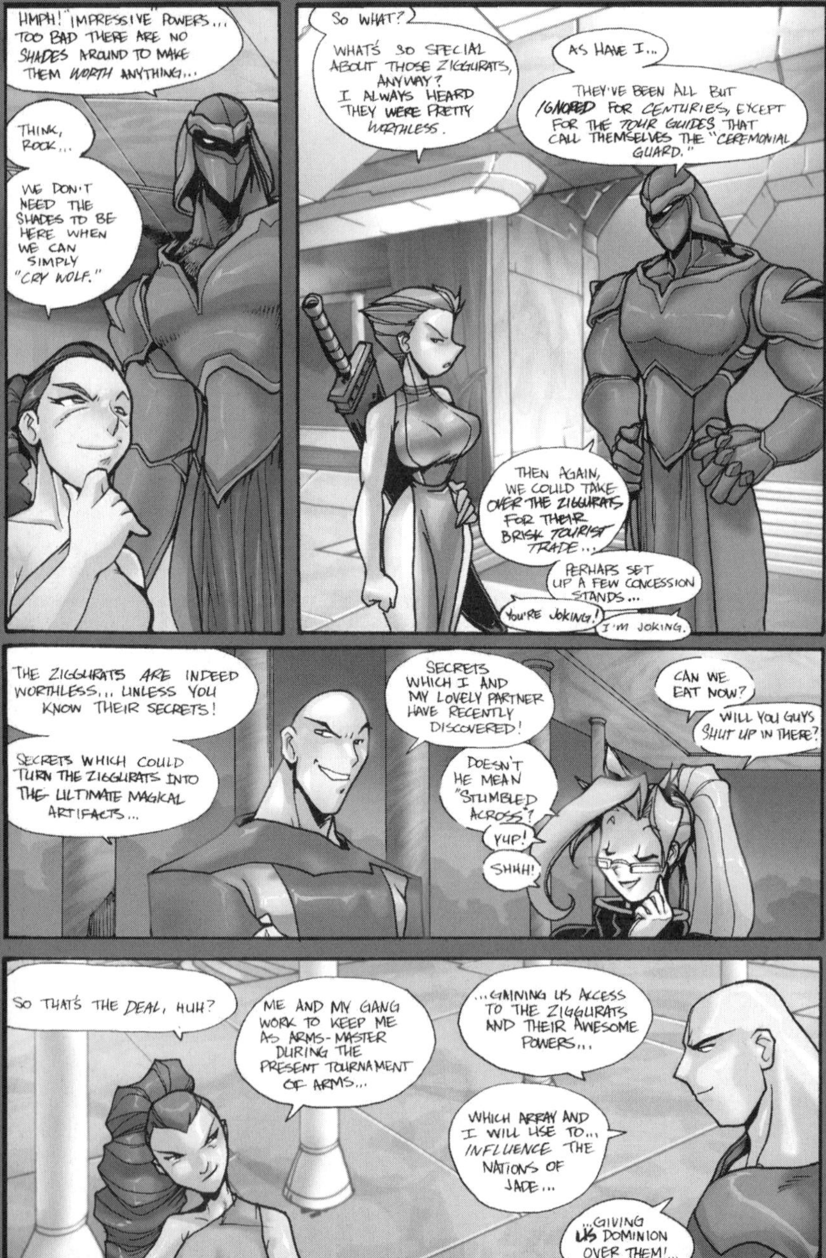

HMPH! "IMPRESSIVE" POWERS... TOO BAD THERE ARE NO SHADES AROUND TO MAKE THEM WORTH ANYTHING...
THINK, ROCK...
WE DON'T NEED THE SHADES TO BE HERE WHEN WE CAN SIMPLY "CRY WOLF."
SO WHAT?
WHAT'S SO SPECIAL ABOUT THOSE ZIGGURATS, ANYWAY? I ALWAYS HEARD THEY WERE PRETTY WORTHLESS.
AS HAVE I...
THEY'VE BEEN ALL BUT IGNORED FOR CENTURIES, EXCEPT FOR THE TOUR GUIDES THAT CALL THEMSELVES THE "CEREMONIAL GUARD."
THEN AGAIN, WE COULD TAKE OVER THE ZIGGURATS FOR THEIR BRISK TOURIST TRADE...
PERHAPS SET UP A FEW CONCESSION STANDS...
YOU'RE JOKING!
I'M JOKING.
THE ZIGGURATS ARE INDEED WORTHLESS... UNLESS YOU KNOW THEIR SECRETS!
SECRETS WHICH COULD TURN THE ZIGGURATS INTO THE ULTIMATE MAGICAL ARTIFACTS...
SECRETS WHICH I AND MY LOVELY PARTNER HAVE RECENTLY DISCOVERED!
DOESN'T HE MEAN "STUMBLED ACROSS"?
YUP!
SHHH!
CAN WE EAT NOW?
WILL YOU GUYS SHUT UP IN THERE?
SO THAT'S THE DEAL, HUH?
ME AND MY GANG WORK TO KEEP ME AS ARMS-MASTER DURING THE PRESENT TOURNAMENT OF ARMS...
...GAINING US ACCESS TO THE ZIGGURATS AND THEIR AWESOME POWERS...
WHICH ARRAY AND I WILL USE TO... INFLUENCE THE NATIONS OF JADE...
...GIVING US DOMINION OVER THEM!...

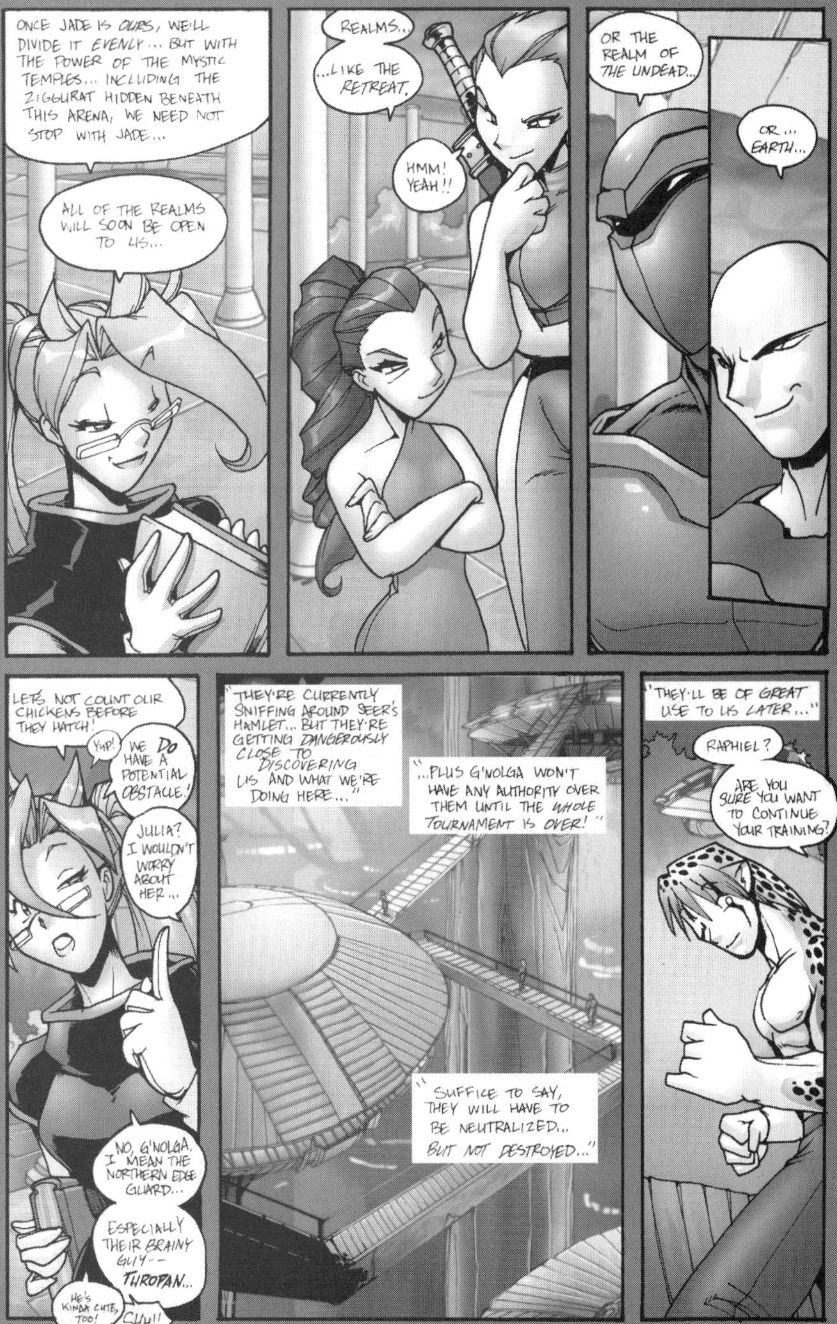
ONCE JADE IS OURS, WE'LL DIVIDE IT EVENLY... BUT WITH THE POWER OF THE MYSTIC TEMPLES... INCLUDING THE ZIGGURAT HIDDEN BENEATH THIS ARENA, WE NEED NOT STOP WITH JADE...
ALL OF THE REALMS WILL SOON BE OPEN TO US...
REALMS...
...LIKE THE RETREAT.
HMM! YEAH!!
OR THE REALM OF THE UNDEAD...
OR... EARTH...
LET'S NOT COUNT OUR CHICKENS BEFORE THEY HATCH!
YUP!
WE DO HAVE A POTENTIAL OBSTACLE!
JULIA? I WOULDN'T WORRY ABOUT HER...
NO, G'NOLGA. I MEAN THE NORTHERN EDGE GUARD...
ESPECIALLY THEIR BRAINY GUY-- THROPAN...
HE'S KINDA CUTE, TOO!
SHH!!
"THEY'RE CURRENTLY SNIFFING AROUND SEER'S HAMLET... BUT THEY'RE GETTING DANGEROUSLY CLOSE TO DISCOVERING US AND WHAT WE'RE DOING HERE..."
"...PLUS G'NOLGA WON'T HAVE ANY AUTHORITY OVER THEM UNTIL THE WHOLE TOURNAMENT IS OVER!"
"SUFFICE TO SAY, THEY WILL HAVE TO BE NEUTRALIZED... BUT NOT DESTROYED..."
"THEY'LL BE OF GREAT USE TO US LATER..."
RAPHIEL?
ARE YOU SURE YOU WANT TO CONTINUE YOUR TRAINING?

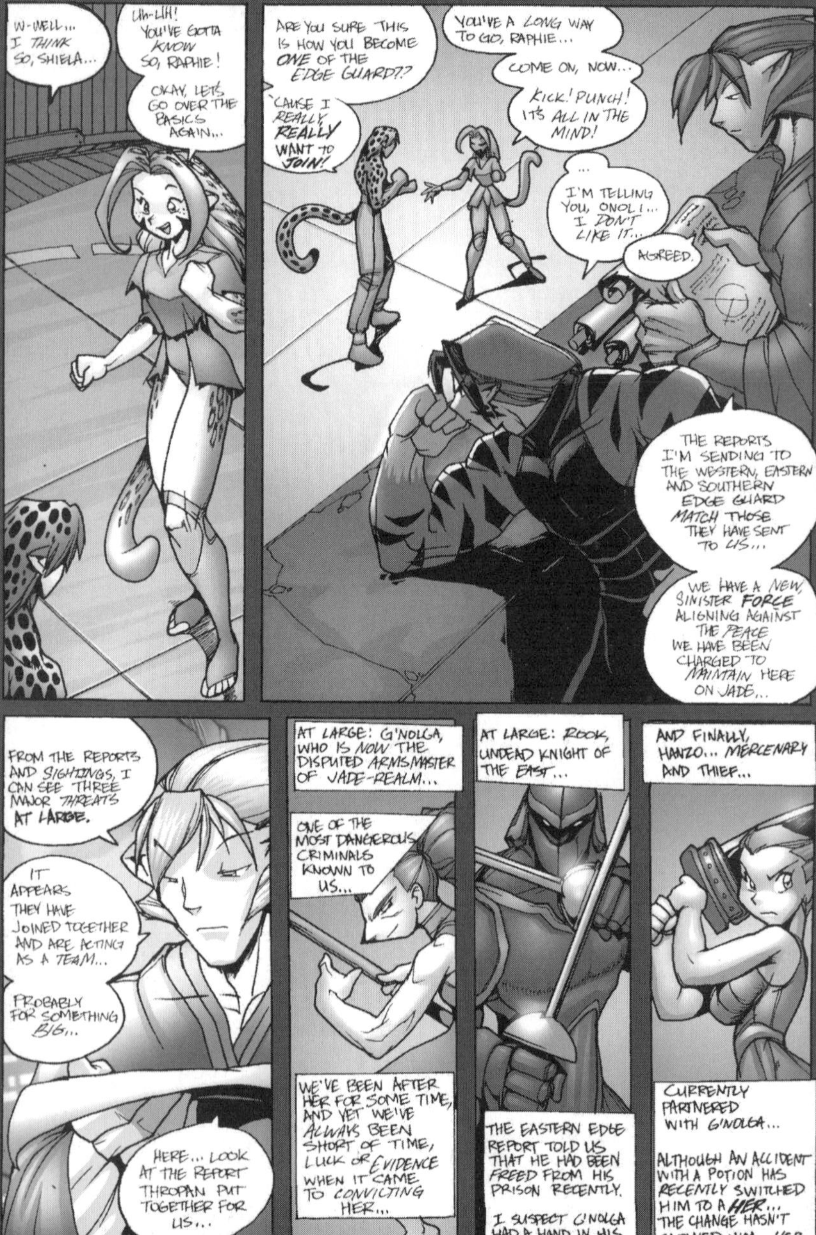
W-WELL... I THINK SO, SHIELA...
UH-UH! YOU'VE GOTTA KNOW SO, RAPHIE!
OKAY, LET'S GO OVER THE BASICS AGAIN...
ARE YOU SURE THIS IS HOW YOU BECOME ONE OF THE EDGE GUARD?!?
'CAUSE I REALLY, REALLY WANT TO JOIN!
YOU'VE A LONG WAY TO GO, RAPHIE...
COME ON, NOW...
KICK! PUNCH! IT'S ALL IN THE MIND!
...
I'M TELLING YOU, ONOLI... I DON'T LIKE IT...
AGREED.
THE REPORTS I'M SENDING TO THE WESTERN, EASTERN AND SOUTHERN EDGE GUARD MATCH THOSE THEY HAVE SENT TO US...
WE HAVE A NEW, SINISTER FORCE ALIGNING AGAINST THE PEACE WE HAVE BEEN CHARGED TO MAINTAIN HERE ON JADE...
FROM THE REPORTS AND SIGHTINGS, I CAN SEE THREE MAJOR THREATS AT LARGE.
IT APPEARS THEY HAVE JOINED TOGETHER AND ARE ACTING AS A TEAM...
PROBABLY FOR SOMETHING BIG...
HERE... LOOK AT THE REPORT THROPAN PUT TOGETHER FOR US...
AT LARGE: G'NOLGA, WHO IS NOW THE DISPUTED ARMS MASTER OF JADE-REALM...
ONE OF THE MOST DANGEROUS CRIMINALS KNOWN TO US...
WE'VE BEEN AFTER HER FOR SOME TIME, AND YET WE'VE ALWAYS BEEN SHORT OF TIME, LUCK OR EVIDENCE WHEN IT CAME TO CONVICTING HER...
AT LARGE: ROOK, UNDEAD KNIGHT OF THE EAST...
THE EASTERN EDGE REPORT TOLD US THAT HE HAD BEEN FREED FROM HIS PRISON RECENTLY.
I SUSPECT G'NOLGA HAD A HAND IN HIS LIBERATION...
AND FINALLY, HANZO... MERCENARY AND THIEF...
CURRENTLY PARTNERED WITH G'NOLGA...
ALTHOUGH AN ACCIDENT WITH A POTION HAS RECENTLY SWITCHED HIM TO A HER... THE CHANGE HASN'T SLOWED HIM-- HER DOWN A BIT...

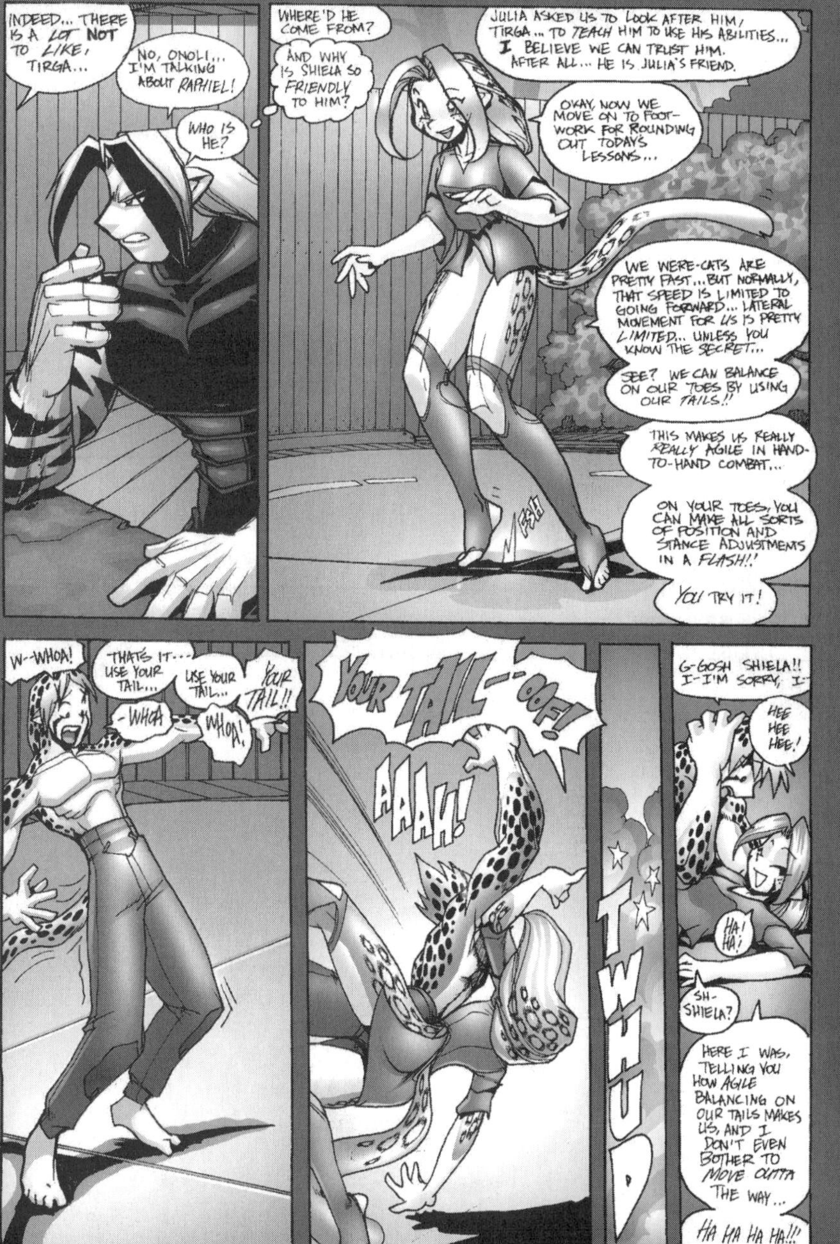

INDEED... THERE IS A LOT NOT TO LIKE, TIRGA...
NO, ONOLI... I'M TALKING ABOUT RAPHIEL!
WHO IS HE?
WHERE'D HE COME FROM?
AND WHY IS SHIELA SO FRIENDLY TO HIM?
JULIA ASKED US TO LOOK AFTER HIM, TIRGA... TO TEACH HIM TO USE HIS ABILITIES... I BELIEVE WE CAN TRUST HIM. AFTER ALL... HE IS JULIA'S FRIEND.
OKAY, NOW WE MOVE ON TO FOOT-WORK FOR ROUNDING OUT TODAY'S LESSONS...
WE WERE-CATS ARE PRETTY FAST... BUT NORMALLY, THAT SPEED IS LIMITED TO GOING FORWARD... LATERAL MOVEMENT FOR US IS PRETTY LIMITED... UNLESS YOU KNOW THE SECRET...
SEE? WE CAN BALANCE ON OUR TOES BY USING OUR TAILS!!
THIS MAKES US REALLY REALLY AGILE IN HAND-TO-HAND COMBAT...
ON YOUR TOES, YOU CAN MAKE ALL SORTS OF POSITION AND STANCE ADJUSTMENTS IN A FLASH!!
YOU TRY IT!
W--WHOA!
THAT'S IT... USE YOUR TAIL...
-WHOA
USE YOUR TAIL...
WHOA!
YOUR TAIL!!
YOUR TAIL--OOF!
AAAH!
TWHUD
G-GOSH SHIELA!! I-I'M SORRY, I-
HEE HEE HEE!
HA! HA!
SH-SHIELA?
HERE I WAS, TELLING YOU HOW AGILE BALANCING ON OUR TAILS MAKES US, AND I DON'T EVEN BOTHER TO MOVE OUTTA THE WAY...
HA HA HA HA!!

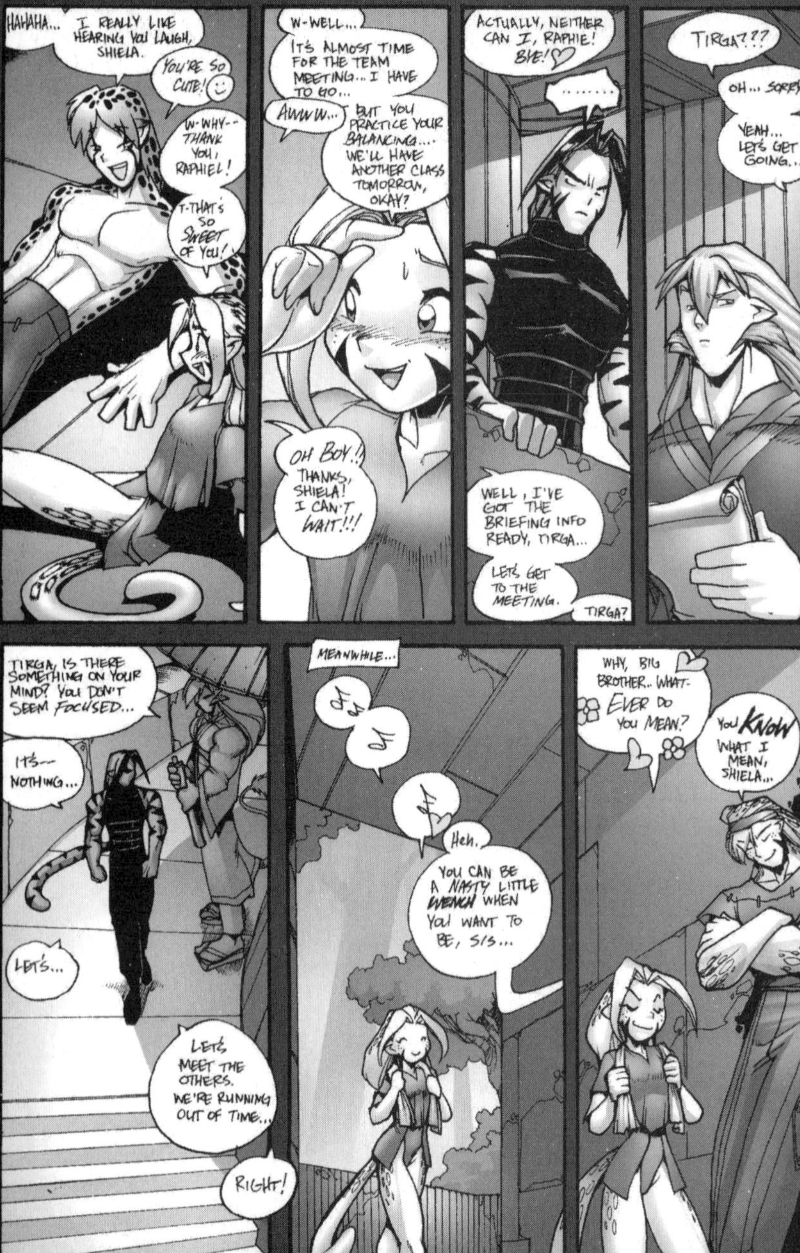
HAHAHA... I REALLY LIKE HEARING YOU LAUGH, SHIELA.
YOU'RE SO CUTE!
W-WHY-- THANK YOU, RAPHIEL!
T-THAT'S SO SWEET OF YOU!
W-WELL... IT'S ALMOST TIME FOR THE TEAM MEETING... I HAVE TO GO...
AWWW...
BUT YOU PRACTICE YOUR BALANCING.... WE'LL HAVE ANOTHER CLASS TOMORROW, OKAY?
OH BOY!! THANKS, SHIELA! I CAN'T WAIT!!!
ACTUALLY, NEITHER CAN I, RAPHIE! BYE!
....
WELL, I'VE GOT THE BRIEFING INFO READY, TIRGA...
LET'S GET TO THE MEETING.
TIRGA?
TIRGA???
OH... SORRY.
YEAH... LET'S GET GOING...
TIRGA, IS THERE SOMETHING ON YOUR MIND? YOU DON'T SEEM FOCUSED...
IT'S-- NOTHING...
LET'S...
LET'S MEET THE OTHERS. WE'RE RUNNING OUT OF TIME...
RIGHT!
MEANWHILE...
Heh.
YOU CAN BE A NASTY LITTLE WENCH WHEN YOU WANT TO BE, SIS...
WHY, BIG BROTHER.. WHAT-EVER DO YOU MEAN?
YOU KNOW WHAT I MEAN, SHIELA...

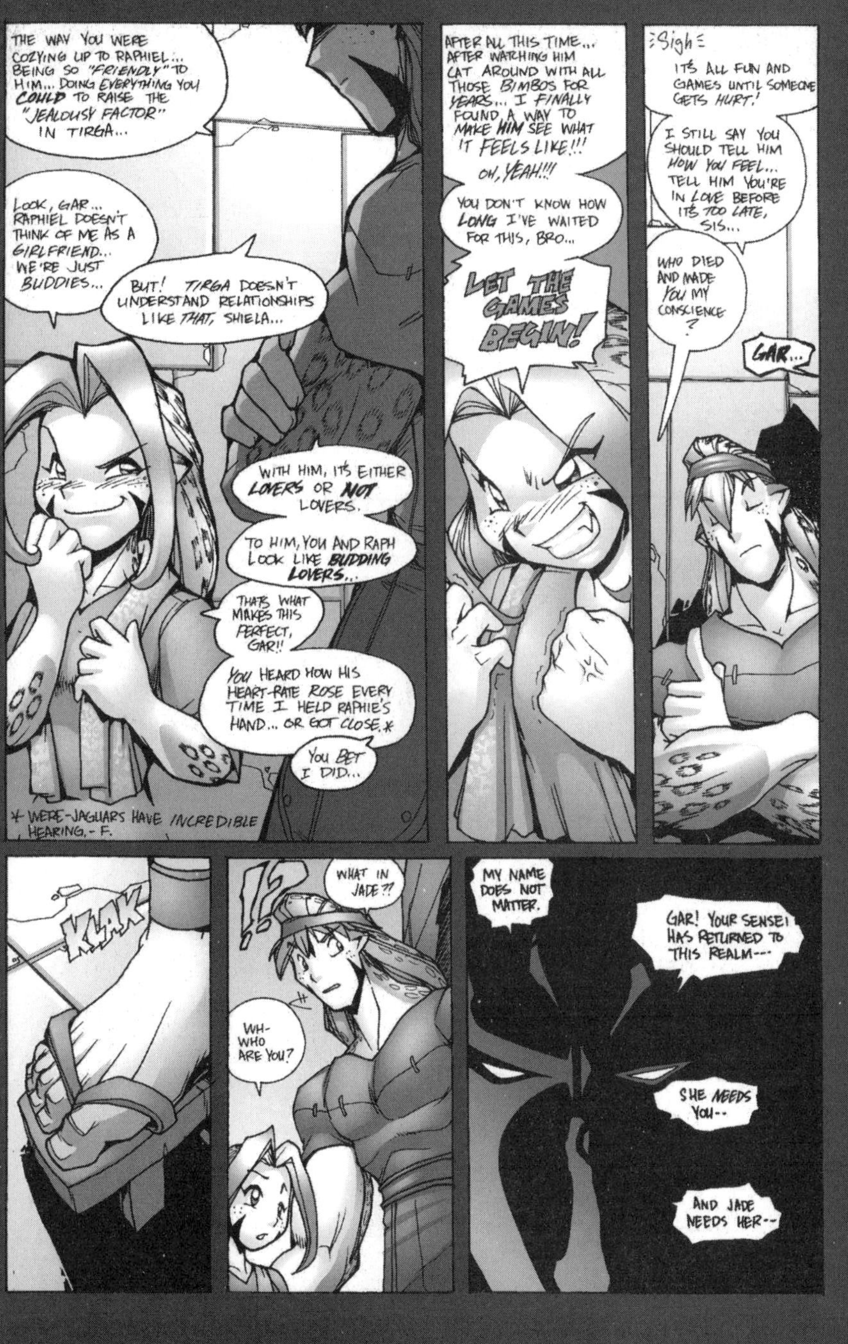
THE WAY YOU WERE COZYING UP TO RAPHIEL... BEING SO "FRIENDLY" TO HIM... DOING EVERYTHING YOU COULD TO RAISE THE "JEALOUSY FACTOR" IN TIRGA...
LOOK, GAR... RAPHIEL DOESN'T THINK OF ME AS A GIRLFRIEND... WE'RE JUST BUDDIES...
BUT! TIRGA DOESN'T UNDERSTAND RELATIONSHIPS LIKE THAT, SHIELA...
WITH HIM, IT'S EITHER LOVERS OR NOT LOVERS.
TO HIM, YOU AND RAPH LOOK LIKE BUDDING LOVERS...
THAT'S WHAT MAKES THIS PERFECT, GAR!!
YOU HEARD HOW HIS HEART-RATE ROSE EVERY TIME I HELD RAPHIE'S HAND... OR GOT CLOSE.*
YOU BET I DID...
* WERE-JAGUARS HAVE INCREDIBLE HEARING. - F.
AFTER ALL THIS TIME... AFTER WATCHING HIM CAT AROUND WITH ALL THOSE BIMBOS FOR YEARS... I FINALLY FOUND A WAY TO MAKE HIM SEE WHAT IT FEELS LIKE!!!
OH, YEAH!!!
YOU DON'T KNOW HOW LONG I'VE WAITED FOR THIS, BRO...
LET THE GAMES BEGIN!
:Sigh:
IT'S ALL FUN AND GAMES UNTIL SOMEONE GETS HURT!
I STILL SAY YOU SHOULD TELL HIM HOW YOU FEEL... TELL HIM YOU'RE IN LOVE BEFORE IT'S TOO LATE, SIS...
WHO DIED AND MADE YOU MY CONSCIENCE?
GAR...
KLAK
!?
WHAT IN JADE??
WH-WHO ARE YOU?
MY NAME DOES NOT MATTER.
GAR! YOUR SENSEI HAS RETURNED TO THIS REALM---
SHE NEEDS YOU--
AND JADE NEEDS HER--

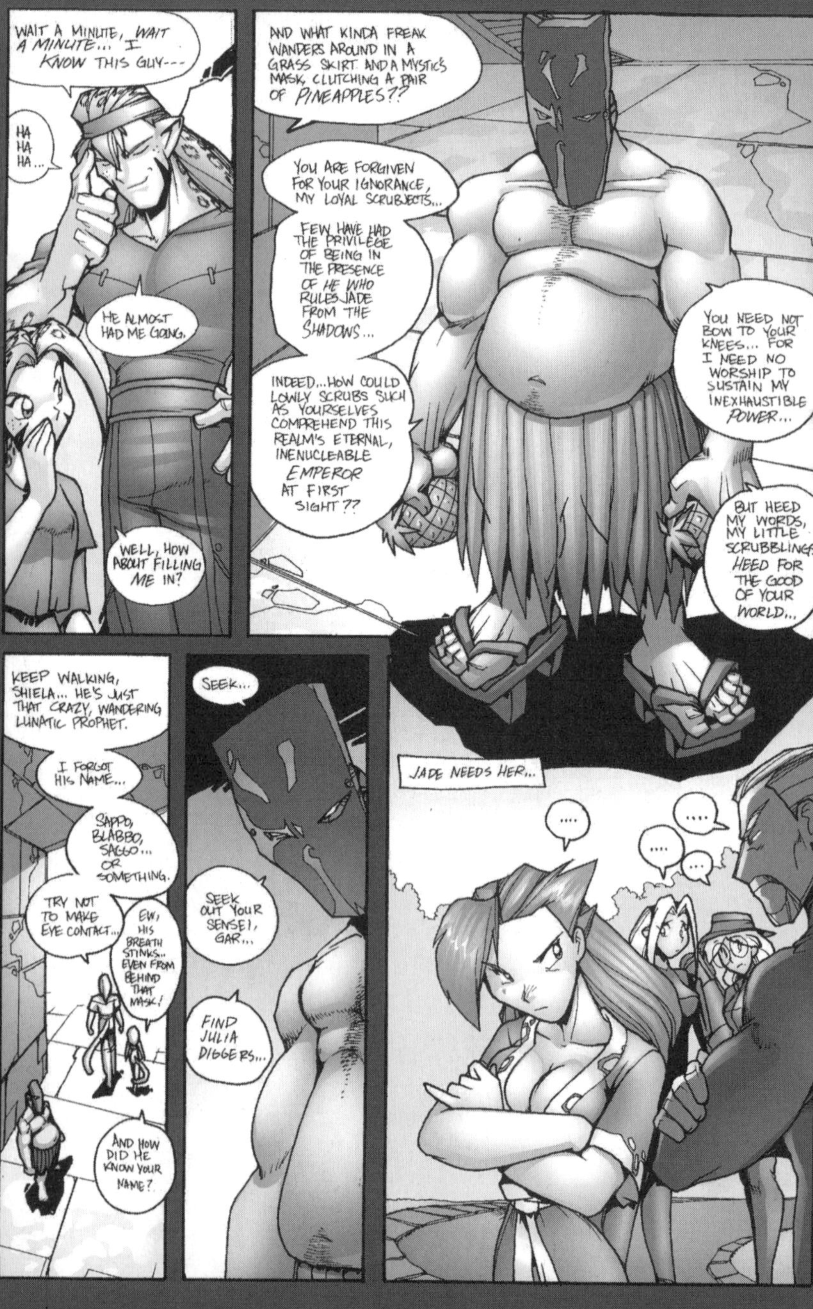
WAIT A MINUTE, WAIT A MINUTE... I KNOW THIS GUY---
HA HA HA HA...
HE ALMOST HAD ME GOING.
WELL, HOW ABOUT FILLING ME IN?
AND WHAT KINDA FREAK WANDERS AROUND IN A GRASS SKIRT AND A MYSTIC'S MASK, CLUTCHING A PAIR OF PINEAPPLES??
YOU ARE FORGIVEN FOR YOUR IGNORANCE, MY LOYAL SCRUBJECTS...
FEW HAVE HAD THE PRIVILEGE OF BEING IN THE PRESENCE OF HE WHO RULES JADE FROM THE SHADOWS...
INDEED...HOW COULD LOWLY SCRUBS SUCH AS YOURSELVES COMPREHEND THIS REALM'S ETERNAL, INENUCLEABLE EMPEROR AT FIRST SIGHT??
YOU NEED NOT BOW TO YOUR KNEES... FOR I NEED NO WORSHIP TO SUSTAIN MY INEXHAUSTIBLE POWER...
BUT HEED MY WORDS, MY LITTLE SCRUBBLINGS, HEED FOR THE GOOD OF YOUR WORLD...
KEEP WALKING, SHIELA... HE'S JUST THAT CRAZY, WANDERING LUNATIC PROPHET.
I FORGOT HIS NAME...
SAPPO, BLABBO, SAGGO... OR SOMETHING.
TRY NOT TO MAKE EYE CONTACT...
EW, HIS BREATH STINKS... EVEN FROM BEHIND THAT MASK!
AND HOW DID HE KNOW YOUR NAME?
SEEK...
SEEK OUT YOUR SENSEI, GAR...
FIND JULIA DIGGERS...
JADE NEEDS HER...
....
....
....
...

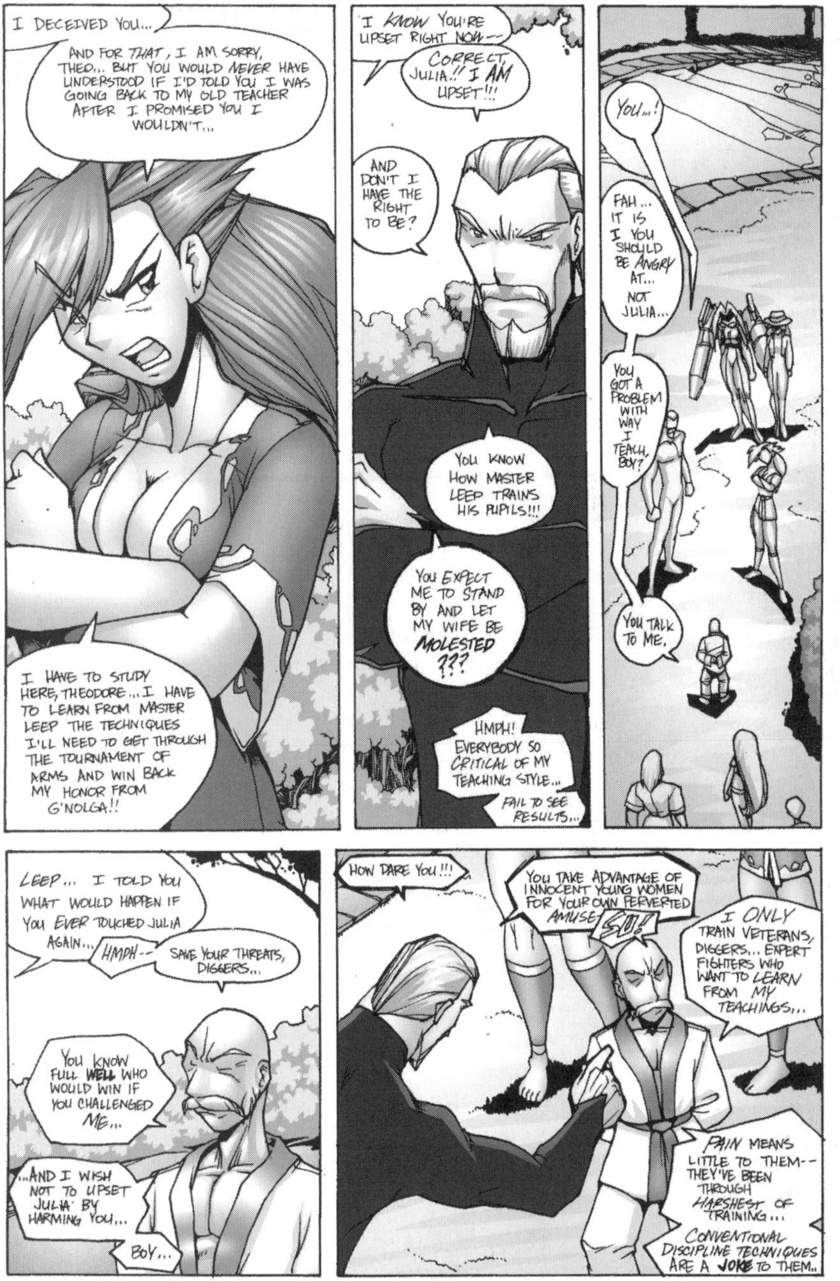
I DECEIVED YOU...
AND FOR THAT, I AM SORRY, THEO... BUT YOU WOULD NEVER HAVE UNDERSTOOD IF I'D TOLD YOU I WAS GOING BACK TO MY OLD TEACHER AFTER I PROMISED YOU I WOULDN'T...
I HAVE TO STUDY HERE, THEODORE... I HAVE TO LEARN FROM MASTER LEEP THE TECHNIQUES I'LL NEED TO GET THROUGH THE TOURNAMENT OF ARMS AND WIN BACK MY HONOR FROM G'NOLGA!!
I KNOW YOU'RE UPSET RIGHT NOW--
CORRECT, JULIA!! I AM UPSET!!!
AND DON'T I HAVE THE RIGHT TO BE?
YOU KNOW HOW MASTER LEEP TRAINS HIS PUPILS!!!
YOU EXPECT ME TO STAND BY AND LET MY WIFE BE MOLESTED???
HMPH! EVERYBODY SO CRITICAL OF MY TEACHING STYLE...
FAIL TO SEE RESULTS...
YOU...!
FAH... IT IS I YOU SHOULD BE ANGRY AT... NOT JULIA...
YOU GOT A PROBLEM WITH WAY I TEACH, BOY?
YOU TALK TO ME.
LEEP... I TOLD YOU WHAT WOULD HAPPEN IF YOU EVER TOUCHED JULIA AGAIN...
HMPH--
SAVE YOUR THREATS, DIGGERS...
YOU KNOW FULL WELL WHO WOULD WIN IF YOU CHALLENGED ME...
...AND I WISH NOT TO UPSET JULIA BY HARMING YOU...
BOY...
HOW DARE YOU!!!
YOU TAKE ADVANTAGE OF INNOCENT YOUNG WOMEN FOR YOUR OWN PERVERTED AMUSE-
SO!
I ONLY TRAIN VETERANS, DIGGERS... EXPERT FIGHTERS WHO WANT TO LEARN FROM MY TEACHINGS...
PAIN MEANS LITTLE TO THEM-- THEY'VE BEEN THROUGH HARSHEST OF TRAINING...
CONVENTIONAL DISCIPLINE TECHNIQUES ARE A JOKE TO THEM..

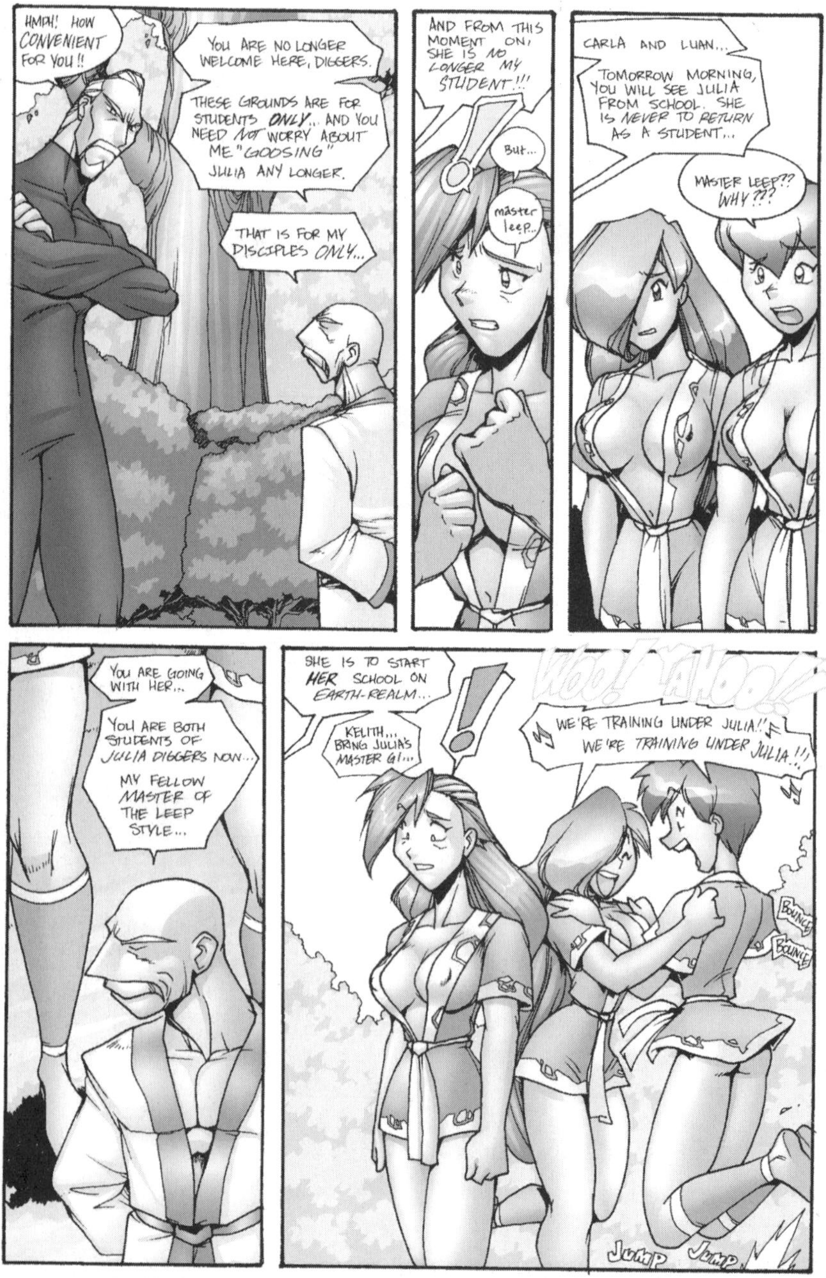
HMPH! HOW CONVENIENT FOR YOU!!
YOU ARE NO LONGER WELCOME HERE, DIGGERS.
THESE GROUNDS ARE FOR STUDENTS ONLY... AND YOU NEED NOT WORRY ABOUT ME "GOOSING" JULIA ANY LONGER.
THAT IS FOR MY DISCIPLES ONLY...
AND FROM THIS MOMENT ON, SHE IS NO LONGER MY STUDENT!!!
But...
master leep...
CARLA AND LUAN...
TOMORROW MORNING, YOU WILL SEE JULIA FROM SCHOOL. SHE IS NEVER TO RETURN AS A STUDENT...
MASTER LEEP?? WHY???
YOU ARE GOING WITH HER...
YOU ARE BOTH STUDENTS OF JULIA DIGGERS NOW...
MY FELLOW MASTER OF THE LEEP STYLE...
SHE IS TO START HER SCHOOL ON EARTH-REALM...
KELITH... BRING JULIA'S MASTER GI...
WOO! YAHOO!!
WE'RE TRAINING UNDER JULIA!!
WE'RE TRAINING UNDER JULIA!!!
BOUNCE
BOUNCE
JUMP
JUMP

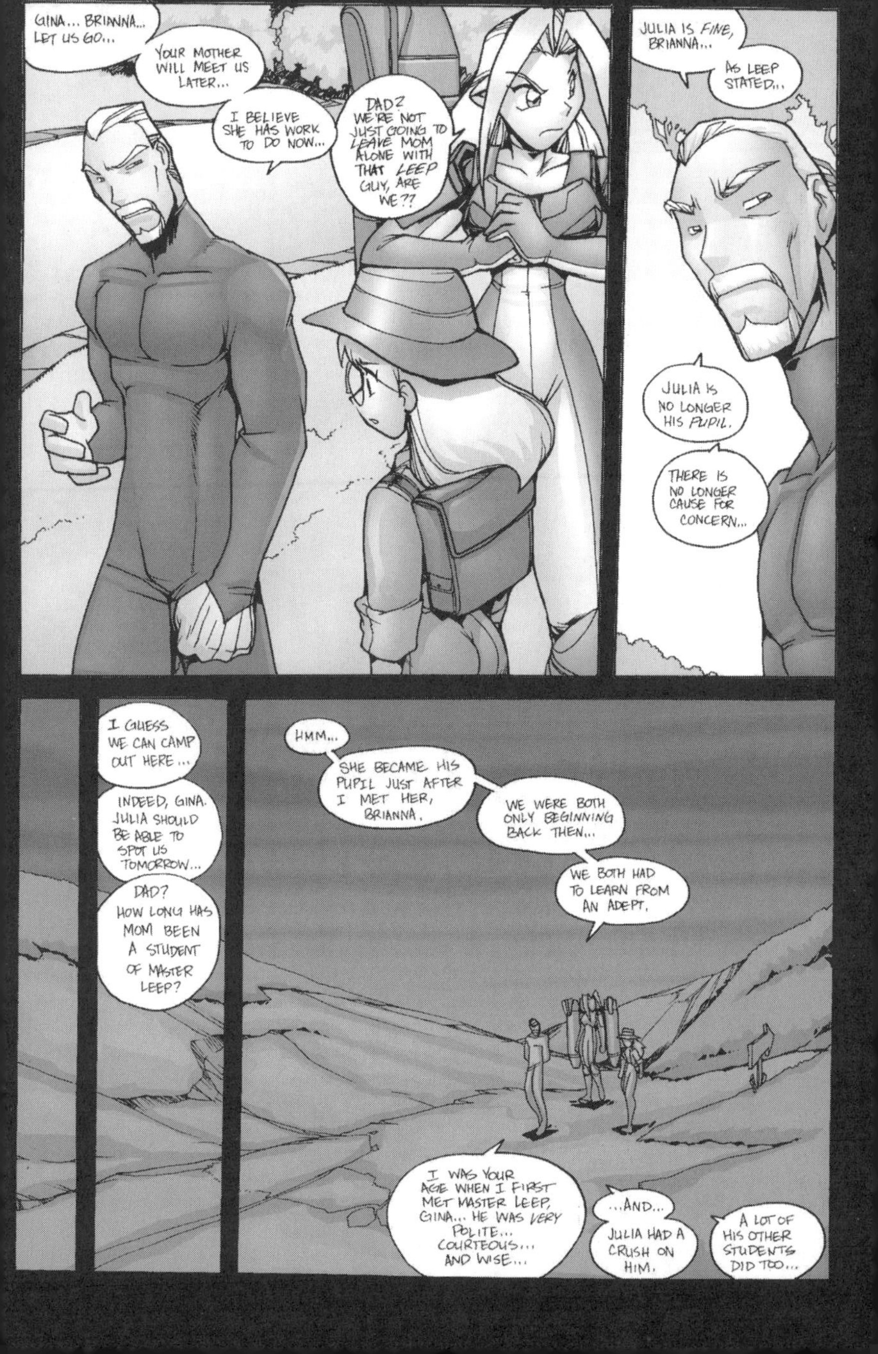
GINA... BRIANNA... LET US GO...
YOUR MOTHER WILL MEET US LATER...
I BELIEVE SHE HAS WORK TO DO NOW...
DAD? WE'RE NOT JUST GOING TO *LEAVE* MOM ALONE WITH THAT *LEEP* GUY, ARE WE??
JULIA IS *FINE*, BRIANNA...
AS LEEP STATED...
JULIA IS NO LONGER HIS *PUPIL*.
THERE IS NO LONGER CAUSE FOR CONCERN...
I GUESS WE CAN CAMP OUT HERE...
INDEED, GINA. JULIA SHOULD BE ABLE TO SPOT US TOMORROW...
DAD? HOW LONG HAS MOM BEEN A STUDENT OF MASTER LEEP?
HMM...
SHE BECAME HIS PUPIL JUST AFTER I MET HER, BRIANNA.
WE WERE BOTH ONLY BEGINNING BACK THEN...
WE BOTH HAD TO LEARN FROM AN ADEPT.
I WAS YOUR AGE WHEN I FIRST MET MASTER LEEP, GINA... HE WAS *VERY* POLITE... COURTEOUS... AND WISE...
...AND... JULIA HAD A CRUSH ON HIM.
A LOT OF HIS OTHER STUDENTS DID TOO...

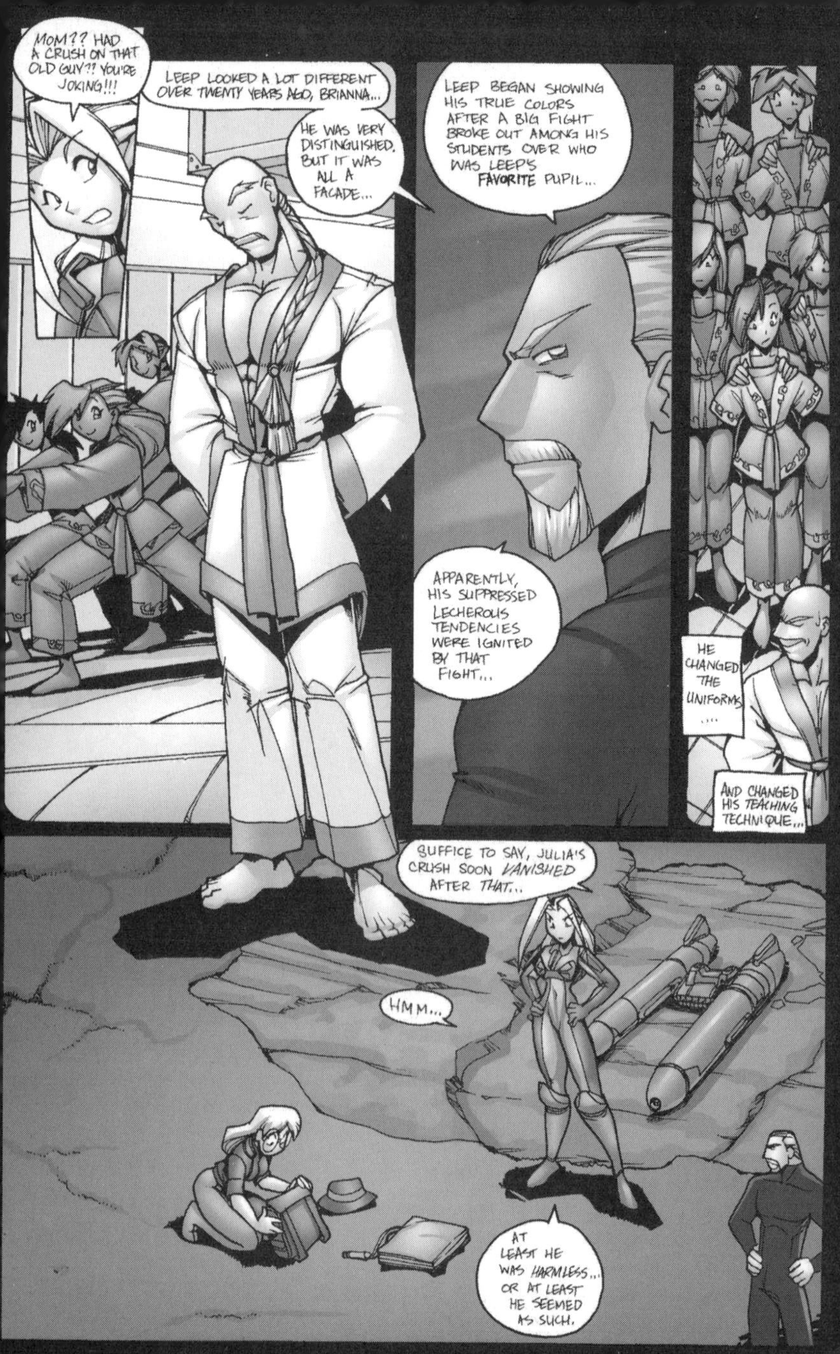
MOM?? HAD A CRUSH ON THAT OLD GUY?? YOU'RE JOKING!!!
LEEP LOOKED A LOT DIFFERENT OVER TWENTY YEARS AGO, BRIANNA...
HE WAS VERY DISTINGUISHED. BUT IT WAS ALL A FACADE...
LEEP BEGAN SHOWING HIS TRUE COLORS AFTER A BIG FIGHT BROKE OUT AMONG HIS STUDENTS OVER WHO WAS LEEP'S FAVORITE PUPIL...
APPARENTLY, HIS SUPPRESSED LECHEROUS TENDENCIES WERE IGNITED BY THAT FIGHT...
HE CHANGED THE UNIFORMS ...
AND CHANGED HIS TEACHING TECHNIQUE...
SUFFICE TO SAY, JULIA'S CRUSH SOON VANISHED AFTER THAT...
HMM...
AT LEAST HE WAS HARMLESS... OR AT LEAST HE SEEMED AS SUCH.

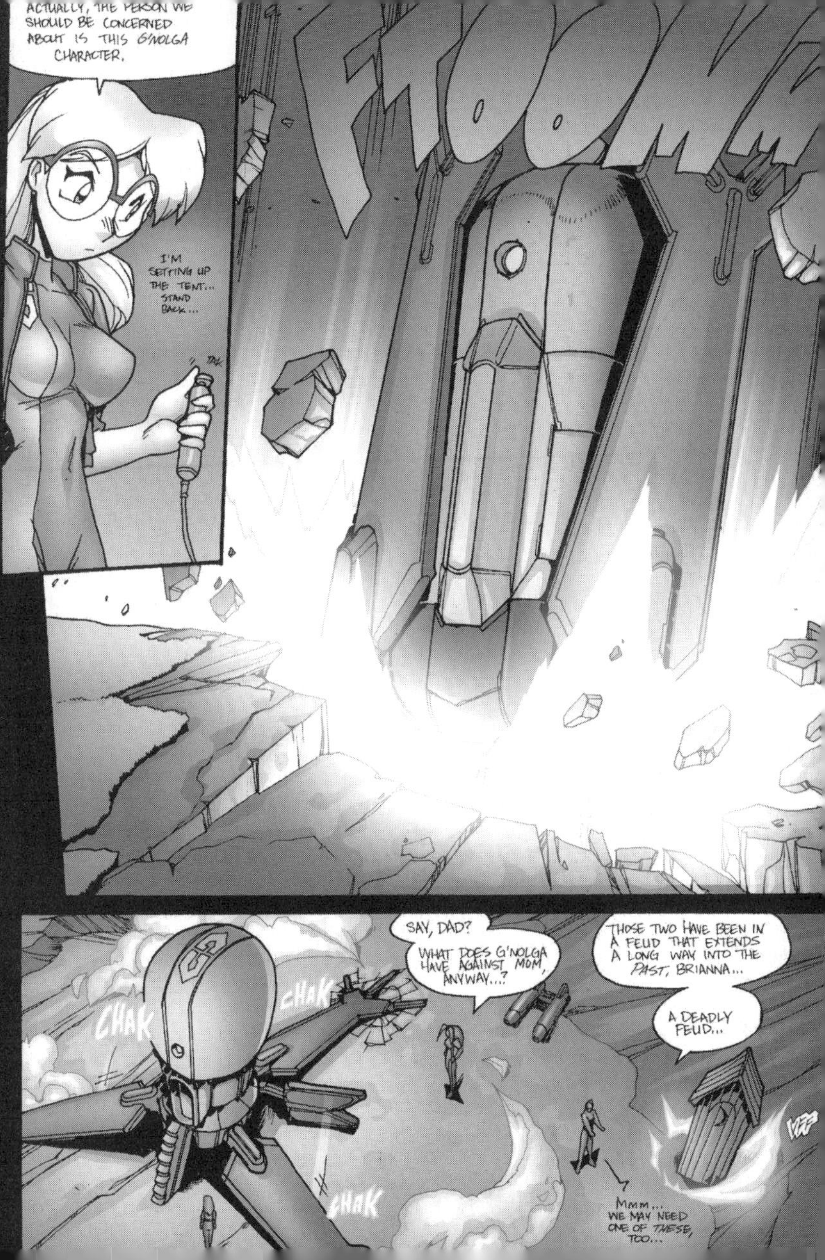
ACTUALLY, THE PERSON WE SHOULD BE CONCERNED ABOUT IS THIS G'NOLGA CHARACTER.
I'M SETTING UP THE TENT... STAND BACK...
FTOOOM
CHAK
CHAK
SAY, DAD?
WHAT DOES G'NOLGA HAVE AGAINST MOM, ANYWAY...?
THOSE TWO HAVE BEEN IN A FEUD THAT EXTENDS A LONG WAY INTO THE PAST, BRIANNA...
A DEADLY FEUD...
CHAK
MMM... WE MAY NEED ONE OF THESE, TOO...

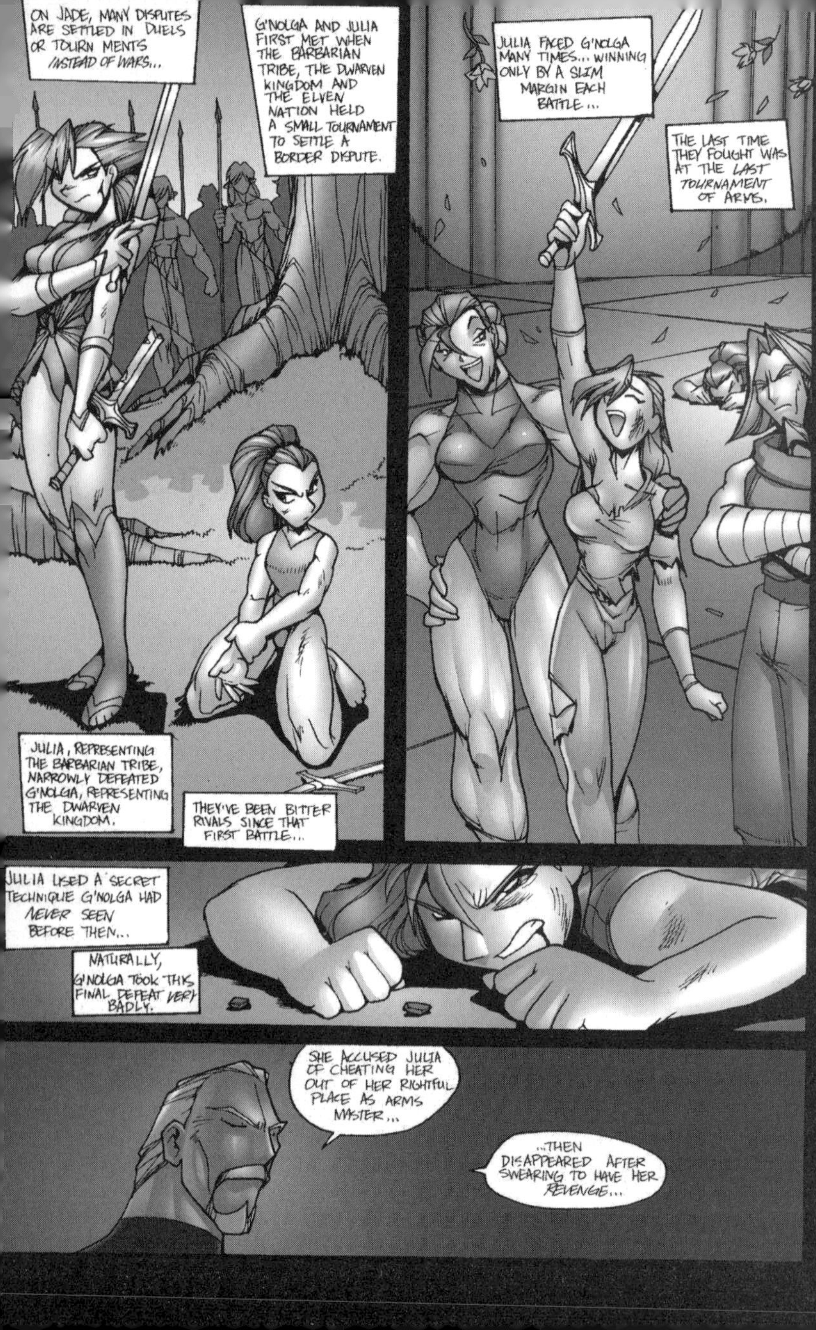

ON JADE, MANY DISPUTES ARE SETTLED IN DUELS OR TOURN MENTS INSTEAD OF WARS...
G'NOLGA AND JULIA FIRST MET WHEN THE BARBARIAN TRIBE, THE DWARVEN KINGDOM AND THE ELVEN NATION HELD A SMALL TOURNAMENT TO SETTLE A BORDER DISPUTE.
JULIA, REPRESENTING THE BARBARIAN TRIBE, NARROWLY DEFEATED G'NOLGA, REPRESENTING THE DWARVEN KINGDOM.
THEY'VE BEEN BITTER RIVALS SINCE THAT FIRST BATTLE...
JULIA FACED G'NOLGA MANY TIMES... WINNING ONLY BY A SLIM MARGIN EACH BATTLE...
THE LAST TIME THEY FOUGHT WAS AT THE LAST TOURNAMENT OF ARMS.
JULIA USED A SECRET TECHNIQUE G'NOLGA HAD NEVER SEEN BEFORE THEN...
NATURALLY, G'NOLGA TOOK THIS FINAL DEFEAT VERY BADLY.
SHE ACCUSED JULIA OF CHEATING HER OUT OF HER RIGHTFUL PLACE AS ARMS MASTER...
...THEN DISAPPEARED AFTER SWEARING TO HAVE HER REVENGE...

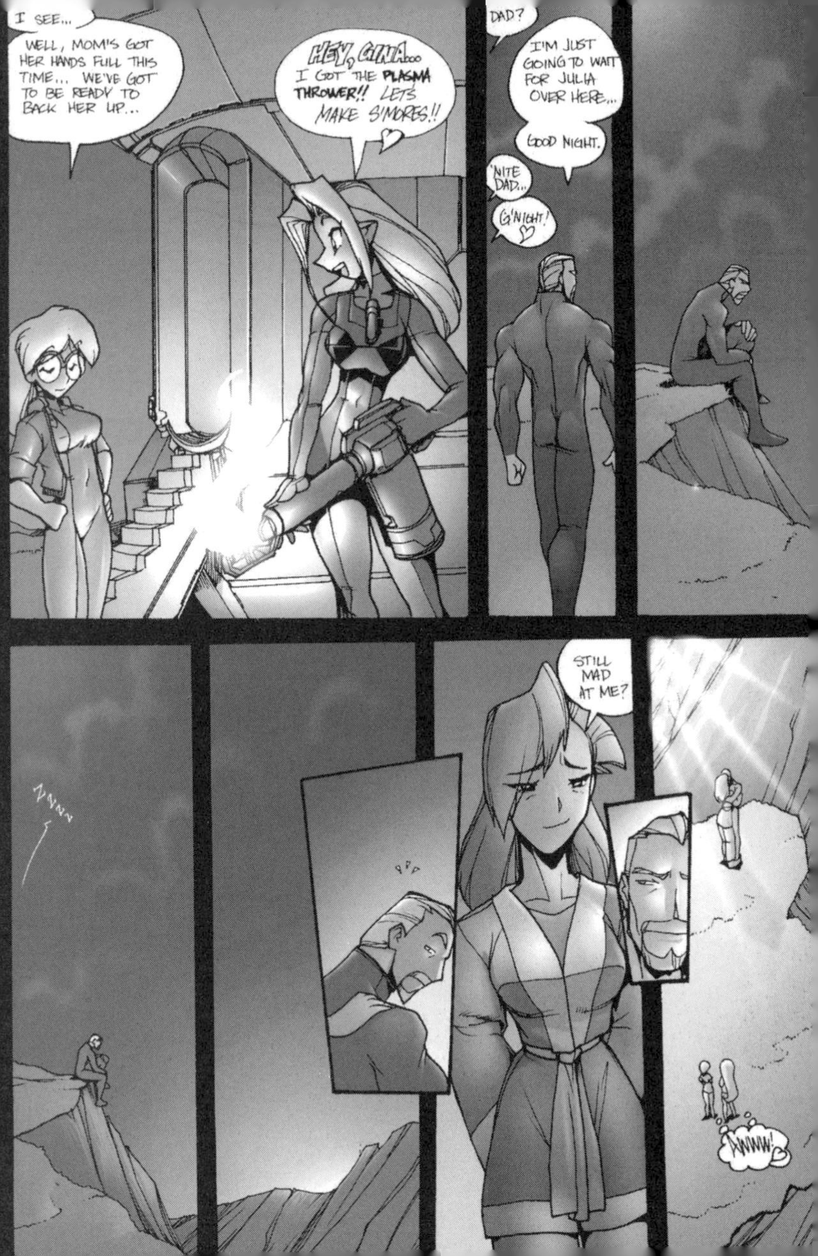
I SEE...
WELL, MOM'S GOT HER HANDS FULL THIS TIME... WE'VE GOT TO BE READY TO BACK HER UP...
HEY, GINA... I GOT THE PLASMA THROWER!! LETS MAKE S'MORES!!
DAD?
I'M JUST GOING TO WAIT FOR JULIA OVER HERE...
GOOD NIGHT.
'NITE DAD...
G'NIGHT!
STILL MAD AT ME?
AWWW!

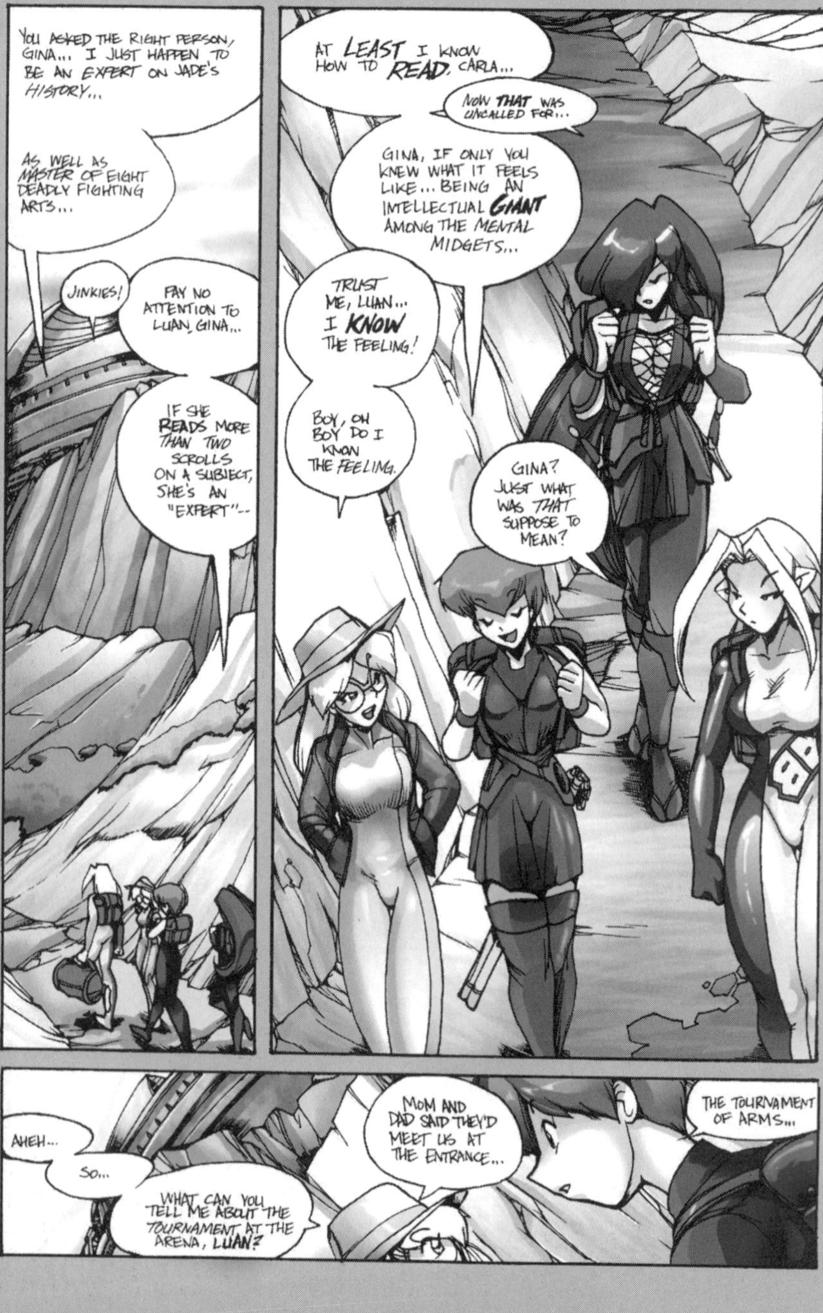
YOU ASKED THE RIGHT PERSON, GINA... I JUST HAPPEN TO BE AN EXPERT ON JADE'S HISTORY...
AS WELL AS MASTER OF EIGHT DEADLY FIGHTING ARTS...
JINKIES!
PAY NO ATTENTION TO LUAN, GINA...
IF SHE READS MORE THAN TWO SCROLLS ON A SUBJECT, SHE'S AN "EXPERT"--
AT LEAST I KNOW HOW TO READ, CARLA...
NOW THAT WAS UNCALLED FOR...
GINA, IF ONLY YOU KNEW WHAT IT FEELS LIKE... BEING AN INTELLECTUAL GIANT AMONG THE MENTAL MIDGETS...
TRUST ME, LUAN... I KNOW THE FEELING!
BOY, OH BOY DO I KNOW THE FEELING.
GINA? JUST WHAT WAS THAT SUPPOSE TO MEAN?
AHEH...
SO...
WHAT CAN YOU TELL ME ABOUT THE TOURNAMENT AT THE ARENA, LUAN?
MOM AND DAD SAID THEY'D MEET US AT THE ENTRANCE...
THE TOURNAMENT OF ARMS...

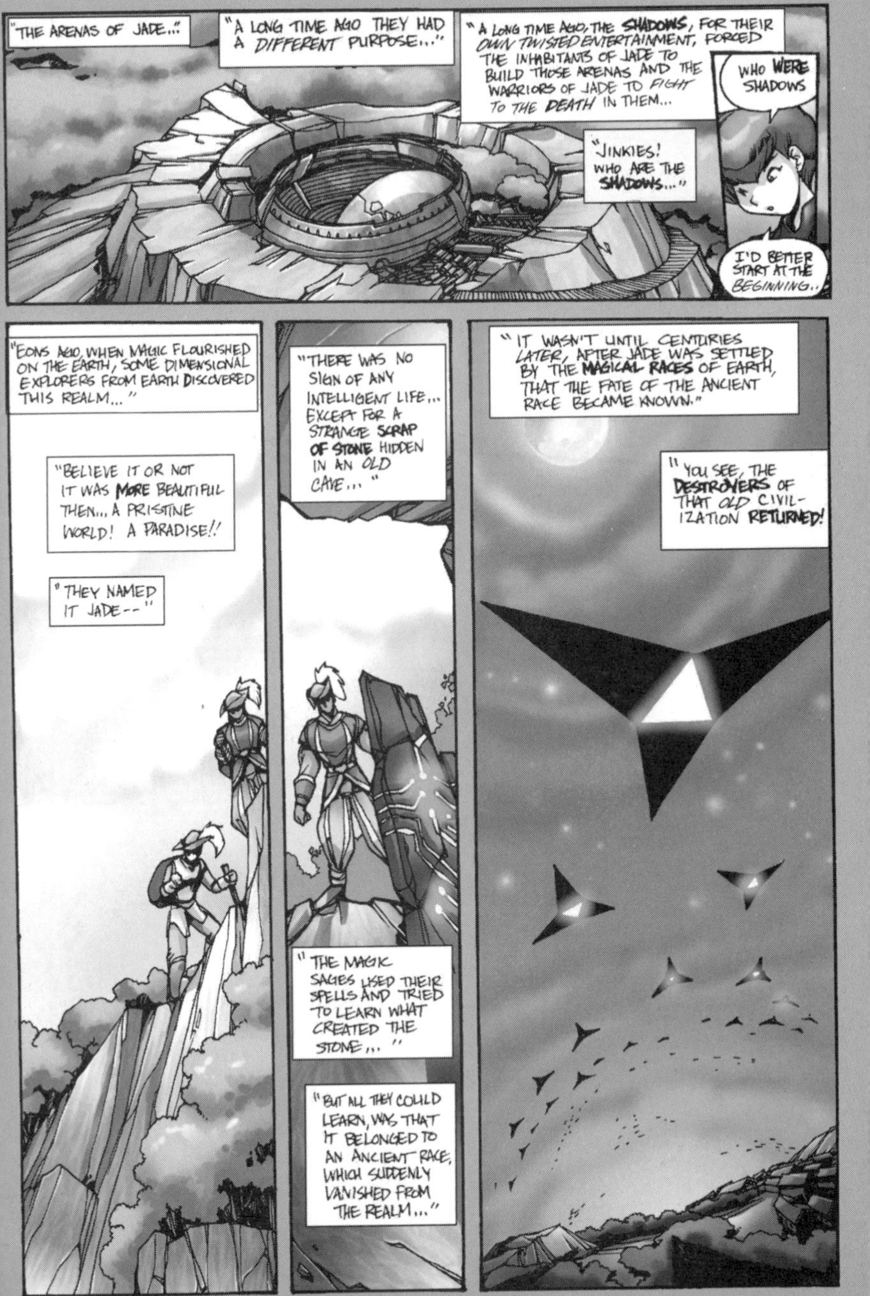
"THE ARENAS OF JADE..."
"A LONG TIME AGO THEY HAD A *DIFFERENT* PURPOSE..."
"A LONG TIME AGO, THE **SHADOWS**, FOR THEIR *OWN TWISTED ENTERTAINMENT*, FORCED THE INHABITANTS OF JADE TO BUILD THOSE ARENAS AND THE WARRIORS OF JADE TO *FIGHT TO THE* **DEATH** IN THEM..."
WHO **WERE** SHADOWS
"JINKIES! WHO ARE THE **SHADOWS**..."
I'D BETTER START AT THE *BEGINNING*...
"EONS AGO, WHEN MAGIC FLOURISHED ON THE EARTH, SOME DIMENSIONAL EXPLORERS FROM EARTH DISCOVERED THIS REALM..."
"BELIEVE IT OR NOT IT WAS **MORE** BEAUTIFUL THEN... A PRISTINE WORLD! A PARADISE!!
"THEY NAMED IT JADE--"
"THERE WAS NO SIGN OF ANY INTELLIGENT LIFE... EXCEPT FOR A STRANGE **SCRAP OF STONE** HIDDEN IN AN *OLD* CAVE..."
"THE MAGIC SAGES USED THEIR SPELLS AND TRIED TO LEARN WHAT CREATED THE STONE..."
"BUT ALL THEY COULD LEARN, WAS THAT IT BELONGED TO AN ANCIENT RACE, WHICH SUDDENLY VANISHED FROM THE REALM..."
"IT WASN'T UNTIL CENTURIES *LATER*, AFTER JADE WAS SETTLED BY THE **MAGICAL RACES** OF EARTH, THAT THE FATE OF THE ANCIENT RACE BECAME KNOWN."
"YOU SEE, THE **DESTROYERS** OF THAT *OLD* CIVILIZATION **RETURNED**!

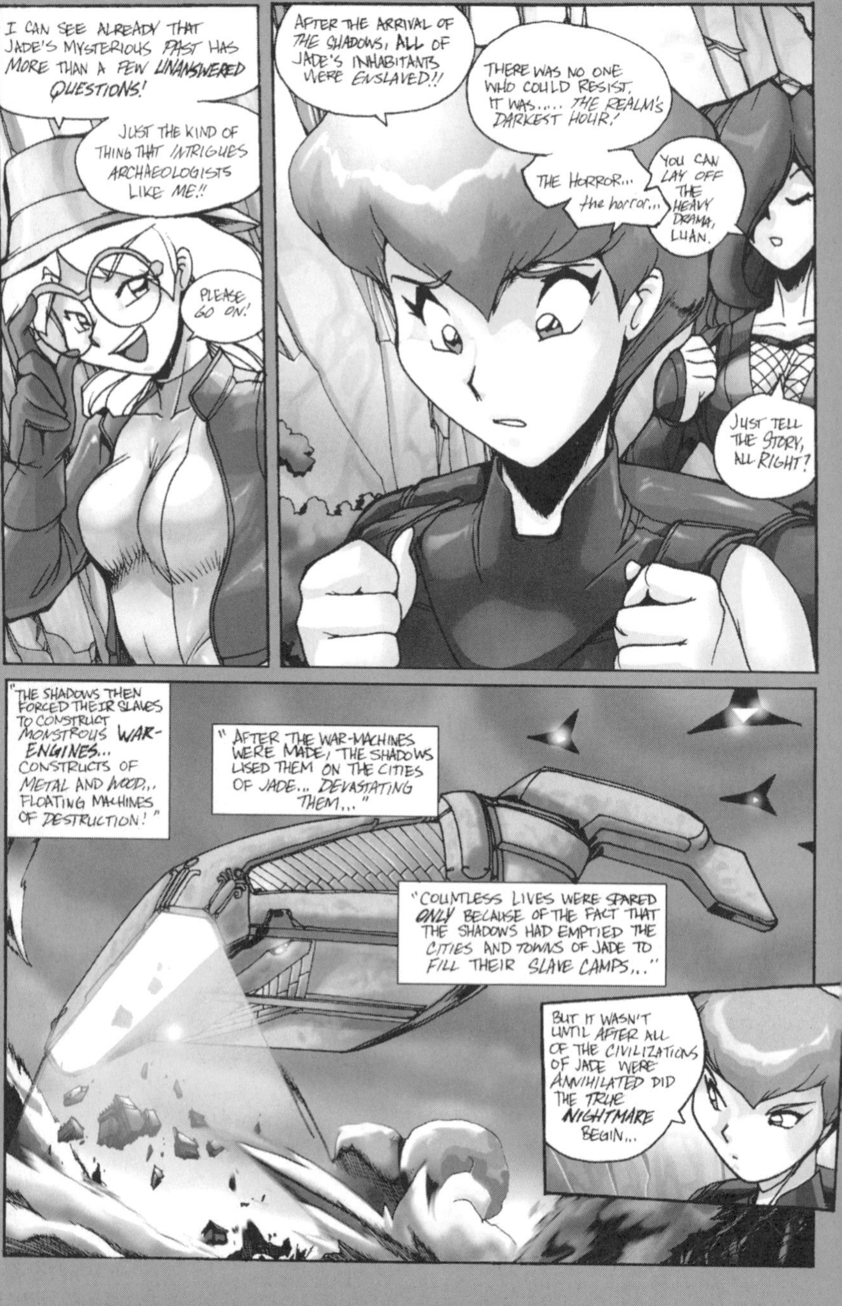
I CAN SEE ALREADY THAT JADE'S MYSTERIOUS PAST HAS MORE THAN A FEW UNANSWERED QUESTIONS!
JUST THE KIND OF THING THAT INTRIGUES ARCHAEOLOGISTS LIKE ME!!
PLEASE GO ON!
AFTER THE ARRIVAL OF THE SHADOWS, ALL OF JADE'S INHABITANTS WERE ENSLAVED!!
THERE WAS NO ONE WHO COULD RESIST. IT WAS..... THE REALM'S DARKEST HOUR!
THE HORROR... the horror...
YOU CAN LAY OFF THE HEAVY DRAMA, LUAN.
JUST TELL THE STORY, ALL RIGHT?
"THE SHADOWS THEN FORCED THEIR SLAVES TO CONSTRUCT MONSTROUS WAR-ENGINES... CONSTRUCTS OF METAL AND WOOD... FLOATING MACHINES OF DESTRUCTION!"
"AFTER THE WAR-MACHINES WERE MADE, THE SHADOWS USED THEM ON THE CITIES OF JADE... DEVASTATING THEM..."
"COUNTLESS LIVES WERE SPARED ONLY BECAUSE OF THE FACT THAT THE SHADOWS HAD EMPTIED THE CITIES AND TOWNS OF JADE TO FILL THEIR SLAVE CAMPS..."
BUT IT WASN'T UNTIL AFTER ALL OF THE CIVILIZATIONS OF JADE WERE ANNIHILATED DID THE TRUE NIGHTMARE BEGIN...

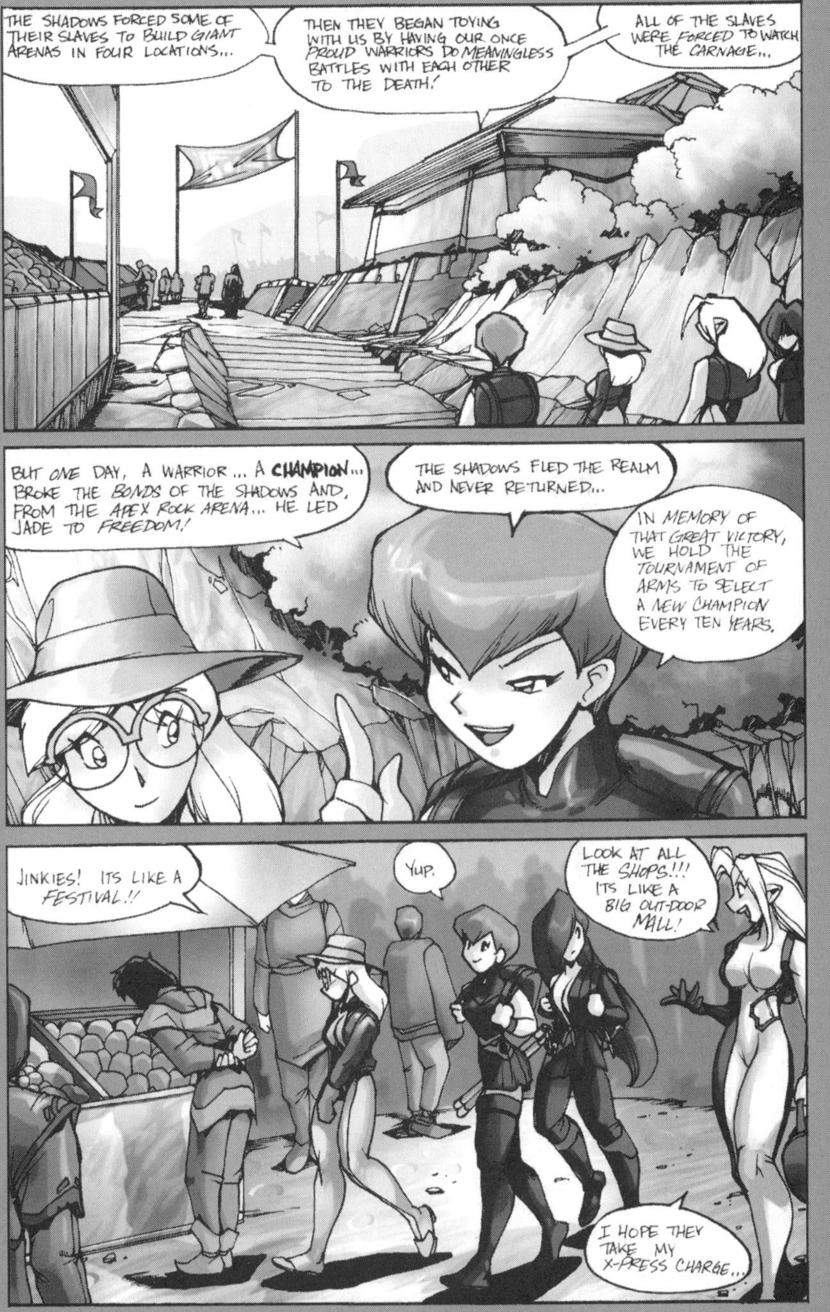
THE SHADOWS FORCED SOME OF THEIR SLAVES TO BUILD GIANT ARENAS IN FOUR LOCATIONS...
THEN THEY BEGAN TOYING WITH US BY HAVING OUR ONCE PROUD WARRIORS DO MEANINGLESS BATTLES WITH EACH OTHER TO THE DEATH!
ALL OF THE SLAVES WERE FORCED TO WATCH THE CARNAGE...
BUT ONE DAY, A WARRIOR... A CHAMPION... BROKE THE BONDS OF THE SHADOWS AND, FROM THE APEX ROCK ARENA... HE LED JADE TO FREEDOM!
THE SHADOWS FLED THE REALM AND NEVER RETURNED...
IN MEMORY OF THAT GREAT VICTORY, WE HOLD THE TOURNAMENT OF ARMS TO SELECT A NEW CHAMPION EVERY TEN YEARS.
JINKIES! ITS LIKE A FESTIVAL!!
YUP.
LOOK AT ALL THE SHOPS!!! ITS LIKE A BIG OUT-DOOR MALL!
I HOPE THEY TAKE MY X-PRESS CHARGE...

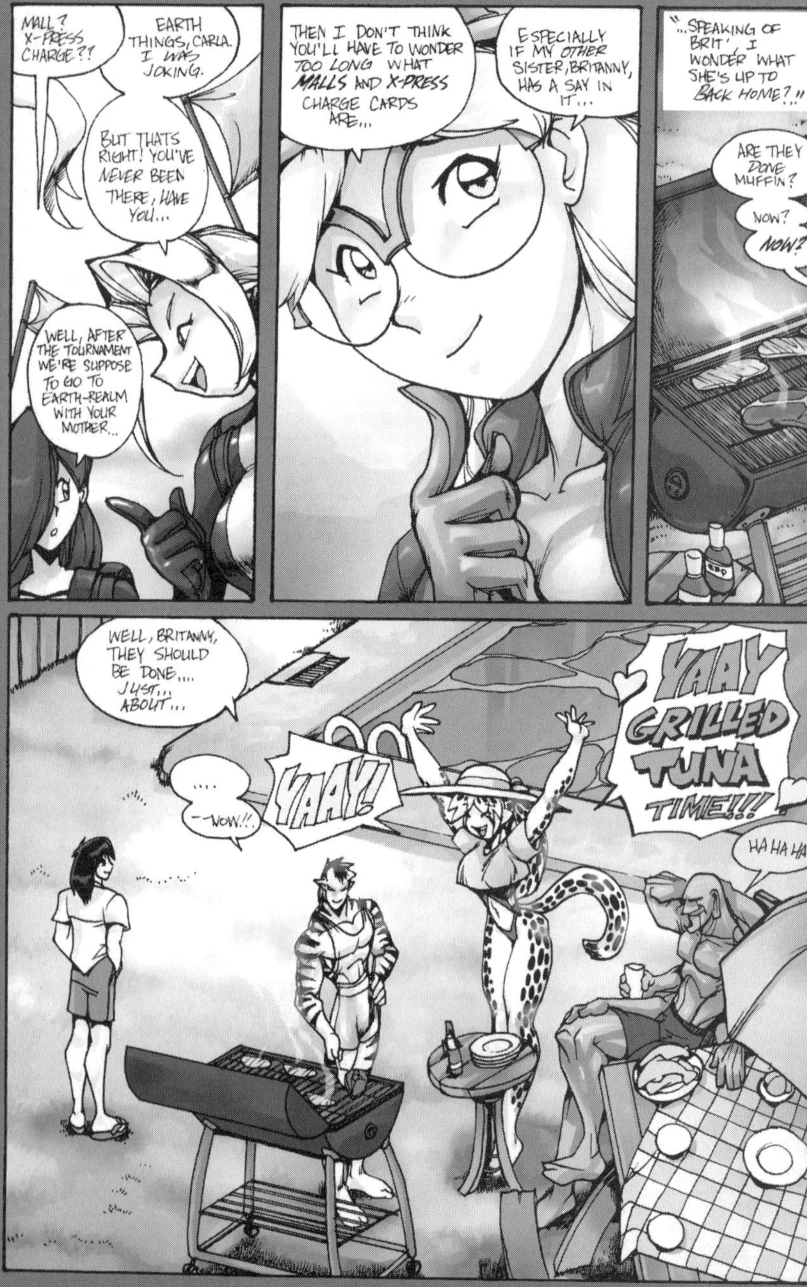
MALL? X-PRESS CHARGE??
EARTH THINGS, CARLA. I WAS JOKING.
BUT THATS RIGHT! YOU'VE NEVER BEEN THERE, HAVE YOU...
WELL, AFTER THE TOURNAMENT WE'RE SUPPOSE TO GO TO EARTH-REALM WITH YOUR MOTHER...
THEN I DON'T THINK YOU'LL HAVE TO WONDER TOO LONG WHAT MALLS AND X-PRESS CHARGE CARDS ARE...
ESPECIALLY IF MY OTHER SISTER, BRITANNY, HAS A SAY IN IT...
"...SPEAKING OF BRIT', I WONDER WHAT SHE'S UP TO BACK HOME?.."
ARE THEY DONE MUFFIN?
NOW? NOW?
WELL, BRITANNY, THEY SHOULD BE DONE.... JUST... ABOUT...
.... --NOW!!
YAAY!
YAAY GRILLED TUNA TIME!!!
HA HA HA!

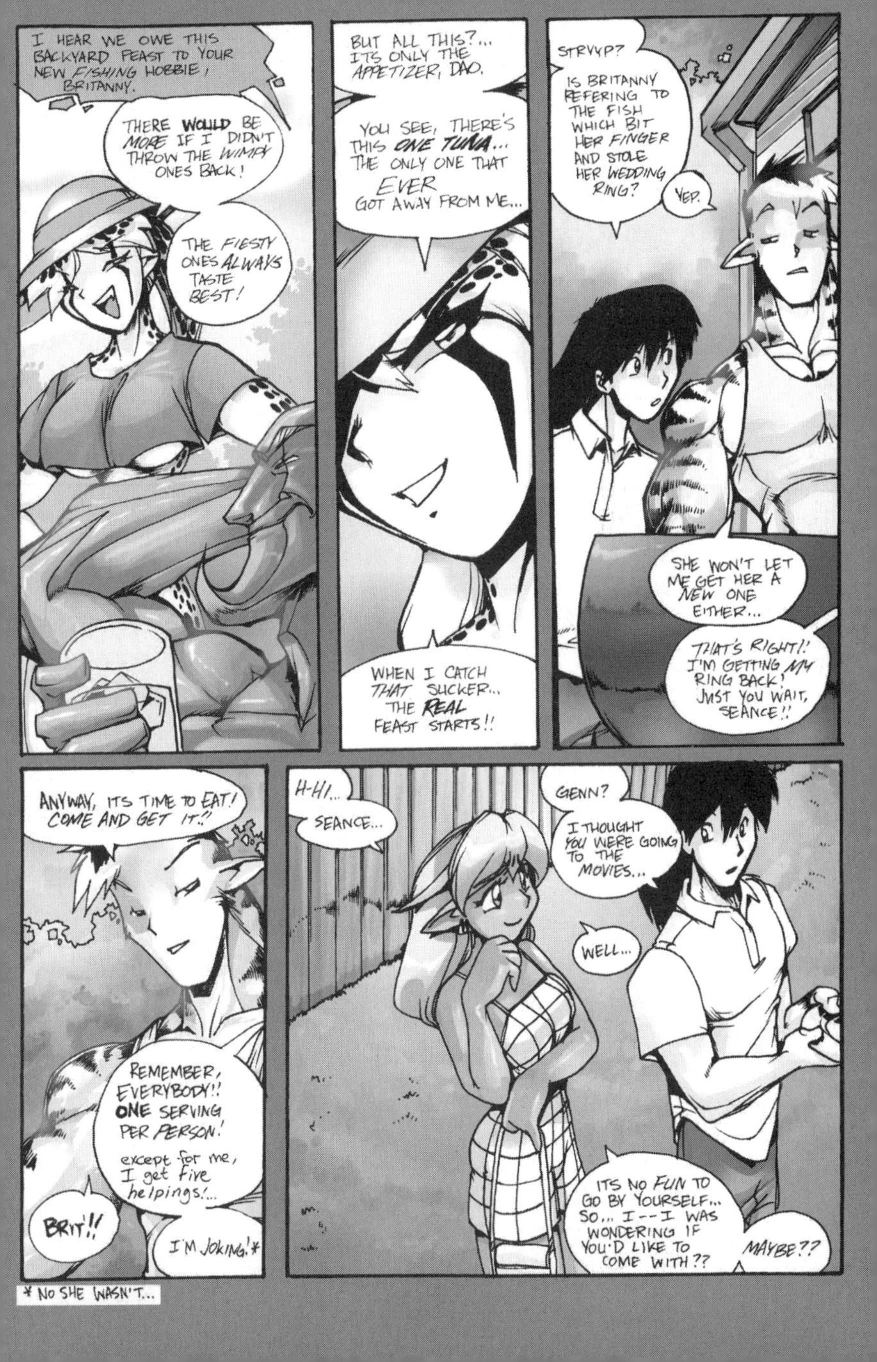
I HEAR WE OWE THIS BACKYARD FEAST TO YOUR NEW FISHING HOBBIE, BRITANNY.
THERE WOULD BE MORE IF I DIDN'T THROW THE WIMPY ONES BACK!
THE FIESTY ONES ALWAYS TASTE BEST!
BUT ALL THIS?... ITS ONLY THE APPETIZER, DAO.
YOU SEE, THERE'S THIS ONE TUNA... THE ONLY ONE THAT EVER GOT AWAY FROM ME...
WHEN I CATCH THAT SUCKER... THE REAL FEAST STARTS!!
STRVYP?
IS BRITANNY REFERING TO THE FISH WHICH BIT HER FINGER AND STOLE HER WEDDING RING?
YEP.
SHE WON'T LET ME GET HER A NEW ONE EITHER...
THAT'S RIGHT!! I'M GETTING MY RING BACK! JUST YOU WAIT, SEANCE!!
ANYWAY, ITS TIME TO EAT! COME AND GET IT!!
REMEMBER, EVERYBODY!! ONE SERVING PER PERSON! except for me, I get five helpings!...
BRIT!!
I'M JOKING!*
H-HI... SEANCE...
GENN?
I THOUGHT YOU WERE GOING TO THE MOVIES...
WELL...
ITS NO FUN TO GO BY YOURSELF... SO... I--I WAS WONDERING IF YOU'D LIKE TO COME WITH??
MAYBE??

* NO SHE WASN'T...

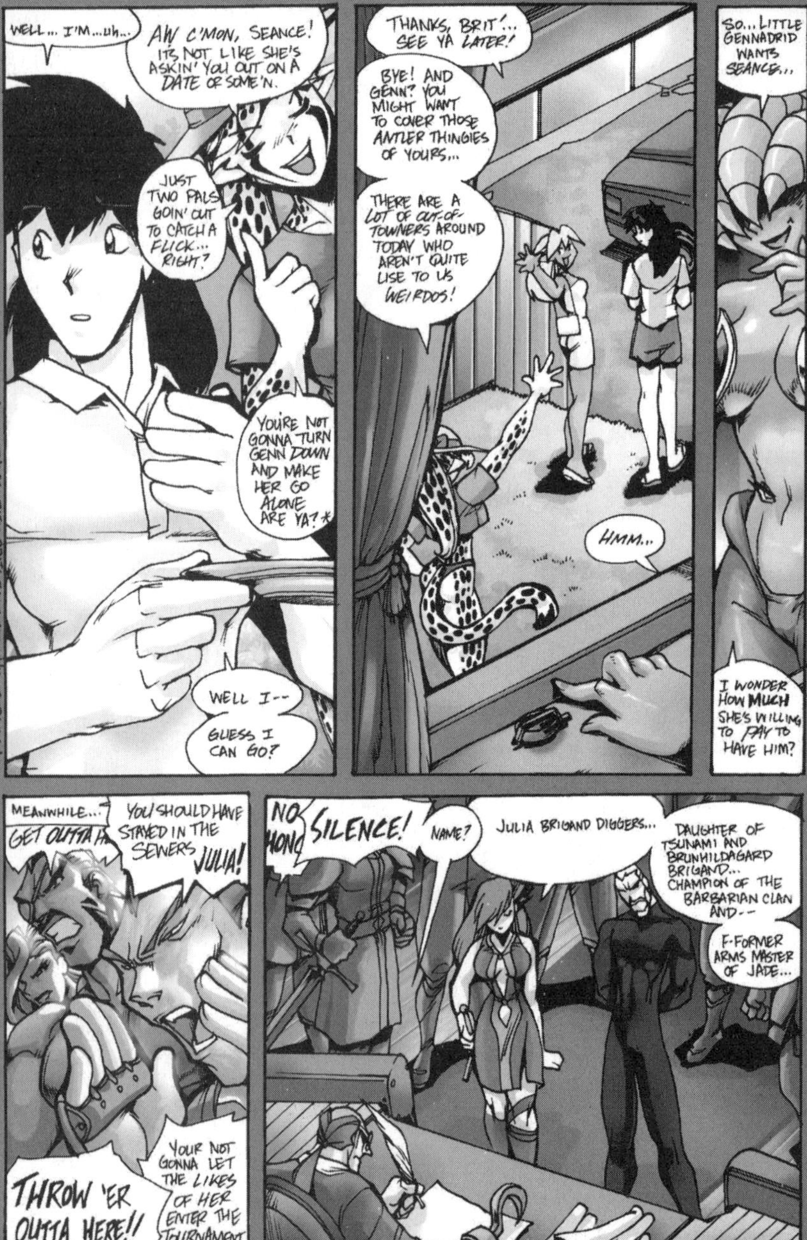
WELL... I'M...uh...
AW C'MON, SEANCE! IT'S NOT LIKE SHE'S ASKIN' YOU OUT ON A DATE OR SOME'N.
JUST TWO PALS GOIN' OUT TO CATCH A FLICK... RIGHT?
YOU'RE NOT GONNA TURN GENN DOWN AND MAKE HER GO ALONE ARE YA? *
WELL I--
GUESS I CAN GO?
* IF SEANCE LEAVES, THEN BRIT CAN SNATCH HIS SERVING!
THANKS, BRIT!... SEE YA LATER!
BYE! AND GENN? YOU MIGHT WANT TO COVER THOSE ANTLER THINGIES OF YOURS...
THERE ARE A LOT OF OUT-OF-TOWNERS AROUND TODAY WHO AREN'T QUITE USE TO US WEIRDOS!
HMM...
SO... LITTLE GENNADRID WANTS SEANCE...
I WONDER HOW MUCH SHE'S WILLING TO PAY TO HAVE HIM?
MEANWHILE...
YOU SHOULD HAVE STAYED IN THE SEWERS JULIA!
THROW 'ER OUTTA HERE!!
YOUR NOT GONNA LET THE LIKES OF HER ENTER THE TOURNAMENT ARE YOU?
NO
SILENCE!
NAME?
JULIA BRIGAND DIGGERS...
DAUGHTER OF TSUNAMI AND BRUNHILDAGARD BRIGAND... CHAMPION OF THE BARBARIAN CLAN AND--
F-FORMER ARMS MASTER OF JADE...

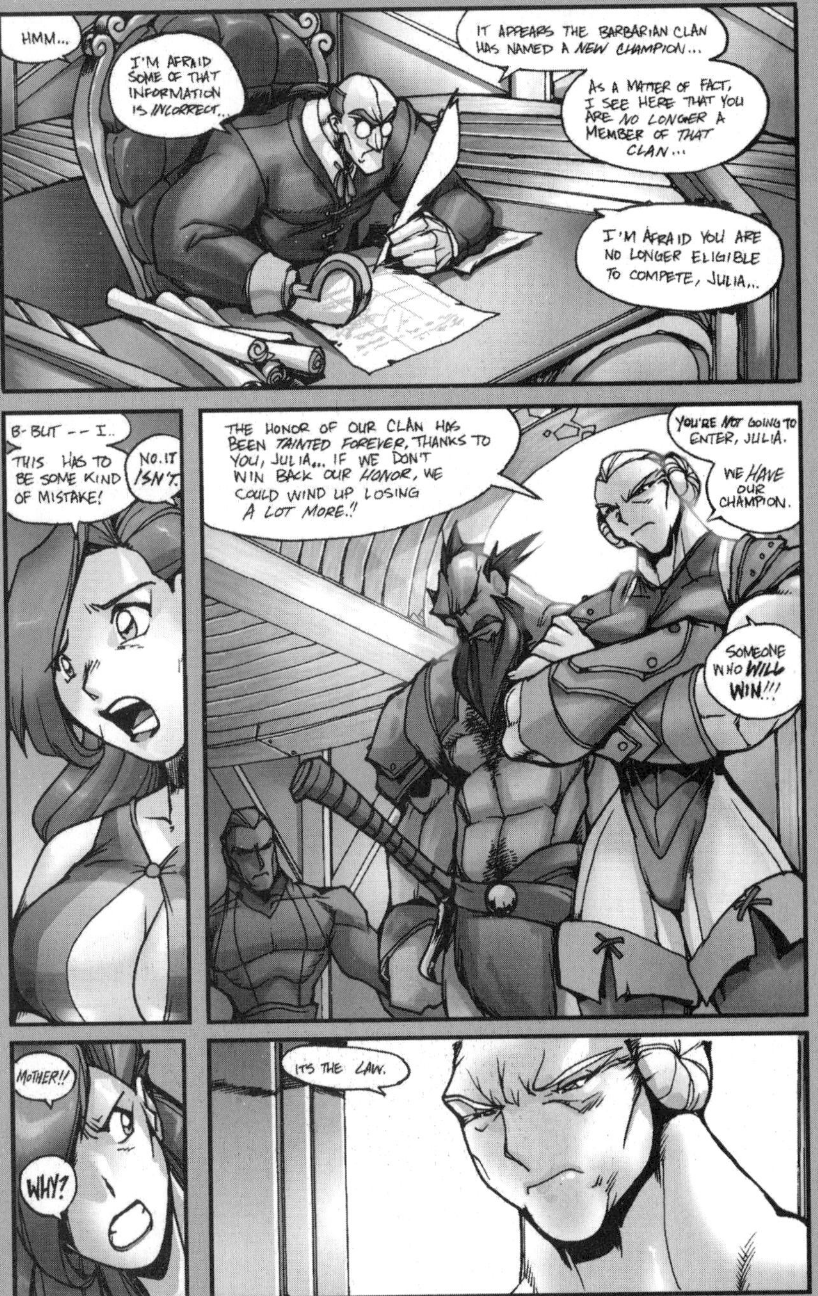
HMM...
I'M AFRAID SOME OF THAT INFORMATION IS INCORRECT...
IT APPEARS THE BARBARIAN CLAN HAS NAMED A NEW CHAMPION...
AS A MATTER OF FACT, I SEE HERE THAT YOU ARE NO LONGER A MEMBER OF THAT CLAN...
I'M AFRAID YOU ARE NO LONGER ELIGIBLE TO COMPETE, JULIA...
B-BUT -- I..
THIS HAS TO BE SOME KIND OF MISTAKE!
NO. IT ISN'T.
THE HONOR OF OUR CLAN HAS BEEN TAINTED FOREVER, THANKS TO YOU, JULIA... IF WE DON'T WIN BACK OUR HONOR, WE COULD WIND UP LOSING A LOT MORE.!
YOU'RE NOT GOING TO ENTER, JULIA.
WE HAVE OUR CHAMPION.
SOMEONE WHO WILL WIN!!!
MOTHER!!
WHY?
ITS THE LAW.

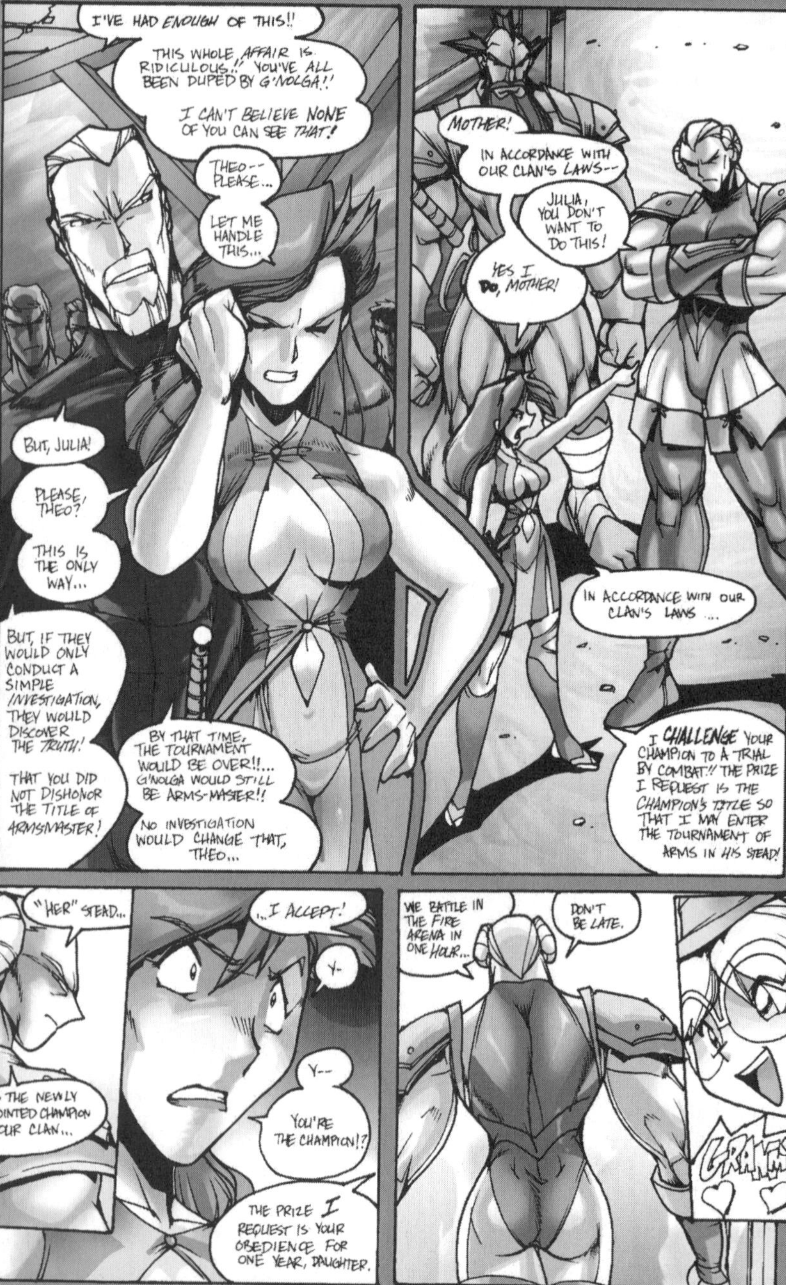
I'VE HAD ENOUGH OF THIS!!
THIS WHOLE AFFAIR IS RIDICULOUS!! YOU'VE ALL BEEN DUPED BY G'NOLGA!!
I CAN'T BELIEVE NONE OF YOU CAN SEE THAT!
THEO-- PLEASE...
LET ME HANDLE THIS...
BUT, JULIA!
PLEASE, THEO?
THIS IS THE ONLY WAY...
BUT, IF THEY WOULD ONLY CONDUCT A SIMPLE INVESTIGATION, THEY WOULD DISCOVER THE TRUTH!
THAT YOU DID NOT DISHONOR THE TITLE OF ARMSMASTER!
BY THAT TIME, THE TOURNAMENT WOULD BE OVER!!... G'NOLGA WOULD STILL BE ARMS-MASTER!!
NO INVESTIGATION WOULD CHANGE THAT, THEO...
MOTHER!
IN ACCORDANCE WITH OUR CLAN'S LAWS--
JULIA, YOU DON'T WANT TO DO THIS!
YES I DO, MOTHER!
IN ACCORDANCE WITH OUR CLAN'S LAWS ...
I CHALLENGE YOUR CHAMPION TO A TRIAL BY COMBAT!! THE PRIZE I REQUEST IS THE CHAMPION'S TITLE SO THAT I MAY ENTER THE TOURNAMENT OF ARMS IN HIS STEAD!
"HER" STEAD...
...I ACCEPT!
Y-
Y--
...AS THE NEWLY APPOINTED CHAMPION OF OUR CLAN...
YOU'RE THE CHAMPION!?
THE PRIZE I REQUEST IS YOUR OBEDIENCE FOR ONE YEAR, DAUGHTER.
WE BATTLE IN THE FIRE ARENA IN ONE HOUR...
DON'T BE LATE.
GRAMMY

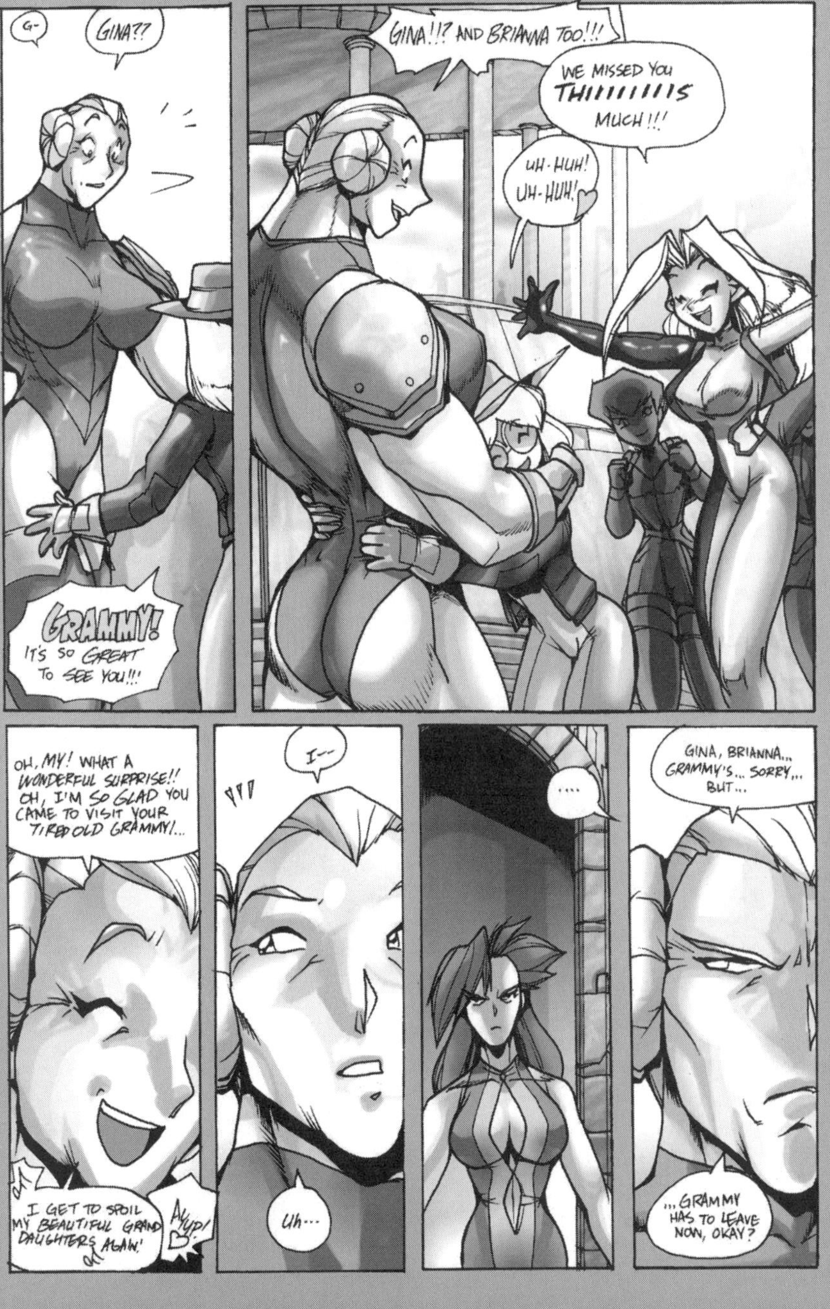
G-
GINA??
GINA!!? AND BRIANNA TOO!!!
WE MISSED YOU THIIIIIIIIS MUCH!!!
UH-HUH! UH-HUH!
GRAMMY! IT'S SO GREAT TO SEE YOU!!!
OH, MY! WHAT A WONDERFUL SURPRISE!! OH, I'M SO GLAD YOU CAME TO VISIT YOUR TIRED OLD GRAMMY!...
I GET TO SPOIL MY BEAUTIFUL GRAND DAUGHTERS AGAIN!
AYUP!
I--
Uh...
....
GINA, BRIANNA... GRAMMY'S... SORRY... BUT...
...GRAMMY HAS TO LEAVE NOW, OKAY?

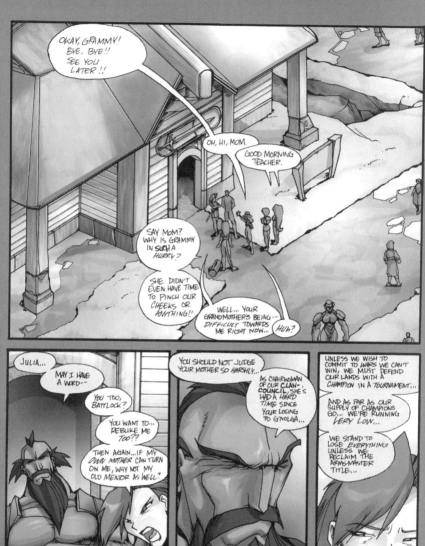

OKAY, GRAMMY! BYE, BYE!! SEE YOU LATER !!

OH, HI, MOM.

GOOD MORNING TEACHER.

SAY MOM? WHY IS GRAMMY IN SUCH A HURRY?

SHE DIDN'T EVEN HAVE TIME TO PINCH OUR CHEEKS OR ANYTHING!!

WELL... YOUR GRANDMOTHER'S BEING-- DIFFICULT TOWARDS ME RIGHT NOW...

HUH?

JULIA... MAY I HAVE A WORD--

YOU TOO, BATTLOCK?

YOU WANT TO... REBUKE ME TOO??

THEN AGAIN...IF MY OWN MOTHER CAN TURN ON ME, WHY NOT MY OLD MENTOR AS WELL?

YOU SHOULD NOT JUDGE YOUR MOTHER SO HARSHLY...

AS CHAIRWOMAN OF OUR CLAN- COUNCIL, SHE'S HAD A HARD TIME SINCE YOUR LOSING TO G'NOLGA...

OUR NEIGHBORS... PARTICULARLY THE SHADOW ELVES AND THE DWARVEN KINGDOM... HAVE SEEN THIS AS A SIGN OF WEAKNESS...

WE'RE BEING CHALLENGED FOR TERRITORY ON EVERY FRONT--

UNLESS WE WISH TO COMMIT TO WARS WE CAN'T WIN, WE MUST DEFEND OUR LANDS WITH A CHAMPION IN A TOURNAMENT...

AND AS FAR AS OUR SUPPLY OF CHAMPIONS GO... WE'RE RUNNING VERY LOW...

WE STAND TO LOSE EVERYTHING UNLESS WE RECLAIM THE ARMS-MASTER TITLE...

TH- THAT'S RIGHT...

WHEN I WAS ARMS-MASTER, NO ONE COULD TRY TO CHALLENGE OUR CLAN FOR PROPERTY WE ALREADY OWN!

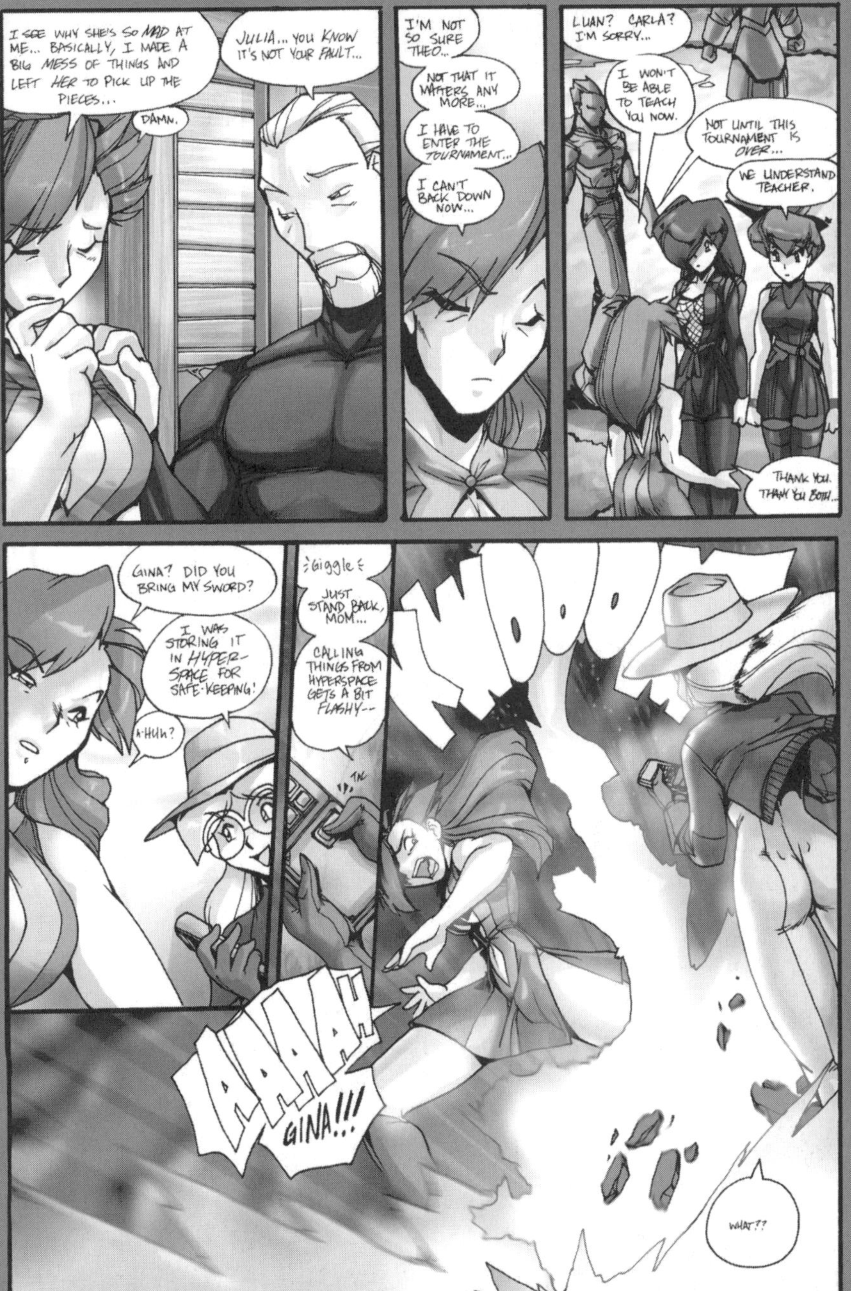
I SEE WHY SHE'S SO MAD AT ME... BASICALLY, I MADE A BIG MESS OF THINGS AND LEFT HER TO PICK UP THE PIECES...
DAMN.
JULIA... YOU KNOW IT'S NOT YOUR FAULT...
I'M NOT SO SURE THEO...
NOT THAT IT MATTERS ANY MORE...
I HAVE TO ENTER THE TOURNAMENT...
I CAN'T BACK DOWN NOW...
LUAN? CARLA? I'M SORRY...
I WON'T BE ABLE TO TEACH YOU NOW.
NOT UNTIL THIS TOURNAMENT IS OVER...
WE UNDERSTAND TEACHER.
THANK YOU. THANK YOU BOTH...
GINA? DID YOU BRING MY SWORD?
I WAS STORING IT IN HYPER-SPACE FOR SAFE-KEEPING!
A-HUH?
GIGGLE
JUST STAND BACK, MOM...
CALLING THINGS FROM HYPERSPACE GETS A BIT FLASHY--
TIK
WHOOOOM
AAAAH
GINA!!!
WHAT??

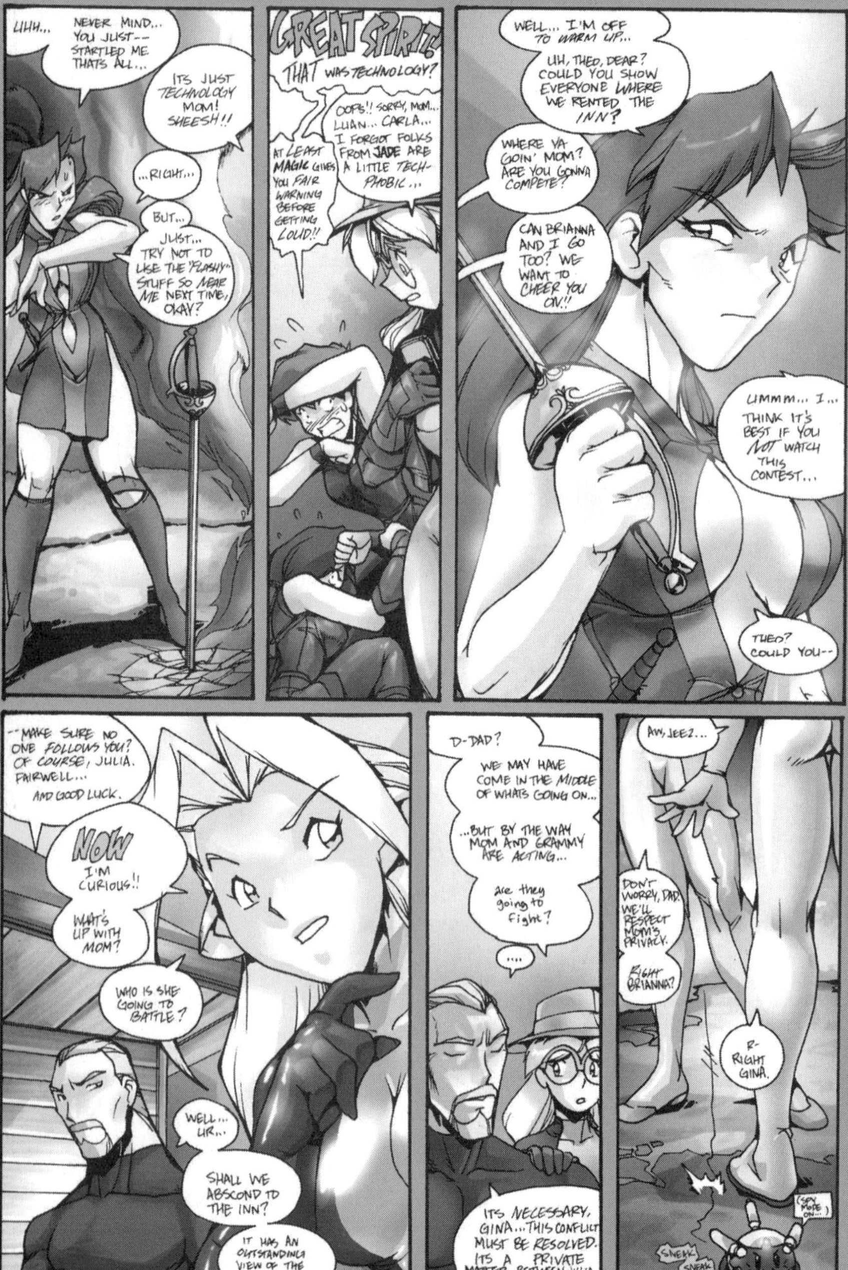
UHH...
NEVER MIND... YOU JUST-- STARTLED ME THATS ALL...
ITS JUST TECHNOLOGY MOM! SHEESH!!
...RIGHT...
BUT... JUST... TRY NOT TO USE THE "FLASHY" STUFF SO NEAR ME NEXT TIME, OKAY?
GREAT SPIRIT!
THAT WAS TECHNOLOGY?
OOPS!! SORRY, MOM... LUAN... CARLA... I FORGOT FOLKS FROM JADE ARE A LITTLE TECH-PHOBIC...
AT LEAST MAGIC GIVES YOU FAIR WARNING BEFORE GETTING LOUD!!
WELL... I'M OFF TO WARM UP...
UH, THEO, DEAR? COULD YOU SHOW EVERYONE WHERE WE RENTED THE INN?
WHERE YA GOIN' MOM? ARE YOU GONNA COMPETE?
CAN BRIANNA AND I GO TOO? WE WANT TO CHEER YOU ON!!
UMMM... I... THINK IT'S BEST IF YOU NOT WATCH THIS CONTEST...
THEO? COULD YOU--
--MAKE SURE NO ONE FOLLOWS YOU? OF COURSE, JULIA. FAIRWELL...
AND GOOD LUCK.
NOW I'M CURIOUS!!
WHAT'S UP WITH MOM?
WHO IS SHE GOING TO BATTLE?
WELL... UR...
SHALL WE ABSCOND TO THE INN?
IT HAS AN OUTSTANDING VIEW OF THE COLOSSIUM...
D-DAD?
WE MAY HAVE COME IN THE MIDDLE OF WHATS GOING ON...
...BUT BY THE WAY MOM AND GRAMMY ARE ACTING...
are they going to fight?
....
ITS NECESSARY, GINA... THIS CONFLICT MUST BE RESOLVED. ITS A PRIVATE MATTER BETWEEN JULIA AND HER MOTHER...
AW, JEEZ...
DON'T WORRY, DAD. WE'LL RESPECT MOM'S PRIVACY.
RIGHT BRIANNA?
R-RIGHT GINA.
(SPY MODE ON...)
SNEAK
SNEAK
SNEAK

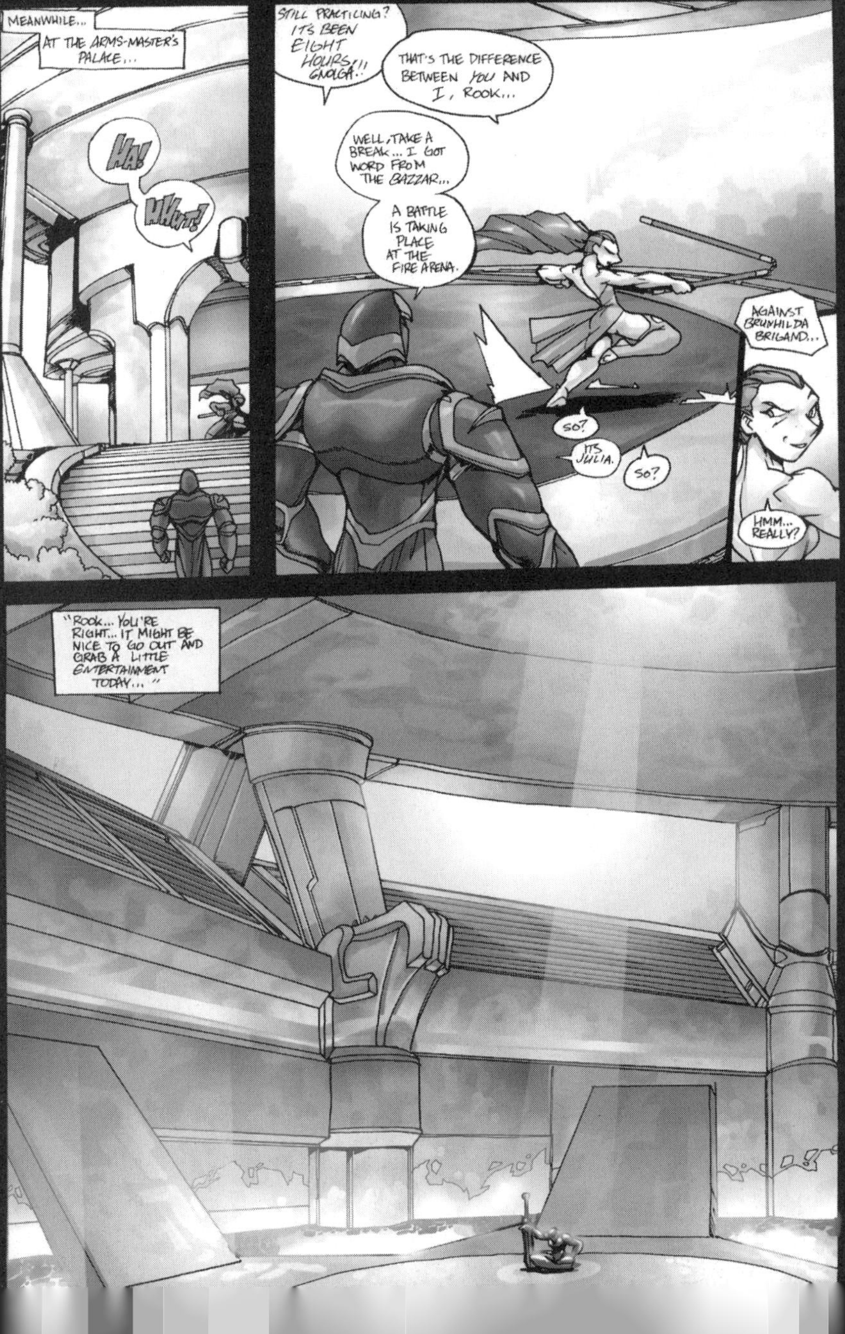
MEANWHILE...
AT THE ARMS-MASTER'S PALACE...
HA!
HHWAT!
STILL PRACTICING? IT'S BEEN EIGHT HOURS, GNOLGA!!
THAT'S THE DIFFERENCE BETWEEN YOU AND I, ROOK...
WELL, TAKE A BREAK... I GOT WORD FROM THE BAZZAR...
A BATTLE IS TAKING PLACE AT THE FIRE ARENA.
SO?
ITS JULIA.
SO?
AGAINST BRUNHILDA BRIGAND...
HMM... REALLY?
"ROOK... YOU'RE RIGHT... IT MIGHT BE NICE TO GO OUT AND GRAB A LITTLE ENTERTAINMENT TODAY..."

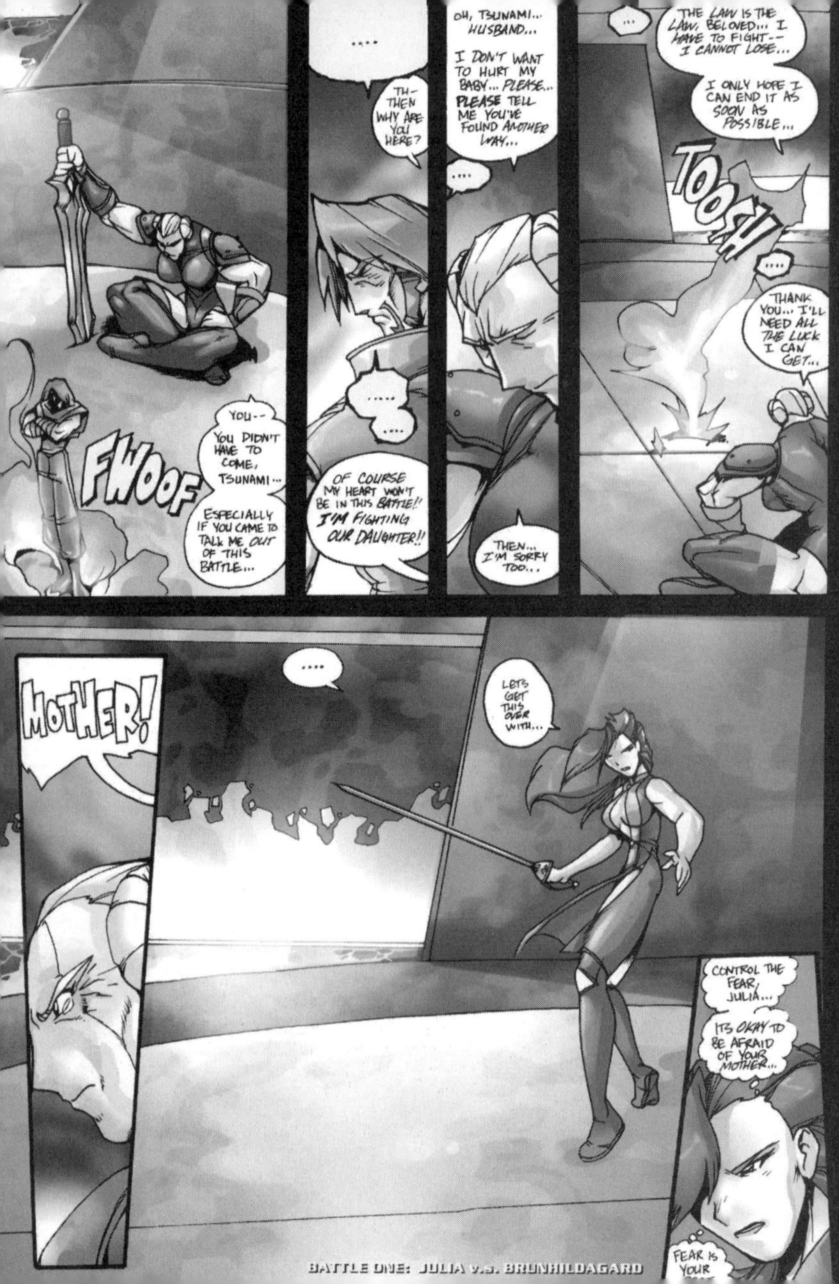
YOU-- YOU DIDN'T HAVE TO COME, TSUNAMI...
FWOOF
ESPECIALLY IF YOU CAME TO TALK ME OUT OF THIS BATTLE...
....
TH-THEN WHY ARE YOU HERE?
.....
....
OF COURSE MY HEART WON'T BE IN THIS BATTLE!! I'M FIGHTING OUR DAUGHTER!!
OH, TSUNAMI... HUSBAND...
I DON'T WANT TO HURT MY BABY... PLEASE... PLEASE TELL ME YOU'VE FOUND ANOTHER WAY...
....
THEN... I'M SORRY TOO...
...
THE LAW IS THE LAW, BELOVED... I HAVE TO FIGHT-- I CANNOT LOSE...
I ONLY HOPE I CAN END IT AS SOON AS POSSIBLE...
TOOSH
....
THANK YOU... I'LL NEED ALL THE LUCK I CAN GET...
MOTHER!
....
LETS GET THIS OVER WITH...
CONTROL THE FEAR, JULIA...
ITS OKAY TO BE AFRAID OF YOUR MOTHER...
FEAR IS YOUR
BATTLE ONE: JULIA v.s. BRUNHILDAGARD

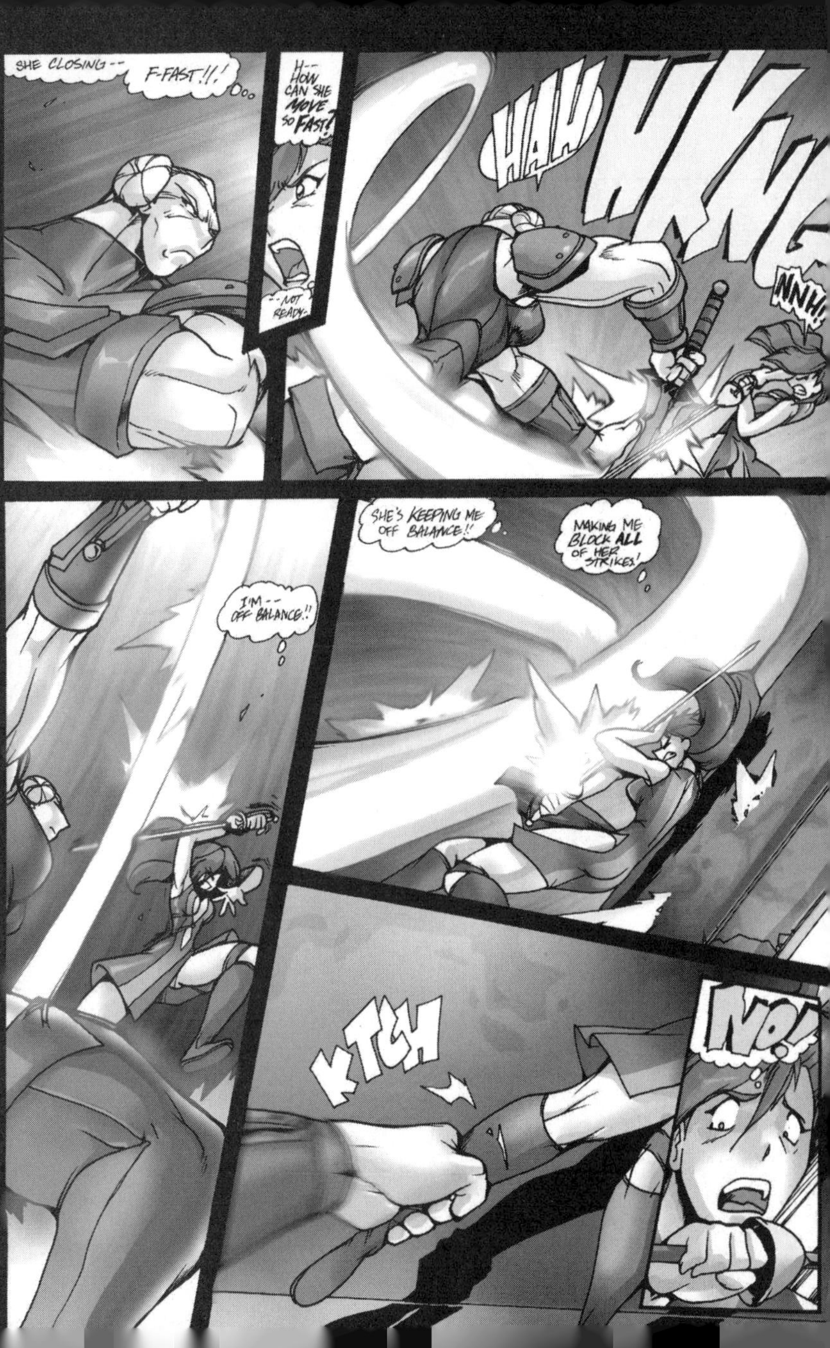
SHE CLOSING --
F-FAST!!
H-- HOW CAN SHE MOVE SO FAST!
--NOT READY-
HAH
HHNG
NNH!
SHE'S KEEPING ME OFF BALANCE!!
MAKING ME BLOCK ALL OF HER STRIKES!
I'M -- OFF BALANCE!!
KTCH
NO!

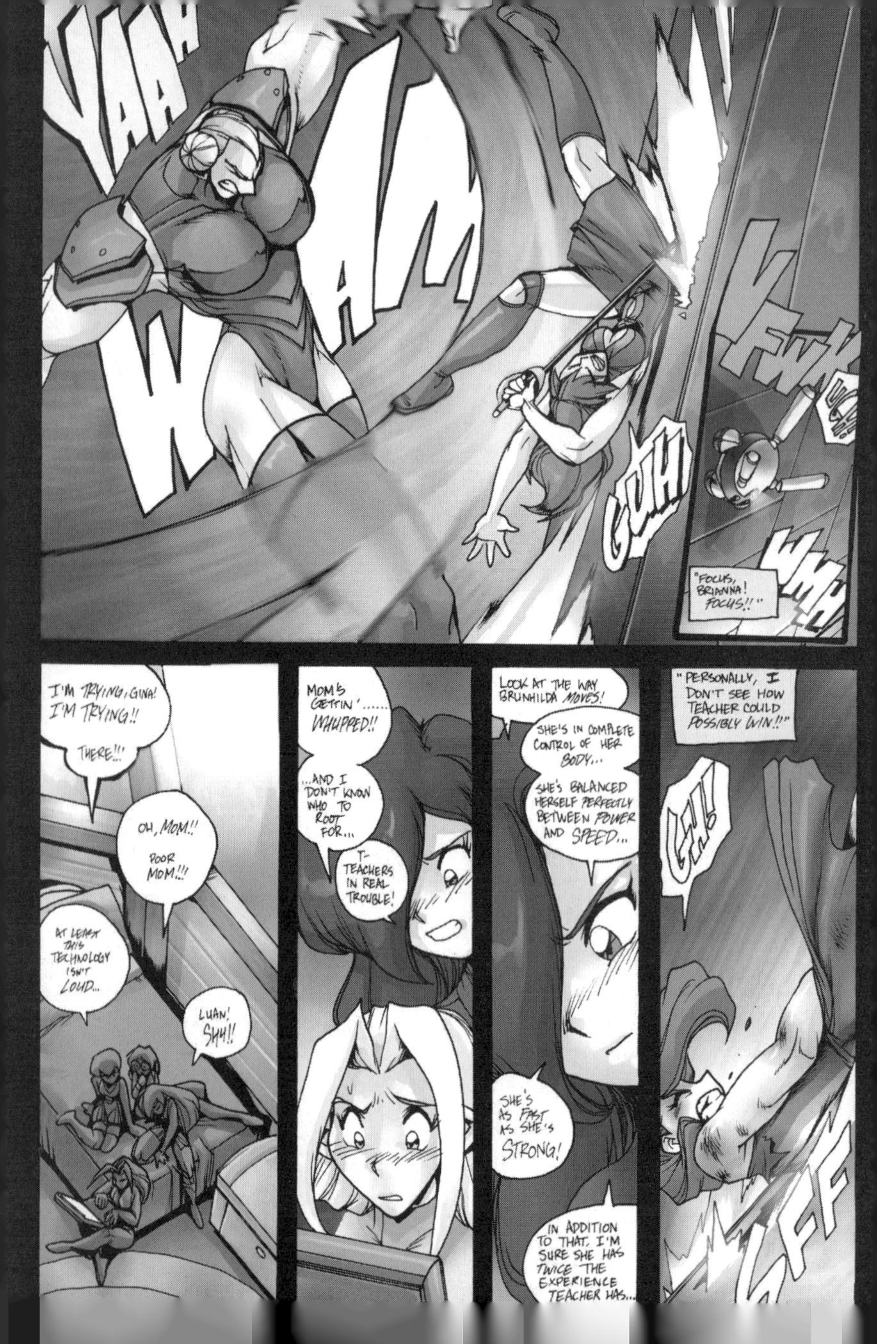
YAAH
WHAM
FWK
UGH
GUH
"FOCUS, BRIANNA! FOCUS!!"
WMH
I'M TRYING, GINA! I'M TRYING!!
THERE!!!
OH, MOM!!
POOR MOM!!!
AT LEAST THIS TECHNOLOGY ISN'T LOUD...
LUAN! SHH!!
MOM'S GETTIN'...... WHUPPED!!
...AND I DON'T KNOW WHO TO ROOT FOR...
T-TEACHERS IN REAL TROUBLE!
LOOK AT THE WAY BRUNHILDA MOVES!
SHE'S IN COMPLETE CONTROL OF HER BODY...
SHE'S BALANCED HERSELF PERFECTLY BETWEEN POWER AND SPEED...
SHE'S AS FAST AS SHE'S STRONG!
IN ADDITION TO THAT, I'M SURE SHE HAS TWICE THE EXPERIENCE TEACHER HAS...
"PERSONALLY, I DON'T SEE HOW TEACHER COULD POSSIBLY WIN!!"
GH!!
OFF

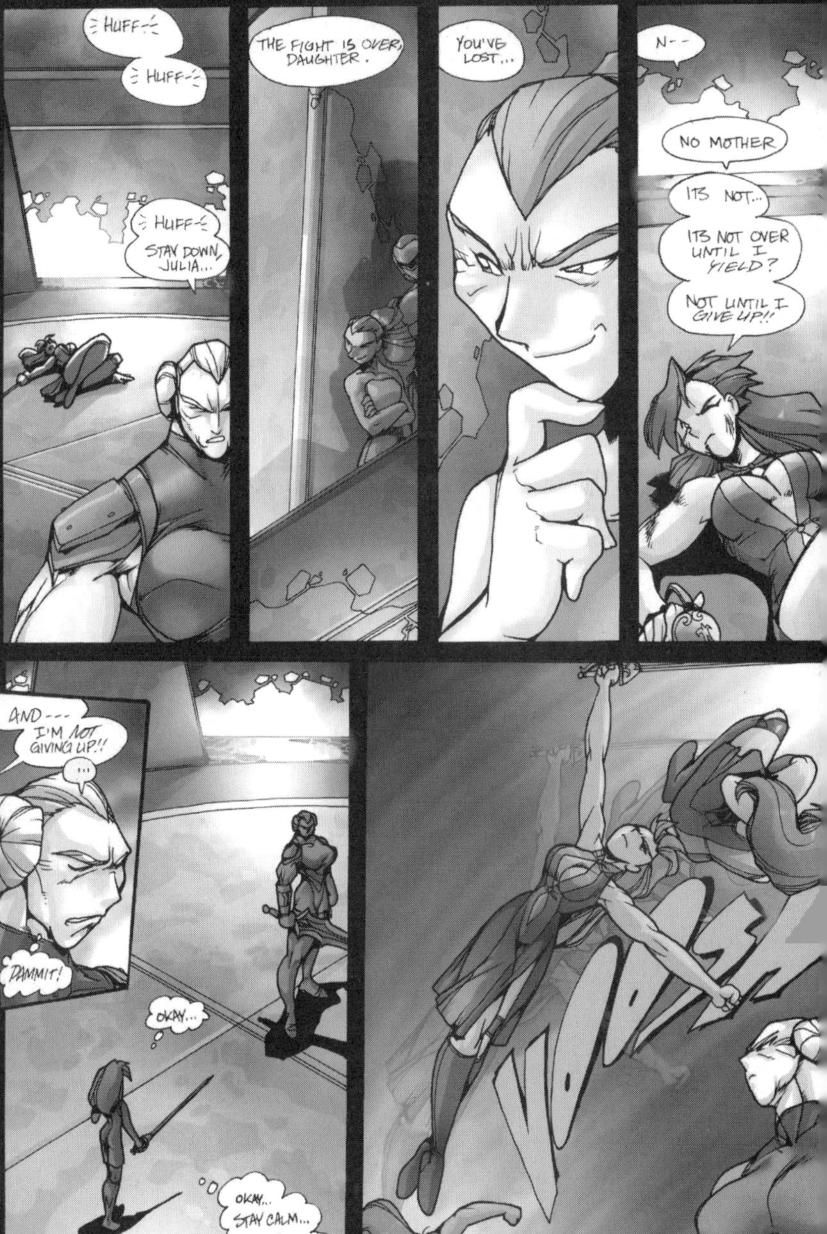
HUFF
HUFF
HUFF
STAY DOWN, JULIA...
THE FIGHT IS OVER, DAUGHTER.
YOU'VE LOST...
N--
NO MOTHER
ITS NOT...
ITS NOT OVER UNTIL I YIELD?
NOT UNTIL I GIVE UP!!
AND---
I'M NOT GIVING UP!!
...
DAMMIT!
OKAY...
OKAY...
STAY CALM...
KEEP IN CONTROL...

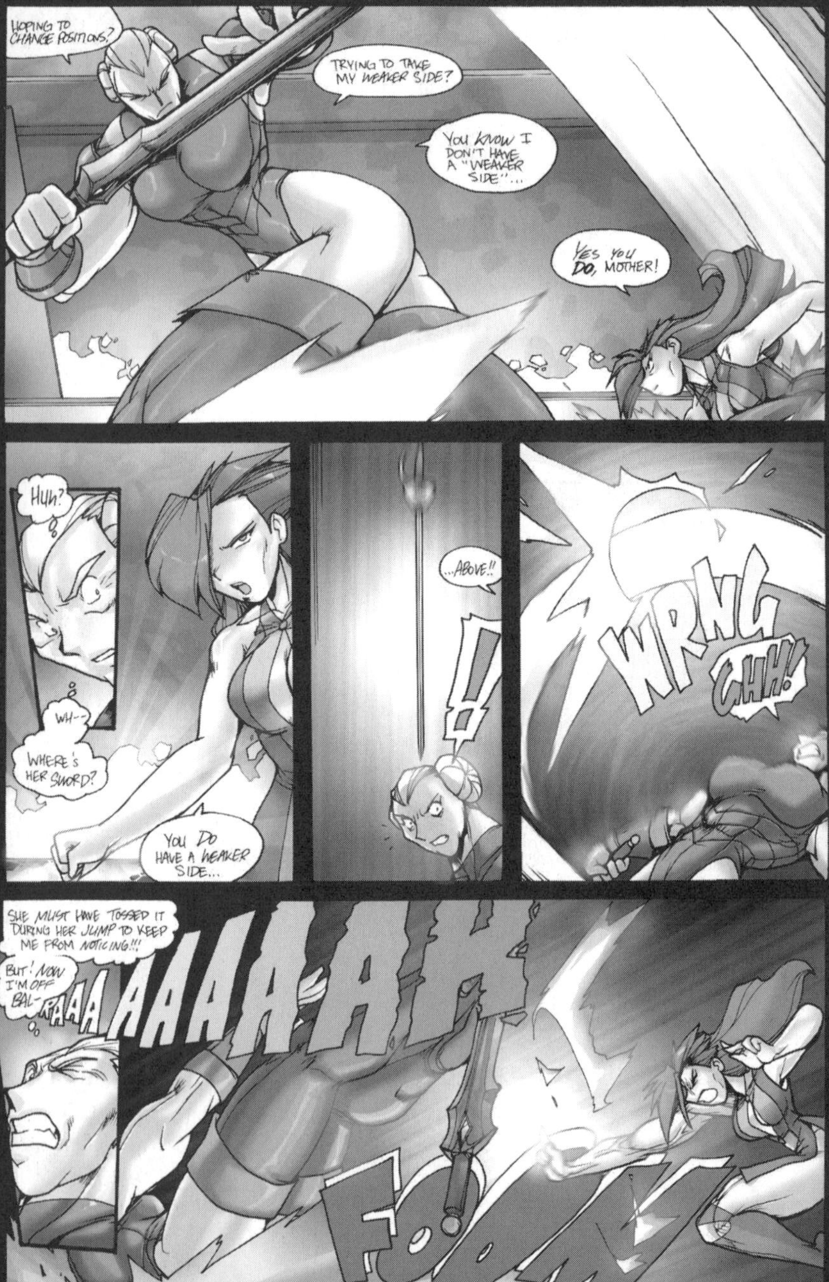
HOPING TO CHANGE POSITIONS?
TRYING TO TAKE MY WEAKER SIDE?
YOU KNOW I DON'T HAVE A "WEAKER SIDE"...
YES YOU DO, MOTHER!
HUH?
WH--
WHERE'S HER SWORD?
YOU DO HAVE A WEAKER SIDE...
...ABOVE!!
!
WRNG CHH!
SHE MUST HAVE TOSSED IT DURING HER JUMP TO KEEP ME FROM NOTICING!!!
BUT! NOW I'M OFF BAL-
RAAA AAAAAH

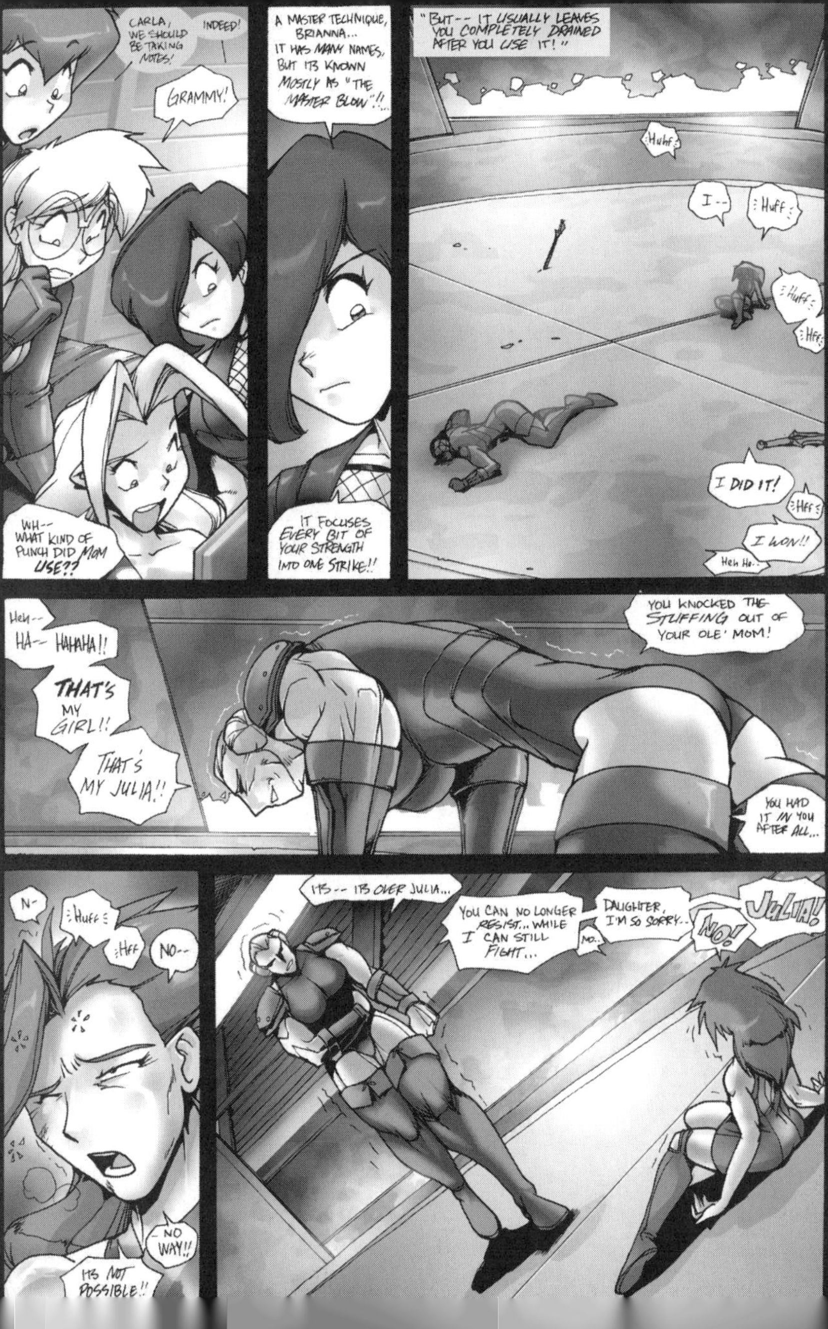
CARLA, WE SHOULD BE TAKING NOTES!
INDEED!
GRAMMY!
WH-- WHAT KIND OF PUNCH DID MOM USE??
A MASTER TECHNIQUE, BRIANNA... IT HAS MANY NAMES, BUT IT'S KNOWN MOSTLY AS "THE MASTER BLOW"!!
IT FOCUSES EVERY BIT OF YOUR STRENGTH INTO ONE STRIKE!!
"BUT-- IT USUALLY LEAVES YOU COMPLETELY DRAINED AFTER YOU USE IT!"
Huhf
I--
Huff
Huff
Hff
I DID IT!
Hff
I WON!!
Heh He..
Heh-- HA-- HAHAHA!!
THAT'S MY GIRL!!
THAT'S MY JULIA!!
YOU KNOCKED THE STUFFING OUT OF YOUR OLE' MOM!
YOU HAD IT IN YOU AFTER ALL...
N-
Huff
Hff
NO--
-NO WAY!!
IT'S NOT POSSIBLE!!
IT'S-- IT'S OVER JULIA...
YOU CAN NO LONGER RESIST... WHILE I CAN STILL FIGHT...
NO..
DAUGHTER, I'M SO SORRY...
NO!
JULIA!

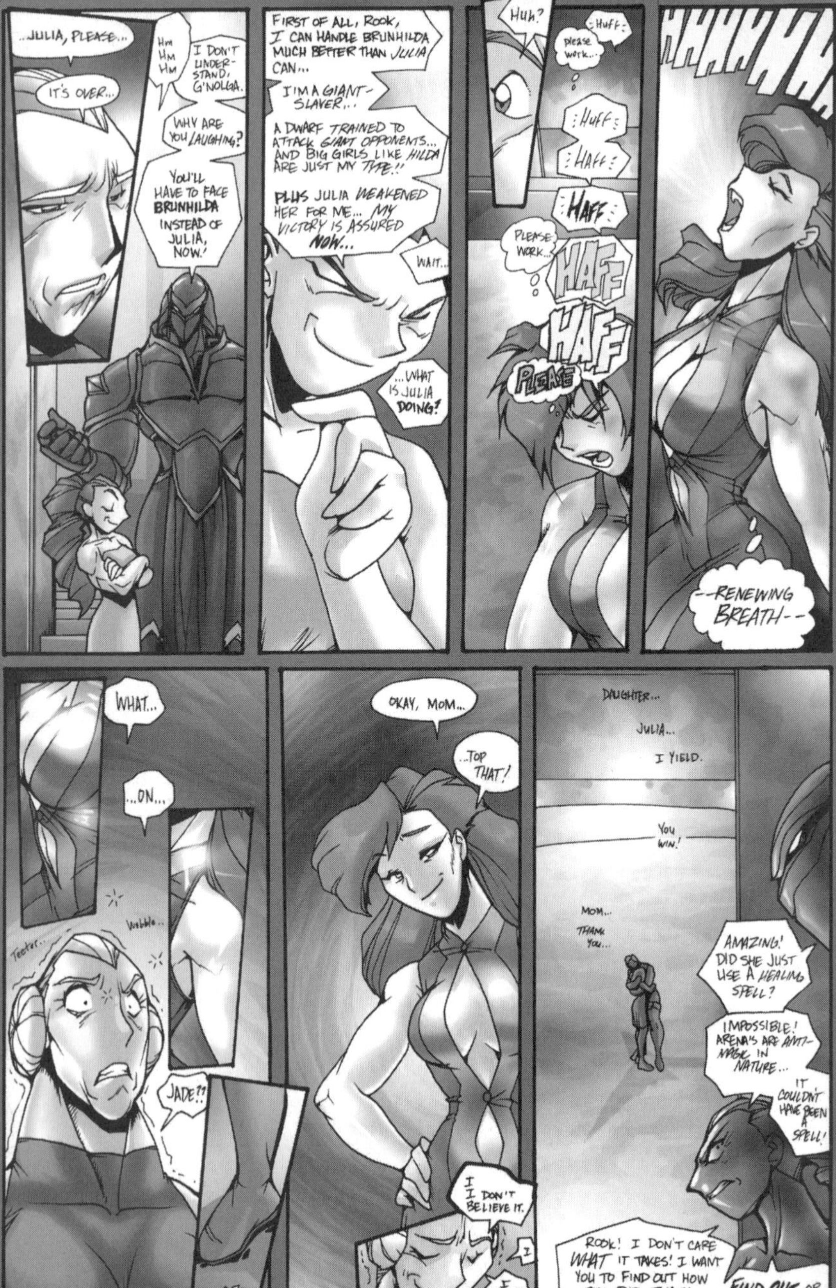
..JULIA, PLEASE...
IT'S OVER...
Hm Hm Hm
I DON'T UNDERSTAND, G'NOLGA.
WHY ARE YOU LAUGHING?
YOU'LL HAVE TO FACE BRUNHILDA INSTEAD OF JULIA, NOW.'
FIRST OF ALL, ROOK, I CAN HANDLE BRUNHILDA MUCH BETTER THAN JULIA CAN...
I'M A GIANT-SLAYER...
A DWARF TRAINED TO ATTACK GIANT OPPONENTS... AND BIG GIRLS LIKE HILDA ARE JUST MY TYPE!!
PLUS JULIA WEAKENED HER FOR ME... MY VICTORY IS ASSURED NOW...
WAIT...
...WHAT IS JULIA DOING?
HUH?
Huff
please work...
HUFF
HAFF
HAFF
PLEASE WORK...
HAFF
HAF
PLEASE
HHHHHHHH
--RENEWING BREATH--
WHAT...
...ON...
Wobble...
Teeter...
JADE?!
SKF
OKAY, MOM...
...TOP THAT!
I... I DON'T BELIEVE IT.
I
I CAN'T WIN...
DAUGHTER...
JULIA...
I YIELD.
YOU WIN!
MOM...
THANK YOU...
AMAZING! DID SHE JUST USE A HEALING SPELL?
IMPOSSIBLE! ARENA'S ARE ANTI-MAGIC IN NATURE...
IT COULDN'T HAVE BEEN A SPELL!
ROOK! I DON'T CARE WHAT IT TAKES! I WANT YOU TO FIND OUT HOW SHE DID THAT!
FIND OUT OR WE'RE FINISHED!!

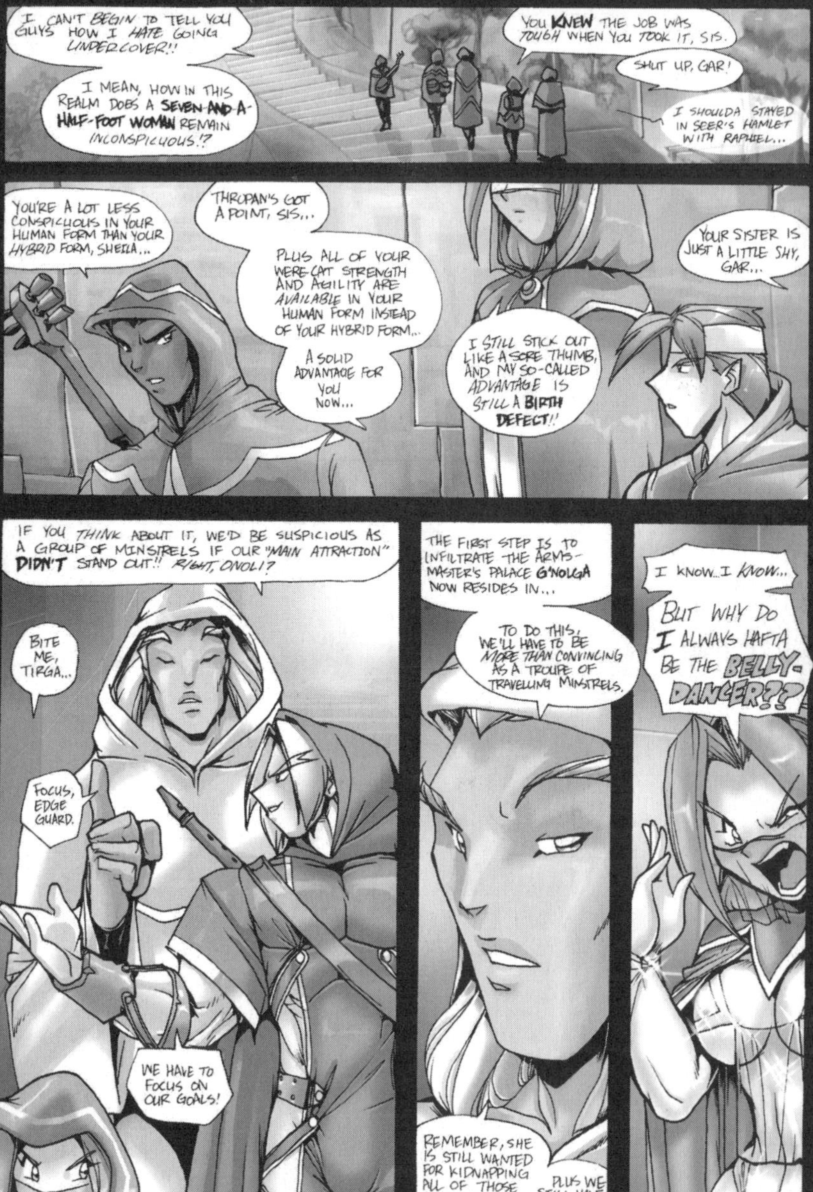
I CAN'T BEGIN TO TELL YOU GUYS HOW I HATE GOING UNDERCOVER!!
I MEAN, HOW IN THIS REALM DOES A SEVEN-AND-A-HALF-FOOT WOMAN REMAIN INCONSPICUOUS!?
YOU KNEW THE JOB WAS TOUGH WHEN YOU TOOK IT, SIS.
SHUT UP, GAR!
I SHOULDA STAYED IN SEER'S HAMLET WITH RAPHIEL...
YOU'RE A LOT LESS CONSPICUOUS IN YOUR HUMAN FORM THAN YOUR HYBRID FORM, SHEILA...
THROPAN'S GOT A POINT, SIS...
PLUS ALL OF YOUR WERE-CAT STRENGTH AND AGILITY ARE AVAILABLE IN YOUR HUMAN FORM INSTEAD OF YOUR HYBRID FORM...
A SOLID ADVANTAGE FOR YOU NOW...
I STILL STICK OUT LIKE A SORE THUMB, AND MY SO-CALLED ADVANTAGE IS STILL A BIRTH DEFECT!!
YOUR SISTER IS JUST A LITTLE SHY, GAR...
IF YOU THINK ABOUT IT, WE'D BE SUSPICIOUS AS A GROUP OF MINSTRELS IF OUR "MAIN ATTRACTION" DIDN'T STAND OUT!! RIGHT, ONOLI!?
BITE ME, TIRGA...
FOCUS, EDGE GUARD.
WE HAVE TO FOCUS ON OUR GOALS!
THE FIRST STEP IS TO INFILTRATE THE ARMS-MASTER'S PALACE G'NOLGA NOW RESIDES IN...
TO DO THIS, WE'LL HAVE TO BE MORE THAN CONVINCING AS A TROUPE OF TRAVELLING MINSTRELS.
REMEMBER, SHE IS STILL WANTED FOR KIDNAPPING ALL OF THOSE MAGIC-USERS...
PLUS WE STILL HAVE TO LOCATE THE VICTIMS.
I KNOW...I KNOW...
BUT WHY DO I ALWAYS HAFTA BE THE BELLY-DANCER??

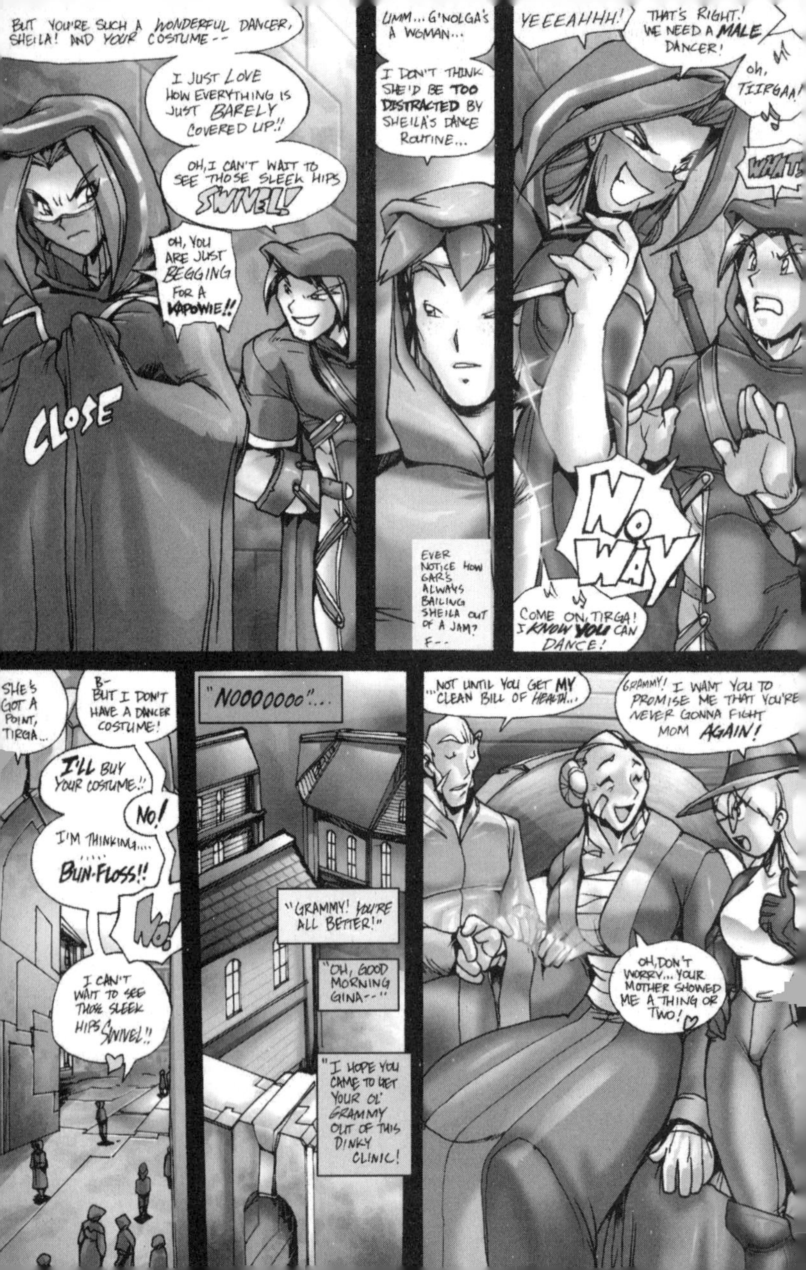
BUT YOU'RE SUCH A WONDERFUL DANCER, SHEILA! AND YOUR COSTUME--
I JUST LOVE HOW EVERYTHING IS JUST BARELY COVERED UP!!
OH, I CAN'T WAIT TO SEE THOSE SLEEK HIPS SWIVEL!
OH, YOU ARE JUST BEGGING FOR A KAPOWIE!!
CLOSE
UMM... G'NOLGA'S A WOMAN...
I DON'T THINK SHE'D BE TOO DISTRACTED BY SHEILA'S DANCE ROUTINE...
EVER NOTICE HOW GAR'S ALWAYS BAILING SHEILA OUT OF A JAM?
F--
YEEEAHHH!
THAT'S RIGHT! WE NEED A MALE DANCER!
oh, TIIRGAA!
WHAT!
NO WAY
COME ON, TIRGA! I KNOW YOU CAN DANCE!
SHE'S GOT A POINT, TIRGA...
B-BUT I DON'T HAVE A DANCER COSTUME!
I'LL BUY YOUR COSTUME!!
NO!
I'M THINKING.... BUN-FLOSS!!
NO!
I CAN'T WAIT TO SEE THOSE SLEEK HIPS SWIVEL!!
"NOOOOOOO"...
"GRAMMY! YOU'RE ALL BETTER!"
"OH, GOOD MORNING GINA--"
"I HOPE YOU CAME TO GET YOUR OL' GRAMMY OUT OF THIS DINKY CLINIC!
...NOT UNTIL YOU GET MY CLEAN BILL OF HEALTH...
GRAMMY! I WANT YOU TO PROMISE ME THAT YOU'RE NEVER GONNA FIGHT MOM AGAIN!
OH, DON'T WORRY... YOUR MOTHER SHOWED ME A THING OR TWO!

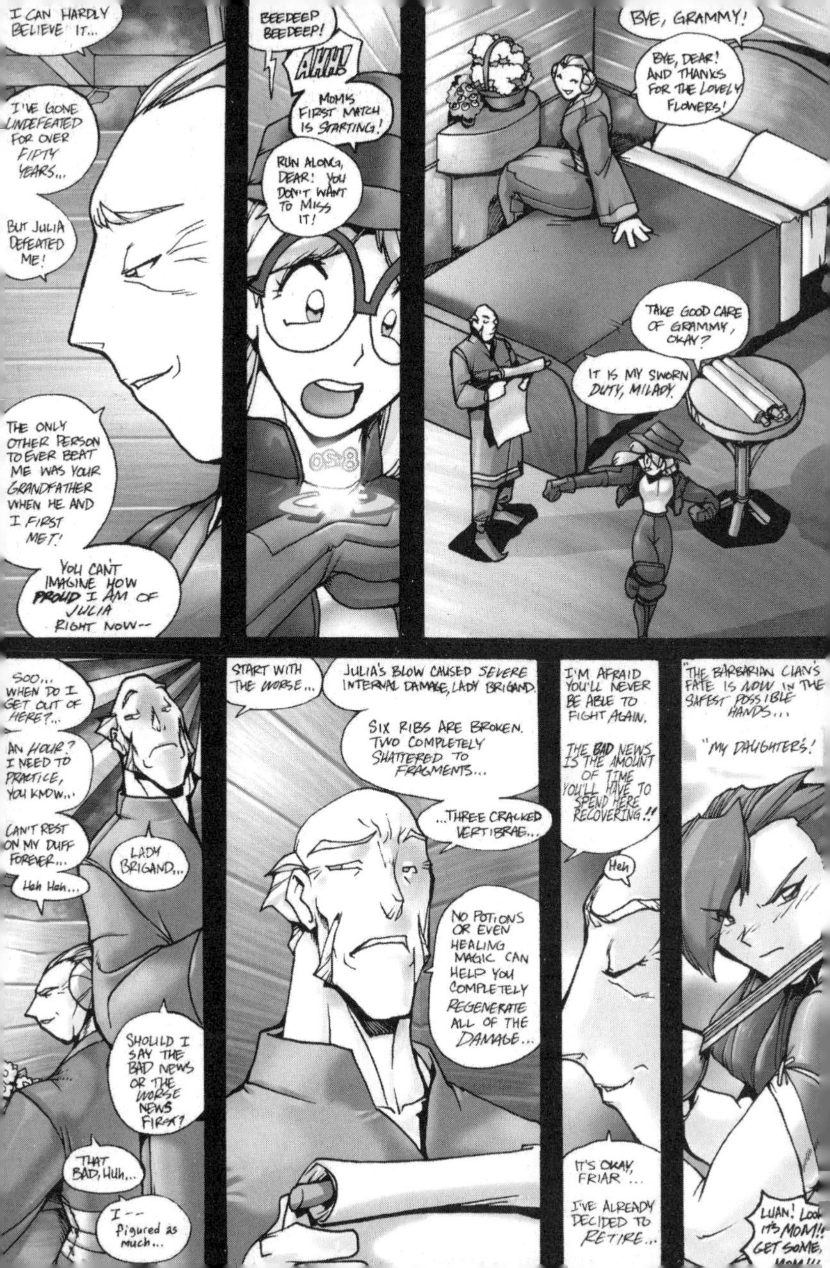

I CAN HARDLY BELIEVE IT...
I'VE GONE UNDEFEATED FOR OVER FIFTY YEARS...
BUT JULIA DEFEATED ME!
THE ONLY OTHER PERSON TO EVER BEAT ME WAS YOUR GRANDFATHER WHEN HE AND I FIRST MET!
YOU CAN'T IMAGINE HOW PROUD I AM OF JULIA RIGHT NOW--
BEEDEEP BEEDEEP!
AHH!
MOM'S FIRST MATCH IS STARTING!
RUN ALONG, DEAR! YOU DON'T WANT TO MISS IT!
BYE, GRAMMY!
BYE, DEAR! AND THANKS FOR THE LOVELY FLOWERS!
TAKE GOOD CARE OF GRAMMY, OKAY?
IT IS MY SWORN DUTY, MILADY.
SOO... WHEN DO I GET OUT OF HERE?...
AN HOUR? I NEED TO PRACTICE, YOU KNOW...
CAN'T REST ON MY DUFF FOREVER...
Heh Heh...
LADY BRIGAND...
SHOULD I SAY THE BAD NEWS OR THE WORSE NEWS FIRST?
THAT BAD, Huh...
I-- figured as much...
START WITH THE WORSE...
JULIA'S BLOW CAUSED SEVERE INTERNAL DAMAGE, LADY BRIGAND.
SIX RIBS ARE BROKEN. TWO COMPLETELY SHATTERED TO FRAGMENTS...
...THREE CRACKED VERTIBRAE...
NO POTIONS OR EVEN HEALING MAGIC CAN HELP YOU COMPLETELY REGENERATE ALL OF THE DAMAGE...
I'M AFRAID YOU'LL NEVER BE ABLE TO FIGHT AGAIN.
THE BAD NEWS IS THE AMOUNT OF TIME YOU'LL HAVE TO SPEND HERE RECOVERING!!
Heh
IT'S OKAY, FRIAR...
I'VE ALREADY DECIDED TO RETIRE...
"THE BARBARIAN CLAN'S FATE IS NOW IN THE SAFEST POSSIBLE HANDS...
"MY DAUGHTER'S!
LUAN! LOOK IT'S MOM!! GET SOME,

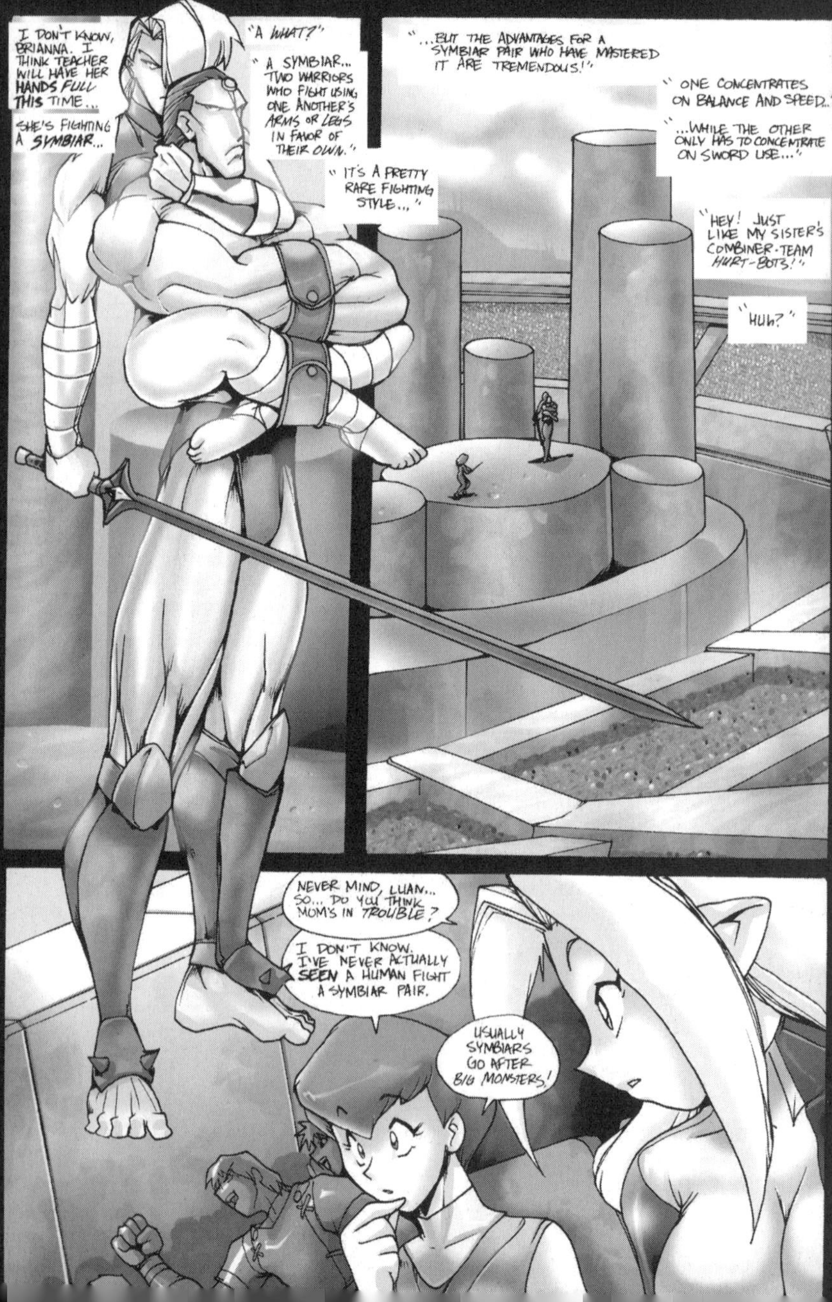
I DON'T KNOW, BRIANNA. I THINK TEACHER WILL HAVE HER HANDS FULL THIS TIME...
SHE'S FIGHTING A SYMBIAR...
"A WHAT?"
"A SYMBIAR... TWO WARRIORS WHO FIGHT USING ONE ANOTHER'S ARMS OR LEGS IN FAVOR OF THEIR OWN."
"IT'S A PRETTY RARE FIGHTING STYLE..."
"...BUT THE ADVANTAGES FOR A SYMBIAR PAIR WHO HAVE MASTERED IT ARE TREMENDOUS!"
"ONE CONCENTRATES ON BALANCE AND SPEED..."
"...WHILE THE OTHER ONLY HAS TO CONCENTRATE ON SWORD USE..."
"HEY! JUST LIKE MY SISTER'S COMBINER-TEAM HURT-BOTS!"
"HUH?"
NEVER MIND, LUAN... SO... DO YOU THINK MOM'S IN TROUBLE?
I DON'T KNOW. I'VE NEVER ACTUALLY SEEN A HUMAN FIGHT A SYMBIAR PAIR.
USUALLY SYMBIARS GO AFTER BIG MONSTERS!

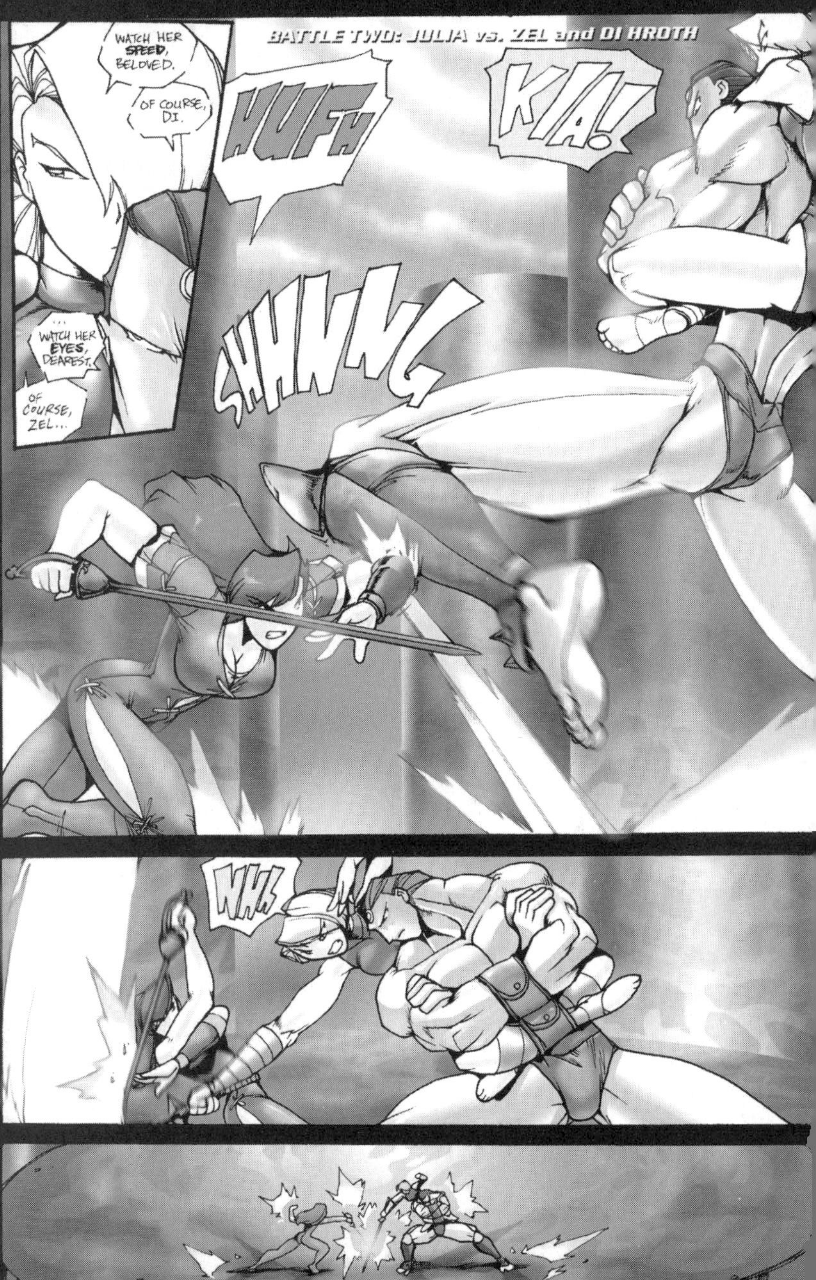
BATTLE TWO: JULIA vs. ZEL and DI HROTH
WATCH HER SPEED, BELOVED.
OF COURSE, DI.
HUFH
KIA!
... WATCH HER EYES, DEAREST.
OF COURSE, ZEL...
SHHNNG
NHH

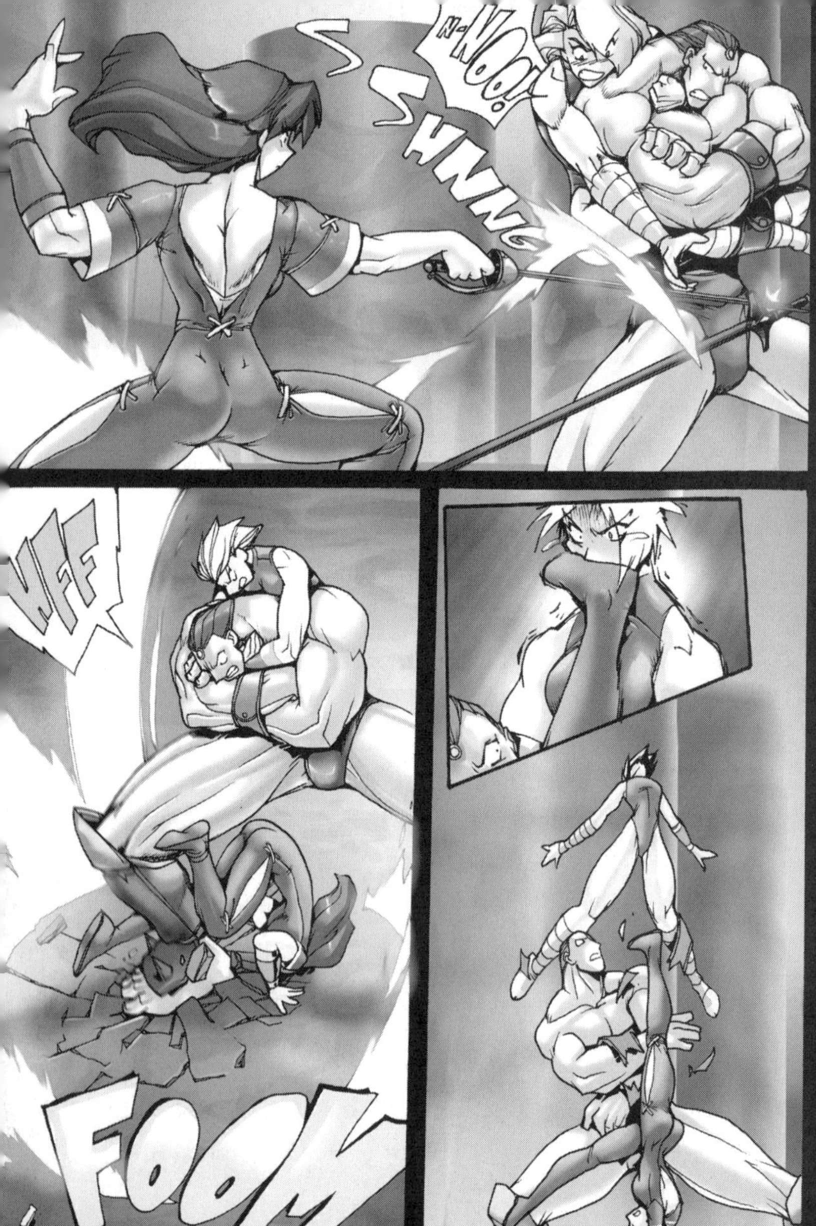
SSHNNG
N-NOOO!
UFF
FOOM

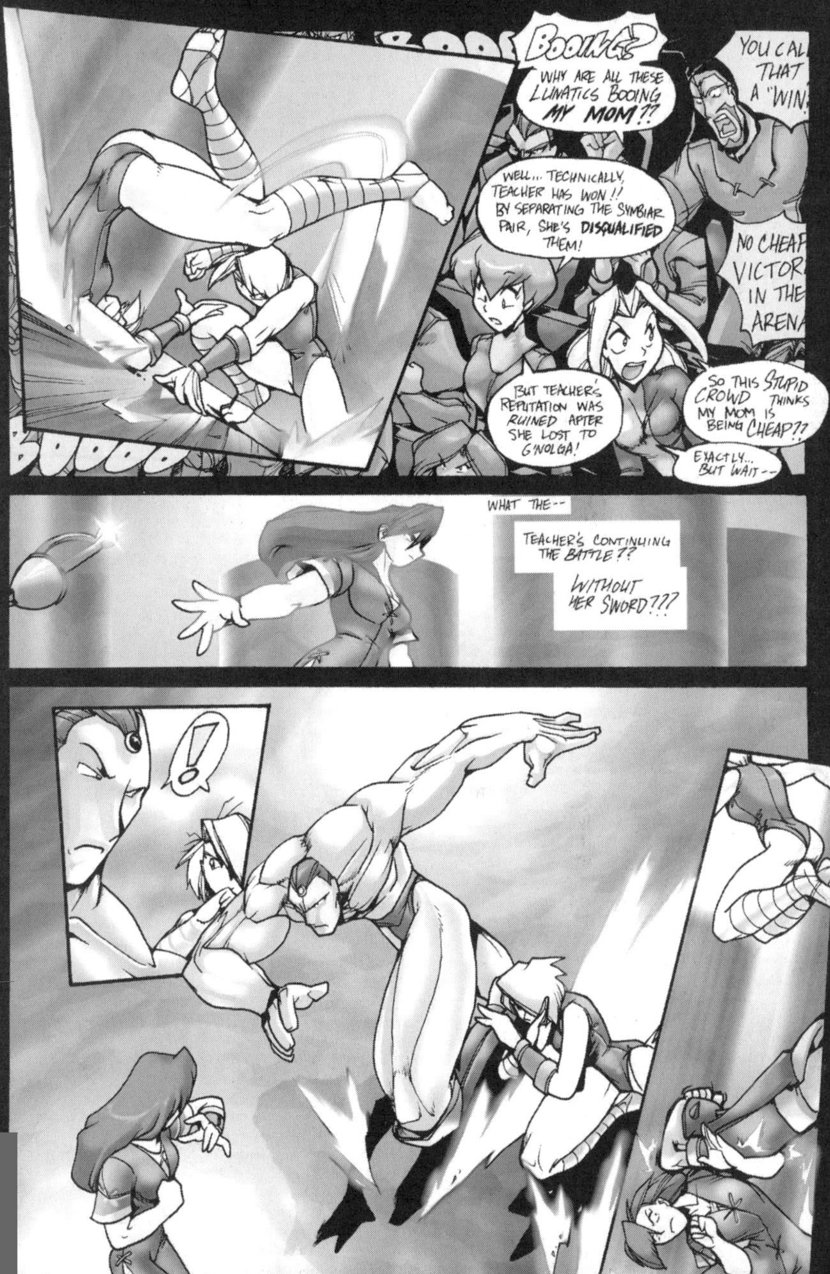

BOOOO
BOOING?
WHY ARE ALL THESE LUNATICS BOOING MY MOM??
YOU CAL THAT A "WIN
WELL... TECHNICALLY, TEACHER HAS WON!! BY SEPARATING THE SYMBIAR PAIR, SHE'S DISQUALIFIED THEM!
NO CHEAP VICTOR IN THE ARENA
BOOOOO
BUT TEACHER'S REPUTATION WAS RUINED AFTER SHE LOST TO G'NOLGA!
SO THIS STUPID CROWD THINKS MY MOM IS BEING CHEAP??
EXACTLY... BUT WAIT--
WHAT THE--
TEACHER'S CONTINUING THE BATTLE??
WITHOUT HER SWORD???
!

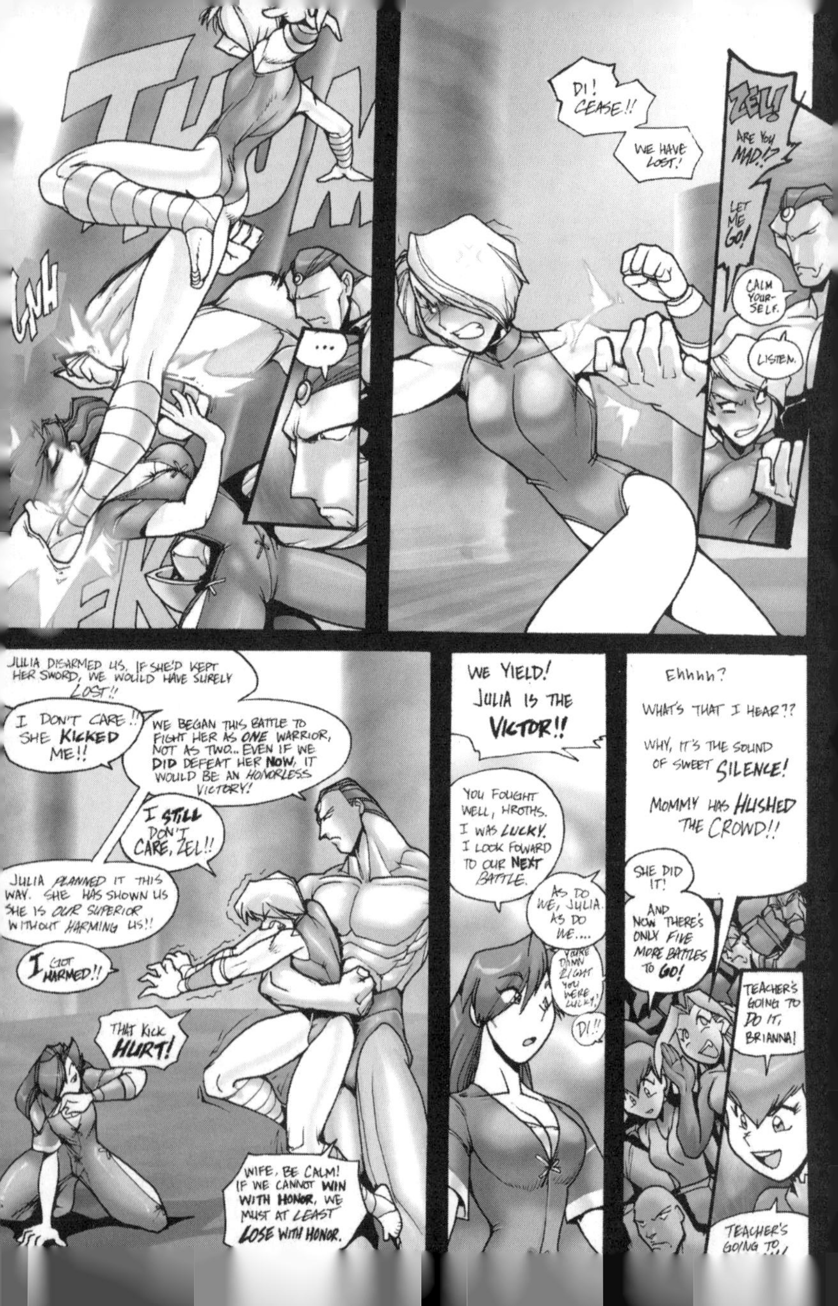
UNH
...
DI! CEASE!!
WE HAVE LOST!
ZEL! ARE YOU MAD!? LET ME GO!
CALM YOURSELF.
LISTEN.
JULIA DISARMED US. IF SHE'D KEPT HER SWORD, WE WOULD HAVE SURELY LOST!!
I DON'T CARE!! SHE KICKED ME!!
WE BEGAN THIS BATTLE TO FIGHT HER AS ONE WARRIOR, NOT AS TWO... EVEN IF WE DID DEFEAT HER NOW, IT WOULD BE AN HONORLESS VICTORY!
I STILL DON'T CARE, ZEL!!
JULIA PLANNED IT THIS WAY. SHE HAS SHOWN US SHE IS OUR SUPERIOR WITHOUT HARMING US!!
I GOT HARMED!!
THAT KICK HURT!
WIFE, BE CALM! IF WE CANNOT WIN WITH HONOR, WE MUST AT LEAST LOSE WITH HONOR.
WE YIELD! JULIA IS THE VICTOR!!
YOU FOUGHT WELL, HROTHS. I WAS LUCKY. I LOOK FOWARD TO OUR NEXT BATTLE.
AS DO WE, JULIA. AS DO WE....
YOU'RE DAMN RIGHT YOU WERE LUCKY!
DI!!
Ehhhh?
WHAT'S THAT I HEAR??
WHY, IT'S THE SOUND OF SWEET SILENCE!
MOMMY HAS HUSHED THE CROWD!!
SHE DID IT!
AND NOW THERE'S ONLY FIVE MORE BATTLES TO GO!
TEACHER'S GOING TO DO IT, BRIANNA!
TEACHER'S GOING TO

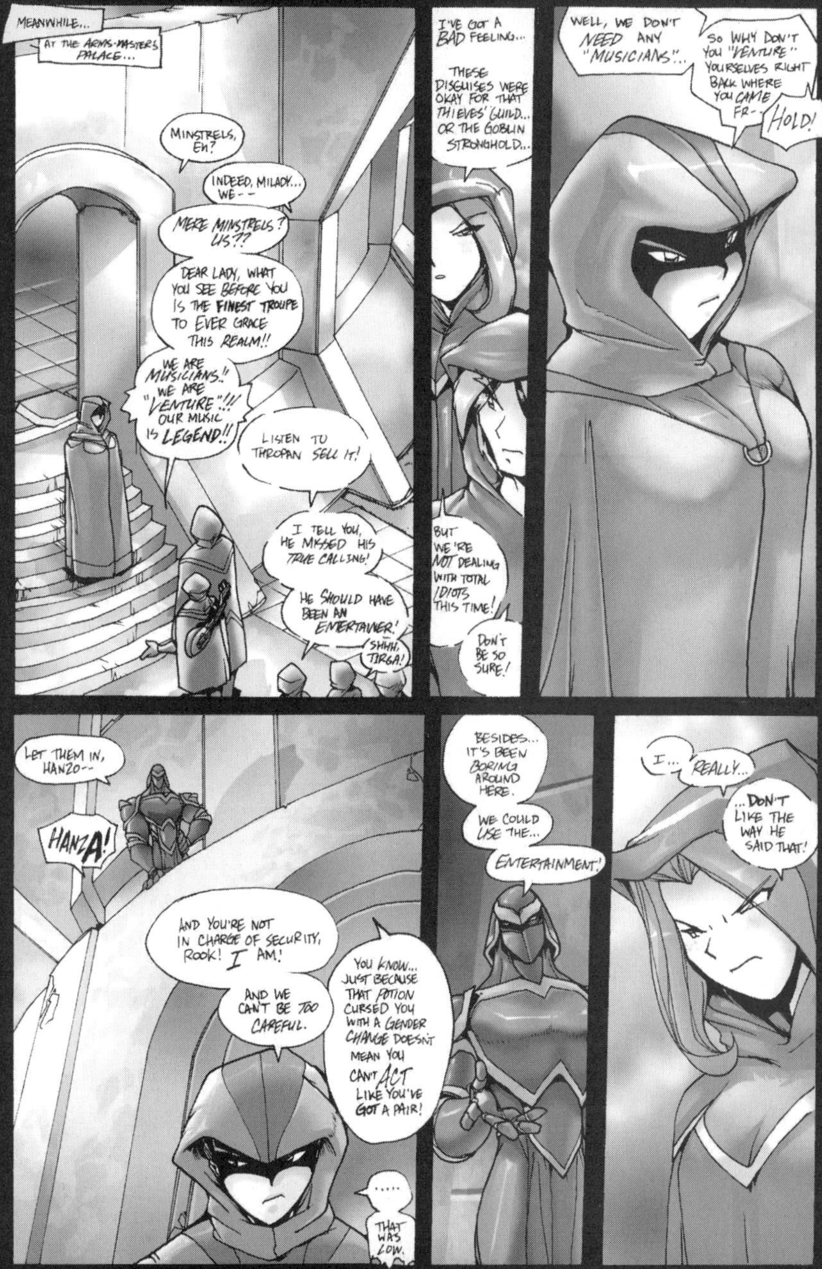

MEANWHILE...
AT THE ARMS-MASTERS PALACE...
MINSTRELS, EH?
INDEED, MILADY... WE--
MERE MINSTRELS? US??
DEAR LADY, WHAT YOU SEE BEFORE YOU IS THE FINEST TROUPE TO EVER GRACE THIS REALM!!
WE ARE MUSICIANS!! WE ARE "VENTURE"!!! OUR MUSIC IS LEGEND!!
LISTEN TO THROPAN SELL IT!
I TELL YOU, HE MISSED HIS TRUE CALLING!
HE SHOULD HAVE BEEN AN ENTERTAINER!
SHHH, TIRGA!
I'VE GOT A BAD FEELING...
THESE DISGUISES WERE OKAY FOR THAT THIEVES' GUILD... OR THE GOBLIN STRONGHOLD...
BUT WE'RE NOT DEALING WITH TOTAL IDIOTS THIS TIME!
DON'T BE SO SURE!
WELL, WE DON'T NEED ANY "MUSICIANS"...
SO WHY DON'T YOU "VENTURE" YOURSELVES RIGHT BACK WHERE YOU CAME FR--
HOLD!
LET THEM IN, HANZO--
HANZA!
AND YOU'RE NOT IN CHARGE OF SECURITY, ROOK! I AM!
AND WE CAN'T BE TOO CAREFUL.
YOU KNOW... JUST BECAUSE THAT POTION CURSED YOU WITH A GENDER CHANGE DOESN'T MEAN YOU CAN'T ACT LIKE YOU'VE GOT A PAIR!
.....
THAT WAS LOW.
BESIDES... IT'S BEEN BORING AROUND HERE.
WE COULD USE THE...
ENTERTAINMENT!
I...
REALLY...
...DON'T LIKE THE WAY HE SAID THAT!

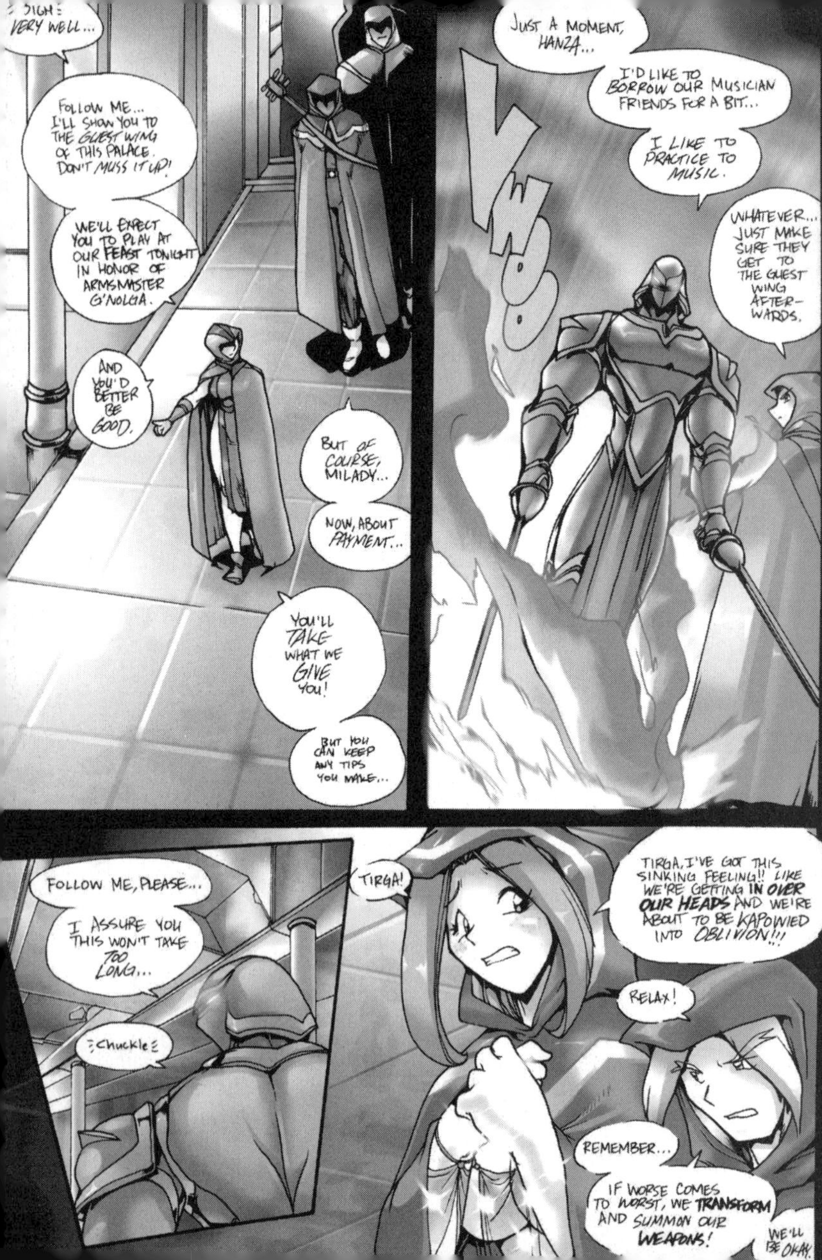
≡SIGH≡ VERY WELL...
FOLLOW ME... I'LL SHOW YOU TO THE GUEST WING OF THIS PALACE. DON'T MUSS IT UP!
WE'LL EXPECT YOU TO PLAY AT OUR FEAST TONIGHT IN HONOR OF ARMSMASTER G'NOLGIA.
AND YOU'D BETTER BE GOOD.
BUT OF COURSE, MILADY...
NOW, ABOUT PAYMENT...
YOU'LL TAKE WHAT WE GIVE YOU!
BUT YOU CAN KEEP ANY TIPS YOU MAKE...
JUST A MOMENT, HANZA...
I'D LIKE TO BORROW OUR MUSICIAN FRIENDS FOR A BIT...
I LIKE TO PRACTICE TO MUSIC.
WHOOO
WHATEVER... JUST MAKE SURE THEY GET TO THE GUEST WING AFTER-WARDS.
FOLLOW ME, PLEASE...
I ASSURE YOU THIS WON'T TAKE TOO LONG...
≡CHUCKLE≡
TIRGA!
TIRGA, I'VE GOT THIS SINKING FEELING!! LIKE WE'RE GETTING IN OVER OUR HEADS AND WE'RE ABOUT TO BE KAPOWIED INTO OBLIVION!!!
RELAX!
REMEMBER...
IF WORSE COMES TO WORST, WE TRANSFORM AND SUMMON OUR WEAPONS!
WE'LL BE OKAY.

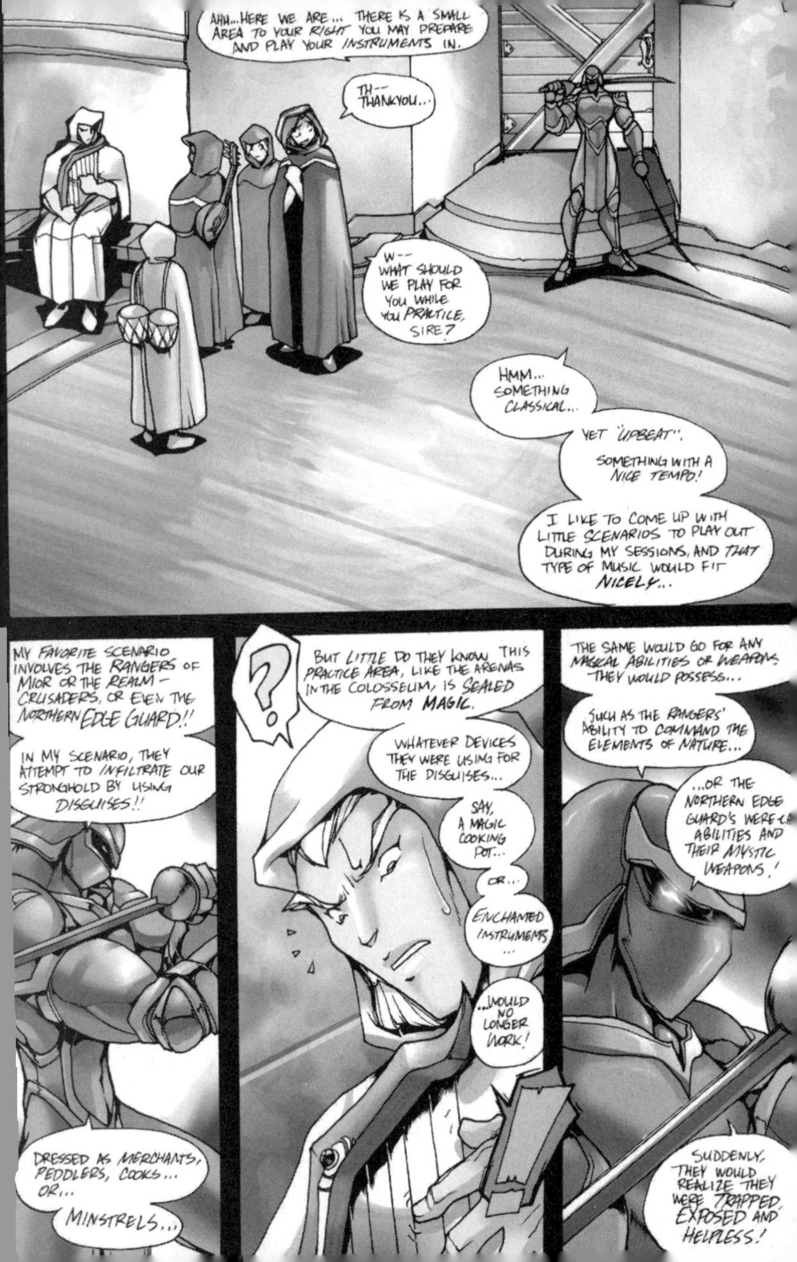
AHH... HERE WE ARE... THERE IS A SMALL AREA TO YOUR RIGHT YOU MAY PREPARE AND PLAY YOUR INSTRUMENTS IN.
TH-- THANKYOU...
W-- WHAT SHOULD WE PLAY FOR YOU WHILE YOU PRACTICE, SIRE?
HMM... SOMETHING CLASSICAL...
YET "UPBEAT". SOMETHING WITH A NICE TEMPO!
I LIKE TO COME UP WITH LITTLE SCENARIOS TO PLAY OUT DURING MY SESSIONS, AND THAT TYPE OF MUSIC WOULD FIT NICELY...
MY FAVORITE SCENARIO INVOLVES THE RANGERS OF MIOR OR THE REALM-CRUSADERS, OR EVEN THE NORTHERN EDGE GUARD!!
IN MY SCENARIO, THEY ATTEMPT TO INFILTRATE OUR STRONGHOLD BY USING DISGUISES!!
DRESSED AS MERCHANTS, PEDDLERS, COOKS... OR...
MINSTRELS...
?
BUT LITTLE DO THEY KNOW THIS PRACTICE AREA, LIKE THE ARENAS IN THE COLOSSEUM, IS SEALED FROM MAGIC.
WHATEVER DEVICES THEY WERE USING FOR THE DISGUISES...
SAY, A MAGIC COOKING POT...
OR...
ENCHANTED INSTRUMENTS...
...WOULD NO LONGER WORK!
THE SAME WOULD GO FOR ANY MAGICAL ABILITIES OR WEAPONS THEY WOULD POSSESS...
SUCH AS THE RANGERS' ABILITY TO COMMAND THE ELEMENTS OF NATURE...
...OR THE NORTHERN EDGE GUARD'S WERE-CA ABILITIES AND THEIR MYSTIC WEAPONS!
SUDDENLY, THEY WOULD REALIZE THEY WERE TRAPPED, EXPOSED AND HELPLESS!

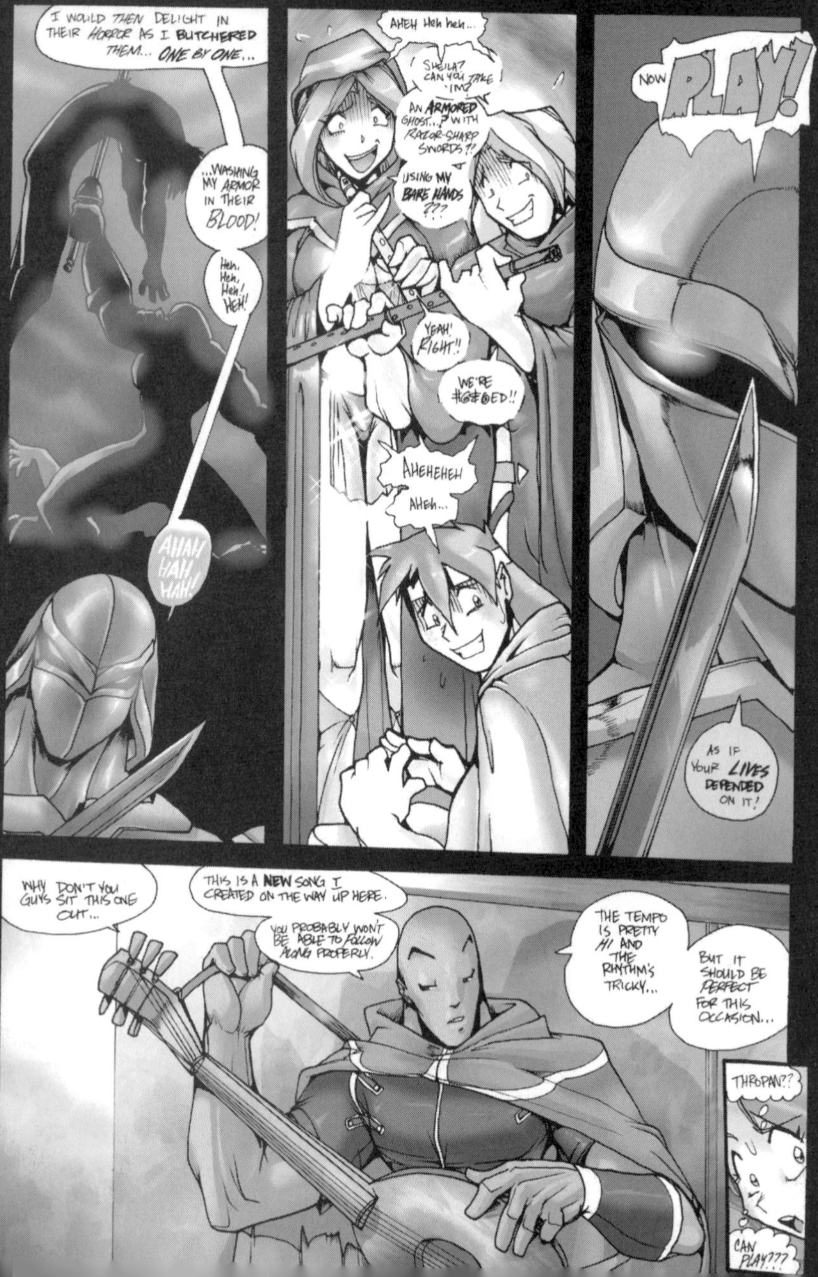
I WOULD THEN DELIGHT IN THEIR HORROR AS I BUTCHERED THEM... ONE BY ONE...
...WASHING MY ARMOR IN THEIR BLOOD!
Heh, Heh, Heh! HEH!
AHAH HAH HAH!
AHEH Heh heh...
SHEILA? CAN YOU TAKE 'IM?
AN ARMORED GHOST...? WITH RAZOR-SHARP SWORDS?!
USING MY BARE HANDS ???
YEAH! RIGHT!!
WE'RE #@$@ED!!
AHEHEHEH AHEh...
NOW PLAY!
AS IF YOUR LIVES DEPENDED ON IT!
WHY DON'T YOU GUYS SIT THIS ONE OUT...
THIS IS A NEW SONG I CREATED ON THE WAY UP HERE.
YOU PROBABLY WON'T BE ABLE TO FOLLOW ALONG PROPERLY.
THE TEMPO IS PRETTY HI AND THE RHYTHM'S TRICKY...
BUT IT SHOULD BE PERFECT FOR THIS OCCASION...
THROPAN??
CAN PLAY???

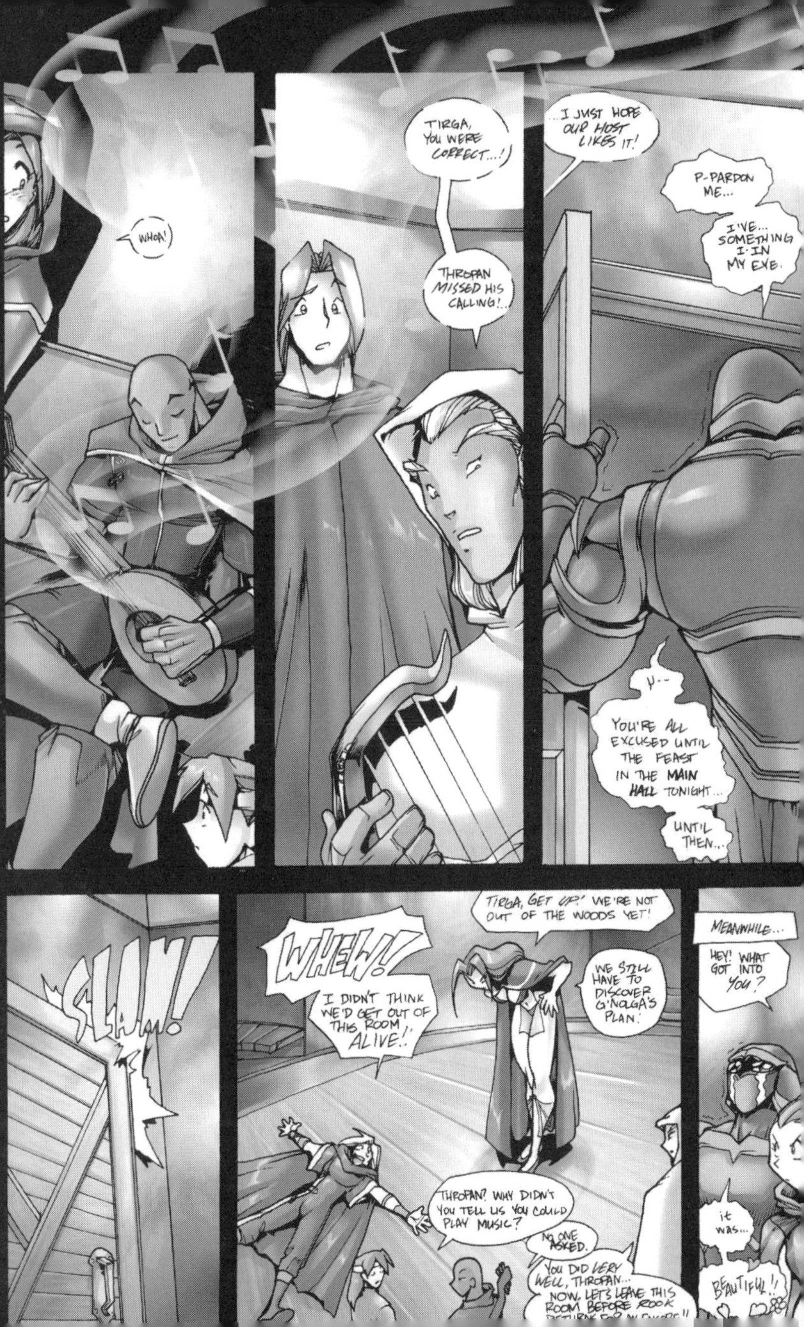
WHOA!
TIRGA, YOU WERE CORRECT...!
THROPAN MISSED HIS CALLING!..
...I JUST HOPE OUR HOST LIKES IT!
P-PARDON ME...
I'VE... SOMETHING I-IN MY EYE.
U...
YOU'RE ALL EXCUSED UNTIL THE FEAST IN THE MAIN HALL TONIGHT...
UNTIL THEN...
SLAM!
WHEW!!
I DIDN'T THINK WE'D GET OUT OF THIS ROOM ALIVE!
TIRGA, GET UP! WE'RE NOT OUT OF THE WOODS YET!
WE STILL HAVE TO DISCOVER G'NOLGA'S PLAN.
THROPAN? WHY DIDN'T YOU TELL US YOU COULD PLAY MUSIC?
NO ONE ASKED.
YOU DID VERY WELL, THROPAN... NOW, LET'S LEAVE THIS ROOM BEFORE ROOK
MEANWHILE...
HEY! WHAT GOT INTO YOU?
it was...
BEAUTIFUL!!

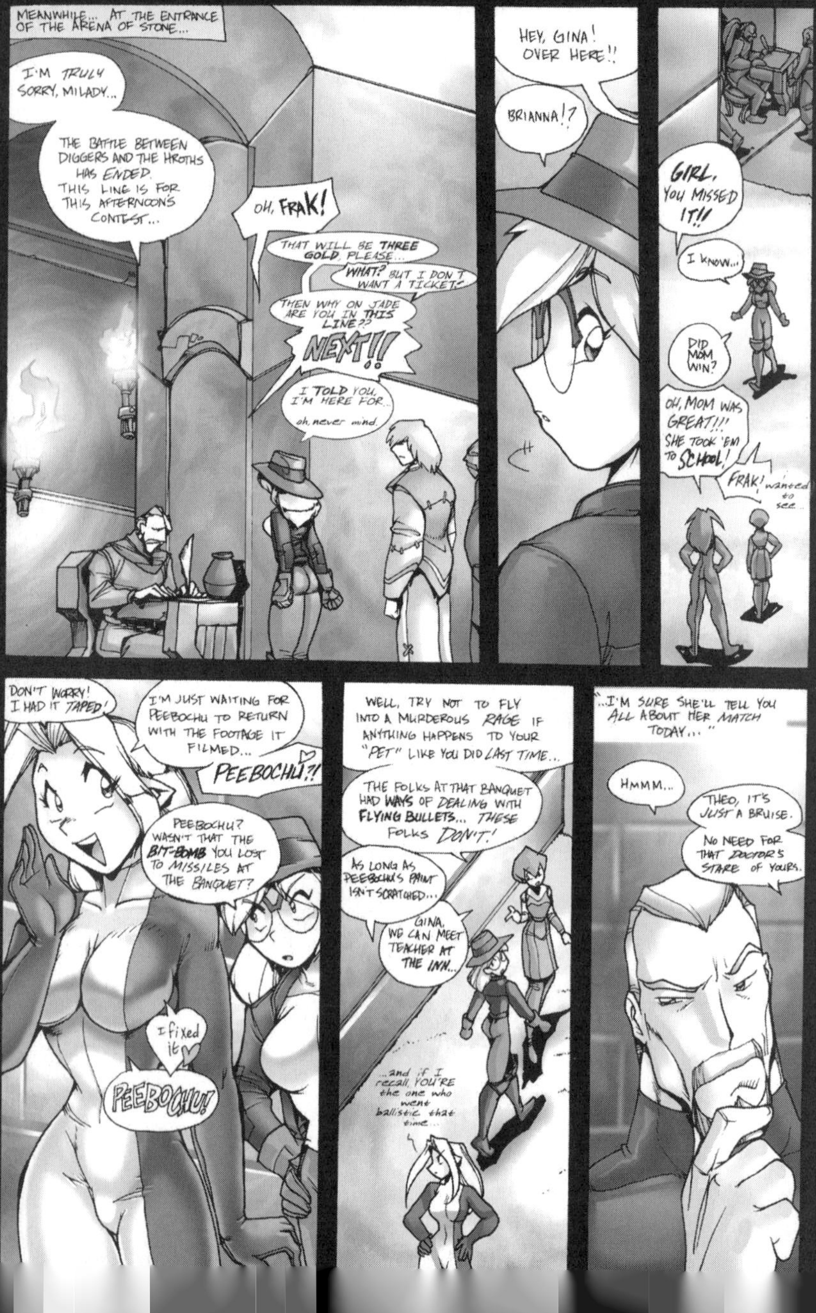
MEANWHILE... AT THE ENTRANCE OF THE ARENA OF STONE...
I'M TRULY SORRY, MILADY...
THE BATTLE BETWEEN DIGGERS AND THE HROTHS HAS ENDED. THIS LINE IS FOR THIS AFTERNOON'S CONTEST...
OH, FRAK!
THAT WILL BE THREE GOLD, PLEASE...
WHAT? BUT I DON'T WANT A TICKET!
THEN WHY ON JADE ARE YOU IN THIS LINE??
NEXT!!
I TOLD YOU, I'M HERE FOR...
oh, never mind.
HEY, GINA! OVER HERE!!
BRIANNA!?
GIRL, YOU MISSED IT!!
I KNOW...
DID MOM WIN?
OH, MOM WAS GREAT!!! SHE TOOK 'EM TO SCHOOL!
FRAK! I wanted to see...
DON'T WORRY! I HAD IT TAPED!
I'M JUST WAITING FOR PEEBOCHU TO RETURN WITH THE FOOTAGE IT FILMED...
PEEBOCHU?!
PEEBOCHU? WASN'T THAT THE BIT-BOMB YOU LOST TO MISSILES AT THE BANQUET?
I fixed it
PEEBOCHU!
WELL, TRY NOT TO FLY INTO A MURDEROUS RAGE IF ANYTHING HAPPENS TO YOUR "PET" LIKE YOU DID LAST TIME...
THE FOLKS AT THAT BANQUET HAD WAYS OF DEALING WITH FLYING BULLETS... THESE FOLKS DON'T!
AS LONG AS PEEBOCHU'S PAINT ISN'T SCRATCHED...
GINA, WE CAN MEET TEACHER AT THE INN...
...and if I recall, YOU'RE the one who went ballistic that time...
"...I'M SURE SHE'LL TELL YOU ALL ABOUT HER MATCH TODAY..."
HMMM...
THEO, IT'S JUST A BRUISE.
NO NEED FOR THAT DOCTOR'S STARE OF YOURS.

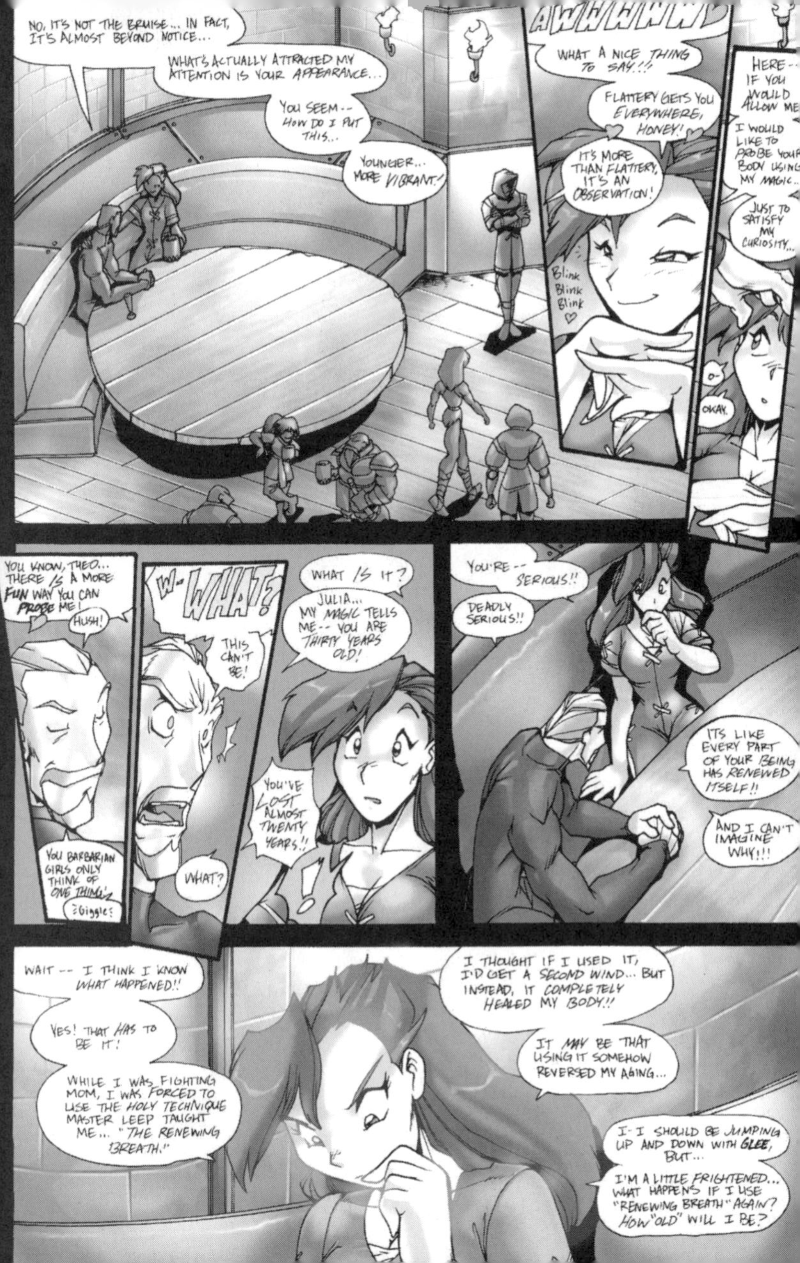
NO, IT'S NOT THE BRUISE... IN FACT, IT'S ALMOST BEYOND NOTICE...
WHAT'S ACTUALLY ATTRACTED MY ATTENTION IS YOUR APPEARANCE...
YOU SEEM-- HOW DO I PUT THIS...
YOUNGER... MORE VIBRANT!
AWWWWWW!
WHAT A NICE THING TO SAY!!!
FLATTERY GETS YOU EVERYWHERE, HONEY!
IT'S MORE THAN FLATTERY, IT'S AN OBSERVATION!
Blink Blink Blink
HERE-- IF YOU WOULD ALLOW ME
I WOULD LIKE TO PROBE YOUR BODY USING MY MAGIC...
JUST TO SATISFY MY CURIOSITY...
OKAY.
YOU KNOW, THEO... THERE IS A MORE FUN WAY YOU CAN PROBE ME!
HUSH!
YOU BARBARIAN GIRLS ONLY THINK OF ONE THING!
Giggle
W-WHAT?
THIS CAN'T BE!
WHAT?
WHAT IS IT?
JULIA... MY MAGIC TELLS ME-- YOU ARE THIRTY YEARS OLD!
YOU'VE LOST ALMOST TWENTY YEARS!!
YOU'RE-- SERIOUS!!
DEADLY SERIOUS!!
ITS LIKE EVERY PART OF YOUR BEING HAS RENEWED ITSELF!!
AND I CAN'T IMAGINE WHY!!!
WAIT -- I THINK I KNOW WHAT HAPPENED!!
YES! THAT HAS TO BE IT!
WHILE I WAS FIGHTING MOM, I WAS FORCED TO USE THE HOLY TECHNIQUE MASTER LEEP TAUGHT ME... "THE RENEWING BREATH."
I THOUGHT IF I USED IT, I'D GET A SECOND WIND... BUT INSTEAD, IT COMPLETELY HEALED MY BODY!!
IT MAY BE THAT USING IT SOMEHOW REVERSED MY AGING...
I-I SHOULD BE JUMPING UP AND DOWN WITH GLEE, BUT...
I'M A LITTLE FRIGHTENED... WHAT HAPPENS IF I USE "RENEWING BREATH" AGAIN? HOW "OLD" WILL I BE?

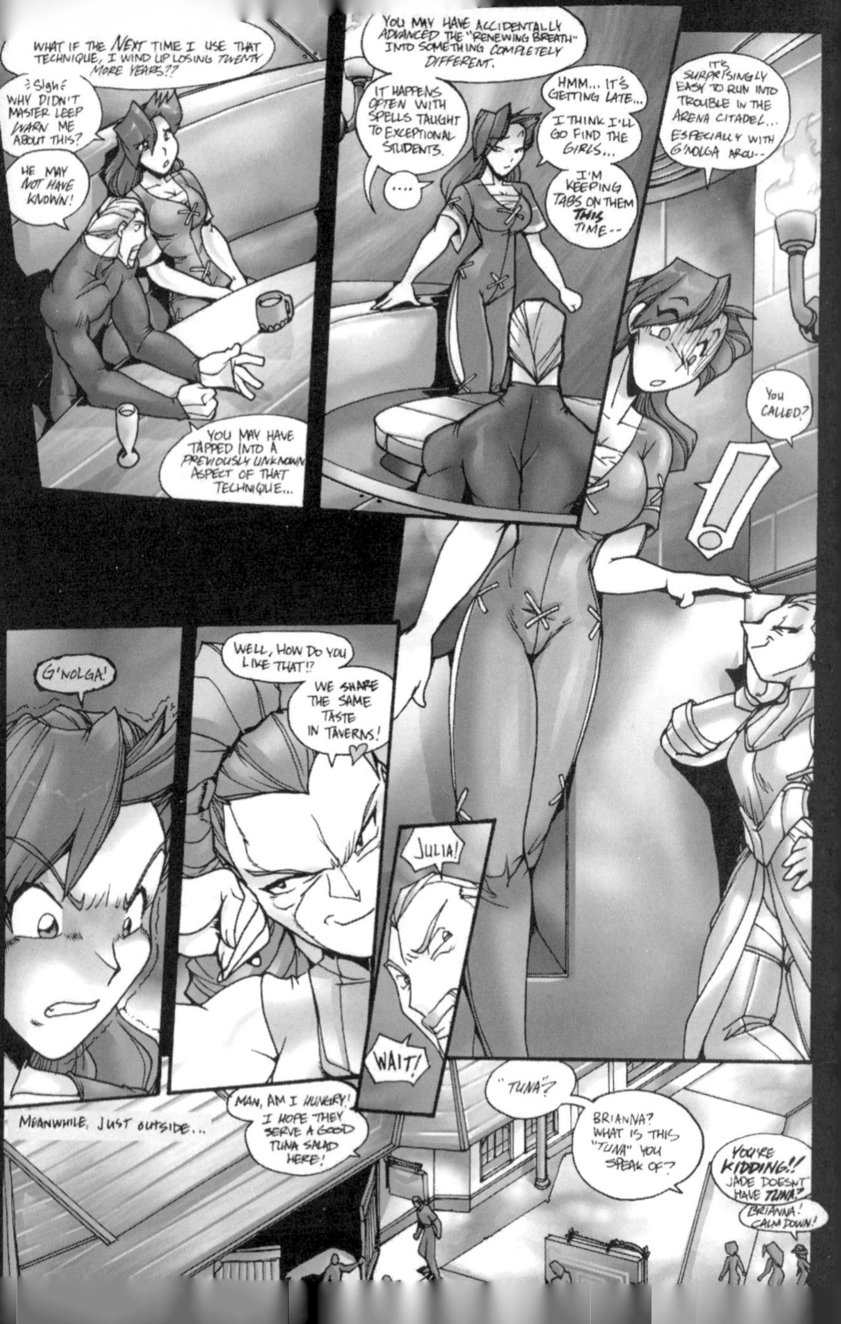

WHAT IF THE NEXT TIME I USE THAT TECHNIQUE, I WIND UP LOSING TWENTY MORE YEARS??
Sigh WHY DIDN'T MASTER LEEP WARN ME ABOUT THIS?
HE MAY NOT HAVE KNOWN!
YOU MAY HAVE TAPPED INTO A PREVIOUSLY UNKNOWN ASPECT OF THAT TECHNIQUE...
YOU MAY HAVE ACCIDENTALLY ADVANCED THE "RENEWING BREATH" INTO SOMETHING COMPLETELY DIFFERENT.
IT HAPPENS OFTEN WITH SPELLS TAUGHT TO EXCEPTIONAL STUDENTS.
....
HMM... IT'S GETTING LATE...
I THINK I'LL GO FIND THE GIRLS...
I'M KEEPING TABS ON THEM THIS TIME--
IT'S SURPRISINGLY EASY TO RUN INTO TROUBLE IN THE ARENA CITADEL...
ESPECIALLY WITH G'NOLGA AROU--
YOU CALLED?
!
G'NOLGA!
WELL, HOW DO YOU LIKE THAT!?
WE SHARE THE SAME TASTE IN TAVERNS!
JULIA!
WAIT!
MEANWHILE, JUST OUTSIDE...
MAN, AM I HUNGRY! I HOPE THEY SERVE A GOOD TUNA SALAD HERE!
"TUNA"?
BRIANNA? WHAT IS THIS "TUNA" YOU SPEAK OF?
YOU'RE KIDDING!! JADE DOESN'T HAVE TUNA?
BRIANNA! CALM DOWN!

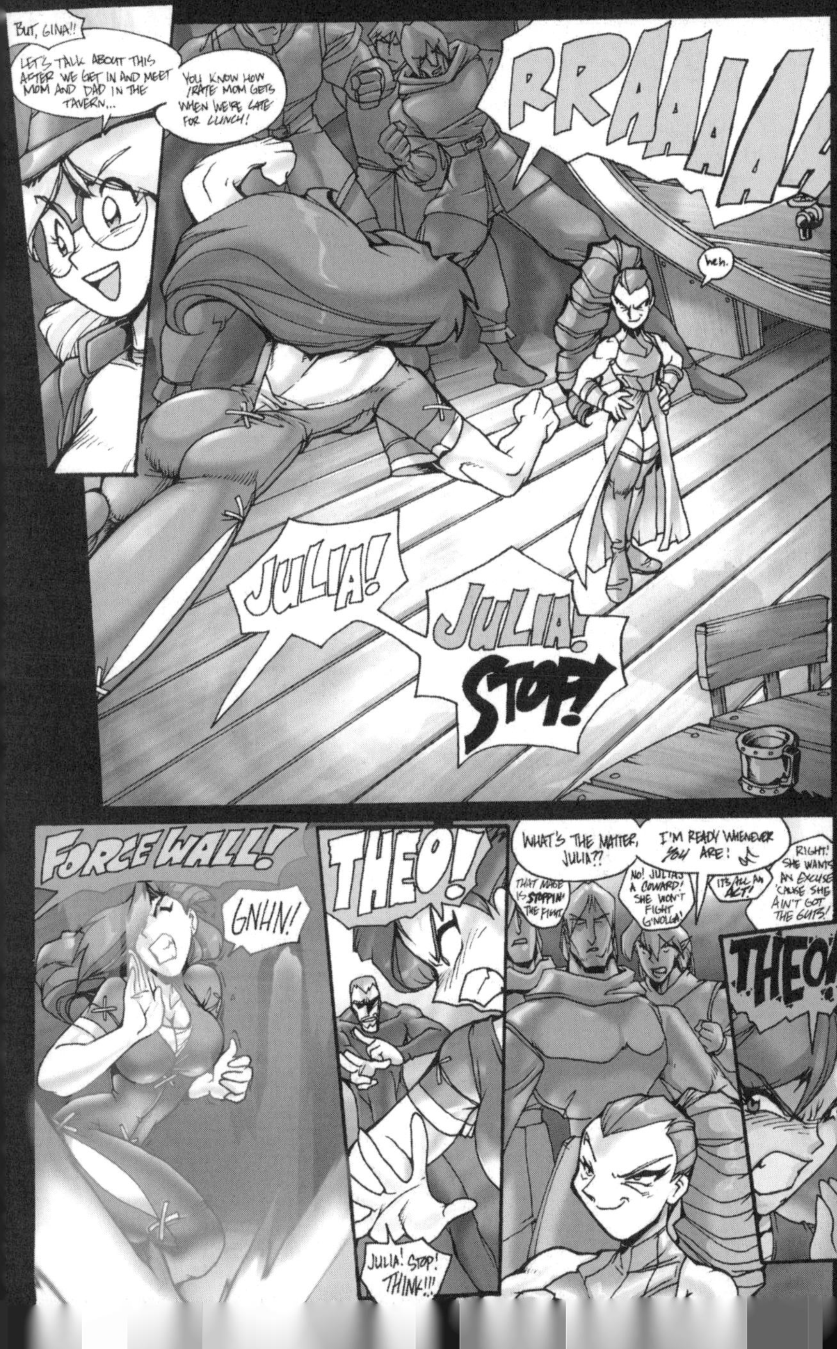
BUT, GINA!!
LET'S TALK ABOUT THIS AFTER WE GET IN AND MEET MOM AND DAD IN THE TAVERN...
YOU KNOW HOW IRATE MOM GETS WHEN WE'RE LATE FOR LUNCH!
RRAAAAAA
heh.
JULIA!
JULIA! STOP!
FORCE WALL!
GNHN!
THEO!
JULIA! STOP! THINK!!!
WHAT'S THE MATTER, JULIA??
I'M READY WHENEVER YOU ARE!
THAT MAGE IS STOPPIN' THE FIGHT.
NO! JULIA'S A COWARD! SHE WON'T FIGHT G'NOLLA!
IT'S ALL AN ACT!
RIGHT! SHE WANTS AN EXCUSE 'CAUSE SHE AIN'T GOT THE GUTS!
THEO!

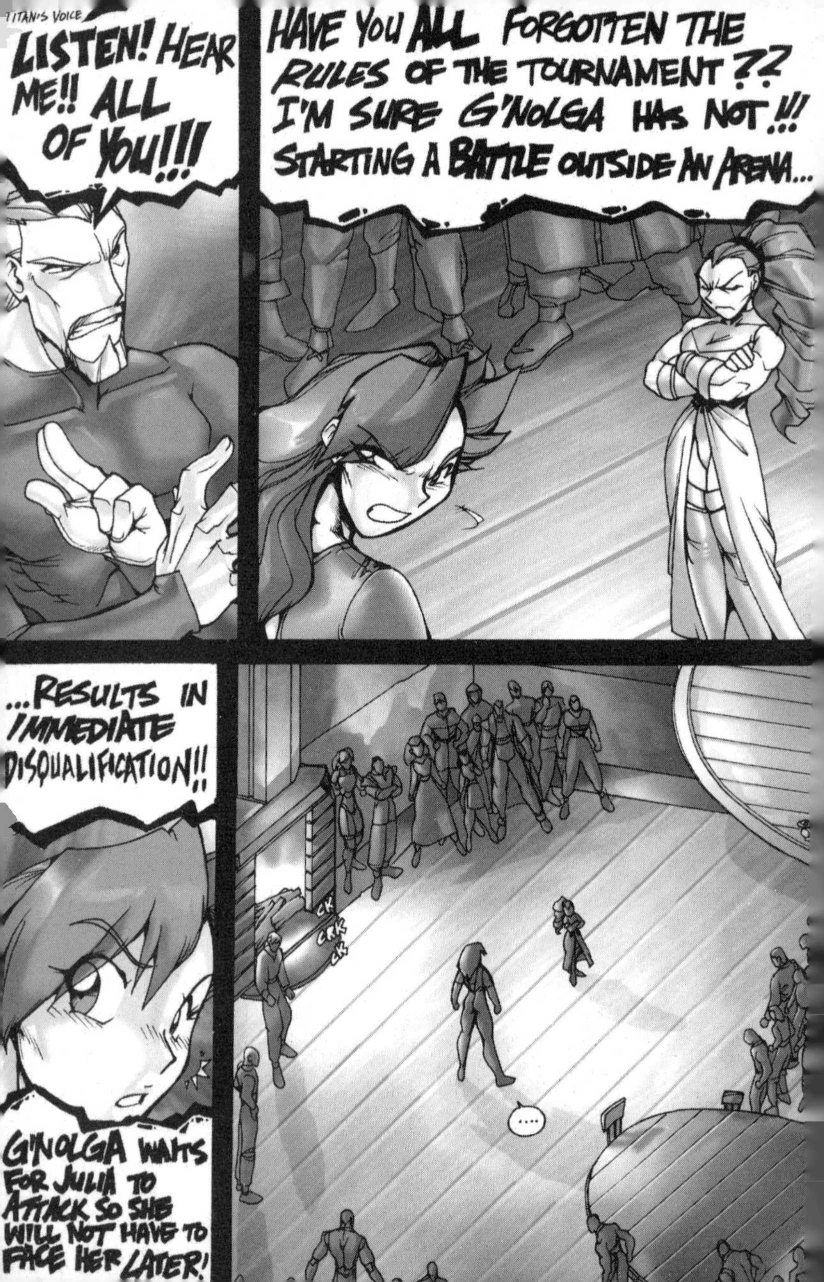
TITAN'S VOICE
LISTEN! HEAR ME!! ALL OF YOU!!!
HAVE YOU ALL FORGOTTEN THE RULES OF THE TOURNAMENT ?? I'M SURE G'NOLGA HAS NOT!!! STARTING A BATTLE OUTSIDE AN ARENA...
...RESULTS IN IMMEDIATE DISQUALIFICATION!!
G'NOLGA WAITS FOR JULIA TO ATTACK SO SHE WILL NOT HAVE TO FACE HER LATER!
CK CRK CK
.....

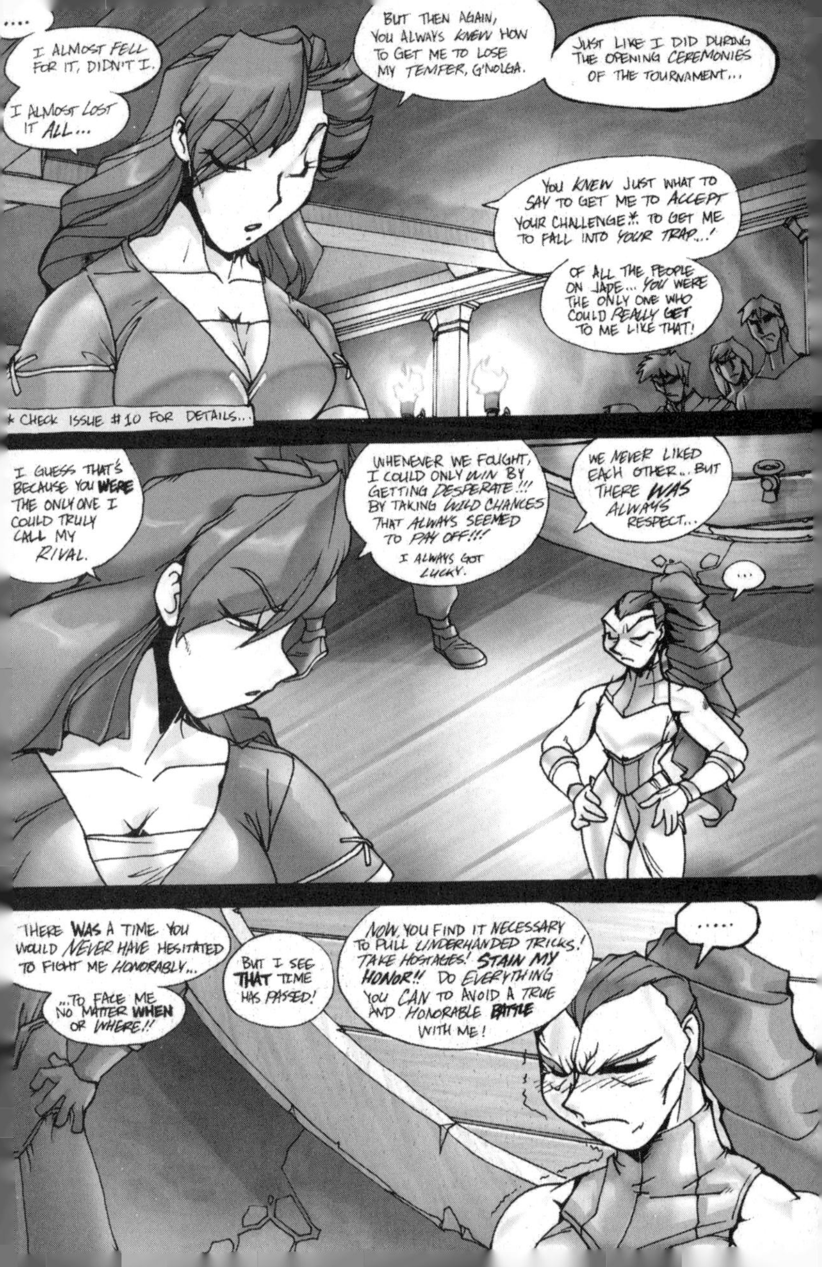
....
I ALMOST FELL FOR IT, DIDN'T I.
I ALMOST LOST IT ALL...
BUT THEN AGAIN, YOU ALWAYS KNEW HOW TO GET ME TO LOSE MY TEMPER, G'NOLGA.
JUST LIKE I DID DURING THE OPENING CEREMONIES OF THE TOURNAMENT...
YOU KNEW JUST WHAT TO SAY TO GET ME TO ACCEPT YOUR CHALLENGE!* TO GET ME TO FALL INTO YOUR TRAP...!
OF ALL THE PEOPLE ON JADE... YOU WERE THE ONLY ONE WHO COULD REALLY GET TO ME LIKE THAT!
* CHECK ISSUE #10 FOR DETAILS...
I GUESS THAT'S BECAUSE YOU WERE THE ONLY ONE I COULD TRULY CALL MY RIVAL.
WHENEVER WE FOUGHT, I COULD ONLY WIN BY GETTING DESPERATE!!! BY TAKING WILD CHANCES THAT ALWAYS SEEMED TO PAY OFF!!!
I ALWAYS GOT LUCKY.
WE NEVER LIKED EACH OTHER... BUT THERE WAS ALWAYS RESPECT...
...
THERE WAS A TIME YOU WOULD NEVER HAVE HESITATED TO FIGHT ME HONORABLY...
...TO FACE ME NO MATTER WHEN OR WHERE!!
BUT I SEE THAT TIME HAS PASSED!
NOW, YOU FIND IT NECESSARY TO PULL UNDERHANDED TRICKS! TAKE HOSTAGES! STAIN MY HONOR!! DO EVERYTHING YOU CAN TO AVOID A TRUE AND HONORABLE BATTLE WITH ME!
.....

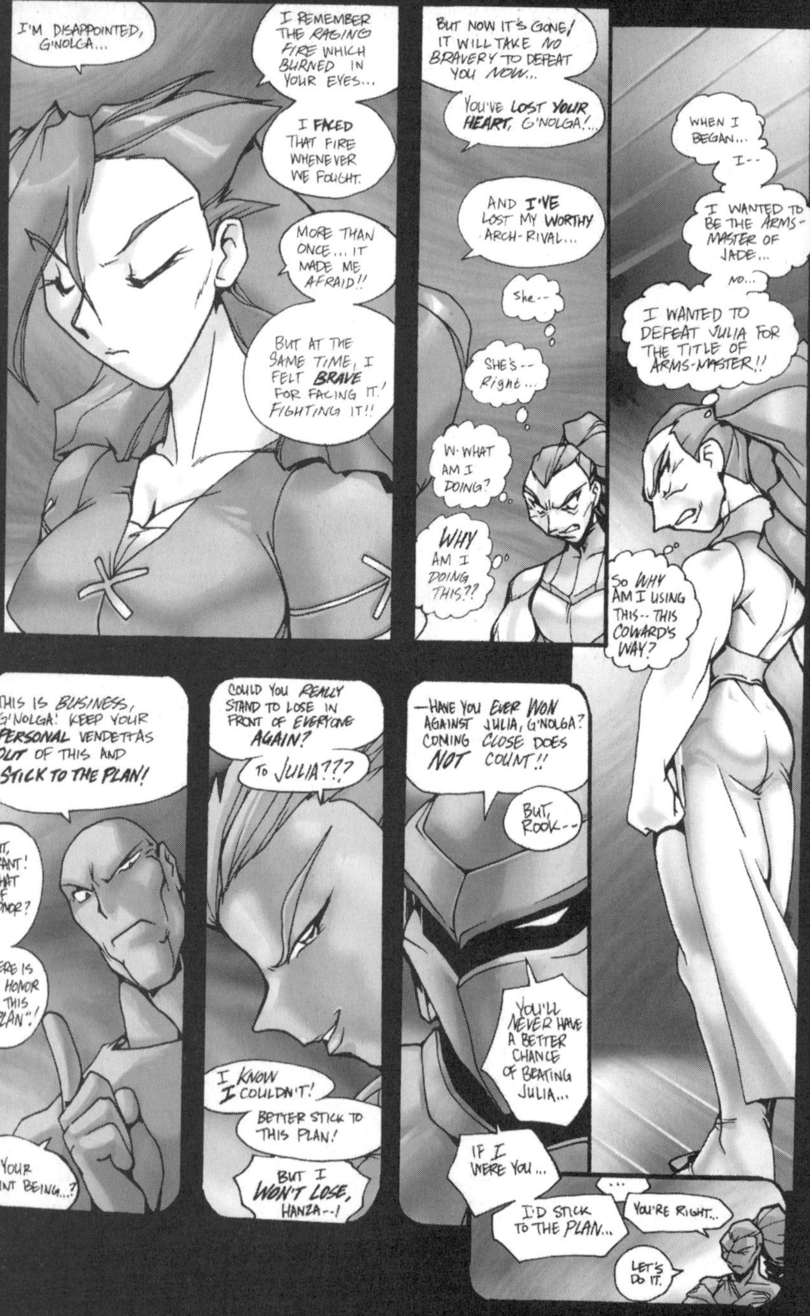
I'M DISAPPOINTED, G'NOLGA...
I REMEMBER THE RAGING FIRE WHICH BURNED IN YOUR EYES...
I FACED THAT FIRE WHENEVER WE FOUGHT.
MORE THAN ONCE... IT MADE ME AFRAID!!
BUT AT THE SAME TIME, I FELT BRAVE FOR FACING IT! FIGHTING IT!!
BUT NOW IT'S GONE! IT WILL TAKE NO BRAVERY TO DEFEAT YOU NOW...
YOU'VE LOST YOUR HEART, G'NOLGA!...
AND I'VE LOST MY WORTHY ARCH-RIVAL...
She--
SHE'S-- Right...
W-WHAT AM I DOING?
WHY AM I DOING THIS??
WHEN I BEGAN...
I--
I WANTED TO BE THE ARMS-MASTER OF JADE...
NO...
I WANTED TO DEFEAT JULIA FOR THE TITLE OF ARMS-MASTER!!
So WHY AM I USING THIS-- THIS COWARD'S WAY?
THIS IS BUSINESS, G'NOLGA! KEEP YOUR PERSONAL VENDETTAS OUT OF THIS AND STICK TO THE PLAN!
BUT, TIRANT! WHAT OF HONOR?
THERE IS NO HONOR IN THIS "PLAN"!
YOUR POINT BEING...?
COULD YOU REALLY STAND TO LOSE IN FRONT OF EVERYONE AGAIN?
TO JULIA???
I KNOW I COULDN'T!
BETTER STICK TO THIS PLAN!
BUT I WON'T LOSE, HANZA--!
—HAVE YOU EVER WON AGAINST JULIA, G'NOLGA? COMING CLOSE DOES NOT COUNT!!
BUT, ROOK--
YOU'LL NEVER HAVE A BETTER CHANCE OF BEATING JULIA...
IF I WERE YOU...
I'D STICK TO THE PLAN...
...
YOU'RE RIGHT...
LET'S DO IT.

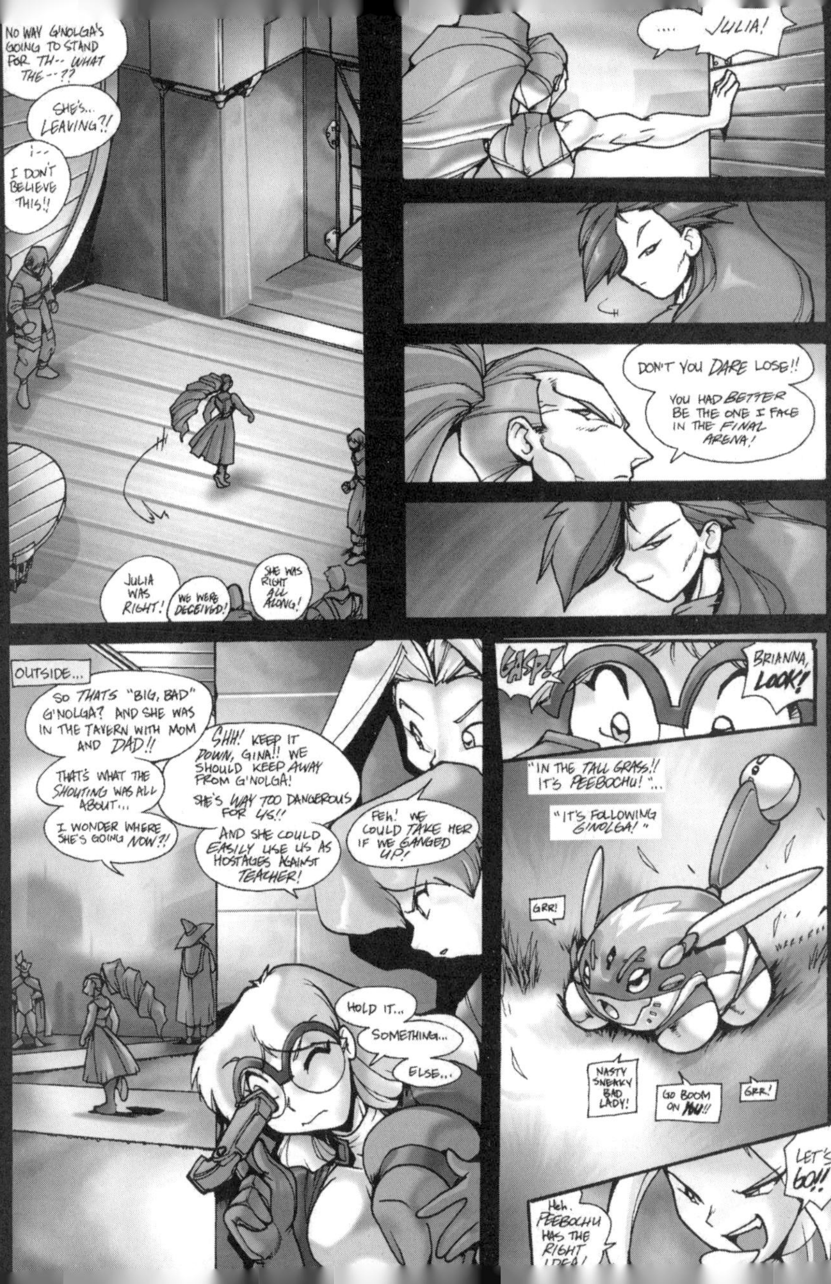
NO WAY G'NOLGA'S GOING TO STAND FOR TH-- WHAT THE--??
SHE'S.. LEAVING?!
I-- I DON'T BELIEVE THIS!!
JULIA WAS RIGHT!
WE WERE DECEIVED!
SHE WAS RIGHT ALL ALONG!
.... JULIA!
DON'T YOU DARE LOSE!!
YOU HAD BETTER BE THE ONE I FACE IN THE FINAL ARENA!
OUTSIDE...
SO THAT'S "BIG, BAD" G'NOLGA? AND SHE WAS IN THE TAVERN WITH MOM AND DAD!!
THAT'S WHAT THE SHOUTING WAS ALL ABOUT...
I WONDER WHERE SHE'S GOING NOW?!
SHH! KEEP IT DOWN, GINA!! WE SHOULD KEEP AWAY FROM G'NOLGA!
SHE'S WAY TOO DANGEROUS FOR US!!
AND SHE COULD EASILY USE US AS HOSTAGES AGAINST TEACHER!
FEH! WE COULD TAKE HER IF WE GANGED UP!
HOLD IT...
SOMETHING...
ELSE...
GASP!
BRIANNA, LOOK!
"IN THE TALL GRASS!! IT'S PEEBOCHU!"...
"IT'S FOLLOWING G'NOLGA!"
GRR!
NASTY SNEAKY BAD LADY!
GO BOOM ON YOU!!
GRR!
LET'S GO!!
Heh.. PEEBOCHU HAS THE RIGHT

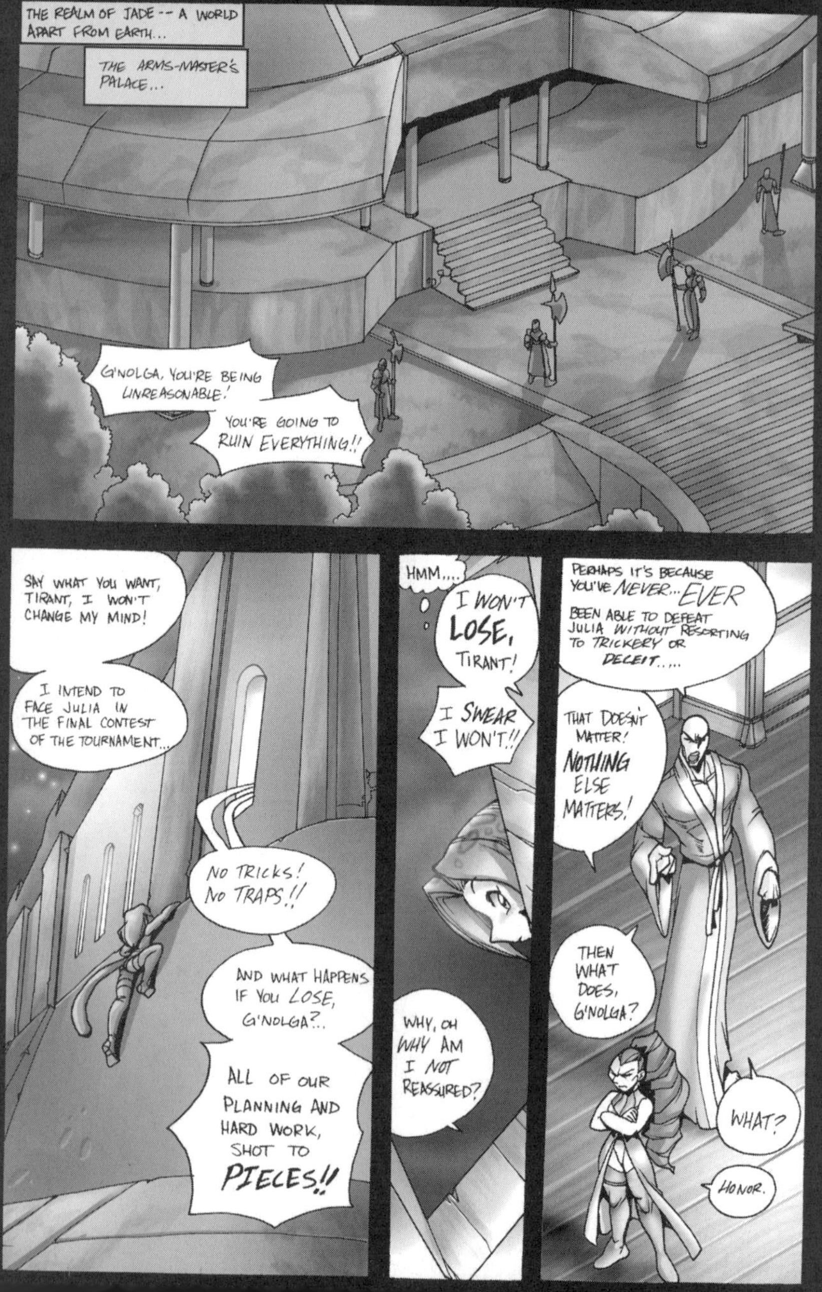
THE REALM OF JADE -- A WORLD APART FROM EARTH...
THE ARMS-MASTER'S PALACE...
G'NOLGA, YOU'RE BEING UNREASONABLE!
YOU'RE GOING TO RUIN EVERYTHING!!
SAY WHAT YOU WANT, TIRANT, I WON'T CHANGE MY MIND!
I INTEND TO FACE JULIA IN THE FINAL CONTEST OF THE TOURNAMENT...
NO TRICKS! NO TRAPS!!
AND WHAT HAPPENS IF YOU LOSE, G'NOLGA?..
ALL OF OUR PLANNING AND HARD WORK, SHOT TO PIECES!!
HMM....
I WON'T LOSE, TIRANT!
I SWEAR I WON'T!!
WHY, OH WHY AM I NOT REASSURED?
PERHAPS IT'S BECAUSE YOU'VE NEVER... EVER BEEN ABLE TO DEFEAT JULIA WITHOUT RESORTING TO TRICKERY OR DECEIT.....
THAT DOESN'T MATTER! NOTHING ELSE MATTERS!
THEN WHAT DOES, G'NOLGA?
WHAT?
HONOR.

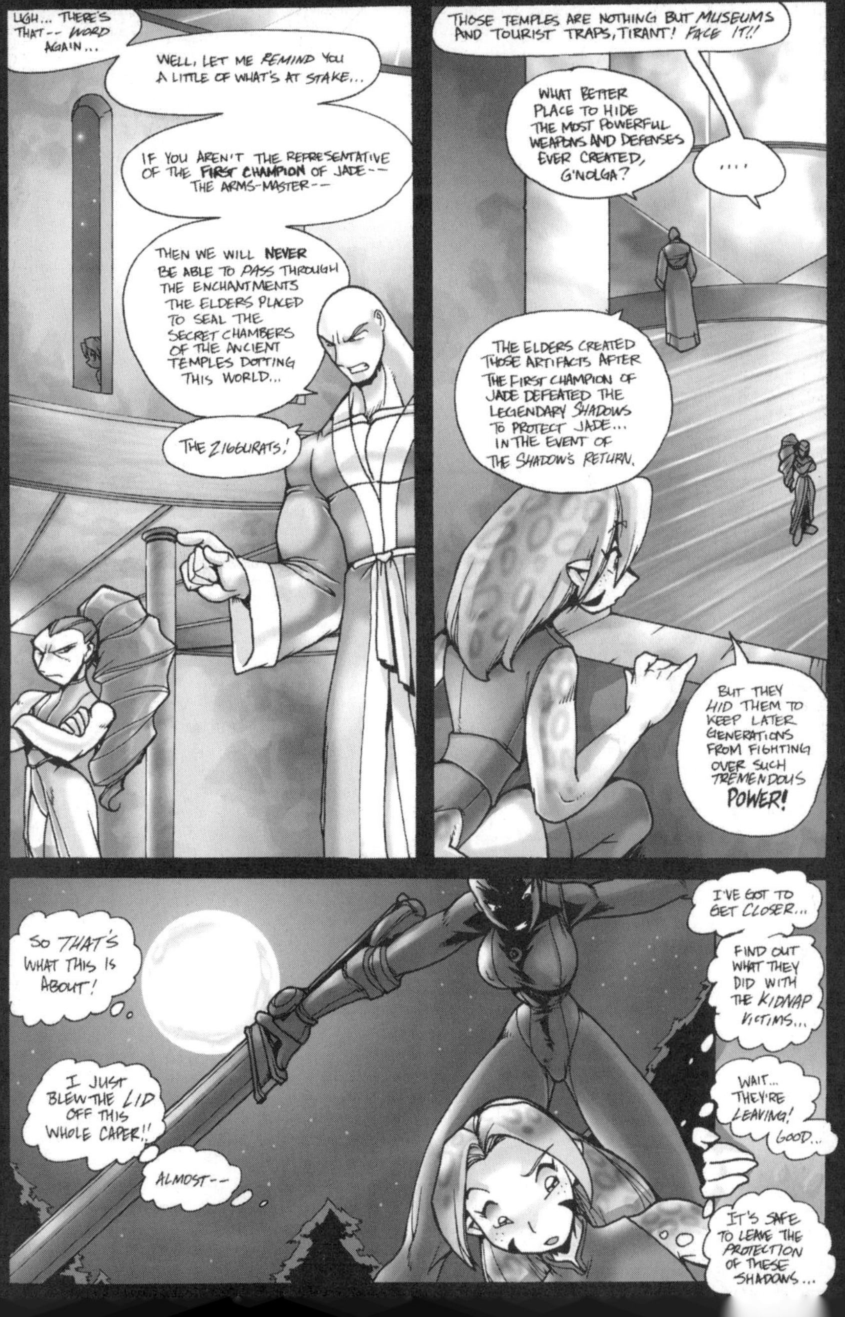
UGH... THERE'S THAT-- WORD AGAIN...
WELL, LET ME REMIND YOU A LITTLE OF WHAT'S AT STAKE...
IF YOU AREN'T THE REPRESENTATIVE OF THE FIRST CHAMPION OF JADE-- THE ARMS-MASTER--
THEN WE WILL NEVER BE ABLE TO PASS THROUGH THE ENCHANTMENTS THE ELDERS PLACED TO SEAL THE SECRET CHAMBERS OF THE ANCIENT TEMPLES DOTTING THIS WORLD...
THE ZIGGURATS!
THOSE TEMPLES ARE NOTHING BUT MUSEUMS AND TOURIST TRAPS, TIRANT! FACE IT!!
WHAT BETTER PLACE TO HIDE THE MOST POWERFUL WEAPONS AND DEFENSES EVER CREATED, G'NOLGA?
....
THE ELDERS CREATED THOSE ARTIFACTS AFTER THE FIRST CHAMPION OF JADE DEFEATED THE LEGENDARY SHADOWS TO PROTECT JADE... IN THE EVENT OF THE SHADOW'S RETURN.
BUT THEY HID THEM TO KEEP LATER GENERATIONS FROM FIGHTING OVER SUCH TREMENDOUS POWER!
SO THAT'S WHAT THIS IS ABOUT!
I JUST BLEW THE LID OFF THIS WHOLE CAPER!!
ALMOST--
I'VE GOT TO GET CLOSER...
FIND OUT WHAT THEY DID WITH THE KIDNAP VICTIMS...
WAIT... THEY'RE LEAVING! GOOD...
IT'S SAFE TO LEAVE THE PROTECTION OF THESE SHADOWS...

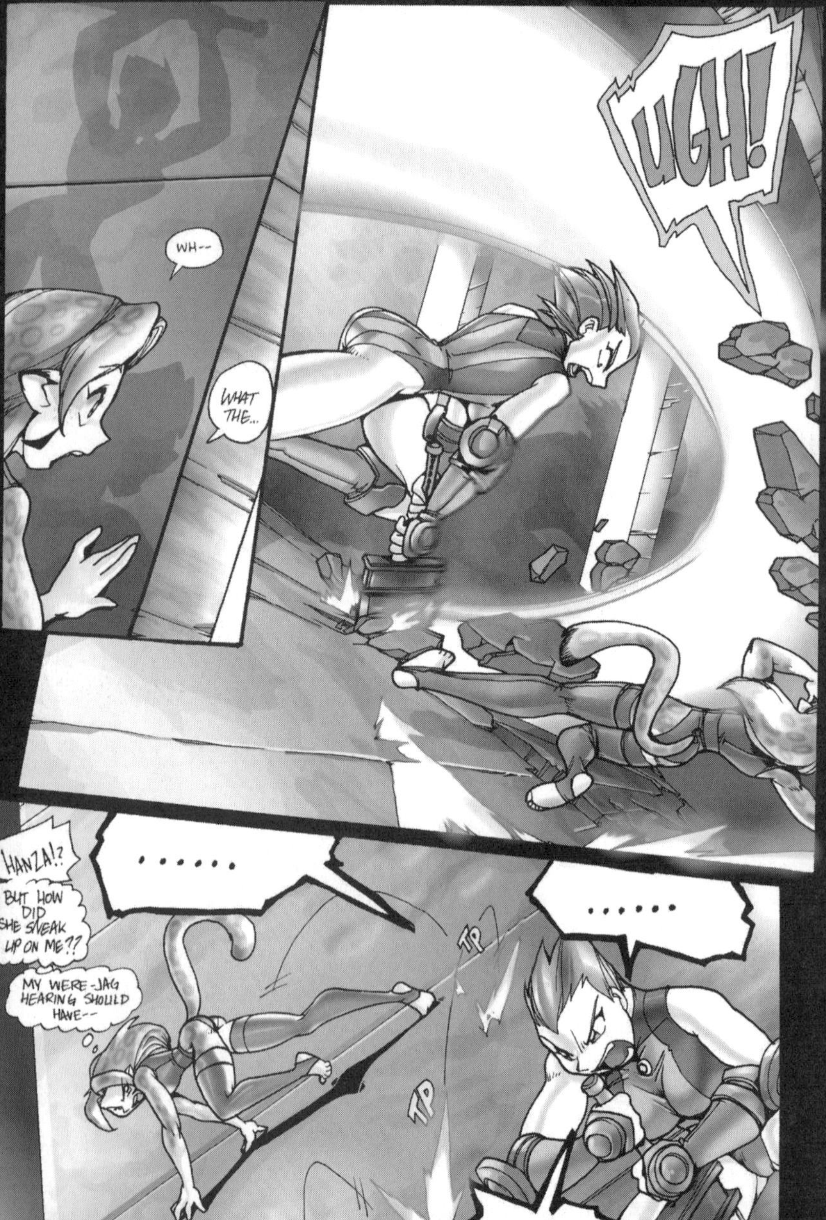
WH--
WHAT THE...
UGH!
HANZA!?
BUT HOW DID SHE SNEAK UP ON ME??
MY WERE-JAG HEARING SHOULD HAVE--
......
TP
TP
......
......

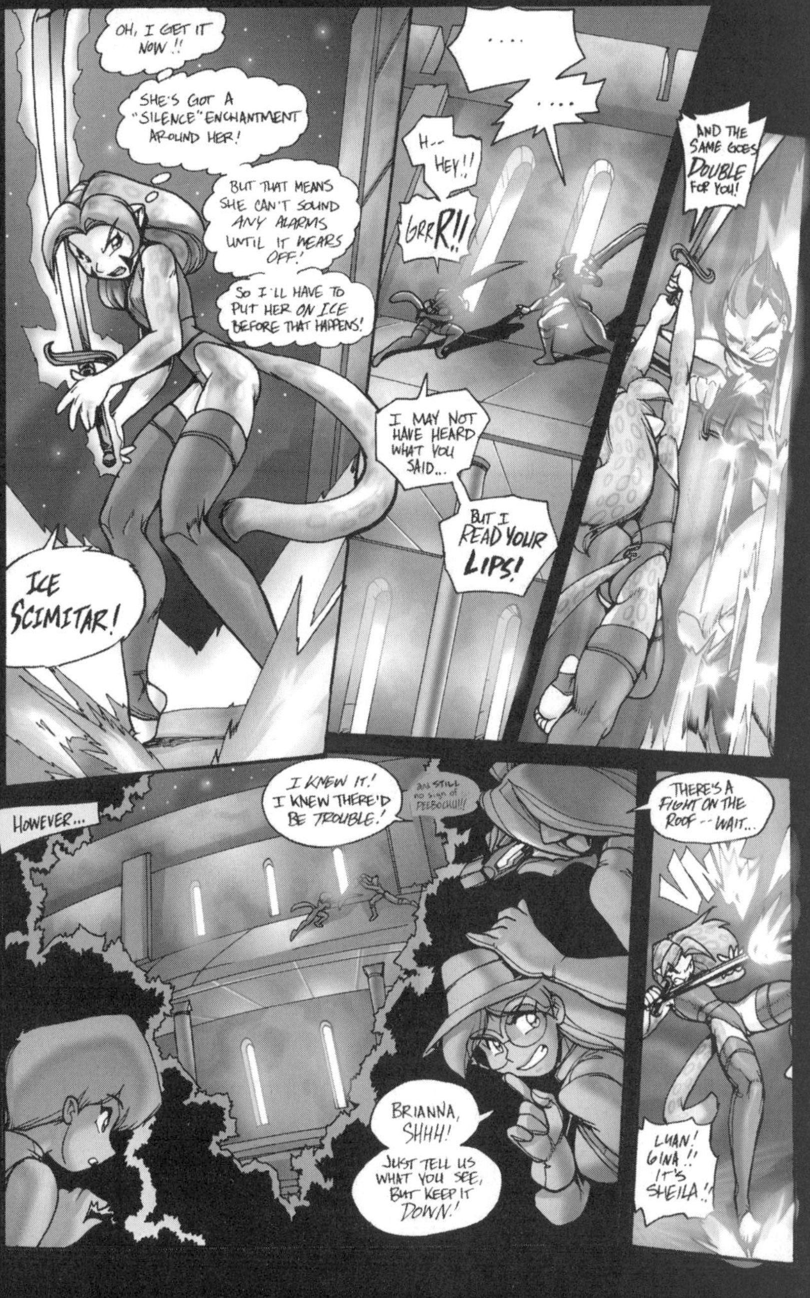

OH, I GET IT NOW!!
SHE'S GOT A "SILENCE" ENCHANTMENT AROUND HER!
BUT THAT MEANS SHE CAN'T SOUND ANY ALARMS UNTIL IT WEARS OFF!
SO I'LL HAVE TO PUT HER ON ICE BEFORE THAT HAPPENS!
ICE SCIMITAR!
....
....
H-- HEY!!
GRRR!!
I MAY NOT HAVE HEARD WHAT YOU SAID...
BUT I READ YOUR LIPS!
AND THE SAME GOES DOUBLE FOR YOU!
HOWEVER...
I KNEW IT! I KNEW THERE'D BE TROUBLE!
BRIANNA, SHHH!
JUST TELL US WHAT YOU SEE, BUT KEEP IT DOWN!
THERE'S A FIGHT ON THE ROOF -- WAIT...
LUAN! GINA!! IT'S SHEILA!!

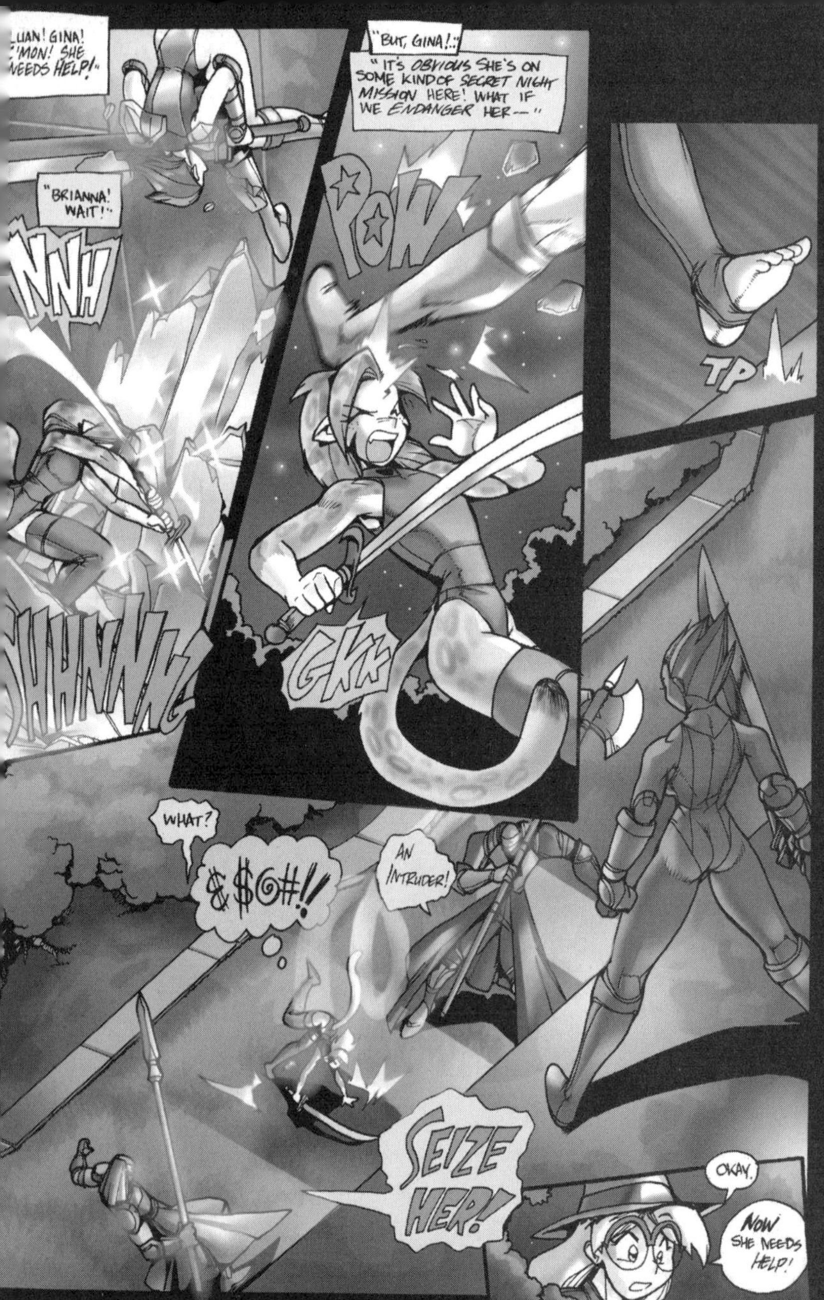
LIAN! GINA! C'MON! SHE NEEDS HELP!
"BRIANNA! WAIT!"
NNH
SHHNNNNG
"BUT, GINA!"
"IT'S OBVIOUS SHE'S ON SOME KIND OF SECRET NIGHT MISSION HERE! WHAT IF WE ENDANGER HER--"
POW
GKK
TP
WHAT?
&$@#!!
AN INTRUDER!
SEIZE HER!
OKAY.
NOW SHE NEEDS HELP!

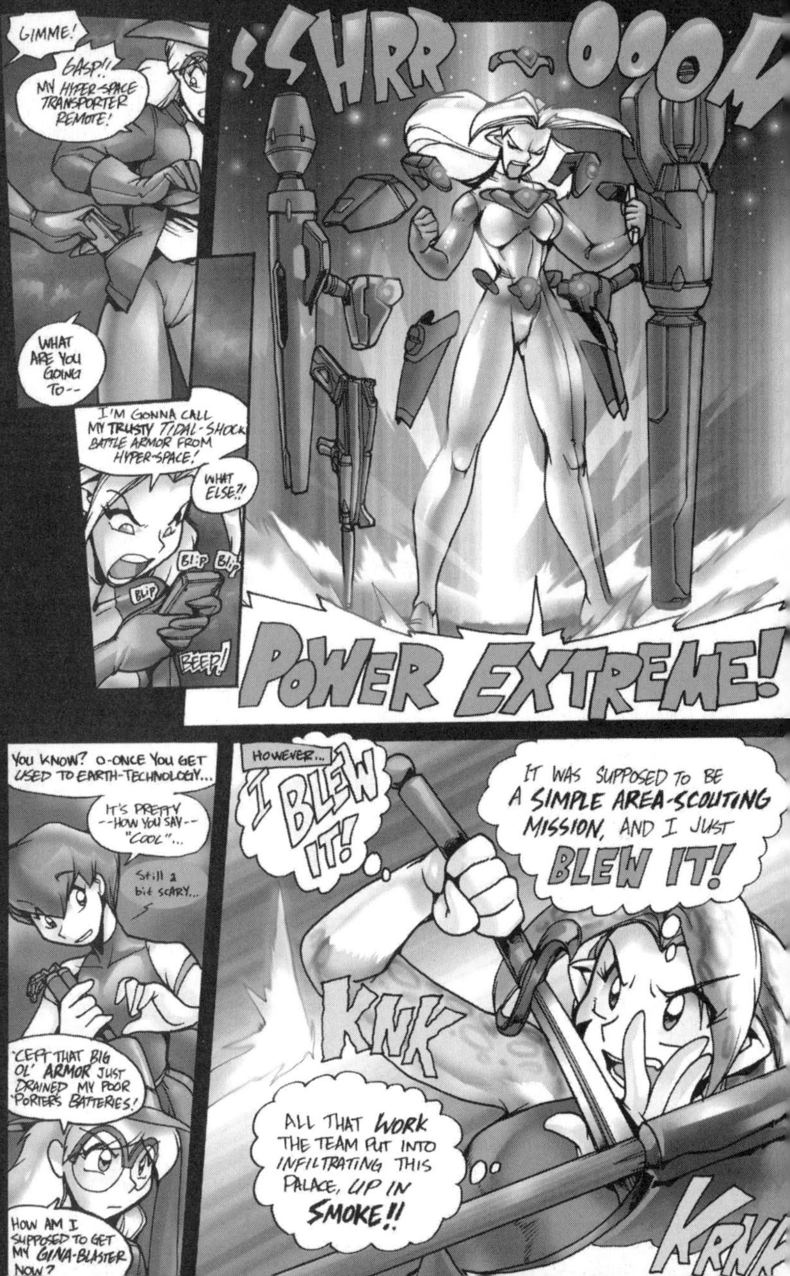
GIMME!
GASP!! .. MY HYPER-SPACE TRANSPORTER REMOTE!
WHAT ARE YOU GOING TO--
I'M GONNA CALL MY TRUSTY TIDAL-SHOCK BATTLE ARMOR FROM HYPER-SPACE!
WHAT ELSE?!
BLIP BLIP
BLIP
BEEP!
SHRR-OOOM
POWER EXTREME!
YOU KNOW? O-ONCE YOU GET USED TO EARTH-TECHNOLOGY...
IT'S PRETTY --HOW YOU SAY-- "COOL"...
Still a bit scary...
'CEPT THAT BIG OL' ARMOR JUST DRAINED MY POOR 'PORTERS BATTERIES!
HOW AM I SUPPOSED TO GET MY GINA-BLASTER NOW?
HOWEVER...
I BLEW IT!
IT WAS SUPPOSED TO BE A SIMPLE AREA-SCOUTING MISSION, AND I JUST BLEW IT!
KNK
ALL THAT WORK THE TEAM PUT INTO INFILTRATING THIS PALACE, UP IN SMOKE!!

KAAKSHH!
YYYATZEE!
AND THOSE WERE JUST THE WARNING SHOTS!
SCAN INDICATES NO LIFE FORMS WERE INSIDE ARMORED TARGETS...
Hee Hee...! NEXT TIME, I'LL CHECK BEFORE I SHOOT!
BETTER KEEP YOUR HEAD DOWN, SHEILA!!
WOULDN'T WANT ANY OF THESE TITANIUM-TIPPED, HIGH-EXPLOSIVE LIL' WARHEADS TO GET YOU TOO!
B.
B--
BRIANNA?!!?
WHAT ARE YOU DOING HE--

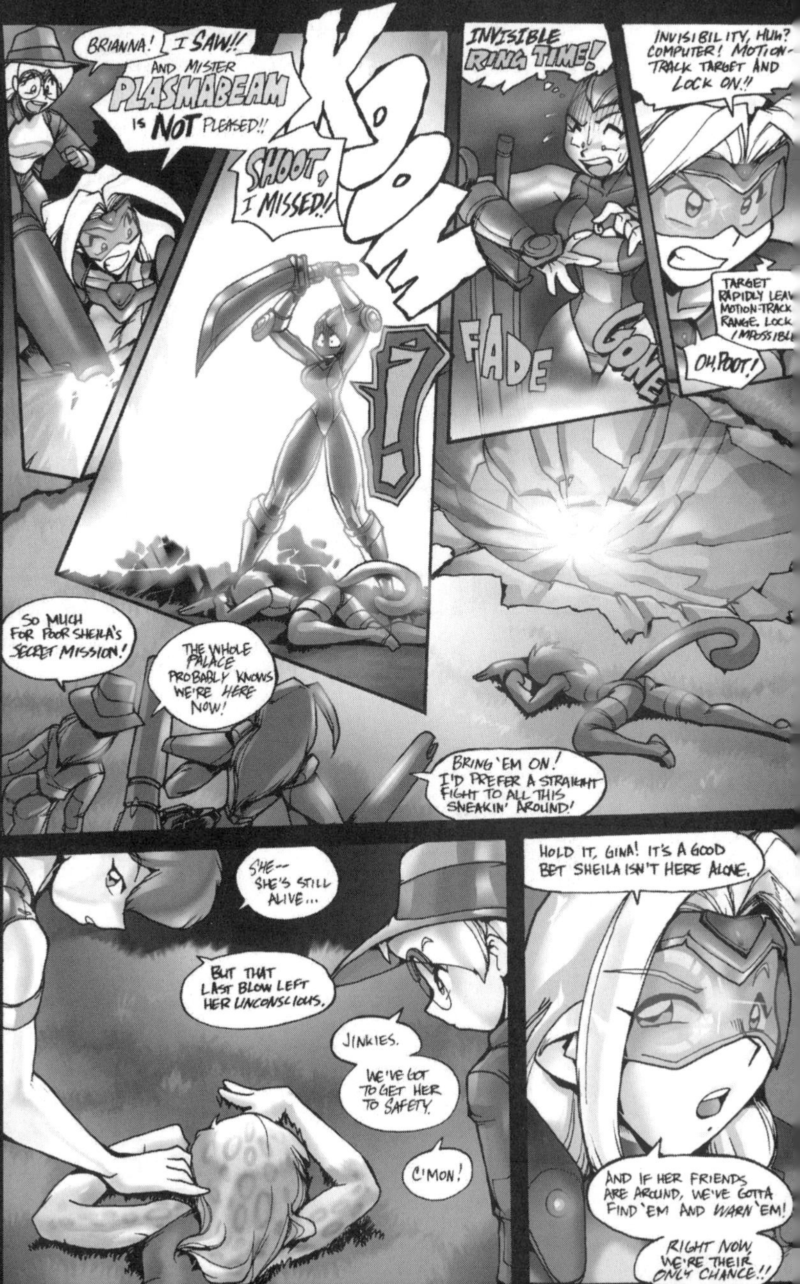
BRIANNA! I SAW!!
AND MISTER PLASMABEAM IS NOT PLEASED!!
XOOM
SHOOT, I MISSED!!
?!
INVISIBLE RING TIME!
FADE
GONE
INVISIBILITY, HUH? COMPUTER! MOTION-TRACK TARGET AND LOCK ON!!
TARGET RAPIDLY LEAV MOTION-TRACK RANGE. LOCK IMPOSSIBL
OH, POOT!
SO MUCH FOR POOR SHEILA'S SECRET MISSION!
THE WHOLE PALACE PROBABLY KNOWS WE'RE HERE NOW!
BRING 'EM ON! I'D PREFER A STRAIGHT FIGHT TO ALL THIS SNEAKIN' AROUND!
SHE-- SHE'S STILL ALIVE...
BUT THAT LAST BLOW LEFT HER UNCONSCIOUS.
JINKIES.
WE'VE GOT TO GET HER TO SAFETY.
C'MON!
HOLD IT, GINA! IT'S A GOOD BET SHEILA ISN'T HERE ALONE.
AND IF HER FRIENDS ARE AROUND, WE'VE GOTTA FIND 'EM AND WARN 'EM!
RIGHT NOW, WE'RE THEIR ONLY CHANCE!!

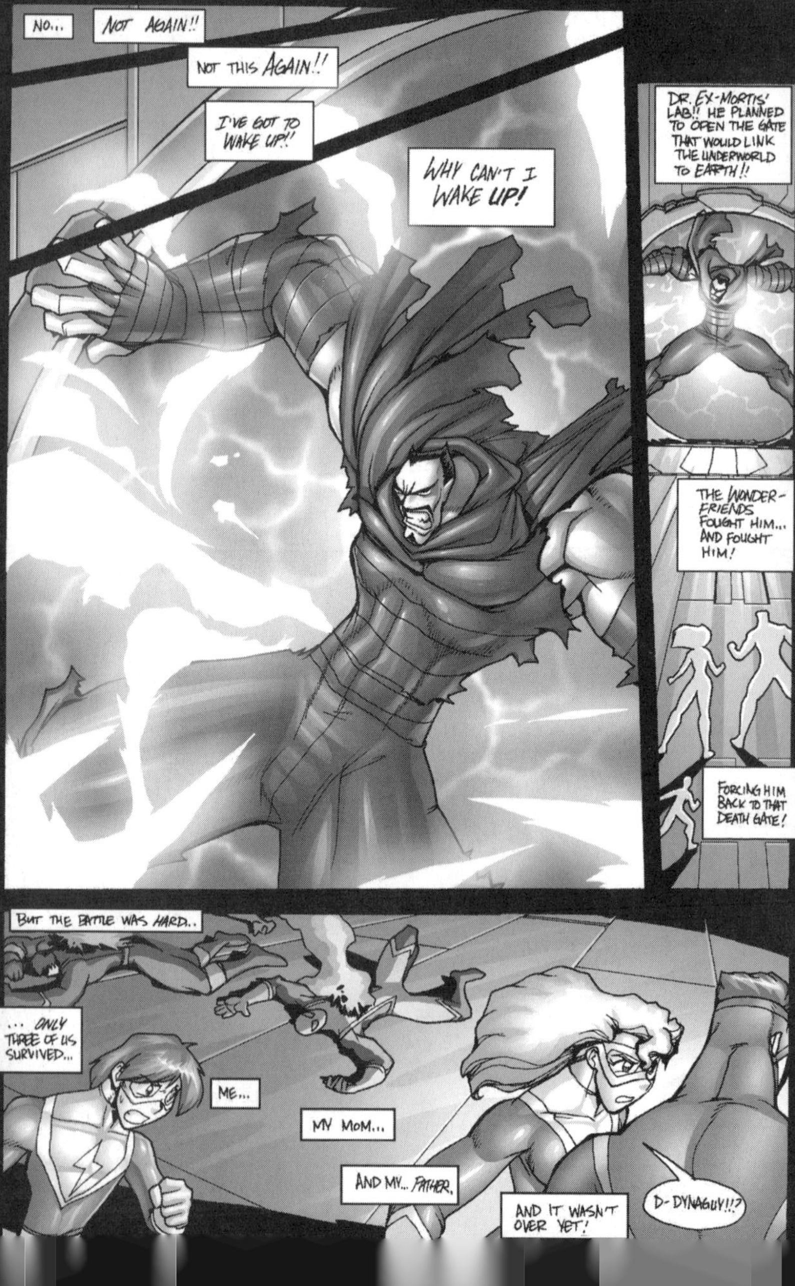
NO...
NOT AGAIN!!
NOT THIS AGAIN!!
I'VE GOT TO WAKE UP!!
WHY CAN'T I WAKE UP!
DR. EX-MORTIS' LAB!! HE PLANNED TO OPEN THE GATE THAT WOULD LINK THE UNDERWORLD TO EARTH!!
THE WONDER-FRIENDS FOUGHT HIM... AND FOUGHT HIM!
FORCING HIM BACK TO THAT DEATH GATE!
BUT THE BATTLE WAS HARD..
... ONLY THREE OF US SURVIVED...
ME...
MY MOM...
AND MY... FATHER.
AND IT WASN'T OVER YET!
D-DYNAGUY!!?

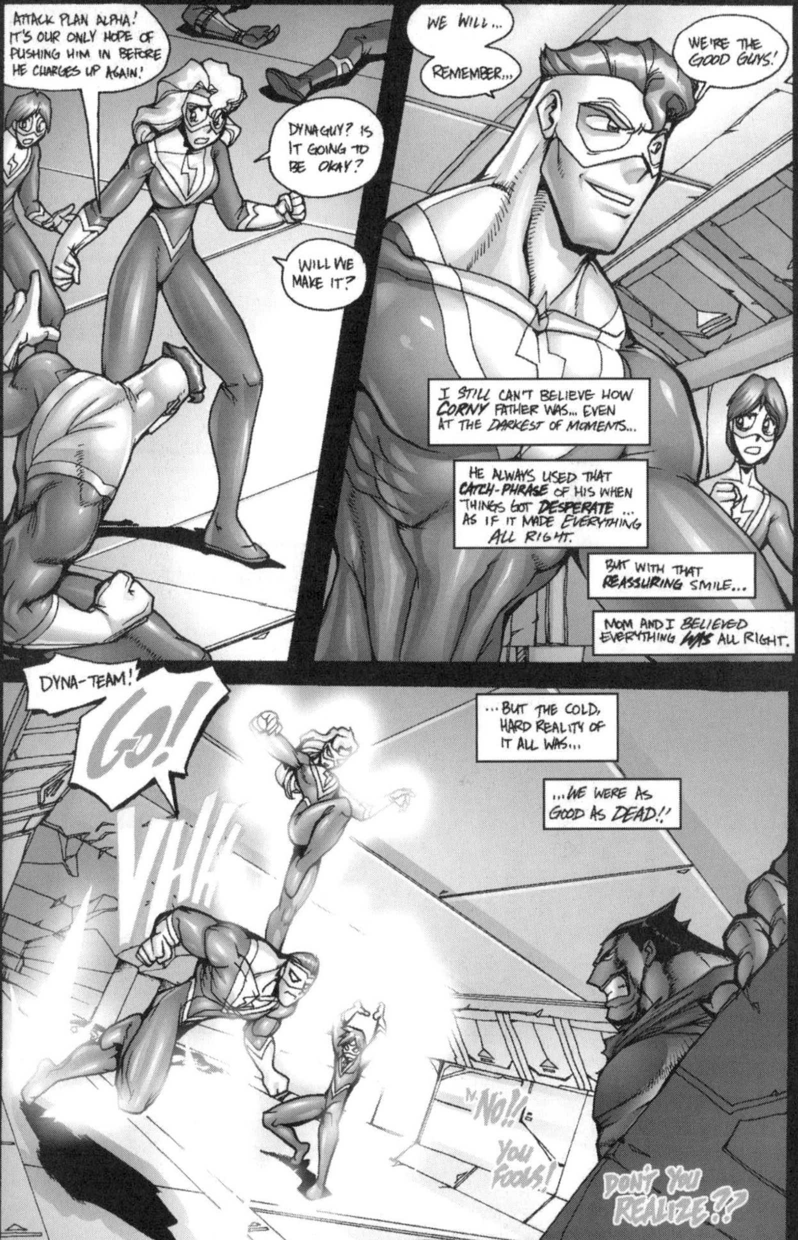
ATTACK PLAN ALPHA! IT'S OUR ONLY HOPE OF PUSHING HIM IN BEFORE HE CHARGES UP AGAIN!
DYNAGUY? IS IT GOING TO BE OKAY?
WILL WE MAKE IT?
WE WILL...
REMEMBER...
WE'RE THE GOOD GUYS!
I STILL CAN'T BELIEVE HOW CORNY FATHER WAS... EVEN AT THE DARKEST OF MOMENTS...
HE ALWAYS USED THAT CATCH-PHRASE OF HIS WHEN THINGS GOT DESPERATE ... AS IF IT MADE EVERYTHING ALL RIGHT.
BUT WITH THAT REASSURING SMILE...
MOM AND I BELIEVED EVERYTHING WAS ALL RIGHT.
DYNA-TEAM!
GO!
...BUT THE COLD, HARD REALITY OF IT ALL WAS...
...WE WERE AS GOOD AS DEAD!!
VHA
NO!!
YOU FOOLS!
DON'T YOU REALIZE?!?

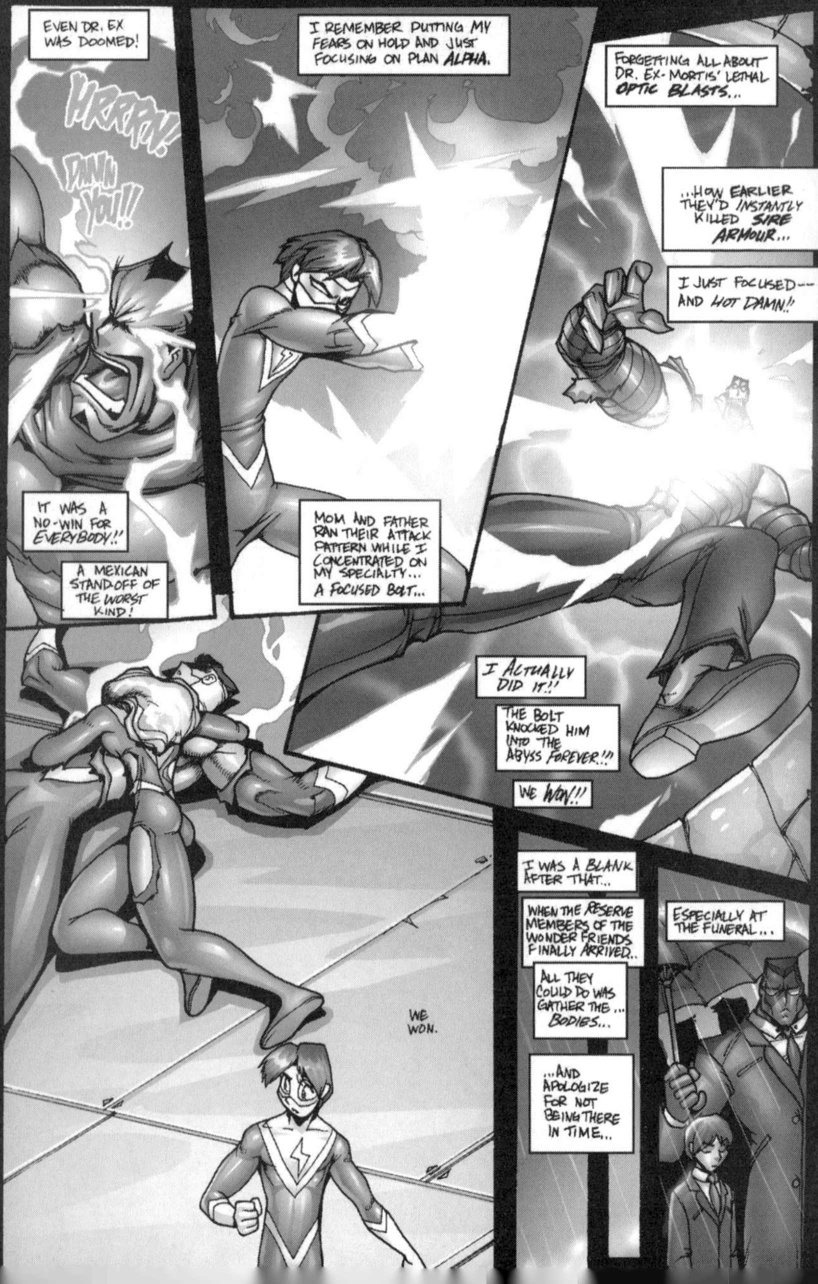
EVEN DR. EX WAS DOOMED!
HRRRN!
DAMN YOU!!
IT WAS A NO-WIN FOR EVERYBODY!!
A MEXICAN STAND-OFF OF THE WORST KIND!
I REMEMBER PUTTING MY FEARS ON HOLD AND JUST FOCUSING ON PLAN ALPHA.
MOM AND FATHER RAN THEIR ATTACK PATTERN WHILE I CONCENTRATED ON MY SPECIALTY...
A FOCUSED BOLT...
FORGETTING ALL ABOUT DR. EX-MORTIS' LETHAL OPTIC BLASTS...
...HOW EARLIER THEY'D INSTANTLY KILLED SIRE ARMOUR...
I JUST FOCUSED--- AND HOT DAMN!!
I ACTUALLY DID IT!!
THE BOLT KNOCKED HIM INTO THE ABYSS FOREVER!!!
WE WON!!
WE WON.
I WAS A BLANK AFTER THAT...
WHEN THE RESERVE MEMBERS OF THE WONDER FRIENDS FINALLY ARRIVED...
ALL THEY COULD DO WAS GATHER THE... BODIES...
...AND APOLOGIZE FOR NOT BEING THERE IN TIME...
ESPECIALLY AT THE FUNERAL...

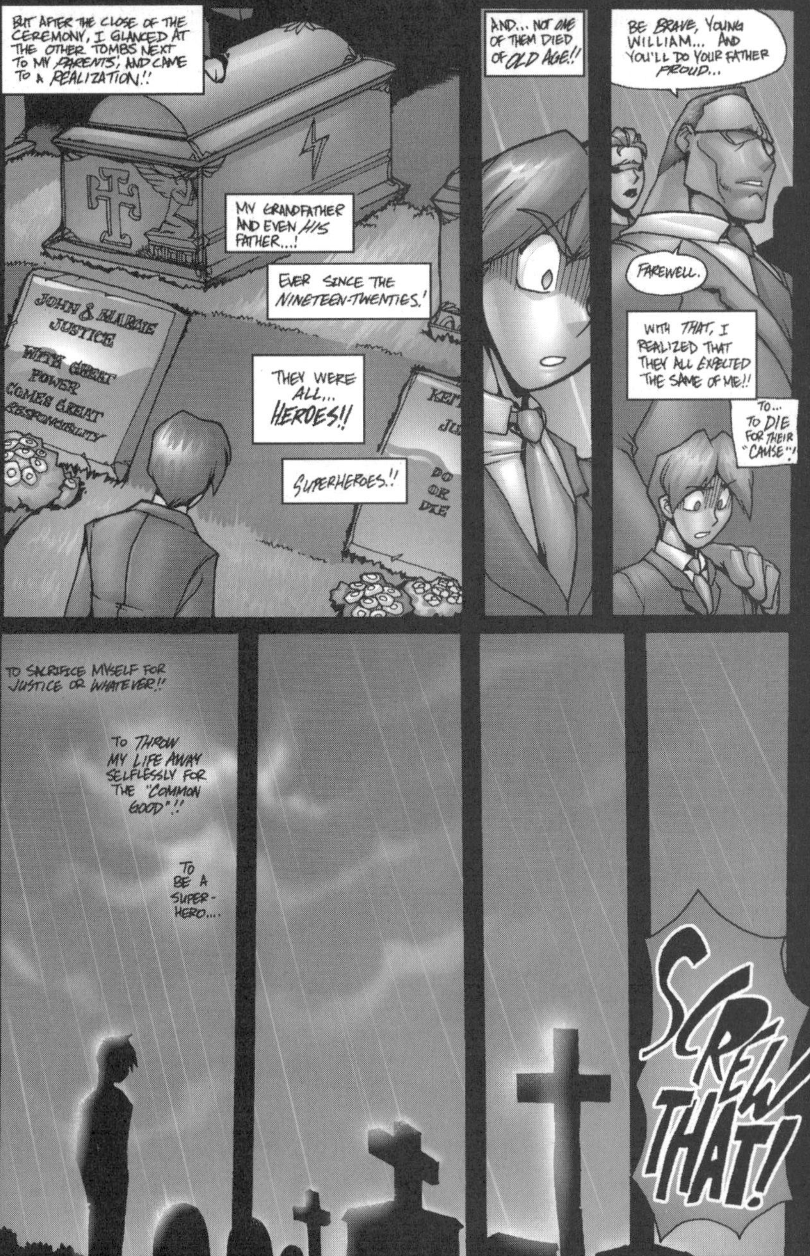
BUT AFTER THE CLOSE OF THE CEREMONY, I GLANCED AT THE OTHER TOMBS NEXT TO MY PARENTS', AND CAME TO A REALIZATION!!
JOHN & MARGIE JUSTICE
WITH GREAT POWER COMES GREAT RESPONSIBILITY
MY GRANDFATHER AND EVEN HIS FATHER...!
EVER SINCE THE NINETEEN-TWENTIES!
THEY WERE ALL... HEROES!!
SUPERHEROES!!
DO OR DIE
AND... NOT ONE OF THEM DIED OF OLD AGE!!
BE BRAVE, YOUNG WILLIAM... AND YOU'LL DO YOUR FATHER PROUD...
FAREWELL.
WITH THAT, I REALIZED THAT THEY ALL EXPECTED THE SAME OF ME!!
TO... TO DIE FOR THEIR "CAUSE"!
TO SACRIFICE MYSELF FOR JUSTICE OR WHATEVER!!
TO THROW MY LIFE AWAY SELFLESSLY FOR THE "COMMON GOOD"!!
TO BE A SUPER-HERO....
SCREW THAT!

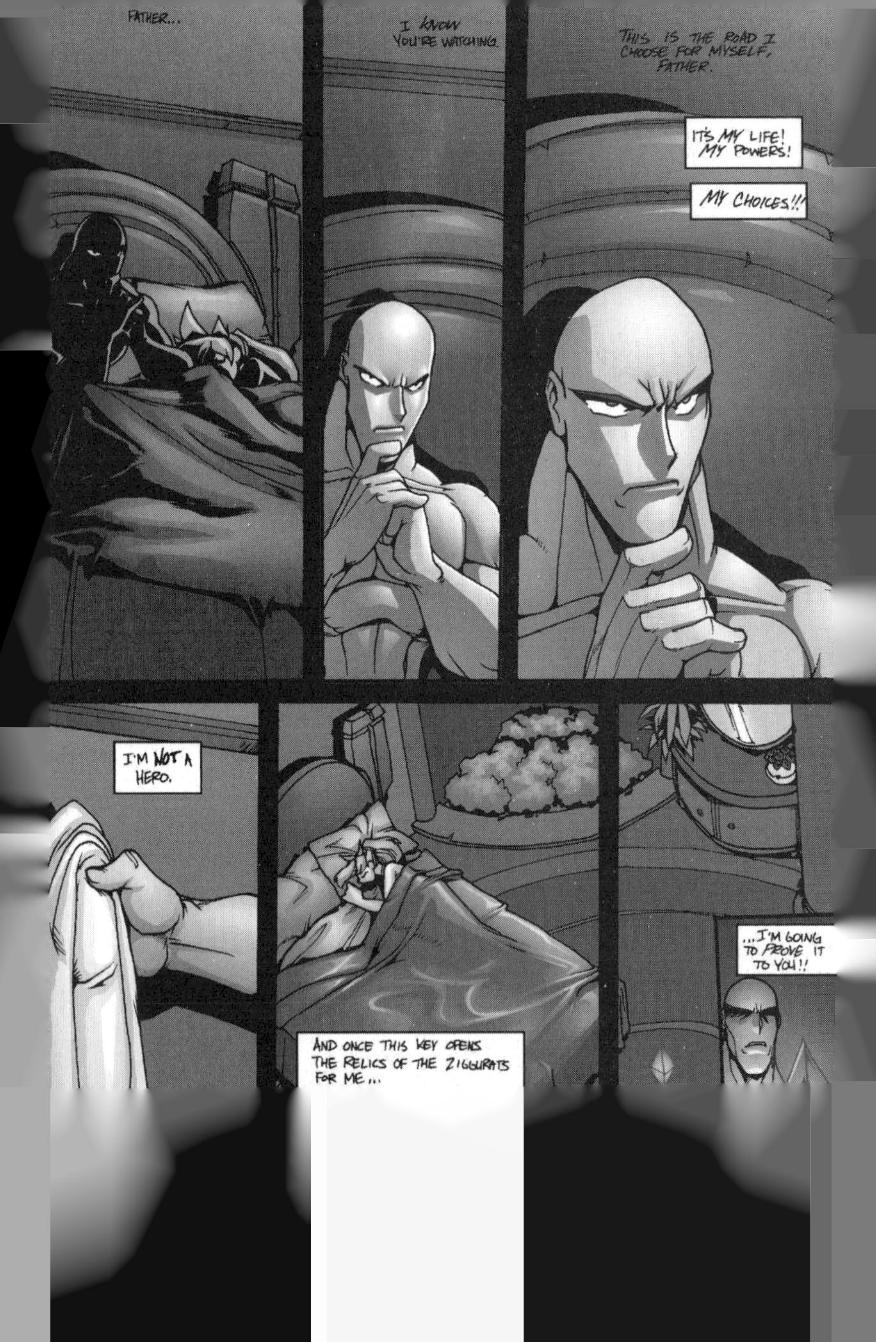
FATHER...
I KNOW YOU'RE WATCHING.
THIS IS THE ROAD I CHOOSE FOR MYSELF, FATHER.
IT'S MY LIFE! MY POWERS!
MY CHOICES!!
I'M NOT A HERO.
AND ONCE THIS KEY OPENS THE RELICS OF THE ZIGGURATS FOR ME...
...I'M GOING TO PROVE IT TO YOU!!

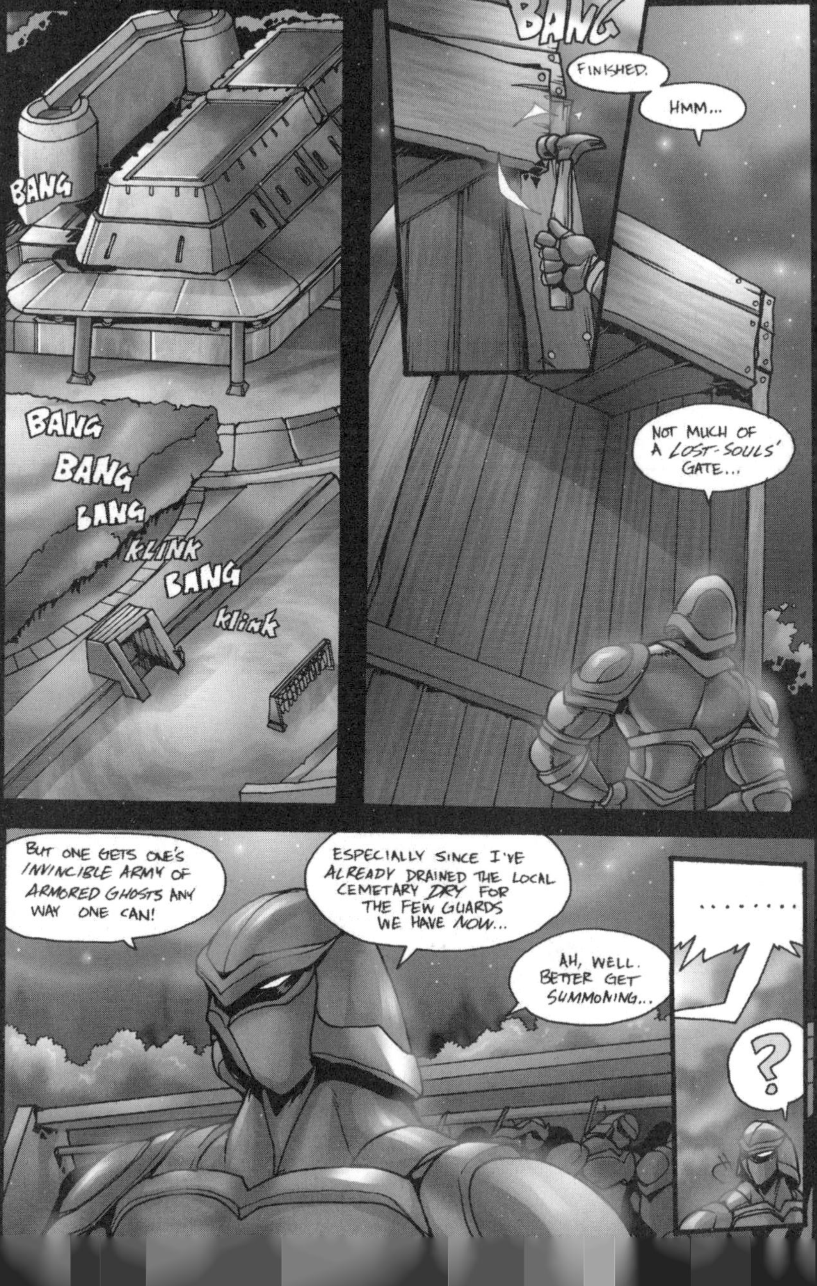

BANG
BANG
BANG
BANG
KLINK
BANG
KLINK
BANG
FINISHED.
HMM...
NOT MUCH OF A LOST-SOULS' GATE...
BUT ONE GETS ONE'S INVINCIBLE ARMY OF ARMORED GHOSTS ANY WAY ONE CAN!
ESPECIALLY SINCE I'VE ALREADY DRAINED THE LOCAL CEMETARY DRY FOR THE FEW GUARDS WE HAVE NOW...
AH, WELL. BETTER GET SUMMONING...
....
?

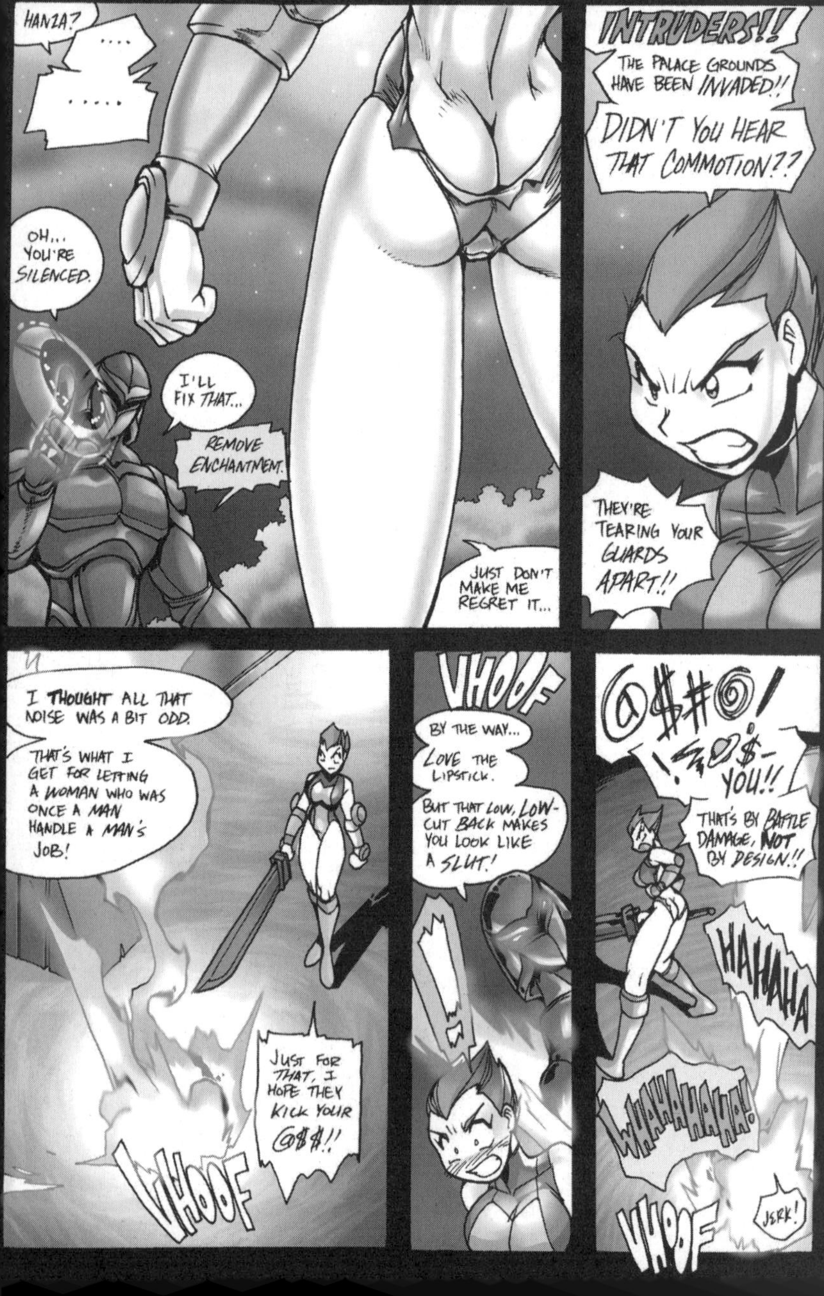
HANZA?
....
.....
OH... YOU'RE SILENCED.
I'LL FIX THAT...
REMOVE ENCHANTMENT.
JUST DON'T MAKE ME REGRET IT...
INTRUDERS!!
THE PALACE GROUNDS HAVE BEEN INVADED!!
DIDN'T YOU HEAR THAT COMMOTION??
THEY'RE TEARING YOUR GUARDS APART!!
I THOUGHT ALL THAT NOISE WAS A BIT ODD.
THAT'S WHAT I GET FOR LETTING A WOMAN WHO WAS ONCE A MAN HANDLE A MAN'S JOB!
JUST FOR THAT, I HOPE THEY KICK YOUR @$$!!
VHOOF
VHOOF
BY THE WAY...
LOVE THE LIPSTICK.
BUT THAT LOW, LOW-CUT BACK MAKES YOU LOOK LIKE A SLUT!
!
@$#@!
!$@$-YOU!!
THAT'S BY BATTLE DAMAGE, NOT BY DESIGN!!
HAHAHA
WAHAHAHAHA!
VHOOF
JERK!

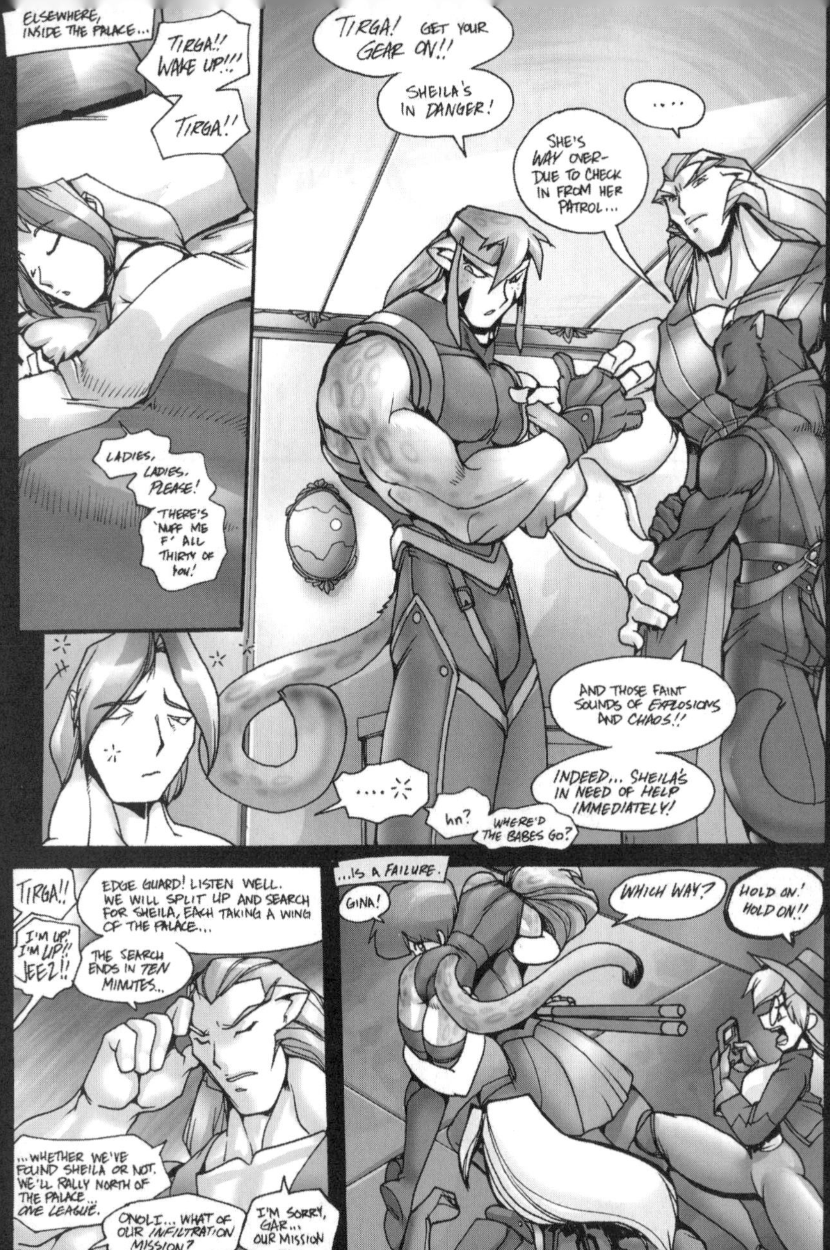

ELSEWHERE, INSIDE THE PALACE...
TIRGA!! WAKE UP!!!
TIRGA!!
LADIES, LADIES, PLEASE!
THERE'S 'NUFF ME F' ALL THIRTY OF YOU!
TIRGA! GET YOUR GEAR ON!!
SHEILA'S IN DANGER!
SHE'S WAY OVER-DUE TO CHECK IN FROM HER PATROL...
....
AND THOSE FAINT SOUNDS OF EXPLOSIONS AND CHAOS!!
INDEED... SHEILA'S IN NEED OF HELP IMMEDIATELY!
....
hn?
WHERE'D THE BABES GO?
TIRGA!!
EDGE GUARD! LISTEN WELL. WE WILL SPLIT UP AND SEARCH FOR SHEILA, EACH TAKING A WING OF THE PALACE...
I'M UP! I'M UP!! JEEZ!!
THE SEARCH ENDS IN TEN MINUTES...
...WHETHER WE'VE FOUND SHEILA OR NOT. WE'LL RALLY NORTH OF THE PALACE... ONE LEAGUE.
ONOLI... WHAT OF OUR INFILTRATION MISSION?
I'M SORRY, GAR... OUR MISSION ...
...IS A FAILURE.
GINA!
WHICH WAY?
HOLD ON! HOLD ON!!

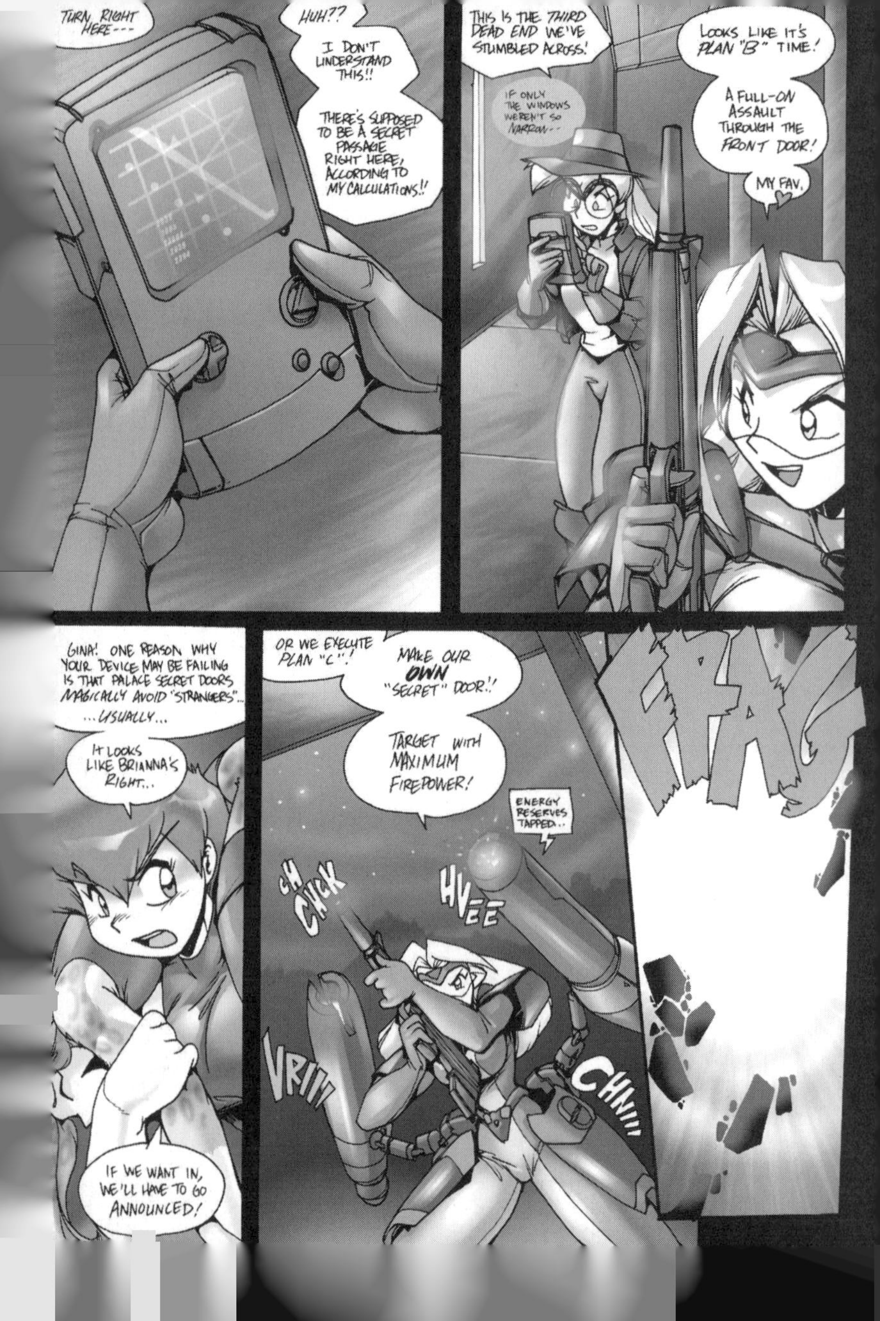

TURN RIGHT HERE---
HUH??
I DON'T UNDERSTAND THIS!!
THERE'S SUPPOSED TO BE A SECRET PASSAGE RIGHT HERE, ACCORDING TO MY CALCULATIONS!!
THIS IS THE THIRD DEAD END WE'VE STUMBLED ACROSS!
IF ONLY THE WINDOWS WEREN'T SO NARROW--
LOOKS LIKE IT'S PLAN "B" TIME!
A FULL-ON ASSAULT THROUGH THE FRONT DOOR!
MY FAV.
GINA! ONE REASON WHY YOUR DEVICE MAY BE FAILING IS THAT PALACE SECRET DOORS MAGICALLY AVOID "STRANGERS"...
...USUALLY...
IT LOOKS LIKE BRIANNA'S RIGHT...
IF WE WANT IN, WE'LL HAVE TO GO ANNOUNCED!
OR WE EXECUTE PLAN "C"!
MAKE OUR OWN "SECRET" DOOR!!
TARGET WITH MAXIMUM FIREPOWER!
ENERGY RESERVES TAPPED..
CH CHCK
HVEE
VRIII
CHNIII
FPAG

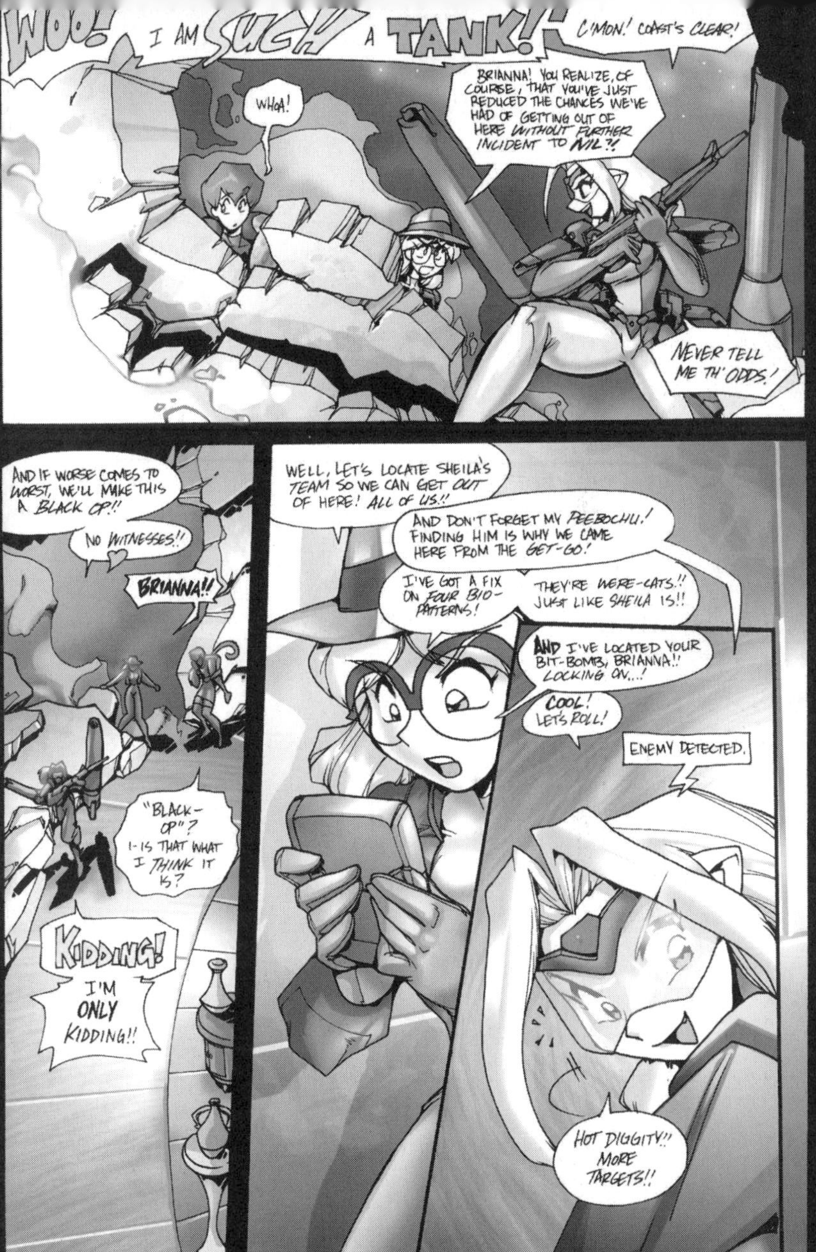
WOO! I AM SUCH!! A TANK!!
C'MON! COAST'S CLEAR!
WHOA!
BRIANNA! YOU REALIZE, OF COURSE, THAT YOU'VE JUST REDUCED THE CHANCES WE'VE HAD OF GETTING OUT OF HERE WITHOUT FURTHER INCIDENT TO NIL?!
NEVER TELL ME TH' ODDS!
AND IF WORSE COMES TO WORST, WE'LL MAKE THIS A BLACK OP!!
NO WITNESSES!!
BRIANNA!!
"BLACK-OP"? I-IS THAT WHAT I THINK IT IS?
KIDDING! I'M ONLY KIDDING!!
WELL, LET'S LOCATE SHEILA'S TEAM SO WE CAN GET OUT OF HERE! ALL OF US!!
AND DON'T FORGET MY PEEBOCHU! FINDING HIM IS WHY WE CAME HERE FROM THE GET-GO!
I'VE GOT A FIX ON FOUR BIO-PATTERNS!
THEY'RE WERE-CATS!! JUST LIKE SHEILA IS!!
AND I'VE LOCATED YOUR BIT-BOMB, BRIANNA!! LOCKING ON...!
COOL! LET'S ROLL!
ENEMY DETECTED.
HOT DIGGITY!! MORE TARGETS!!

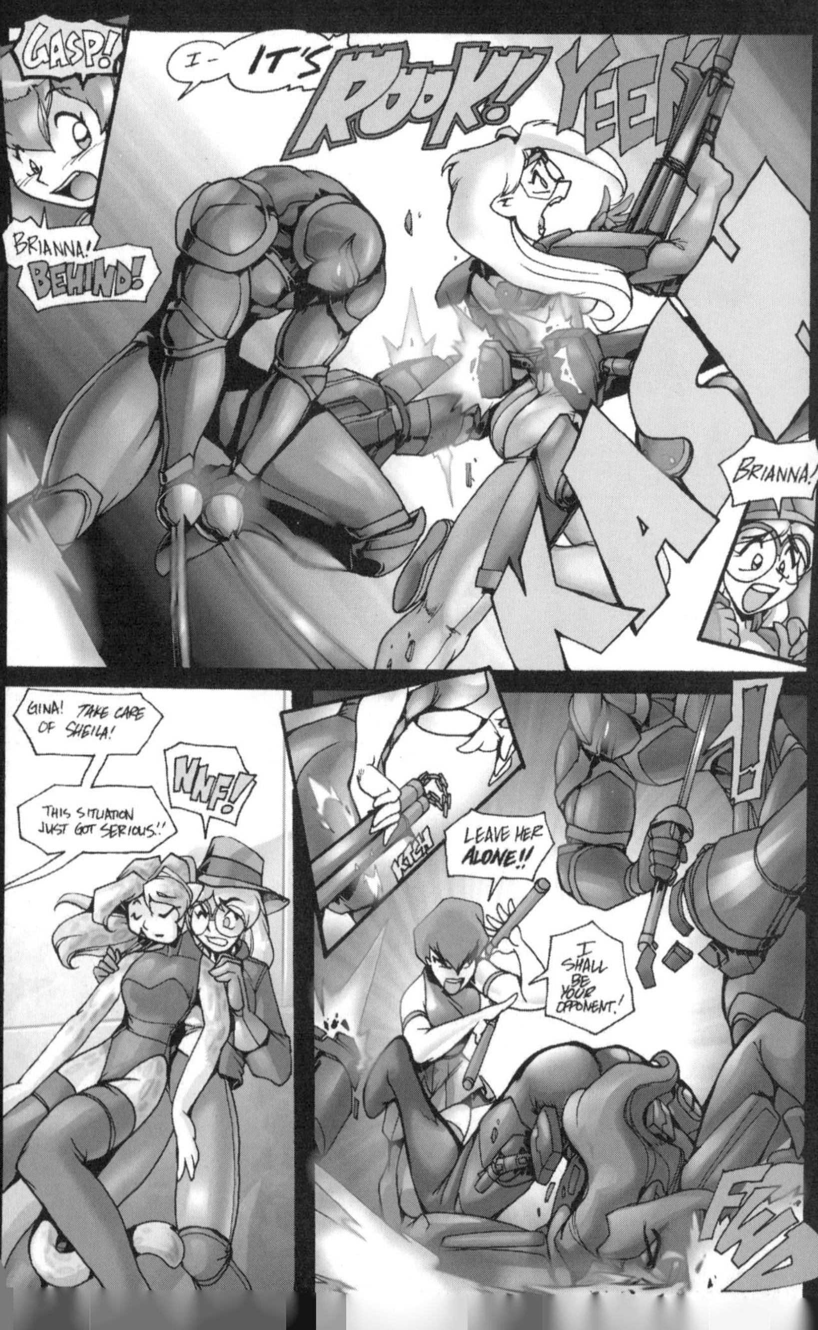
GASP!
I- IT'S
ROOK!!
YEEK!
BRIANNA! BEHIND!
BRIANNA!
GINA! TAKE CARE OF SHEILA!
THIS SITUATION JUST GOT SERIOUS!!
NNF!
KTCH
LEAVE HER ALONE!!
!
I SHALL BE YOUR OPPONENT!

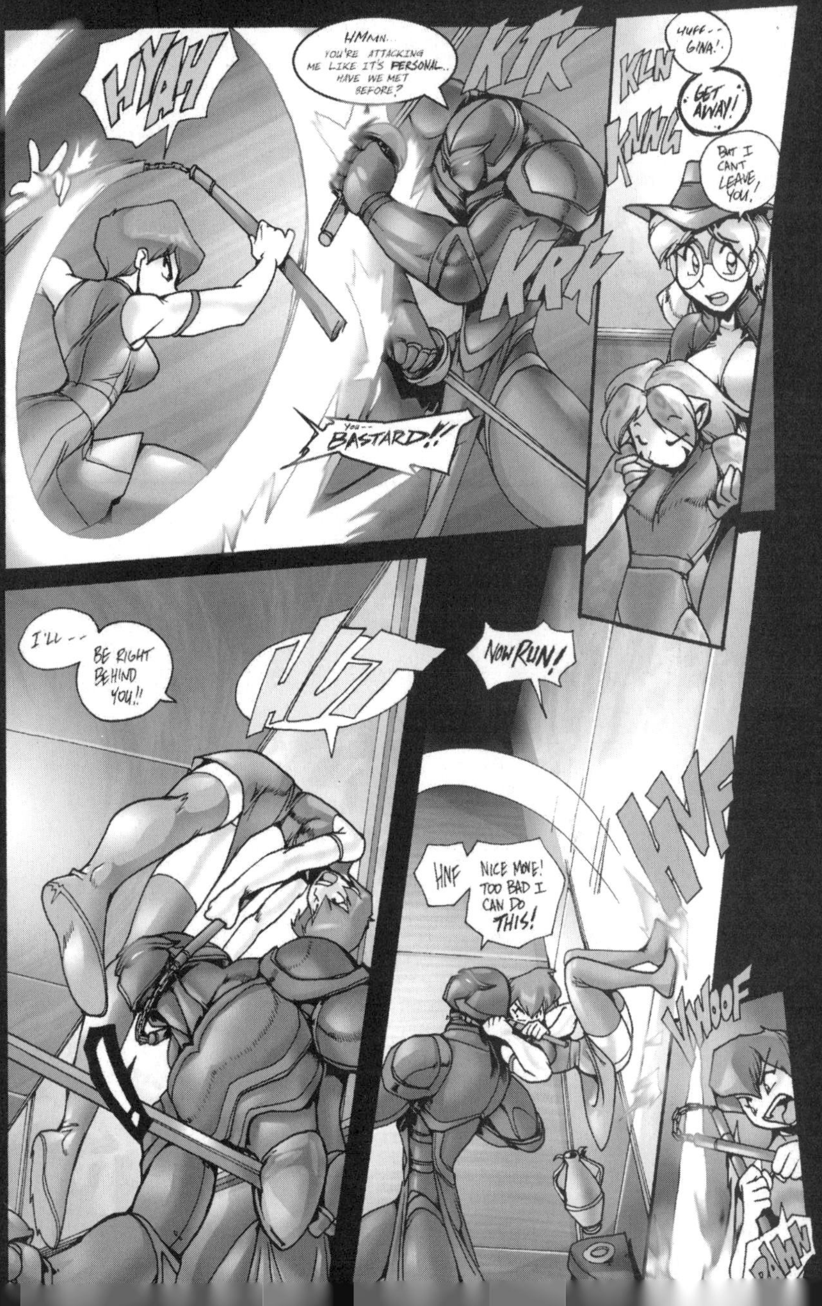
HIYAH
HMMN.. YOU'RE ATTACKING ME LIKE IT'S PERSONAL.. HAVE WE MET BEFORE?
KLIK
KRK
YOU-- BASTARD!!
KLN
KNNG
HUFF-- GINA!
GET AWAY!
BUT I CANT LEAVE YOU!
I'LL-- BE RIGHT BEHIND YOU!!
HUT
NOW RUN!
HNF
NICE MOVE! TOO BAD I CAN DO THIS!
WHOOF

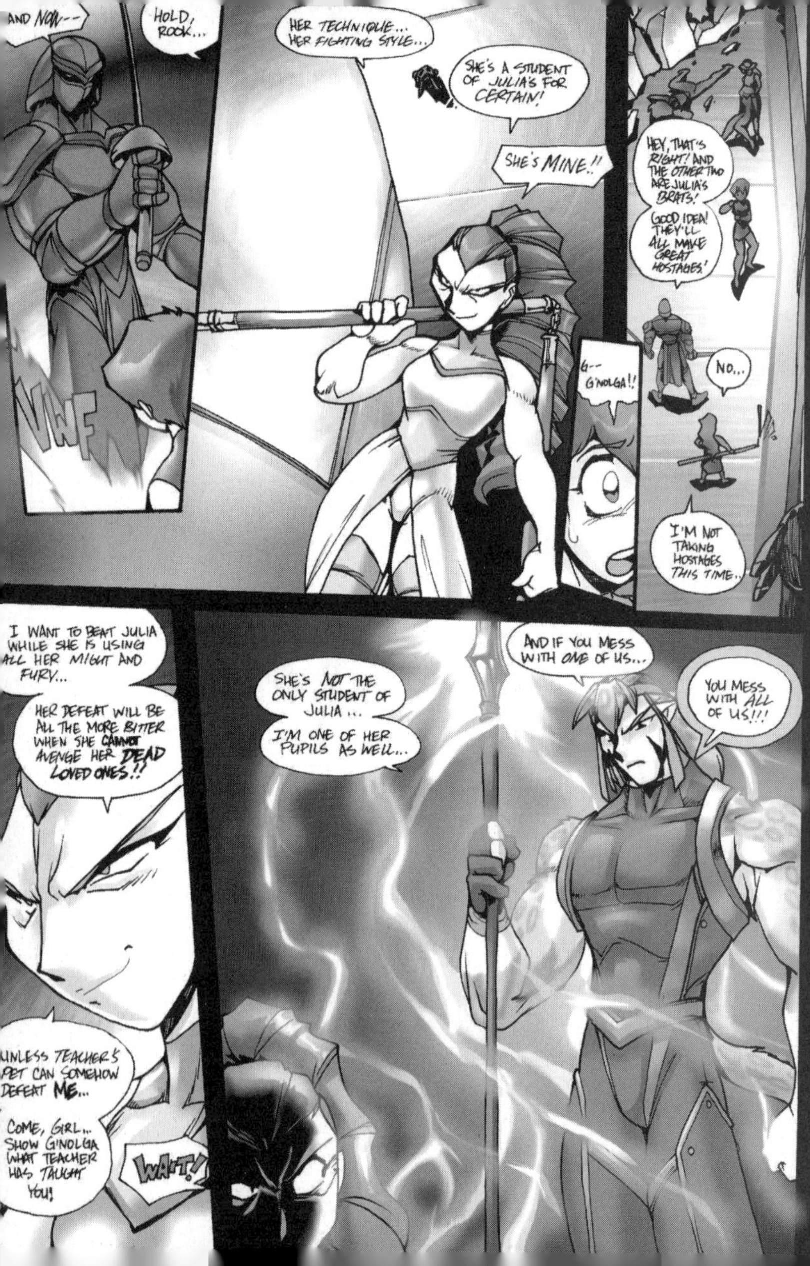
AND NOW--
HOLD, ROOK...
VWF
HER TECHNIQUE... HER FIGHTING STYLE...
SHE'S A STUDENT OF JULIA'S FOR CERTAIN!
SHE'S MINE!!
G-- G'NOLGA!!
HEY, THAT'S RIGHT! AND THE OTHER TWO ARE JULIA'S BRATS!
GOOD IDEA! THEY'LL ALL MAKE GREAT HOSTAGES!
NO...
I'M NOT TAKING HOSTAGES THIS TIME...
I WANT TO BEAT JULIA WHILE SHE IS USING ALL HER MIGHT AND FURY...
HER DEFEAT WILL BE ALL THE MORE BITTER WHEN SHE CANNOT AVENGE HER DEAD LOVED ONES!!
UNLESS TEACHER'S PET CAN SOMEHOW DEFEAT ME...
COME, GIRL... SHOW G'NOLGA WHAT TEACHER HAS TAUGHT YOU!
WAIT!
SHE'S NOT THE ONLY STUDENT OF JULIA...
I'M ONE OF HER PUPILS AS WELL...
AND IF YOU MESS WITH ONE OF US...
YOU MESS WITH ALL OF US!!!

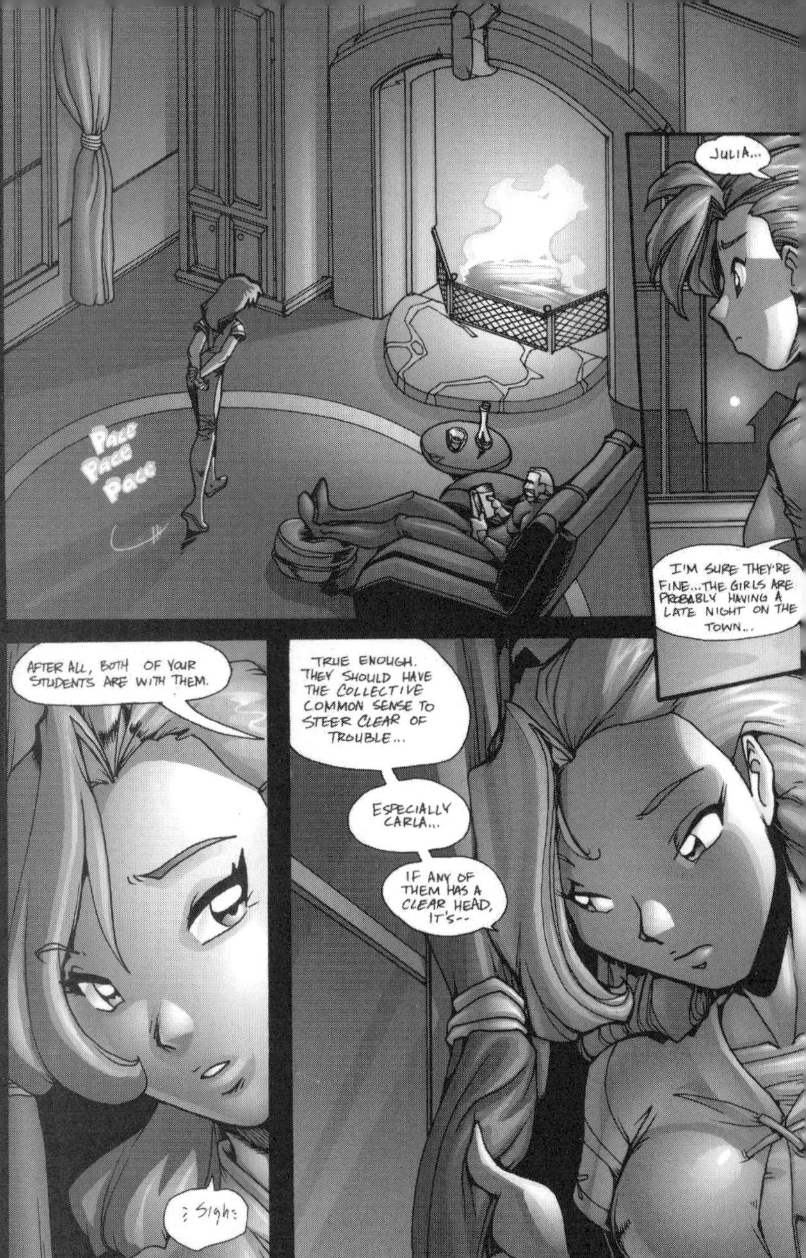
Pace
Pace
Pace
JULIA...
I'M SURE THEY'RE FINE... THE GIRLS ARE PROBABLY HAVING A LATE NIGHT ON THE TOWN...
AFTER ALL, BOTH OF YOUR STUDENTS ARE WITH THEM.
:Sigh:
TRUE ENOUGH. THEY SHOULD HAVE THE COLLECTIVE COMMON SENSE TO STEER CLEAR OF TROUBLE...
ESPECIALLY CARLA...
IF ANY OF THEM HAS A CLEAR HEAD, IT'S--

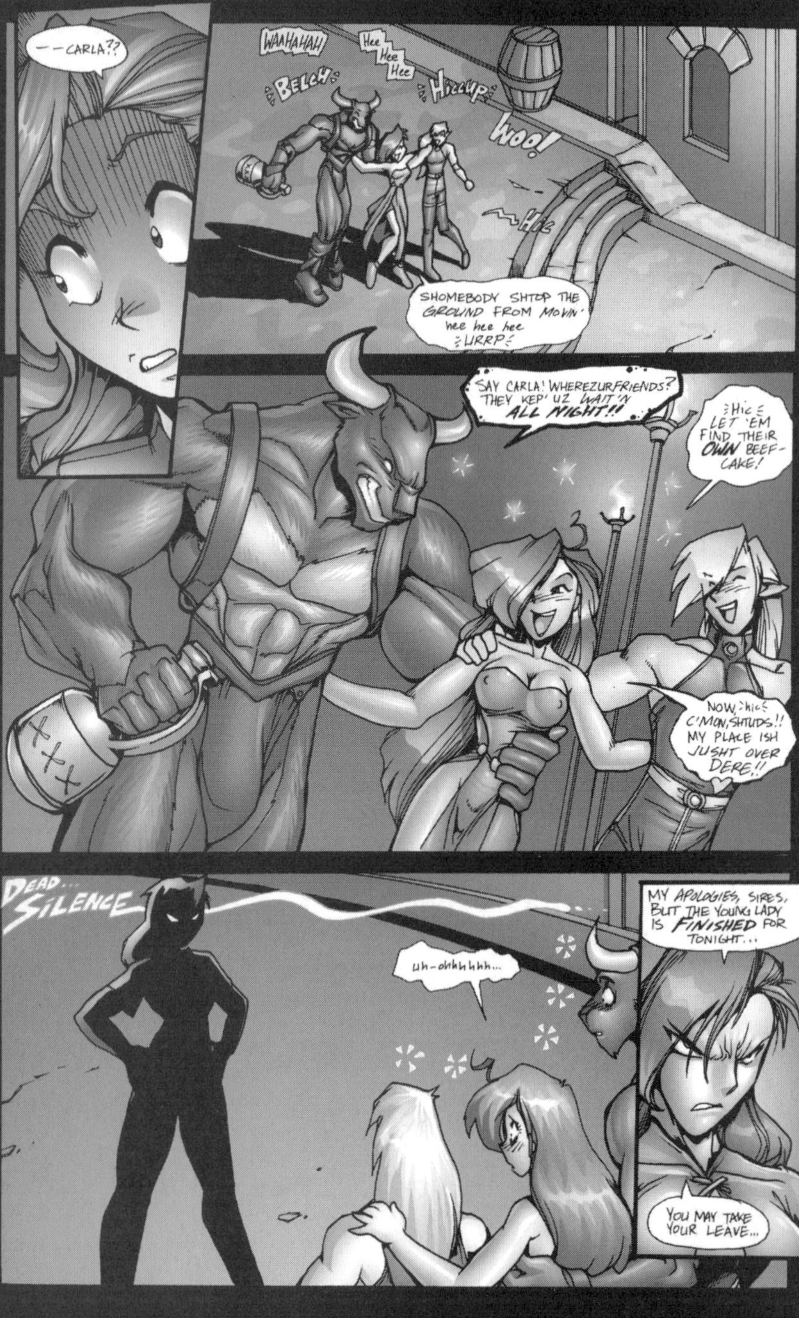
--CARLA??
WAAHAHAH
Hee Hee Hee
BELCH
HICCUP
WOO!
HIC
SHOMEBODY SHTOP THE GROUND FROM MOVIN' hee hee hee URRP
SAY CARLA! WHEREZURFRIENDS? THEY KEP' UZ WAIT'N ALL NIGHT!!
Hic LET 'EM FIND THEIR OWN BEEF-CAKE!
NOW, hic C'MON, SHTUDS!! MY PLACE ISH JUSHT OVER DERE!!
DEAD... SILENCE
uh-ohhhhhh...
MY APOLOGIES, SIRES, BUT THE YOUNG LADY IS FINISHED FOR TONIGHT...
YOU MAY TAKE YOUR LEAVE...

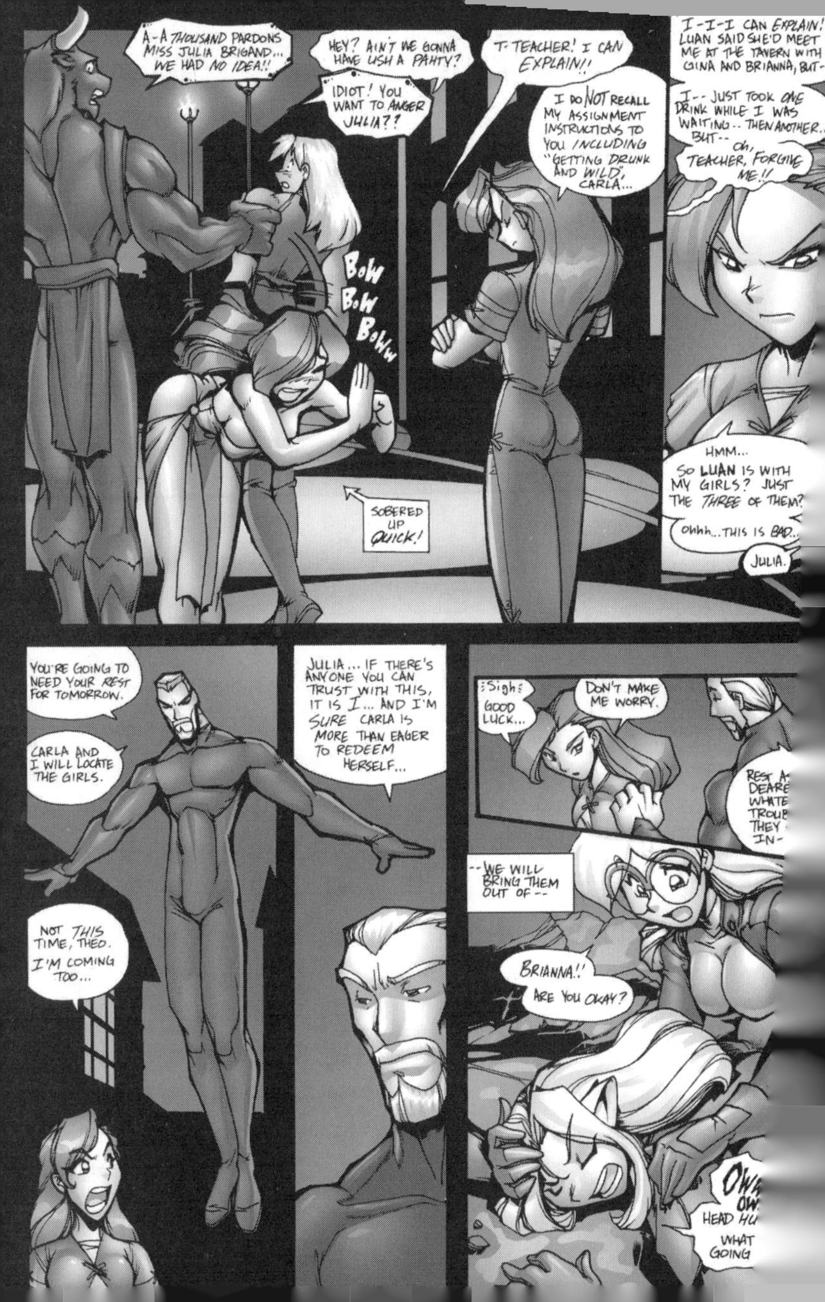
A-A THOUSAND PARDONS MISS JULIA BRIGAND... WE HAD NO IDEA!!
HEY? AIN'T WE GONNA HAVE USH A PAHTY?
IDIOT! YOU WANT TO ANGER JULIA??
BoW BoW BoWW
SOBERED UP QUICK!
T-TEACHER! I CAN EXPLAIN!!
I DO NOT RECALL MY ASSIGNMENT INSTRUCTIONS TO YOU INCLUDING "GETTING DRUNK AND WILD", CARLA...
I-I-I CAN EXPLAIN! LUAN SAID SHE'D MEET ME AT THE TAVERN WITH GINA AND BRIANNA, BUT--
I-- JUST TOOK ONE DRINK WHILE I WAS WAITING.. THEN ANOTHER... BUT-- oh, TEACHER, FORGIVE ME!!
HMM... SO LUAN IS WITH MY GIRLS? JUST THE THREE OF THEM?
Ohhh... THIS IS BAD...
JULIA.
YOU'RE GOING TO NEED YOUR REST FOR TOMORROW.
CARLA AND I WILL LOCATE THE GIRLS.
NOT THIS TIME, THEO. I'M COMING TOO...
JULIA... IF THERE'S ANYONE YOU CAN TRUST WITH THIS, IT IS I... AND I'M SURE CARLA IS MORE THAN EAGER TO REDEEM HERSELF...
:Sigh: GOOD LUCK...
DON'T MAKE ME WORRY.
REST A DEARE WHATE TROUB THEY IN-
--WE WILL BRING THEM OUT OF--
BRIANNA!! ARE YOU OKAY?
OWA OW HEAD HU WHAT GOING

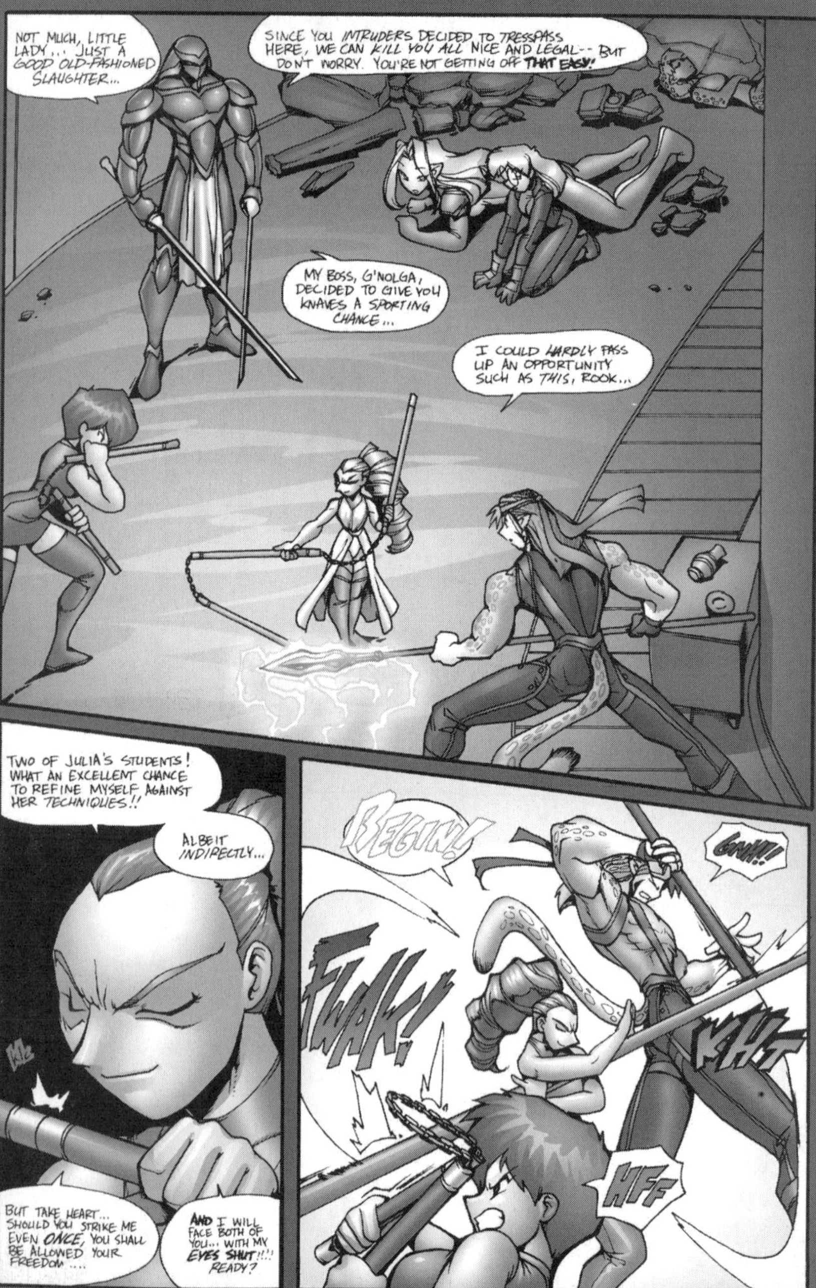
NOT MUCH, LITTLE LADY... JUST A GOOD OLD-FASHIONED SLAUGHTER...
SINCE YOU INTRUDERS DECIDED TO TRESSPASS HERE, WE CAN KILL YOU ALL NICE AND LEGAL-- BUT DON'T WORRY. YOU'RE NOT GETTING OFF THAT EASY!
MY BOSS, G'NOLGA, DECIDED TO GIVE YOU KNAVES A SPORTING CHANCE...
I COULD HARDLY PASS UP AN OPPORTUNITY SUCH AS THIS, ROOK...
TWO OF JULIA'S STUDENTS! WHAT AN EXCELLENT CHANCE TO REFINE MYSELF AGAINST HER TECHNIQUES!!
ALBEIT INDIRECTLY...
BUT TAKE HEART... SHOULD YOU STRIKE ME EVEN ONCE, YOU SHALL BE ALLOWED YOUR FREEDOM....
AND I WILL FACE BOTH OF YOU... WITH MY EYES SHUT!!!! READY?
BEGIN!
GNH!!
FWAK!
WHT
HFF

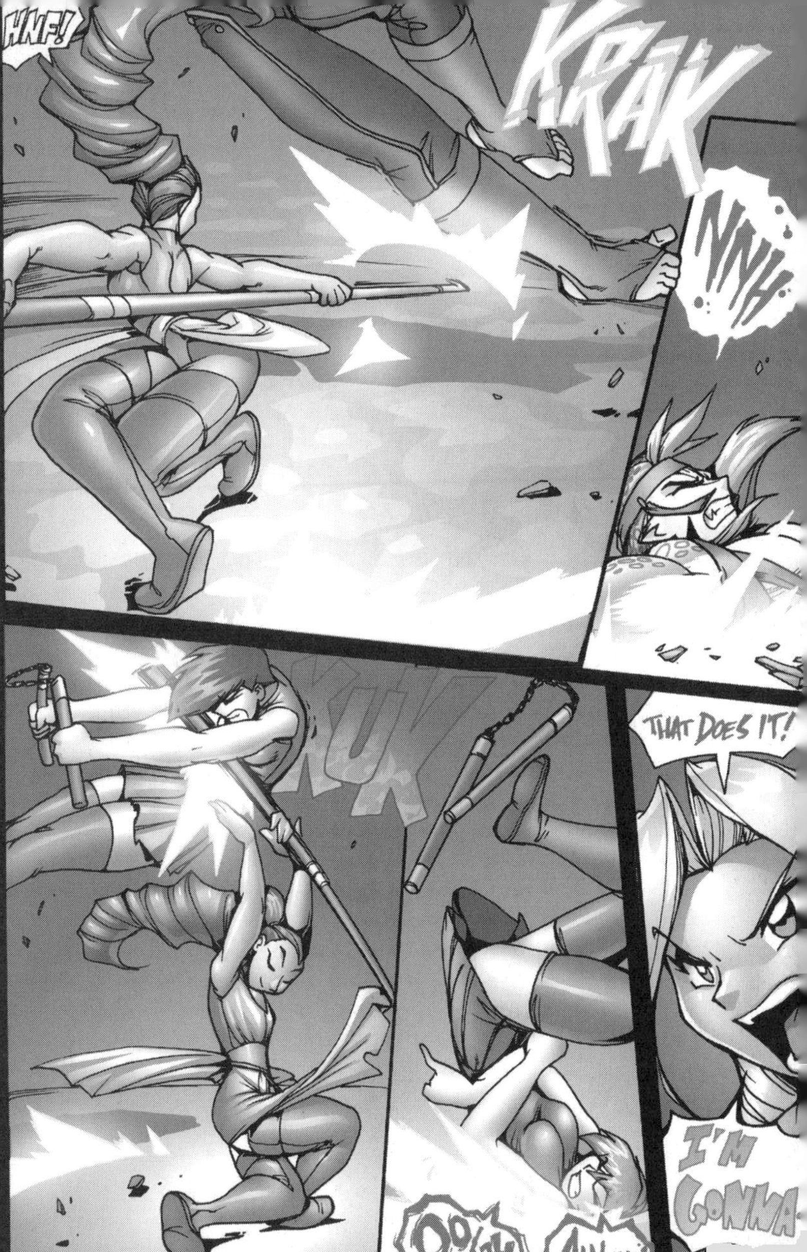
HNF!
KRAK
NNH!
OOGH
THAT DOES IT!
I'M GONNA

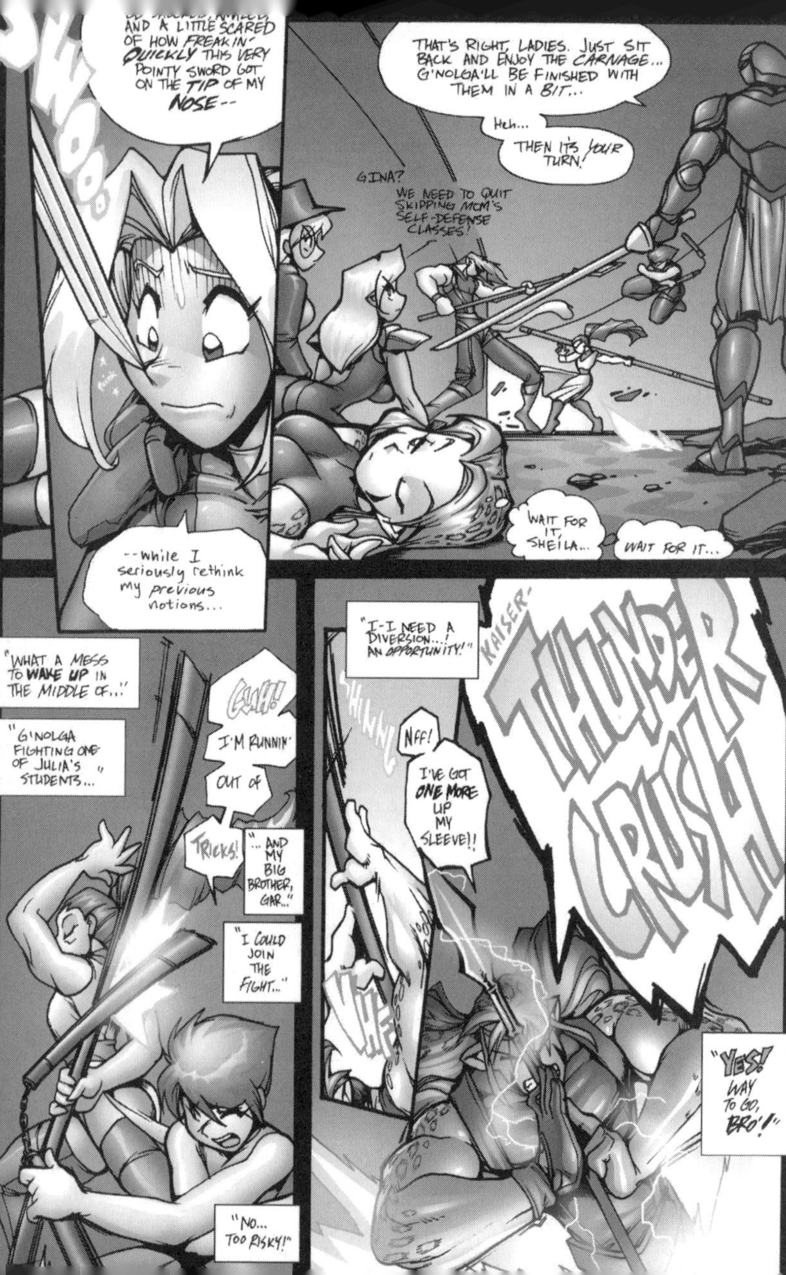
AND A LITTLE SCARED OF HOW FREAKIN' QUICKLY THIS VERY POINTY SWORD GOT ON THE TIP OF MY NOSE--
--while I seriously rethink my previous notions...
THAT'S RIGHT, LADIES. JUST SIT BACK AND ENJOY THE CARNAGE... G'NOLGA'LL BE FINISHED WITH THEM IN A BIT...
Heh...
THEN IT'S YOUR TURN!
GINA? WE NEED TO QUIT SKIPPING MOM'S SELF-DEFENSE CLASSES!
WAIT FOR IT, SHEILA...
WAIT FOR IT...
"WHAT A MESS TO WAKE UP IN THE MIDDLE OF..."
"G'NOLGA FIGHTING ONE OF JULIA'S STUDENTS..."
GAH!
I'M RUNNIN' OUT OF TRICKS!
"...AND MY BIG BROTHER, GAR..."
"I COULD JOIN THE FIGHT..."
"NO... TOO RISKY!"
"I-I NEED A DIVERSION...! AN OPPORTUNITY!"
Nff!
I'VE GOT ONE MORE UP MY SLEEVE!!
KAISER-THUNDER CRUSH!!
"YES! WAY TO GO, BRO'!"

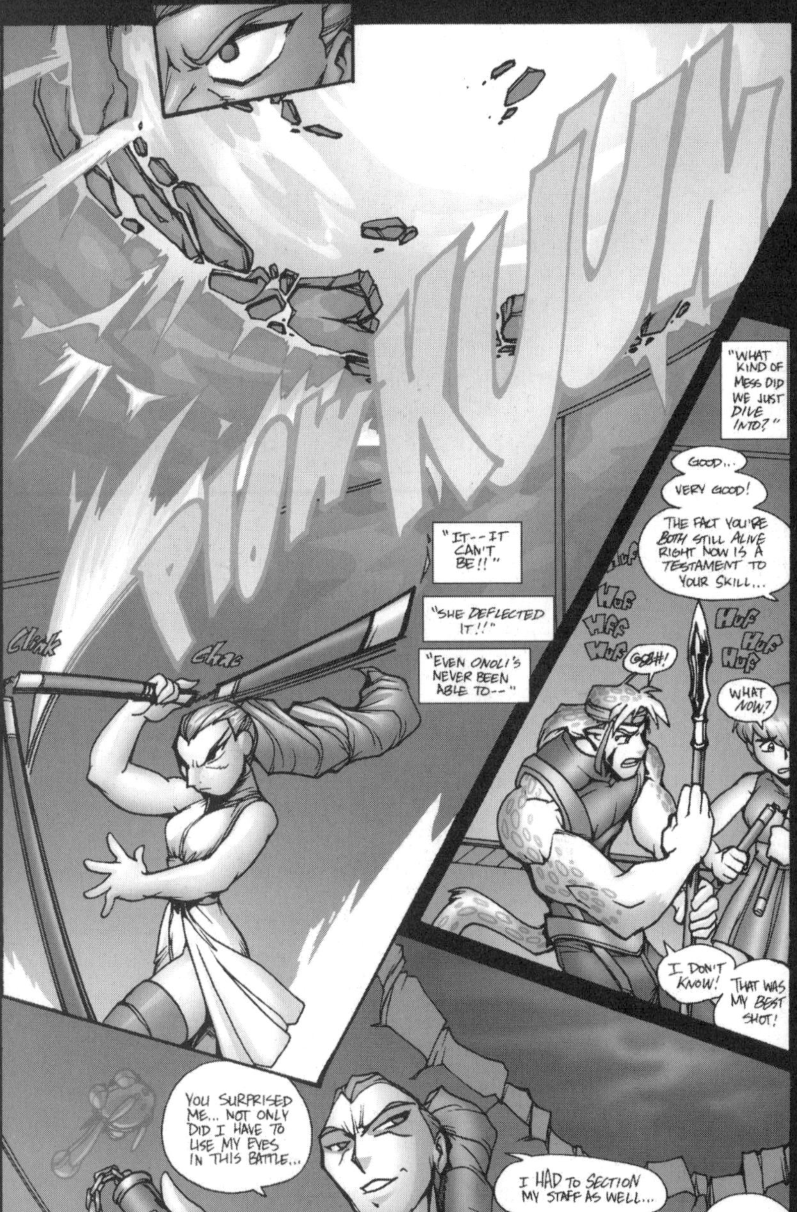
"IT--IT CAN'T BE!!"
"SHE DEFLECTED IT!!"
"EVEN ONOLI'S NEVER BEEN ABLE TO--"
"WHAT KIND OF MESS DID WE JUST DIVE INTO?"
GOOD...
VERY GOOD!
THE FACT YOU'RE BOTH STILL ALIVE RIGHT NOW IS A TESTAMENT TO YOUR SKILL...
HUF HUF HUF
HUF HUF HUF
GOSH!
WHAT NOW?
I DON'T KNOW!
THAT WAS MY BEST SHOT!
YOU SURPRISED ME... NOT ONLY DID I HAVE TO USE MY EYES IN THIS BATTLE...
I HAD TO SECTION MY STAFF AS WELL...
SOMETHING I DON'T DO UNLESS I FEEL... THREATENED.
YOU SHOULD FEEL HONORED!

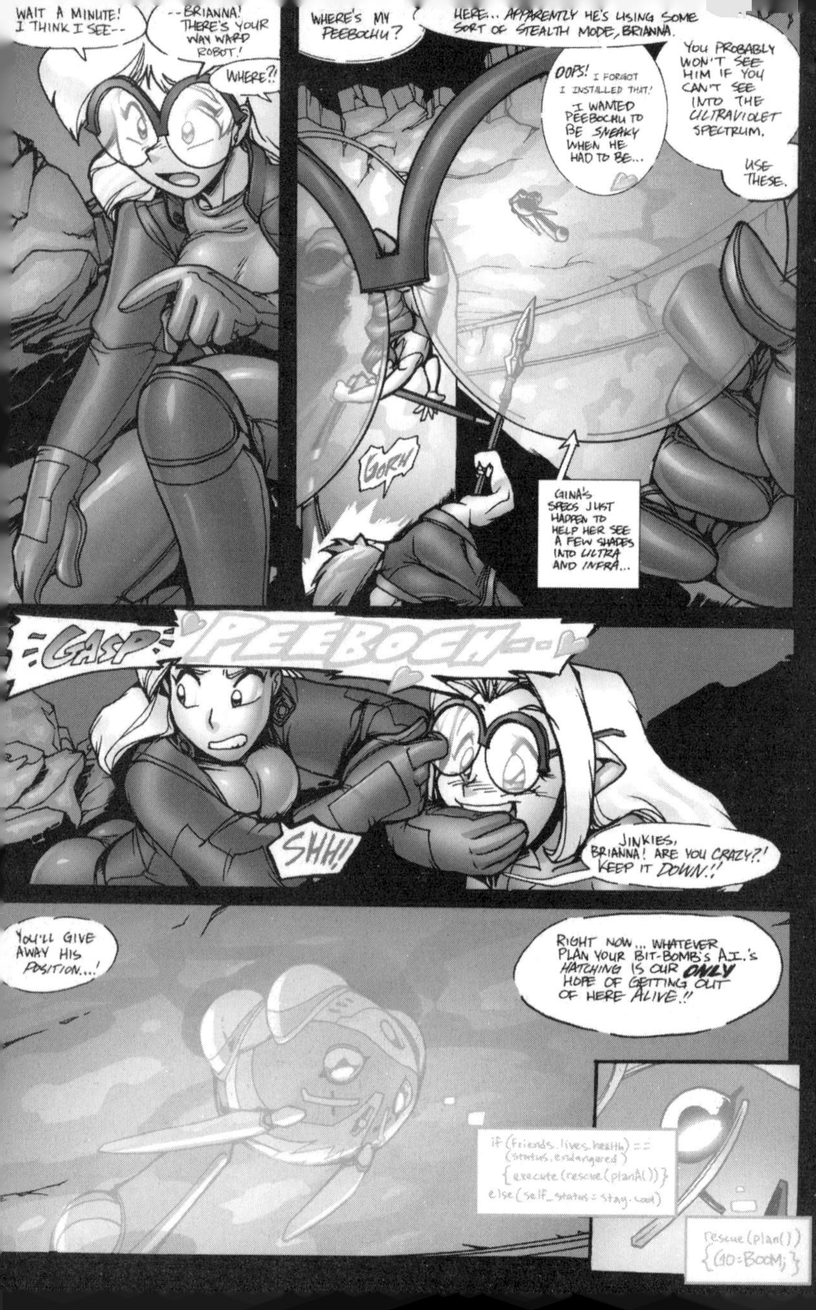

WAIT A MINUTE! I THINK I SEE--
--BRIANNA! THERE'S YOUR WAYWARD ROBOT!
WHERE?!
WHERE'S MY PEEBOCHU?
HERE... APPARENTLY HE'S USING SOME SORT OF STEALTH MODE, BRIANNA.
OOPS! I FORGOT I INSTALLED THAT! I WANTED PEEBOCHU TO BE SNEAKY WHEN HE HAD TO BE...
YOU PROBABLY WON'T SEE HIM IF YOU CAN'T SEE INTO THE ULTRAVIOLET SPECTRUM.
USE THESE.
GORK
GINA'S SPECS JUST HAPPEN TO HELP HER SEE A FEW SHADES INTO ULTRA AND INFRA...
GASP
PEEBOCH--
SHH!
JINKIES, BRIANNA! ARE YOU CRAZY?! KEEP IT DOWN!!
YOU'LL GIVE AWAY HIS POSITION...!
RIGHT NOW... WHATEVER PLAN YOUR BIT-BOMB'S A.I.'s HATCHING IS OUR ONLY HOPE OF GETTING OUT OF HERE ALIVE!!
if (friends.lives.health) == (status.endangered) {execute(rescue(planA())} else(self_status = stay.cool)
rescue(plan()) {go:BOOM;}

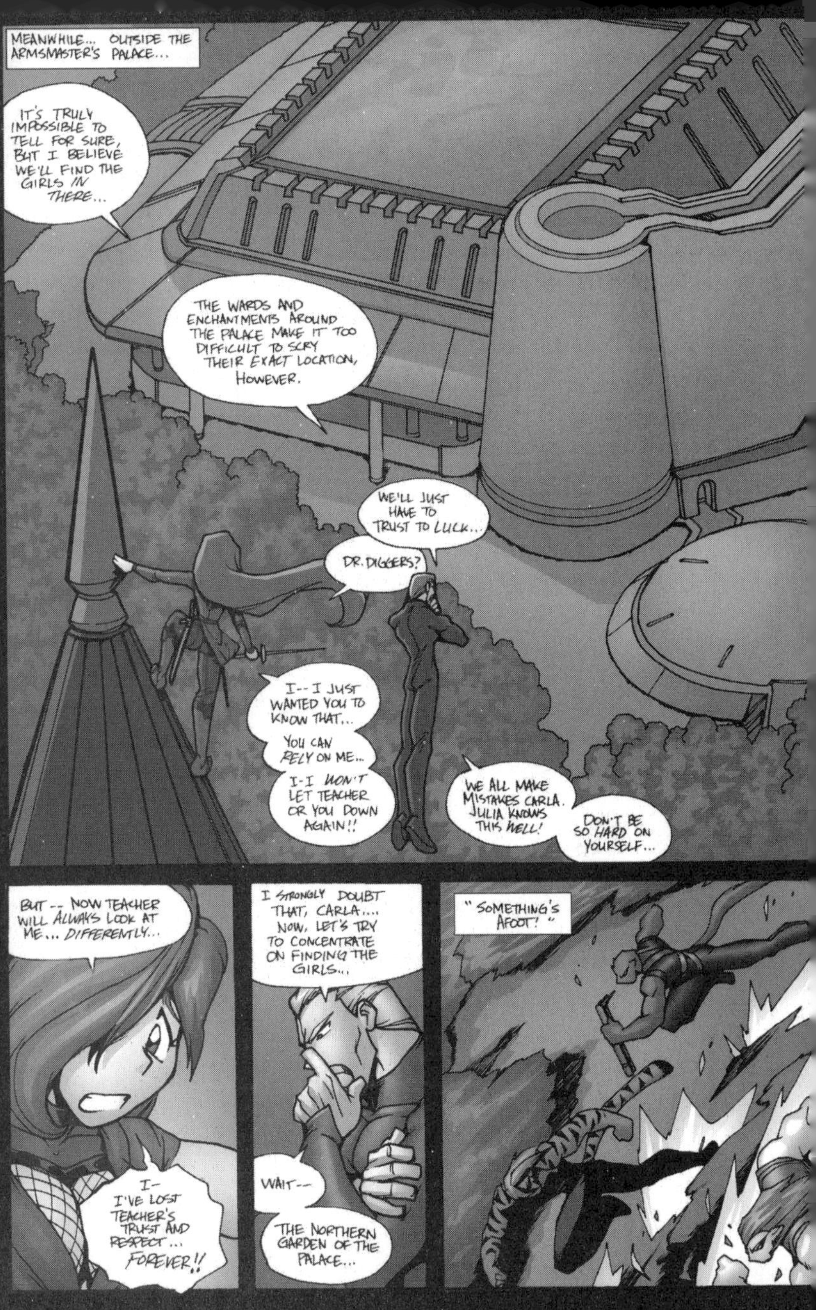
MEANWHILE... OUTSIDE THE ARMSMASTER'S PALACE...
IT'S TRULY IMPOSSIBLE TO TELL FOR SURE, BUT I BELIEVE WE'LL FIND THE GIRLS IN THERE...
THE WARDS AND ENCHANTMENTS AROUND THE PALACE MAKE IT TOO DIFFICULT TO SCRY THEIR EXACT LOCATION, HOWEVER.
WE'LL JUST HAVE TO TRUST TO LUCK...
DR. DIGGERS?
I-- I JUST WANTED YOU TO KNOW THAT...
YOU CAN RELY ON ME...
I-I WON'T LET TEACHER OR YOU DOWN AGAIN!!
WE ALL MAKE MISTAKES CARLA. JULIA KNOWS THIS WELL!
DON'T BE SO HARD ON YOURSELF...
BUT -- NOW TEACHER WILL ALWAYS LOOK AT ME... DIFFERENTLY...
I- I'VE LOST TEACHER'S TRUST AND RESPECT... FOREVER!!
I STRONGLY DOUBT THAT, CARLA.... NOW, LET'S TRY TO CONCENTRATE ON FINDING THE GIRLS...
WAIT--
THE NORTHERN GARDEN OF THE PALACE...
"SOMETHING'S AFOOT!"

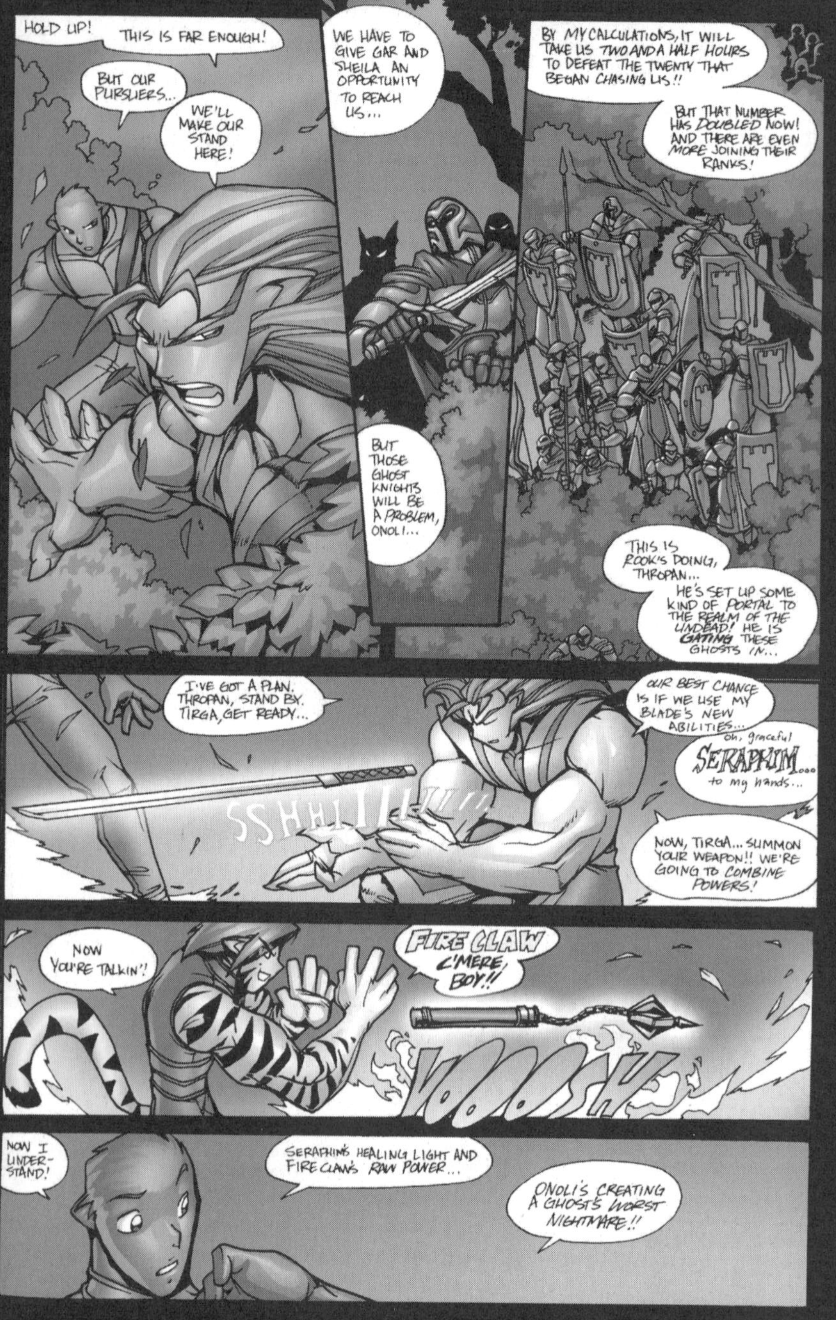
HOLD UP!
THIS IS FAR ENOUGH!
BUT OUR PURSUERS...
WE'LL MAKE OUR STAND HERE!
WE HAVE TO GIVE GAR AND SHEILA AN OPPORTUNITY TO REACH US...
BUT THOSE GHOST KNIGHTS WILL BE A PROBLEM, ONOLI...
BY MY CALCULATIONS, IT WILL TAKE US TWO AND A HALF HOURS TO DEFEAT THE TWENTY THAT BEGAN CHASING US!!
BUT THAT NUMBER HAS DOUBLED NOW! AND THERE ARE EVEN MORE JOINING THEIR RANKS!
THIS IS ROOK'S DOING, THROPAN...
HE'S SET UP SOME KIND OF PORTAL TO THE REALM OF THE UNDEAD! HE IS GATING THESE GHOSTS IN...
I'VE GOT A PLAN. THROPAN, STAND BY. TIRGA, GET READY...
OUR BEST CHANCE IS IF WE USE MY BLADE'S NEW ABILITIES...
oh, graceful SERAPHIM... to my hands...
SSHHIIIII
NOW, TIRGA... SUMMON YOUR WEAPON!! WE'RE GOING TO COMBINE POWERS!
NOW YOU'RE TALKIN'!
FIRE CLAW C'MERE, BOY!!
VOOOSH
NOW I UNDER-STAND!
SERAPHIM'S HEALING LIGHT AND FIRE CLAW'S RAW POWER...
ONOLI'S CREATING A GHOST'S WORST NIGHTMARE!!

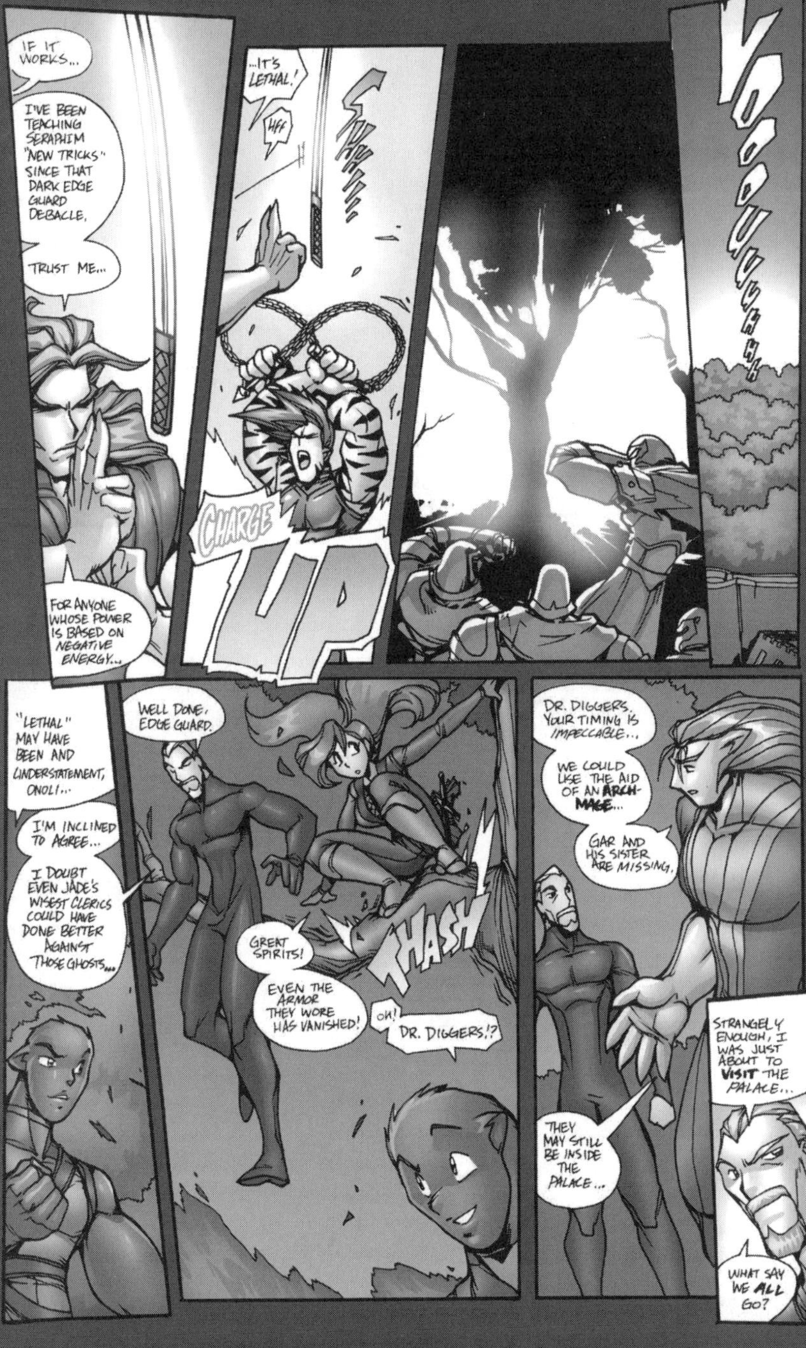
IF IT WORKS...
I'VE BEEN TEACHING SERAPHIM "NEW TRICKS" SINCE THAT DARK EDGE GUARD DEBACLE.
TRUST ME...
FOR ANYONE WHOSE POWER IS BASED ON NEGATIVE ENERGY...
...IT'S LETHAL!
HFF
SHHH!!!
CHARGE UP
VOOOOUUUHHH
"LETHAL" MAY HAVE BEEN AND UNDERSTATEMENT, ONOLI...
I'M INCLINED TO AGREE...
I DOUBT EVEN JADE'S WISEST CLERICS COULD HAVE DONE BETTER AGAINST THOSE GHOSTS...
WELL DONE, EDGE GUARD.
THASH
GREAT SPIRITS!
EVEN THE ARMOR THEY WORE HAS VANISHED!
OH!
DR. DIGGERS!?
DR. DIGGERS, YOUR TIMING IS IMPECCABLE...
WE COULD USE THE AID OF AN ARCH-MAGE...
GAR AND HIS SISTER ARE MISSING.
THEY MAY STILL BE INSIDE THE PALACE...
STRANGELY ENOUGH, I WAS JUST ABOUT TO VISIT THE PALACE...
WHAT SAY WE ALL GO?

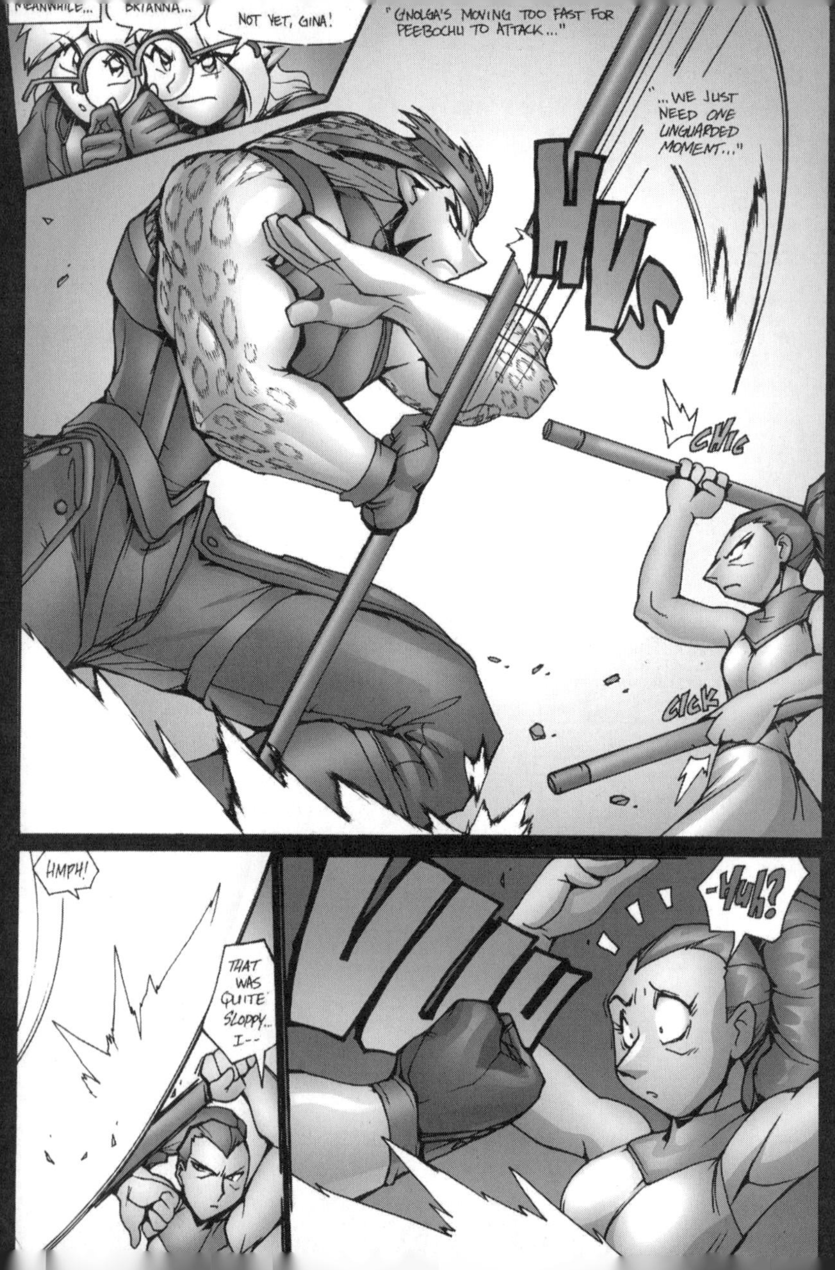
MEANWHILE...
BRIANNA...
NOT YET, GINA!
"GNOLGA'S MOVING TOO FAST FOR PEEBOCHU TO ATTACK..."
"...WE JUST NEED ONE UNGUARDED MOMENT..."
HUS
CHIG
CICK
HMPH!
THAT WAS QUITE SLOPPY... I--
-HUH?

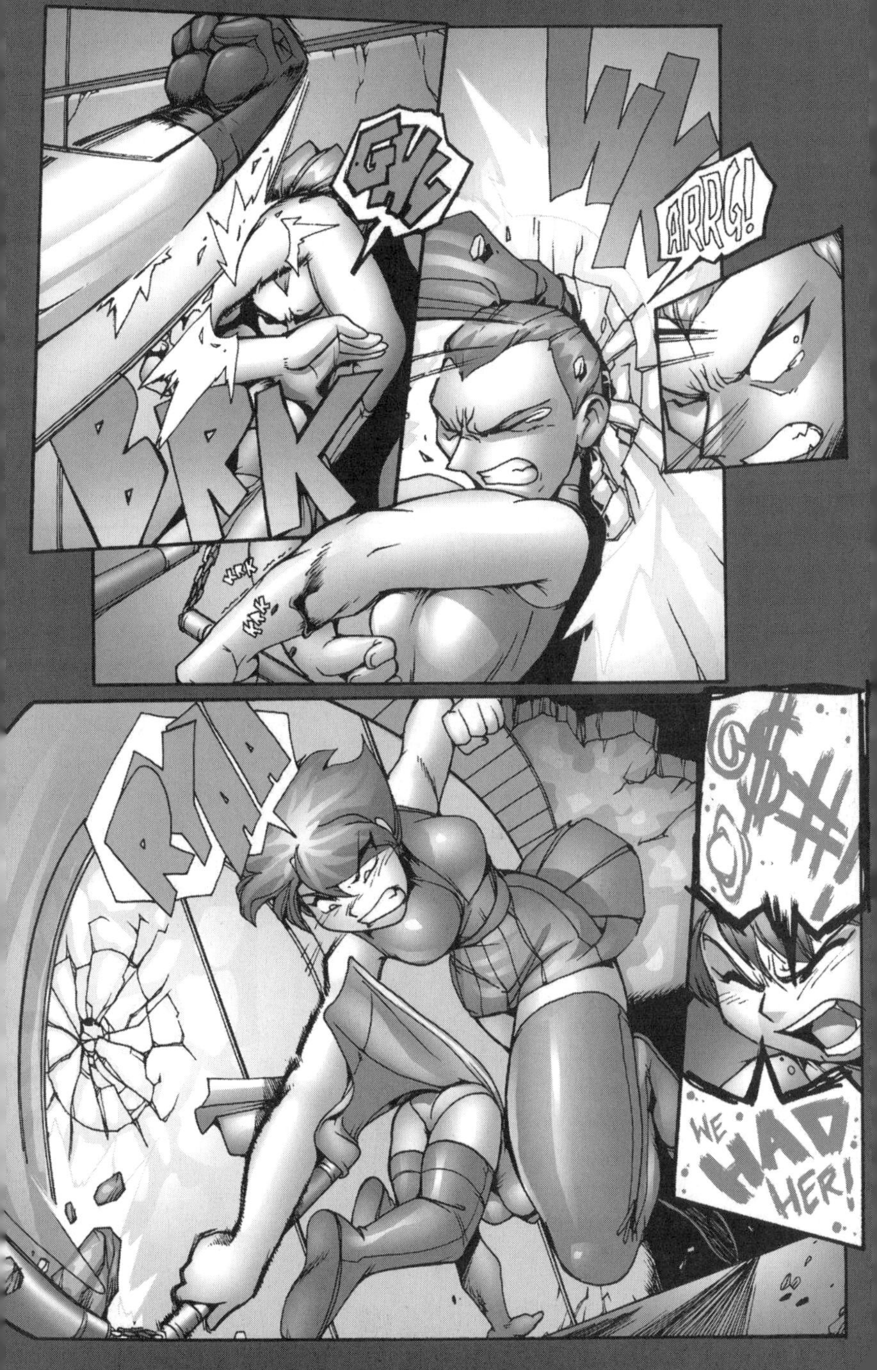
ARRG!
BRK
KRK
KRK
WE HAD HER!

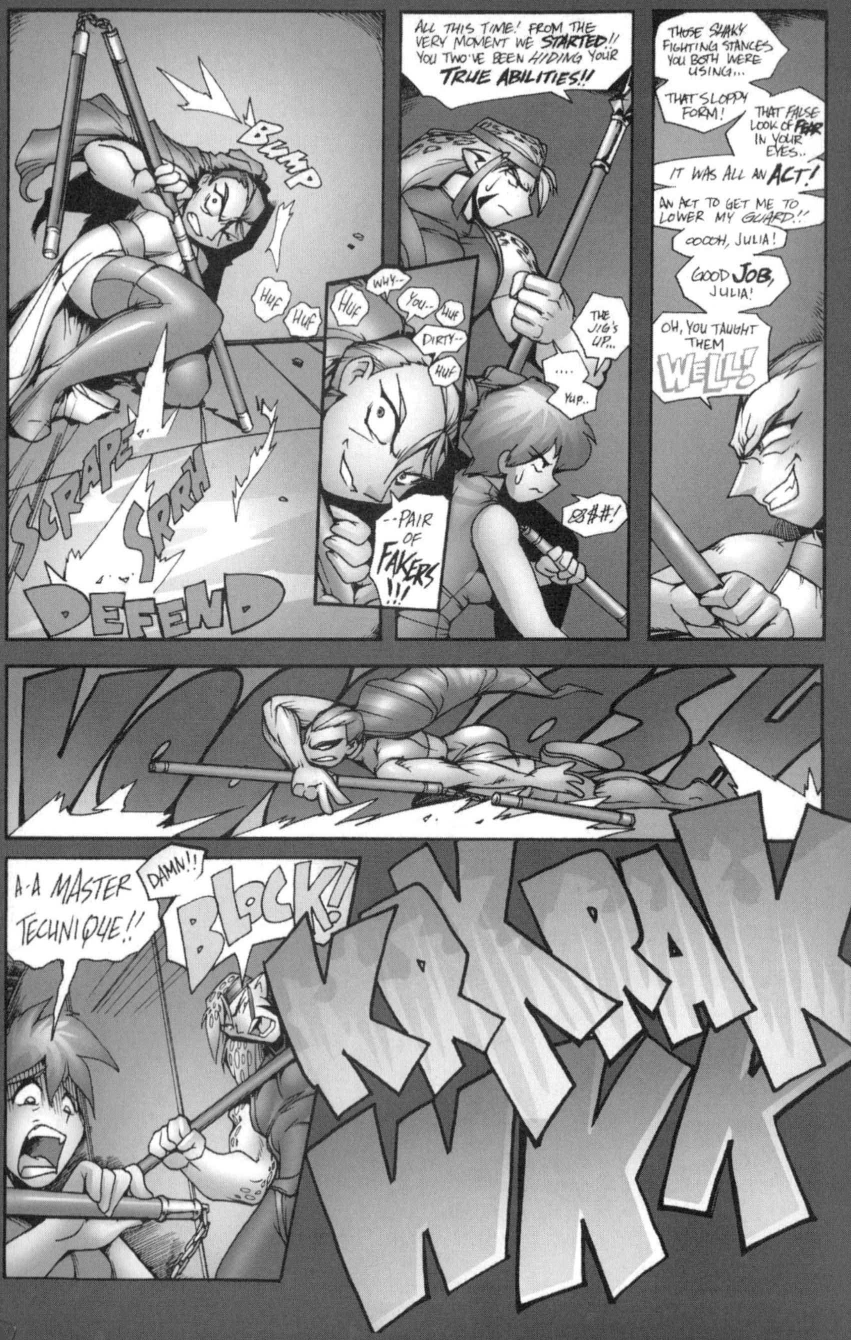

BUMP
SCRAPE
SRRH
DEFEND
HUF
HUF
ALL THIS TIME! FROM THE VERY MOMENT WE STARTED!! YOU TWO'VE BEEN HIDING YOUR TRUE ABILITIES!!
HUF
WHY--
YOU--
HUF
DIRTY--
HUF
--PAIR OF FAKERS!!!
THE JIG'S UP...
....
YUP..
@$#!
THOSE SHAKY FIGHTING STANCES YOU BOTH WERE USING...
THAT'S SLOPPY FORM!
THAT FALSE LOOK OF FEAR IN YOUR EYES..
IT WAS ALL AN ACT!
AN ACT TO GET ME TO LOWER MY GUARD!!
OOOOH, JULIA!
GOOD JOB, JULIA!
OH, YOU TAUGHT THEM WELL!
A-A MASTER TECHNIQUE!!
DAMN!!
BLOCK!!
KRAK

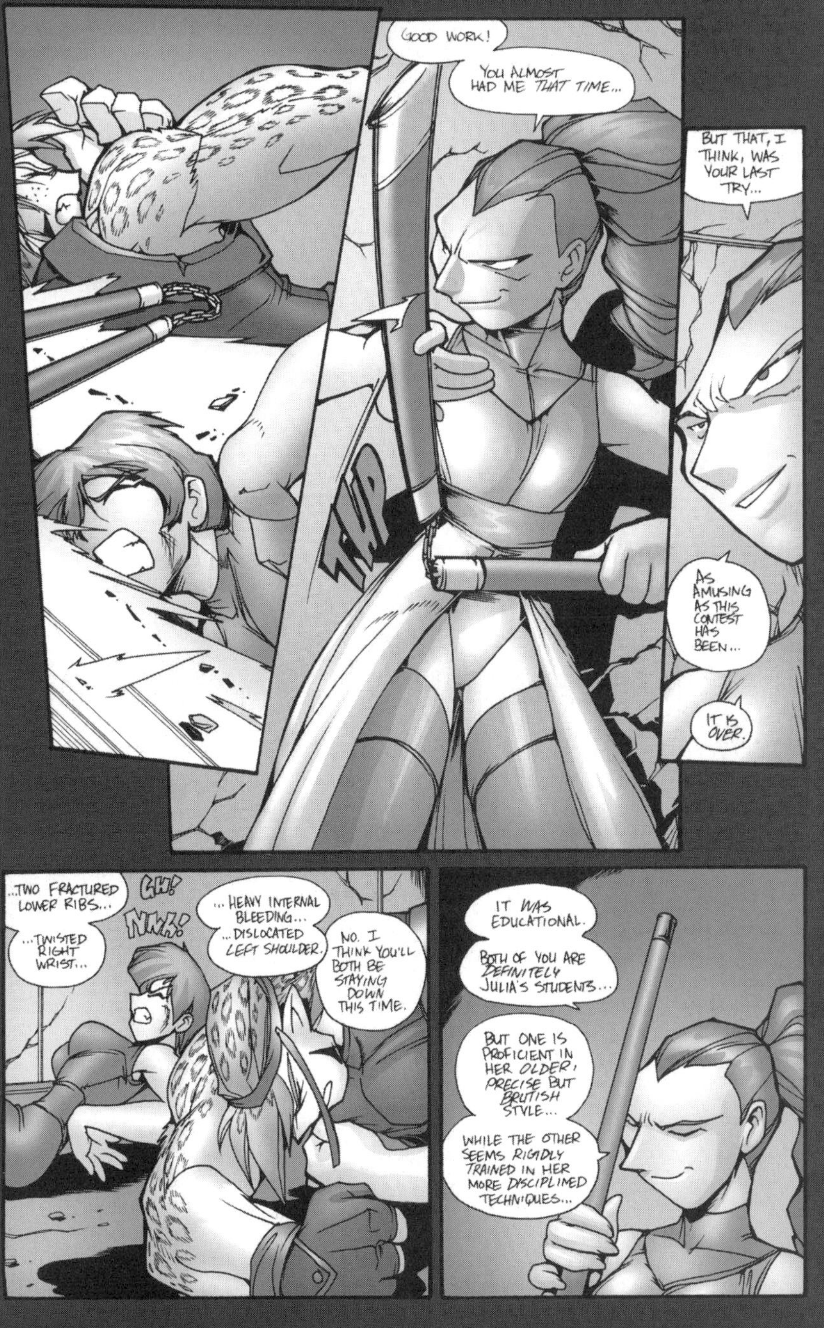
GOOD WORK!
YOU ALMOST HAD ME *THAT* TIME...
THUP
BUT THAT, I THINK, WAS YOUR LAST TRY...
AS AMUSING AS THIS CONTEST HAS BEEN...
IT IS *OVER.*
...TWO FRACTURED LOWER RIBS...
...TWISTED RIGHT WRIST...
GH!
NNG!
...HEAVY INTERNAL BLEEDING... ...DISLOCATED *LEFT SHOULDER.*
NO. I THINK YOU'LL BOTH BE STAYING DOWN THIS TIME.
IT *WAS* EDUCATIONAL.
BOTH OF YOU ARE *DEFINITELY* JULIA'S STUDENTS...
BUT ONE IS PROFICIENT IN HER *OLDER, PRECISE* BUT *BRUTISH* STYLE...
WHILE THE OTHER SEEMS *RIGIDLY TRAINED* IN HER MORE *DISCIPLINED* TECHNIQUES...

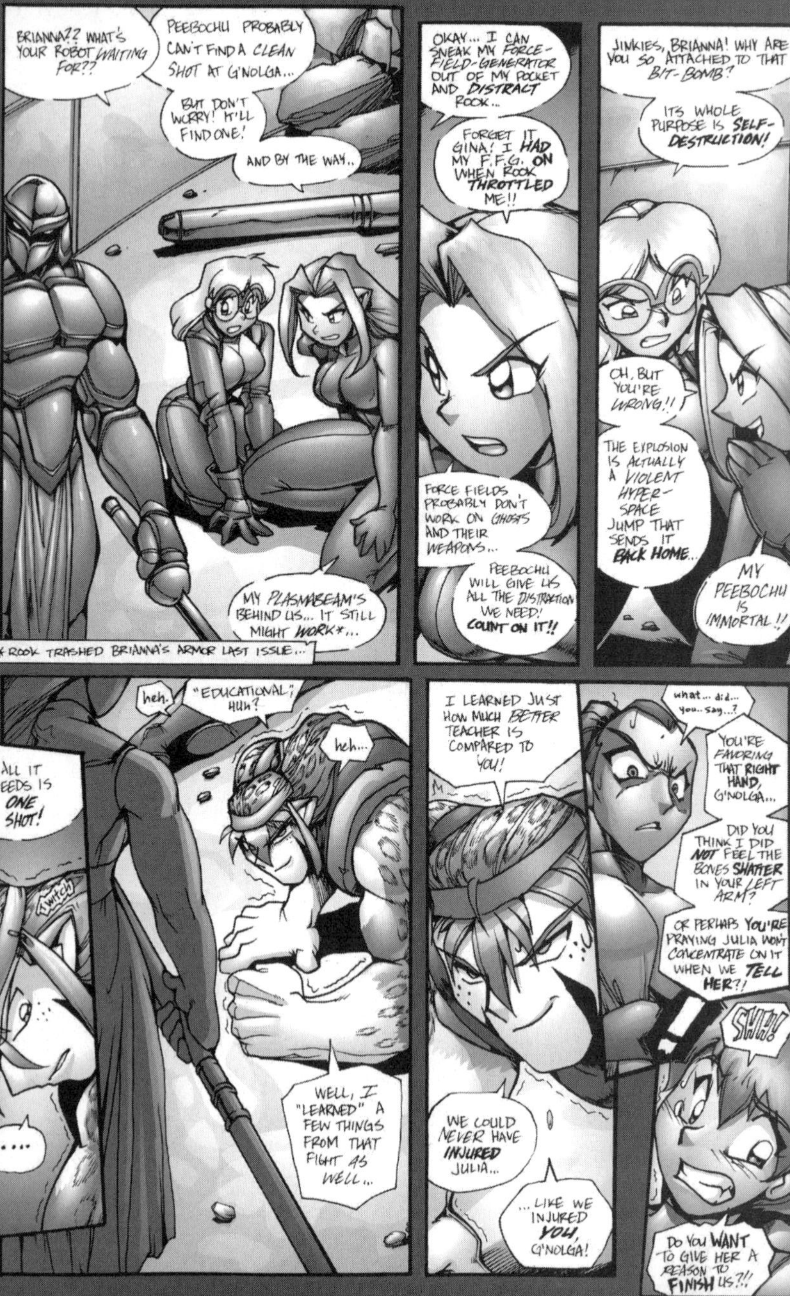
BRIANNA?? WHAT'S YOUR ROBOT WAITING FOR??
PEEBOCHU PROBABLY CAN'T FIND A CLEAN SHOT AT G'NOLGA...
BUT DON'T WORRY! IT'LL FIND ONE!
AND BY THE WAY..
MY PLASMABEAM'S BEHIND US... IT STILL MIGHT WORK*...
*ROOK TRASHED BRIANNA'S ARMOR LAST ISSUE...
OKAY... I CAN SNEAK MY FORCE-FIELD-GENERATOR OUT OF MY POCKET AND DISTRACT ROOK...
FORGET IT GINA! I HAD MY F.F.G. ON WHEN ROOK THROTTLED ME!!
FORCE FIELDS PROBABLY DON'T WORK ON GHOSTS AND THEIR WEAPONS...
PEEBOCHU WILL GIVE US ALL THE DISTRACTION WE NEED! COUNT ON IT!!
JINKIES, BRIANNA! WHY ARE YOU SO ATTACHED TO THAT BIT-BOMB?
ITS WHOLE PURPOSE IS SELF-DESTRUCTION!
OH, BUT YOU'RE WRONG!!
THE EXPLOSION IS ACTUALLY A VIOLENT HYPER-SPACE JUMP THAT SENDS IT BACK HOME...
MY PEEBOCHU IS IMMORTAL!!
heh.
"EDUCATIONAL," HUH?
heh...
ALL IT NEEDS IS ONE SHOT!
twitch
WELL, I "LEARNED" A FEW THINGS FROM THAT FIGHT AS WELL...
...
I LEARNED JUST HOW MUCH BETTER TEACHER IS COMPARED TO YOU!
what... did... you... say...?
YOU'RE FAVORING THAT RIGHT HAND, G'NOLGA...
DID YOU THINK I DID NOT FEEL THE BONES SHATTER IN YOUR LEFT ARM?
OR PERHAPS YOU'RE PRAYING JULIA WON'T CONCENTRATE ON IT WHEN WE TELL HER?!
SHH!
WE COULD NEVER HAVE INJURED JULIA...
...LIKE WE INJURED YOU, G'NOLGA!
DO YOU WANT TO GIVE HER A REASON TO FINISH US?!!

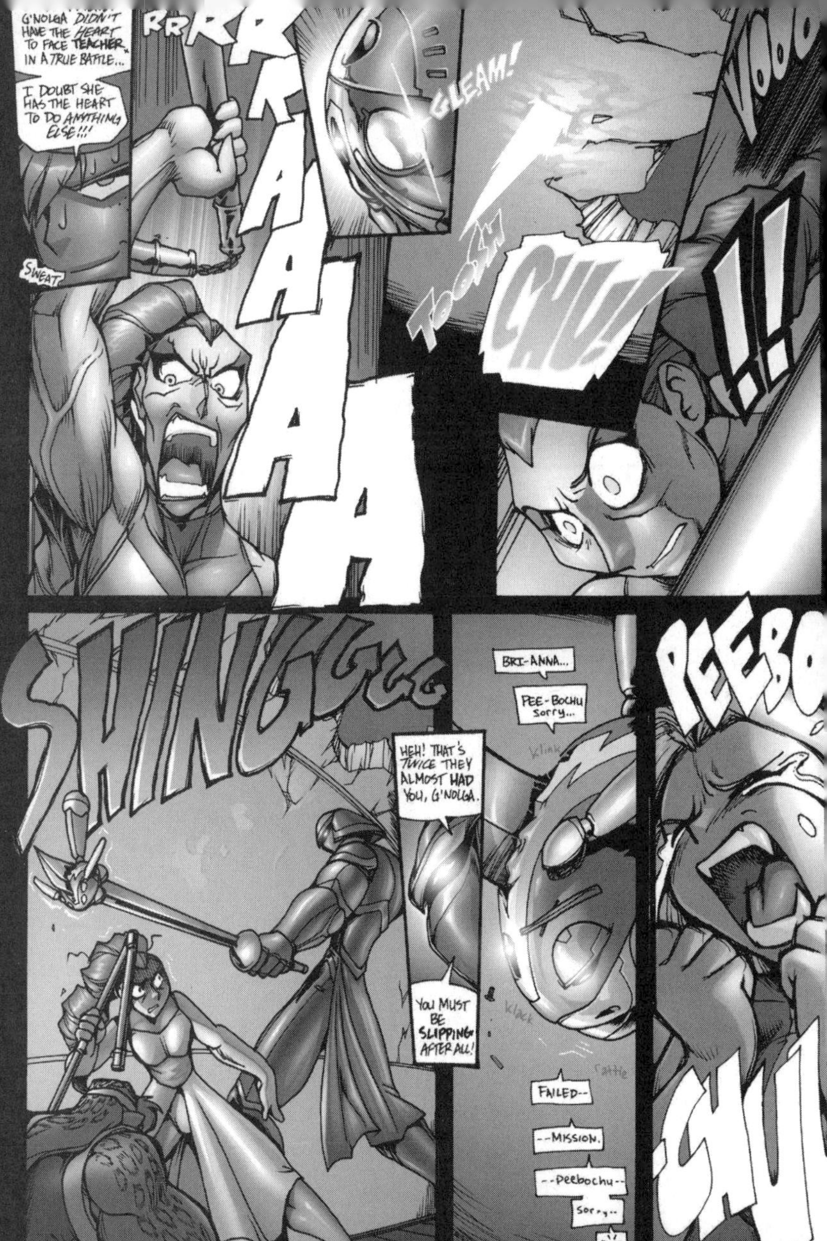
G'NOLGA DIDN'T HAVE THE HEART TO FACE TEACHER IN A TRUE BATTLE...
I DOUBT SHE HAS THE HEART TO DO ANYTHING ELSE!!!
SWEAT
RRRR
AAAA
GLEAM!
CHU!
!!!
SHINGGGG
BRI-ANNA...
PEE-BOCHU sorry...
HEH! THAT'S TWICE THEY ALMOST HAD YOU, G'NOLGA.
YOU MUST BE SLIPPING AFTER ALL!
klack
rattle
FAILED--
--MISSION.
--Peebochu--
Sorry...
PEEBO
-CHU!

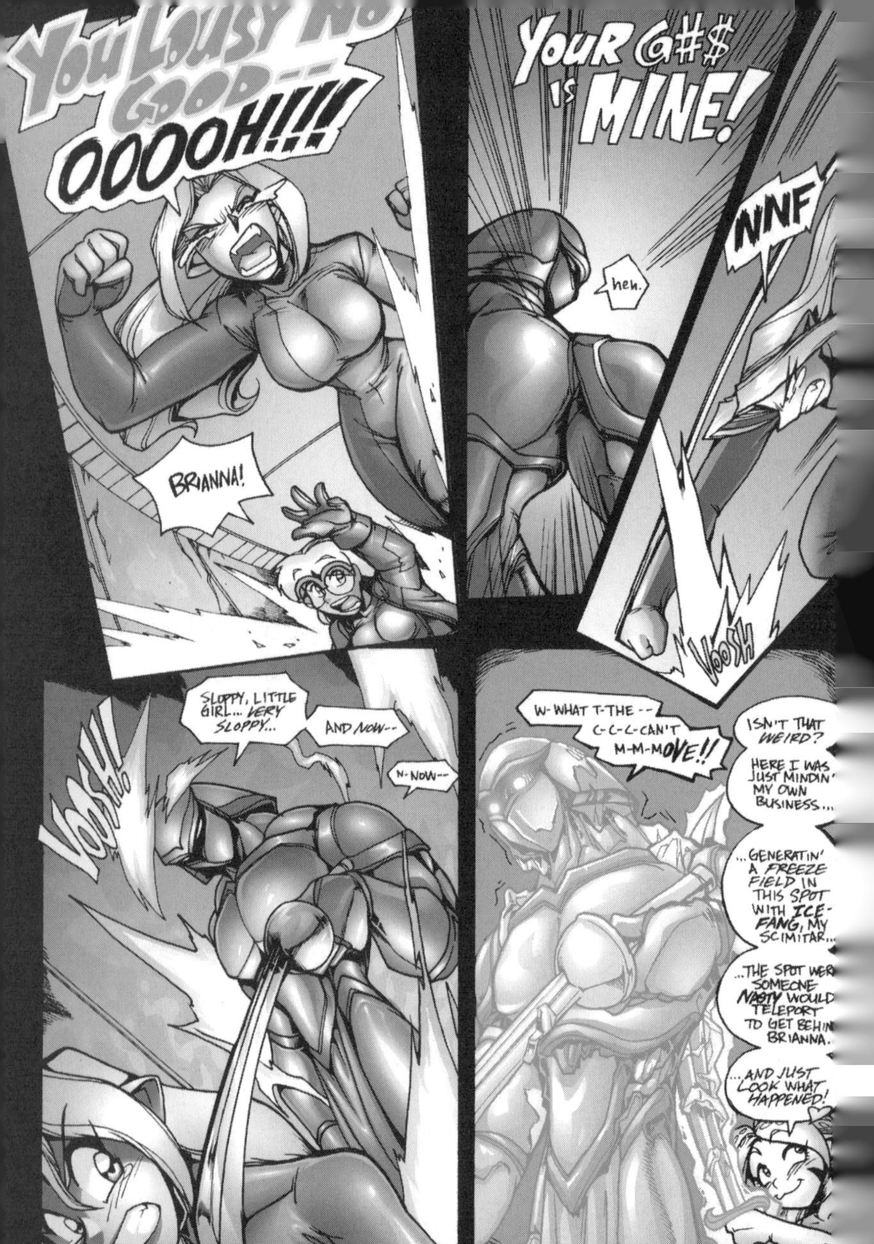
YOU LOUSY NO GOOD--
OOOOH!!!!
BRIANNA!
YOUR @#$ IS MINE!
heh.
NNF
VOOSH
SLOPPY, LITTLE GIRL... VERY SLOPPY...
AND NOW--
N-NOW--
VOOSH!
W-WHAT T-THE --
C-C-C-CAN'T M-M-MOVE!!
ISN'T THAT WEIRD?
HERE I WAS JUST MINDIN' MY OWN BUSINESS...
...GENERATIN' A FREEZE FIELD IN THIS SPOT WITH ICE-FANG, MY SCIMITAR...
...THE SPOT WERE SOMEONE NASTY WOULD TELEPORT TO GET BEHIND BRIANNA.
...AND JUST LOOK WHAT HAPPENED!

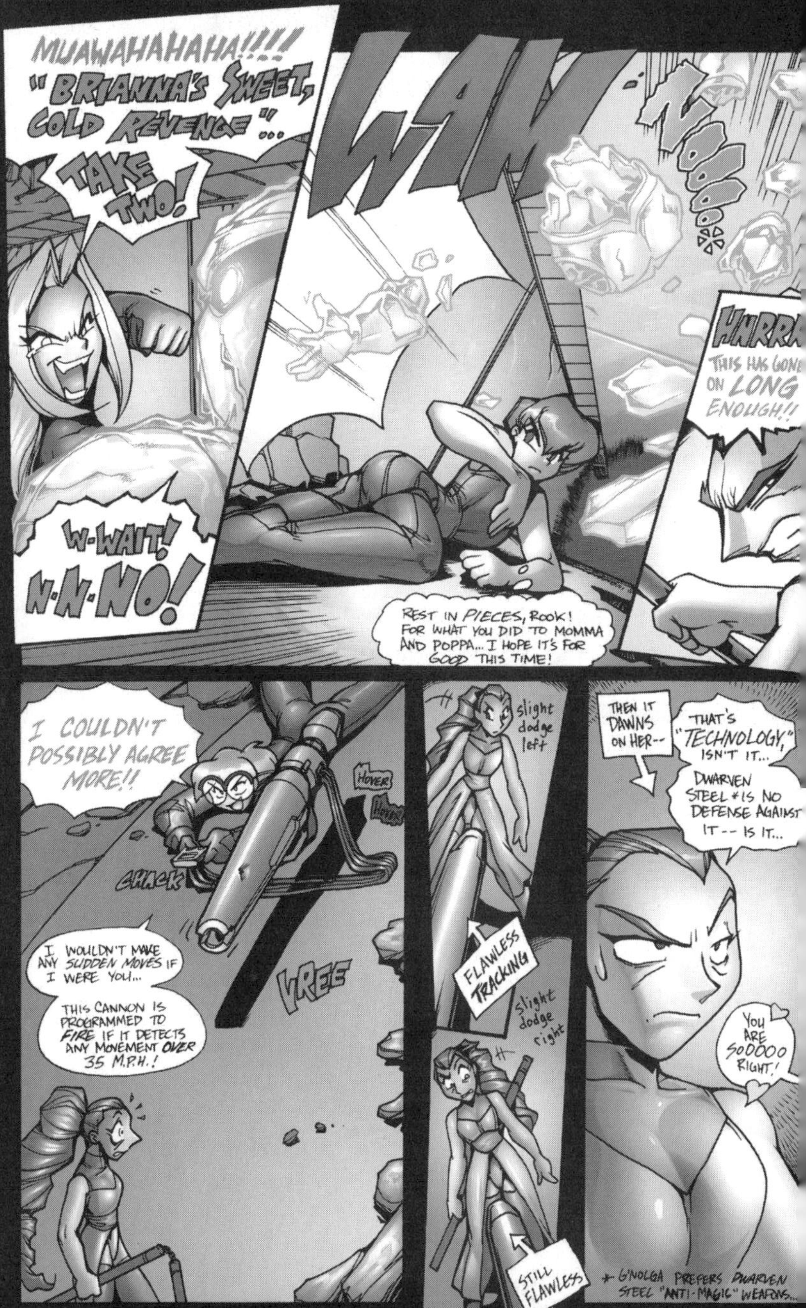

MUAWAHAHAHA!!!!! "BRIANNA'S SWEET, COLD REVENGE"...
TAKE TWO!
W-WAIT! N-N-NO!
WAM
NOOOOO
REST IN PIECES, ROOK! FOR WHAT YOU DID TO MOMMA AND POPPA... I HOPE IT'S FOR GOOD THIS TIME!
HNRRR
THIS HAS GONE ON LONG ENOUGH!!
I COULDN'T POSSIBLY AGREE MORE!!
HOVER
HOVER
CHACK
I WOULDN'T MAKE ANY SUDDEN MOVES IF I WERE YOU...
THIS CANNON IS PROGRAMMED TO FIRE IF IT DETECTS ANY MOVEMENT OVER 35 M.P.H.!
VREE
slight dodge left
FLAWLESS TRACKING
slight dodge right
STILL FLAWLESS
THEN IT DAWNS ON HER--
THAT'S "TECHNOLOGY," ISN'T IT...
DWARVEN STEEL * IS NO DEFENSE AGAINST IT -- IS IT...
YOU ARE SOOOOO RIGHT!
* G'NOLGA PREFERS DWARVEN STEEL "ANTI-MAGIC" WEAPONS...

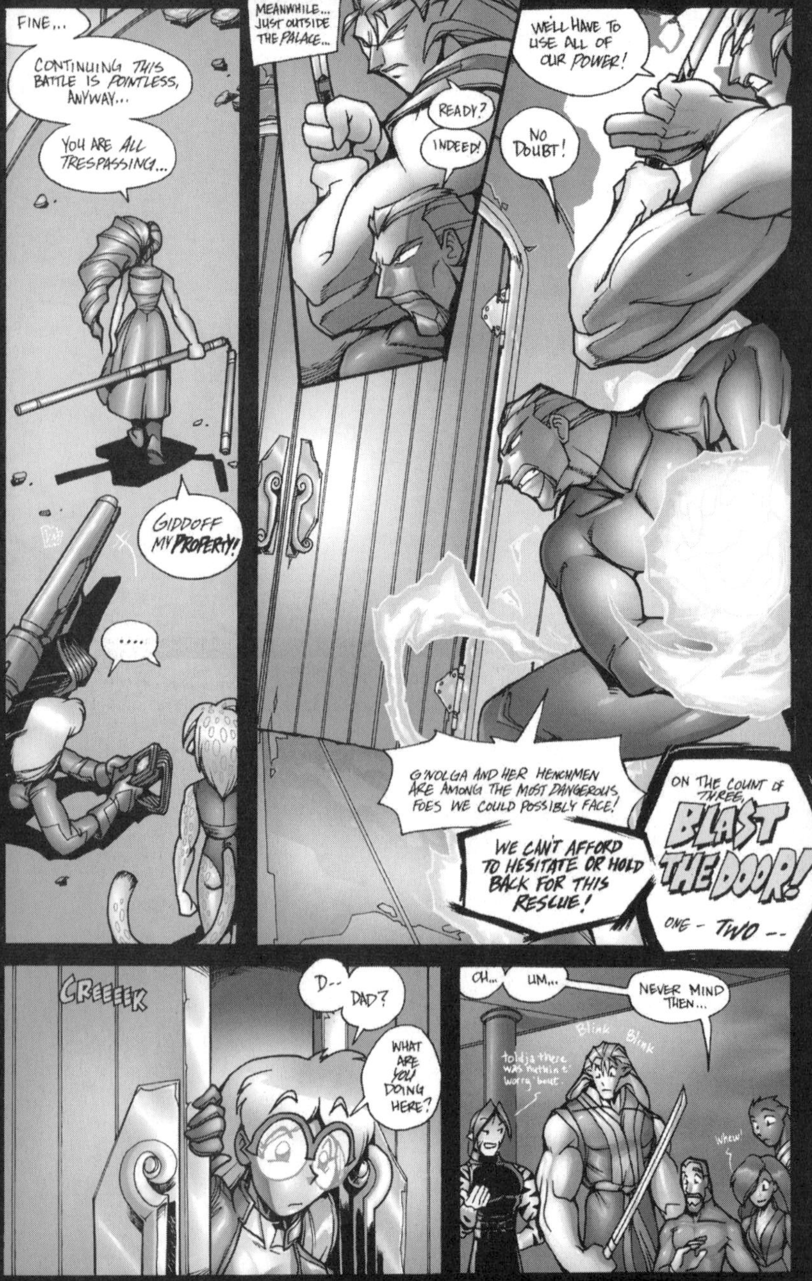
FINE...
CONTINUING THIS BATTLE IS POINTLESS, ANYWAY...
YOU ARE ALL TRESPASSING...
GIDDOFF MY PROPERTY!
....
MEANWHILE... JUST OUTSIDE THE PALACE...
READY?
INDEED!
WE'LL HAVE TO USE ALL OF OUR POWER!
NO DOUBT!
G'NOLGA AND HER HENCHMEN ARE AMONG THE MOST DANGEROUS FOES WE COULD POSSIBLY FACE!
WE CAN'T AFFORD TO HESITATE OR HOLD BACK FOR THIS RESCUE!
ON THE COUNT OF THREE, BLAST THE DOOR!
ONE - TWO --
CREEEEK
D--
DAD?
WHAT ARE YOU DOING HERE?
OH...
UM...
NEVER MIND THEN...
Blink Blink
toldja there was nuthin t' worry 'bout.
Whew!

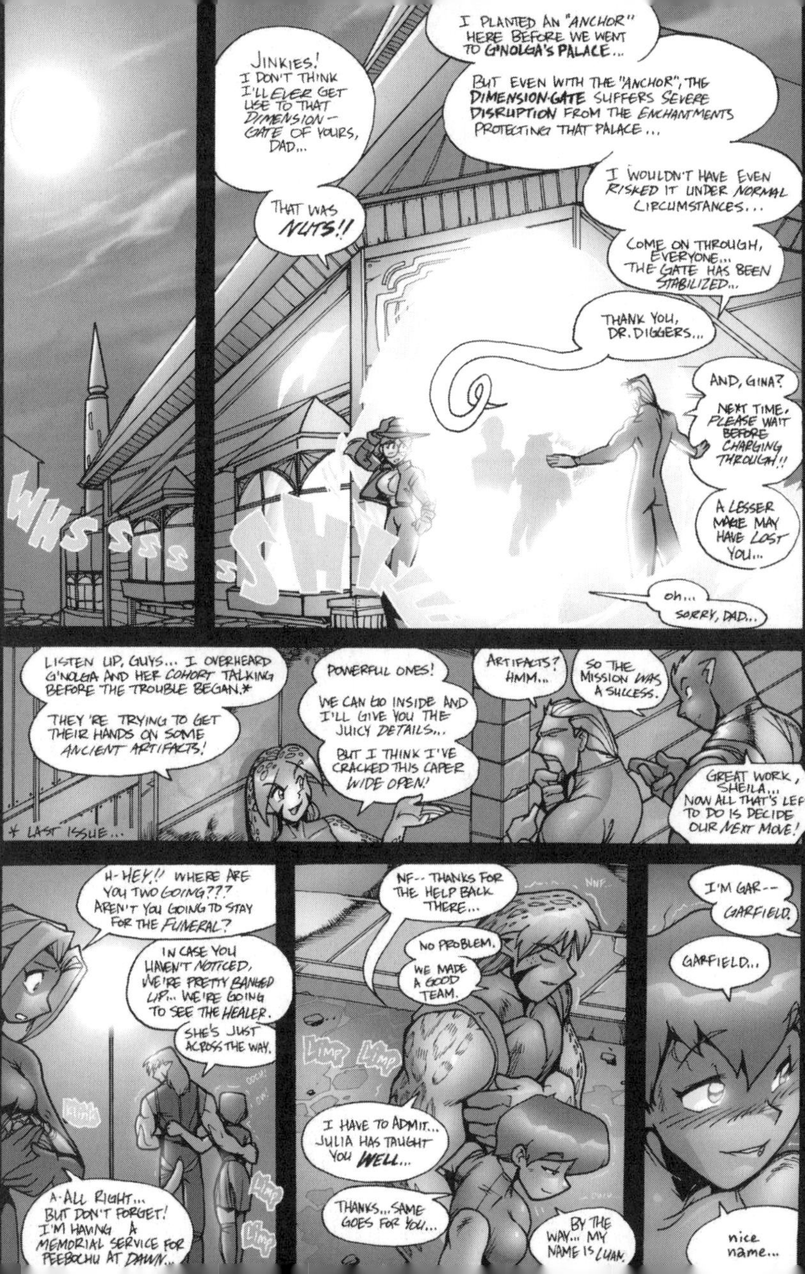

JINKIES! I DON'T THINK I'LL EVER GET USE TO THAT DIMENSION-GATE OF YOURS, DAD...
THAT WAS NUTS!!
WHSSSSSSHH
I PLANTED AN "ANCHOR" HERE BEFORE WE WENT TO G'NOLGA'S PALACE...
BUT EVEN WITH THE "ANCHOR", THE DIMENSION-GATE SUFFERS SEVERE DISRUPTION FROM THE ENCHANTMENTS PROTECTING THAT PALACE...
I WOULDN'T HAVE EVEN RISKED IT UNDER NORMAL CIRCUMSTANCES...
COME ON THROUGH, EVERYONE... THE GATE HAS BEEN STABILIZED...
THANK YOU, DR. DIGGERS...
AND, GINA?
NEXT TIME, PLEASE WAIT BEFORE CHARGING THROUGH!!
A LESSER MAGE MAY HAVE LOST YOU...
oh... SORRY, DAD...
LISTEN UP, GUYS... I OVERHEARD G'NOLGA AND HER COHORT TALKING BEFORE THE TROUBLE BEGAN.*
THEY'RE TRYING TO GET THEIR HANDS ON SOME ANCIENT ARTIFACTS!
POWERFUL ONES!
WE CAN GO INSIDE AND I'LL GIVE YOU THE JUICY DETAILS...
BUT I THINK I'VE CRACKED THIS CAPER WIDE OPEN!
* LAST ISSUE...
ARTIFACTS? HMM...
SO THE MISSION WAS A SUCCESS.
GREAT WORK, SHEILA... NOW ALL THAT'S LEFT TO DO IS DECIDE OUR NEXT MOVE!
H-HEY!! WHERE ARE YOU TWO GOING??? AREN'T YOU GOING TO STAY FOR THE FUNERAL?
IN CASE YOU HAVEN'T NOTICED, WE'RE PRETTY BANGED UP... WE'RE GOING TO SEE THE HEALER.
SHE'S JUST ACROSS THE WAY.
LIMP
A-ALL RIGHT... BUT DON'T FORGET! I'M HAVING A MEMORIAL SERVICE FOR PEEBOCHU AT DAWN...
LIMP
NF-- THANKS FOR THE HELP BACK THERE...
NNF.
NO PROBLEM.
WE MADE A GOOD TEAM.
LIMP LIMP
I HAVE TO ADMIT... JULIA HAS TAUGHT YOU WELL...
THANKS... SAME GOES FOR YOU...
BY THE WAY... MY NAME IS LUAN.
I'M GAR-- GARFIELD.
GARFIELD...
nice name...

NEXT:

Julia continues to battle through the Arms-master Tournament, facing ever-tougher opponents on her way to confronting G'nolga. But while Julia fights for her honor, Tirant and his cohorts make their move to ensure she can't possibly win! With powers beyond science AND magic at Tirant's command, he and Array's conquest of Jade is unstoppable!

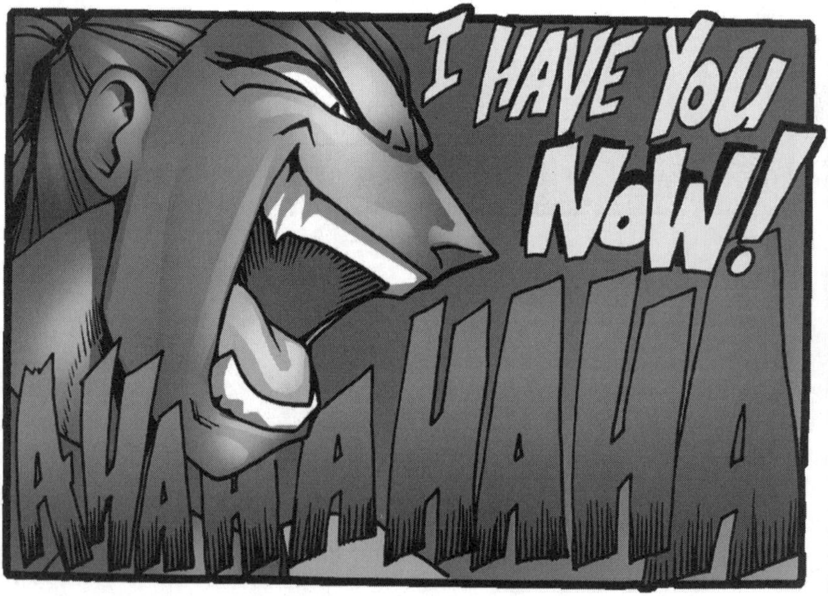
I HAVE YOU NOW!
AHAHAHAHAHA